D0820736

CAMBRIDGE LATIN AMERICAN STUDIES

EDITORS

DAVID JOSLIN   TIMOTHY KING
CLIFFORD T. SMITH   JOHN STREET

9

AN ECONOMIC HISTORY OF COLOMBIA 1845-1930

THE SERIES

AN ECONOMIC HISTORY
OF COLOMBIA
1845-1930

BY

WILLIAM PAUL McGREEVEY
University of California

CAMBRIDGE

AT THE UNIVERSITY PRESS

1971

Published by the Syndics of the Cambridge University Press
Bentley House, 200 Euston Road, London N.W.1
American Branch: 32 East 57th Street, New York, N.Y.10022

Library of Congress Catalogue Card Number: 70–116844

ISBN: 0 521 07909 8

Set in Great Britain
at the Aberdeen University Press
Printed in the United States of America

To Aletha, Sean and Alicia

CONTENTS

TABLES

ix

Tables

FIGURES

MAPS

ACKNOWLEDGEMENTS

In the fall of 1964 I finished work on a doctoral dissertation which bore the pretentious name, 'The Economic Development of Colombia'. In the interim I have sought to correct some of the weaknesses of that work and have as a consequence found myself doing a new and very different book, different that is from the earlier effort and its concentration on the past as a simple prologue to current problems of economic development in Colombia – and by extension in the less developed countries. In the course of changing directions and emphasis I amassed an impressive collection of intellectual debts which I am most happy to acknowledge.

The early supervisors of my work of course bear no responsibility for the current product, but if there is merit in this work it owes much to their guidance. Everett E. Hagen, Charles P. Kindleberger and Simon Kuznets all provided friendly advice and encouragement at the beginning stages of my work. In Colombia I received the friendly assistance and advice of Miguel Urrutia, R. Albert Berry, Indalecio Liévano Aguirre, Luis Ospina Vásquez and Alfredo Gutiérrez. My debt to them and to many other Colombian economists and friends can only partially be indicated in the references to their published works which appear in my footnotes.

A number of friends read earlier drafts of the manuscript and made valuable comments. These include D. A. Brading, Woodrow Borah, Albert Fishlow, Herbert Klein and James Parsons. Their kindnesses have at times been above and beyond the call of collegial duty.

The numerous calculations and quantitative investigations which were carried out as part of the research for this book could never have been accomplished without the assistance of a number of able graduate students at the University of California. These include Harry Cross, Eul Soo Pang, David C. Johnson, Michael Conniff and Jorge Rodriguez. The last mentioned were particularly helpful in the preparation of land use estimates and the revised estimates of Colombian foreign trade. I cannot estimate the diffuse and substantial benefits I derived from seminars and classes with Berkeley students. It is hard to imagine a more stimulating – or distracting – atmosphere for scholarship.

I am particularly grateful to Dr Jaime Duarte French, Director of the Biblioteca Luis Angel Arango, and Armando Moreno Matos, Punto Central de Información, Departamento Administrativo Nacional de

Acknowledgements

Estadística, for the use of their library facilities and access to statistical material.

No one – except possibly for me – has worked as long and willingly at the preparation of this book as has Sharon Sandberg. She has helped with typing, research and moral support as at times the whole enterprise seemed to be too much to complete. During my years at the Center for Latin American Studies Anne Fleming, Administrative Assistant, has done her best to facilitate the work. To her and other members of the Center staff, my thanks.

And of course all this has not been done without financial assistance. My first journey to Colombia was aided by the Department of Economics at MIT and the Foreign Area Fellowship Program. Another stay in 1965 was aided by the Institute of International Studies of the University of Oregon. Subsequently, I have received support from the Center for Latin American Studies, University of California, Berkeley, the Conference on Latin American History and the Joint Committee on Latin American Studies of the Social Science Research Council and American Council of Learned Societies. Most of the grants administered by the foregoing organizations are from money made available to them through grants from the Ford Foundation. To that organization must all scholars working on Latin America be grateful.

Berkeley, 1969   W.P.M.

CHAPTER I

INTRODUCTION

In 1930 Colombia faced its first great crisis caused by a fall in the price and demand for coffee. But Colombia had suffered earlier crises which had arisen in her export sector – the tobacco crisis of 1875/76, for example. In this she shared a common fate with other Latin American countries which produced primary commodities for export. There were spectacular cases of growth led by an expanding export sector all over Latin America in the years between 1850 and 1930. But in virtually all cases that expansion failed to transform local economies. The smaller crises which preceded the Great Depression often brought an export cycle to an end leaving local economic conditions no better (perhaps worse) than they had been prior to the export boom. The famous opera house of Manáus built during the Amazon rubber boom is mute testimony to the failure of the external sector to transform the local economy.

Despite this failure the external sector has proved to be the primary influence on the process of economic change in Latin America. The growth in world demand for primary products and the flow of capital, goods and people into (and out of) Latin America continue to be principal determinants of the 'growth-poles' and of the timing of economic change. In the past local policymakers tried to influence the course of events and were successful in minor ways, but they could do little to alter international demand or the movements of goods and people. The wide variety of ideologies and policies followed in Argentina, Brazil, Chile, Colombia, Cuba, Mexico and Jamaica produced no great differences in the rate of economic progress: these seven countries had virtually the same rank-order positions with respect to per capita income in 1950 that they had had in 1850.[1] With the growing export sector dependent on foreign demand and the availability of foreign capital there was little room for local initiative in policymaking. The ideology of *laissez-faire* and nineteenth-century liberalism complemented the weakness of independent governments prior to 1930.

Although the timing differs substantially for the several countries of

[1] See William Paul McGreevey, 'Recent Research on the Economic History of Latin America', *Latin American Research Review*, III (1968), 89–117. The data summarized in Table II, p. 98, of that article are the basis for the comment on rank correlations.

Introduction

Latin America, at some time between 1850 and 1930 they greatly increased their dependence on trade. In a simple statistical sense this occurred because the value of exports and imports grew much more rapidly than local production.

As foreign trade grew in value and volume, the local economy grew more dependent on foreign influence. The ebb and flow of foreign capital produced wide swings in the balance of payments. The growth of imports, particularly British textiles, disrupted local economies. Artisan handicrafts had to adapt to new competition or go out of business. Fluctuations in foreign demand and competition from other primary producers added further to the gyrations of the balance of payments and the instability of the external sector. The cyclical oscillations of foreign trade struck societies with little capacity to adjust rapidly to changing economic conditions. Even the rural peasantry with only occasional market contacts were subject to rude shocks; for example, from the rise and fall of demand for food in the export sector. As foreign trade grew, the instability and dependence of the local economy expanded proportionately. The growth and fluctuations of the external sector caused grave domestic crises as well as considerable development.

The ideology of the period opposed any effort to dampen the oscillations or promote development by central direction. Had local policy-makers had it in their power, they would not generally have tampered with the economy. With few exceptions the ideology of *laissez-faire* dominated economic policy in Latin America over the years 1850 to 1930. It took the crisis of the 1930s to open up the prospects for planned economic development in terms of the objectives of Latin Americans themselves.

In this book I deal with the relations between the external sector and the domestic economy by treating the economic history of Colombia between 1850 and 1930. Some special features distinguish events in Colombia from those in other countries; e.g. there was little foreign immigration or direct investment in the export sector. Colombian history has nonetheless been tied with the same threads as the rest of Latin America to the industrialized North Atlantic economy. And the pull of those threads has been the motive force for economic change within the country.

Despite emphasis on the export sector I am most interested in exploring economic change in the domestic economy. Since agricultural activities employed the bulk of the population, I have emphasized agrarian change and specifically devote Chapters 3, 6 and 9 to rural problems. I have tried

Introduction

to understand the manner in which changes in the external sector (the demand for exports and the growing supply of imports) have affected rural Colombia. But I have also dealt with the conditions of production in agriculture, i.e. the way in which food and rural exports have been produced and how that method of production has influenced the path of economic change. Quantitatively, rural Colombia is the most important component of the country's economic history; unfortunately, the details of agrarian economic and social history remain to be dug out of local archives, notarial records and other sources. Here I have only scratched the surface.

THE PROBLEMS

There are three sets of problems in Colombian economic history which occupy me in this book. All are related to the impact of the external sector and foreign ideas on the domestic economy and economic welfare of the Colombians. To some extent the three sets of problems determine a set of periods for Colombian economic history and suggest the general organization of the book.

Colonial survivals

The area now known as Colombia and occupied by Spaniards in the 1530s became an export economy when the first conquerors diverted labor from local production of foodstuffs and handicrafts and forced Indians to mine for gold. (Colombia produced more gold than any other of Spain's colonies.) The native population paid a terrible price for that first entry into world trade. In two areas for which data are now available – and one may suppose the same was true of other areas as well – the native population declined at a rate not unlike that of Central Mexico in the sixteenth century.[1] Much of the population decline must be attributed to the introduction of pulmonary diseases by the Spaniards. But the diversion of sedentary peoples to work in lowland placer mines was also a cause of the demographic disaster.[2]

In the mid-eighteenth century Spanish imperial policy began to require

---

[1] Among other works by the same authors see Woodrow Borah and Sherburne Cook, *The Population of Central Mexico in 1548* (Berkeley 1960), and Woodrow Borah, 'The Historical Demography of Aboriginal and Colonial Latin America: An attempt at Perspective' (unpub. MS., n.d.).

[2] See Juan Friede, *Los Quimbayas bajo la dominación española* (Bogotá 1963), p. 258; and Germán Colmenares, *Encomienda y población en la Provincia de Pamplona (1549–1650)* (Bogotá 1960), p. 47 and *passim*.

3

more resources from the Americas. Since military expenditures were being made more in the Old World than in the New, when taxes were increased in the colonies, real resources had to be transferred to Europe. The transfer mechanism required that exports be increased above the level of imports in the colonies so that on balance Spain would have more resources and America less. The process was equivalent to capital export from colony to metropolis. Spanish America (and Colombia as a part thereof) was sapped of resources which might have been used to add to the stock of capital.

The movement for independence ended the capital outflow to Spain by 1820. Foreign wars continued to be a drain on the economy of Nueva Granada until 1824 since the Army of the North fought in Peru and Bolivia.[1] But it was not until after 1845 – more than a quarter century after the Battle of Boyacá which in 1819 established *criollo* hegemony in northern South America – that Colombian foreign trade rose above colonial levels. There was nothing which attracted foreign capital. Although independence wrenched Colombia free from colonial exploitation, political freedom did not prove to be synonymous with accelerated economic and social development. Many characteristics of the *ancien régime* went unaltered: the colonial system of taxation remained virtually intact; dependence on gold mining for foreign exchange went unchallenged as no new export products came onto the scene; fractionated local markets for food products were the rule as before; the system of transportation and internal communications went unimproved. From the point of view of economic history and development the achievement of political independence brought no radical change. The central hypothesis advanced in Chapter 2 is that change was muted and slow because the external sector failed to grow after independence and hence could effect little change in the domestic economy.

After the initial demographic catastrophe the Spaniards initiated a social policy to avert total decimation of the native population.[2] The Hapsburgs developed the *resguardo de indios*, lands reserved for use of the Indian communities and legally inaccessible to Spaniards. They provided the legal fiction of protection for Indian land and labor. Royal protection of native rights, limited though it was, was scorned by the *criollos* (the

---

[1] For a general outline of the economic consequences of the wars for independence see Charles Griffin, 'Economic and Social Aspects of the Era of Spanish-American Independence', *Hispanic American Historical Review*, XXXIX (1949), 170–87.

[2] They acted too late in the Caribbean despite the efforts of Las Casas. For a discussion of population estimates on the islands and an analysis of the causes of population decline see Carl O. Sauer, *The Early Spanish Main* (Berkeley 1966), pp. 65–9, 155–60.

white native-born population) who lived by the exploitation of native labor. As the demands of the criollos for access to Indian lands intensified in the eighteenth century, a policy of protection gave way to a policy of exploitation. A radically new social policy evolved in the third quarter of the eighteenth century.

Because land was still plentiful and labor scarce, the social policy of the Bourbons was directed as much at assuring workers for the haciendas as it was in taking lands from the Indians and handing them over to *mestizos* and Spanish colonists. Although the policy was radical in its implications since it spelled the death of the traditional mode of community land tenure, its limited application muted its immediate impact. The slow process of change toward fuller exploitation of Indian labor begun in the eighteenth century continued into the first quarter century of political independence. As in the case of the commercial and fiscal position of the newly independent state, no radical change in agrarian social policy came with political independence. The real break with the past came after 1845.

The questions dealt with in Chapter 3 have an obvious continuity with events which occurred after 1850. Public land policies were born in the late colonial period, grew in the early nineteenth century and matured in the Reforms of 1850 and the seizure of church lands in 1861. The story of those policies has a smoothness of flow not characteristic of the ups and downs of foreign trade, the rise and decline of foreign dependence. The policies had their continuity because of the consistent effort of the well-to-do merchant and landowning classes to exploit other groups in Colombia – Indians, artisans and rural peasants. They were not always equally successful in their exploitation, but they were always at it. And since Chapter 3 deals largely with the establishment of *policies* and less with the realities of exploitation, it is a prelude to the analysis which follows in Chapters 4 through 7.

The problem in the first part of this book is to gauge the movement in the average level of well-being, the impact of the external sector and the patterns of agrarian social policy in the years prior to 1845. Chapters 2 and 3 constitute an introduction and contrast to the periods after 1845; they are not offered as complete analyses of the years 1760 to 1845.

Economic decline

In his survey of Brazilian economic history Celso Furtado suggests that the period of export expansion based on coffee was preceded by a long period of economic decline (1775–1850) during which Brazilian per capita product fell. He ascribes the fall to the inability to find a successful export product.

There are some indications that the rate of growth of the Brazilian economy was relatively stable throughout the past century[1850–1950]. Another interesting observation is that if the Brazilian economy had attained a rate of growth in the first half of the nineteenth century identical with that for the second half, taking the aforementioned fifty-dollar figure as a starting point, a per capita income of 224 dollars a year would have been attained at the turn of the century. And if the same rate had been maintained for the first half of this century, the real per capita income of the Brazilian population as of 1950 would have been about five hundred dollars – in other words, it would have been comparable to the average for the countries of Western Europe in that same year.

The data presented in the preceding paragraph throw some light on the problem of the present-day relative backwardness of the Brazilian economy. *That backwardness has its roots not in the rate of development for the past century, which seems to have been reasonably rapid, but in the reversal which occurred in the previous three-quarters of a century.* Since Brazil was unable to integrate herself into the expanding currents of world trade during that period of fast transformation of the economic structures of more progressive countries, sharp disparities were created between the Brazilian economic system and those of Western Europe.[1]

The problem of integrating a backward economy into the rapidly changing matrix of international trade was simply too overwhelming for Brazilians.

Profitability in mining tended to fall off to nothing, and the liquidation of productive enterprises was complete. Many of the former entrepreneurs became mere prospectors, and eventually reverted to a mere subsistence activity. A few decades were enough for the entire mining economy to collapse, with the decline of urban nuclei and the dispersal of most of their inhabitants throughout a zone of subsistence economy – a vast region with difficult means of communication, in which small groups were isolated from each other. ... In no other part of the Western Hemisphere was there an instance of so rapid and so complete a process of involution from an economic system chiefly composed of population of European stock.[2]

An export cycle came to an end and the local economy returned to subsistence activities because it could not generate new exports with better economic prospects.

Much the same conditions prevailed in Jamaica in the decades after emancipation of the slaves. Per capita product fell from 1832 until 1870 largely because of the decline in the value of exports.[3] Per capita personal

[1] Celso Furtado, *The Economic Growth of Brazil* (Berkeley 1963), pp. 164–5. Italics added.
[2] Furtado, *The Economic Growth of Brazil*, p. 94.
[3] Gisela Eisner, *Jamaica, 1830–1930: A Study in Economic Growth* (Manchester, England 1961), pp. 119, 134, 319.

Introduction

consumption was lower in 1870 than it had been in 1830 despite the distribution of income away from the plantation owners and to rural laborers. In his introduction to Mrs Eisner's book, W. Arthur Lewis analyzes the reasons for Jamaica's decline and subsequent failure to grow:

> Jamaica did not cope with her economic problems in the half century before 1930 because her leaders did not try to cope with them. ... The nationalist Jamaican leaders of the day, of whatever race, were not much concerned about the economic and social questions which are here discussed; they were preoccupied with questions of political power, and with protecting their respective middle or upper class positions. ... Not until the 1930s did Jamaica find among her own people spokesmen whose primary concern was economic and social development.[1]

Lewis' analysis, and by implication the data presented by Eisner, support the view that the lack of entrepreneurial initiative in supplying of export products, food for domestic consumption and local manufactures lay at the heart of Jamaica's failure to grow economically. It was not the deficiencies of world demand faced by a dependent economy which explain underdevelopment, but the inflexibility of the local economy in the face of change. Perhaps conditions in Jamaica were not so different from those in the American South where per capita income also fell in the years between 1840 and 1880, that is, over the interval which included emancipation and restructuring of the rural economy.[2]

After adjusting the national product estimates made by Humboldt and Quirós for Mexico for the first decade of the nineteenth century, Clark Reynolds suggests that Mexico may have suffered a decline in per capita product between 1810 and 1875: 'One must conclude that if the earlier figures are correct then either there was no net increase in per capita income over the course of the nineteenth century or that per capita income actually *declined* over the long period despite the gains of the Porfiriato.'[3] The gains of the Porfirian period (1876–1910) must certainly have been substantial. From 1895 to 1910 per capita product in Mexico increased at an average annual rate of 1·6 per cent, and the more

---

[1] Eisner, *Jamaica*, pp. xxii–xxiii.

[2] On the trends in Southern per capita income see Richard Easterlin, 'Interregional Differences in Per Capita Income, Population and Total Income, 1840–1950', *Trends in the American Economy in the Nineteenth Century* (National Bureau of Economic Research, Princeton 1960), pp. 73–140.

[3] Clark Reynolds, 'The Per Capita Income of New Spain Before Independence and After the Revolution' (unpub. MS. 1967). Reynolds reviews the earlier analyses of Henry G. Aubrey, 'The National Income of Mexico', *Estadística* (Mexico 1950), pp. 185–98, and Fernando Rosenzweig Hernández, 'La economía novo-hispana al comenzar el siglo XIX', *Ciencias políticas y sociales*, IX (1963), 455–94.

Introduction

limited data available for the previous score of years indicate that per capita product was growing slowly throughout the last quarter of the nineteenth century.[1] Unless the 1800–10 level of per capita product was lower than that of 1910, then per capita product would have to have declined between 1810 and 1875.[2] Inasmuch as periods of decline were registered for other Latin American countries, it becomes feasible to entertain the hypothesis of decline in Colombia.

I believed some years ago that there was a period of economic decline – a fall in average per capita product or income – in Colombia which ended with the nineteenth century and began with the Reforms of 1850. The belief was difficult to support with hard evidence.[3] There were the data on real wages for six highland haciendas which are discussed in Chapter 6. They certainly support the argument but refer only to agriculture in the eastern highlands. The frequency of armed conflict, though civil and political in nature, suggests that the economy may also have been ill. Again, however, the qualitative assessments are contradictory. The Reforms of 1850 – particularly governmental decentralization, the abolition of Indian resguardos and the expansion of foreign trade – had profound effects on the distribution of income; to some extent the gains of one group offset the losses of another.

With such change it is doubtful that contemporary observers could make a correct assessment of the direction (let alone the magnitude) of movement of total and average per capita income. Scholars who have come later (I was among them) have tended to study a particular group making their general assessments on the basis of how that group fared. For example, several studies of the Antioqueño area have shown the rapid expansion of population, the southward movement of the frontier and the growing cultivation and export of coffee as signs of economic development. Yet even at the end of the nineteenth century the Antioqueños constituted but 23 per cent of the total of Colombian population (the regional share was only 13·5 per cent in 1870), so that the progress

---

[1] Enrique Pérez López, 'The National Product of Mexico: 1895 to 1964', *Mexico's Recent Economic Growth: A Mexican View* (Austin, Texas n.d.), p. 27; Fernando Rosenzweig Hernández, 'El desarrollo económico de México de 1877 a 1911', *El trimestre económico*, XXXII (1965), 405–54.

[2] The possibility that the Reynolds calculations for per capita product, 1800–10, may be too high is recognized and discussed in McGreevey, 'Recent Research on the Economic History of Latin America', pp. 99–100.

[3] Some of the early arguments which I considered are presented in Chapter 5 of my doctoral dissertation, 'The Economic Development of Colombia' (Ph.D. diss., M.I.T. 1965), pp. 109–36. Some of the arguments made there are weak, but the lack of empirical support for decline is the most serious omission. I believe I have rectified the error here.

of that region alone tells but a part of the Colombian story.[1] The success of the merchant class is undeniable, but its gains have not been set against the losses of other groups to calculate the net effects of the international trade from which they drew their profits.

In Chapters 4 through 7 I have tried to draw together such information as there is to make an overall assessment of the movement of per capita product between 1845 and 1885. The first phase of the work is the analysis of political and economic issues which divided Colombians along regional, interest-group and class lines during the nineteenth century. The issues provide one means of identifying groups and the coincidence or opposition of their interests with the policies enunciated in the Reforms and the subsequent period of Radical hegemony. In Chapter 4 I attempt to set out the political basis for the divergence between the general interest and the policies of the period.

Chapter 5 takes up the role of the external sector in undercutting handicraft industries and generating the conditions for persistent disequilibrium in the balance of payments. The problem of adjusting the internal economy to international trade probably caused more difficulties than did limitations or fluctuations of foreign demand. The opening up of trade did not itself cause 'underdevelopment'; but the failure to achieve rapid growth of exports does suggest that internal adjustments were slow and difficult. Rising unemployment was one result. The slow growth of exports was itself evidence of a low capacity for transformation in Colombian society in that era. Thus the statistical analysis of trade contributes directly to an interpretation of domestic economic conditions.

In order to carry out the study of the impact of trade on Colombian economic development, I assembled data on foreign trade from the statistical records of Colombia's major trading partners – Britain, the United States, France and Germany. Based on those data and others available in Colombian government publications, consular reports and other sources, I assembled a new set of estimates of Colombia's foreign trade from 1845 to 1930. The result is a much more reliable set of estimates of Colombian trade than has been available at any previous date.

The principal differences between the new data and those formerly available lie in the much greater value of imports than had previously been indicated by official statistics. The new values prove to be consistent

---

[1] The percentages indicated are for the population of the State of Antioquia in 1870 and for the two Departments of Antioquia and Caldas in 1912. Using a slightly broader geographical definition of the Antioqueño area, Parsons puts the Antioqueño share in national population at 26·4 per cent in 1938. (James J. Parsons, *Antioqueño Colonization in Western Colombia* (Berkeley 1949), p. 104.)

with other quantitative and qualitative evidence about the Colombian economy in the last half of the nineteenth century.

The changing use and demand for land provides one of the principal clues to the process of economic change in the second half of the nineteenth century. Cropping by peasant smallholders in the eastern highlands gave way to stockraising by owners of vast estates. The peasants were being driven out of the rich river bottoms and up the hillsides. There was a scarcity of good land brought on by the monopolization of river bottoms by stockmen even though only a small percentage of cultivable land was in use. The shift to stockraising with its lesser demand for labor tended to increase the floating population of beggars and vagrants who roamed about the countryside in search of occasional work.

For a general assessment of the impact of the Reforms and other events in the second half of the nineteenth century I offer in Chapter 7 an anatomy of economic decline. This includes some calculations of the difference between what total output was in 1870 and what it might have been if the Reforms of 1850 had not been adopted. These calculations indicate that 1870 output was lower than it might have been had the former policies of autarchy, concessions to communal Indians and political compromise been followed.

The evidence from Colombia adds another country to the list of Brazil, Jamaica and Mexico which may have experienced periods of decline prior to their twentieth-century experience of growth. Although there are good reasons to believe that unique circumstances in each case have caused the period of decline, it is tempting to generalize. Might not a common condition of external dependence explain all these cases of decline? The trouble with this view is that it ignores the possibility of a common set of internal circumstances – the failure of supply response because of the limitations of entrepreneurial initiative. The comparative study of coffee and tobacco in the Colombian context which appears in Chapter 9 provides one preliminary investigation of the conditions of production which hinder or promote economic progress.

Transition to growth

The best-known international comparisons of the early phases of modern economic growth are those of Gerschenkron, Kuznets and Rostow.[1] All agree that there *may* be a fairly short period (up to 30 years) when the

---

[1] Alexander Gerschenkron, *Economic Backwardness in Historical Perspective* (New York 1965), especially pp. 5–30; Simon Kuznets, *Economic Growth and Structure: Selected Essays* (New York 1965), pp. 213–35, 20–3; W. W. Rostow, *The Stages of Economic Growth* (Cambridge,

rate of growth of total and per capita product accelerates. From that point onward there seems to be some assurance, judging from the experience of the developed countries, that further development will continue indefinitely. Hence the achievement of take-off (Rostow's phrase) or the occurrence of the great spurt (Gerschenkron's) becomes the key to economic development. Whatever the differences between these interpretations they all emphasize a swift, once-and-for-all transition. Where does Colombia fit in this picture?

Between 1890 and 1930 Colombia did experience a very important transition – from an economy largely composed of subsistence production without much specialization and exchange to a market-oriented agriculture with a greater division of labor and more extensive network of trade. The rate of change was particularly rapid between 1911 and 1929 when the value of exports grew at an average annual rate above 10 per cent. The transition was effected in large part by the very rapid growth of coffee exports. Yet this 'pre-industrial' transition did not automatically produce the desired end of self-sustaining growth. Further growth occurred after 1930 and into the 1960s but few Colombians believe an irreversible development threshold has been crossed.[1] Most would accept the conclusion of Kuznets in viewing both sustaining and limiting implications of economic growth:

Given the two sets of impacts of economic growth, the outcome is uncertain, and the process can never be *purely* self-sustained since it always generates *some* self-limiting effects. In this sense, economic growth is always a struggle; it is misleading to convey the impression of easy automaticity, a kind of soaring euphoria of self-sustained flight to higher economic levels.[2]

Important as was the transition in Colombia it cannot be classed with the Industrial Revolution in England, or North America in the antebellum period. The aggregate impact on the Colombian population was not as great as the social and economic transformations which the developed

---

England 1960). Kuznets is the most doubtful of the three about the rapidity of acceleration, but he agrees that some form of transition from the 'late premodern phase' to the 'early growth phase' is recognizable even in the aggregate statistics.

[1] Estimates of the gross domestic product of Colombia go back only as far as 1925 and for years prior to 1945 consist of extrapolations based on samples of total output. The source of those data is United Nations Economic Commission for Latin America, *Analyses and Projections of Economic Development*, III. *The Economic Development of Colombia* (Geneva 1957). An unpublished statistical appendix is available and has been used in this book. Both are referred to hereafter as ECLA *Study*.

[2] Kuznets, *Economic Growth and Structure*, p. 231. The quotation is from an essay entitled 'Notes on the Take-off'.

Introduction

countries have experienced. This should in no way reduce one's estimate of the importance of the transition in Colombia.

In Chapters 8, 9 and 10 I deal with the special roles of the *Antioqueños*, of coffee and of transport improvements in facilitating the process of transition. This trio does not consist of comparable 'inputs' to which one might ascribe relative responsibility for 'causing' economic development to occur. The historiography of Colombian economic history is still too primitive for such a careful analysis. These three important elements in the story are, as a consequence, treated in serial fashion rather than in a multivariate analysis of the sources of economic growth.

No myth has more currency in Colombia than that which holds that the Antioqueños alone are responsible for the country's economic development. Certainly their contribution is out of proportion to their numbers, but other regional groups and the trickle of foreign immigrants produced successful entrepreneurs as well.[1] The special feature of the Antioqueño experience was their rapid exploitation of coffee as an export crop, and then their seizure of the opportunity to industrialize as local demand grew with the export-generated income. Whatever the appeal of the psychological explanations of the Antioqueños' success, such explanations must still be supplemented with quantitative descriptions of the process by which economic development was achieved. That description is the task undertaken in Chapter 8. My reading of the economic history of the transition leads me to concentrate in that description on the traditional model of trade as an engine of economic growth.[2]

The next step in analyzing the transition is to pursue an analysis of the coffee export economy. In Chapter 9 I proceed by formulating a general model of agricultural supply conditions for export products and then comparing two types from Colombian experience – the period of tobacco export expansion and the phase of coffee's growth to predominance as the principal export product. I emphasize the influence of supply conditions which seem almost to determine the development potential of a given volume of export expansion. Since much of the literature on the export economy has emphasized the level and fluctuations of demand for

---

[1] On the role of German immigrants in the nineteenth century in one region see Horacio Rodríguez Plata, *La inmigración alemana al estado soberano de Santander en el siglo XIX* (Bogotá 1968).

[2] D. H. Robertson, 'The Future of International Trade', *Economic Journal*, XLVIII (1938), 1–14, and Ragnar Nurkse, *Patterns of Trade and Development* (Oxford 1962), p. 14, discuss the application of this term, the latter providing quantitative appraisals of the expansion of trade in this century and the last.

exports, my analysis provides something of a different perspective on the problem of economic dependence.

In Chapter 10 I turn to the impact of the railways. Because the data on railway freight movements are superior to most other sources of quantitative data on the Colombian economy, the study of internal improvements lends itself reasonably well to the methods of the new economic history – the integration of empirical-quantitative data, statistical inference and economic theory. Since the public and private investments made in Colombian railways may have constituted the most significant additions to the stock of social overhead capital in the country's history, the quantitative emphasis has not been misplaced. The railways were particularly important because they facilitated the rapid expansion of coffee exports and the widening of internal markets.

Finally, in Chapter 2 I offer a theoretical analysis of the process by which decline was turned into development. It draws on the interrelationship of population expansion and economic development with the added element of interdependence and external economies.

Before continuing into the heart of the book it would be well to say a few words about the methods employed in analyzing and presenting this work on Colombian economic history.

METHODS

A principle I have attempted to follow is that one's work must be presented in such form that it can be replicated by other competent investigators in the field. Adherence to this principle assures that any conclusions can be challenged by repeating the necessary investigation. I have used no materials which would not be available to any scholar.

Wherever possible I have worked with and presented quantitative data. To some readers it may appear that this book is indeed littered with numbers, charts and tables. Most of the quantitative materials are syntheses of primary sources. In the case of transport costs, for example, I have taken data from travelers' accounts and official sources reported in a multitude of volume and distance units and converted them all to costs per ton-kilometer, i.e. the cost of moving one ton a distance of one kilometer. This process of conversion makes the disparate original sources roughly comparable. At the same time one can check for consistency of data. In estimating the growth of port cities it became obvious that the population censuses for Cartagena contained such large errors that no clear estimate of the city's growth could be made. Despite these checks one cannot be entirely confident about the reliability of the data. All censuses probably contain a biased error of underestimation.[1]

The census data are used in presenting data on per capita trade, in estimating schooling and literacy rates and in calculating the impact of coffee expansion on the rural population. Whatever the limitations of those data they play a central role in the analysis presented in this book. Despite their general use throughout my work the ratios calculated are not generally very sensitive to errors of perhaps 10 per cent in population figures. The reader will, however, want to view all the data critically keeping in mind that statistics can lie.

Limitations of the data on the Colombian economy restrict the range of hypotheses which can be submitted to statistical test. I have used a number of such tests, however, in conditions when they are appropriate. In some cases commonly available variables are used as proxies to test socially significant relationships between variables which are not measurable directly. For example, I show in Chapter 4 the increasing stability of the Colombian government over time by testing whether terms of office served by presidents in various periods varied significantly from the constitutionally established term. Government stability is of course not necessarily coincident with full terms in presidential office. Given the limited data – there is little information on the structure and functioning of the bureaucracy – this approach seemed to be the best available. Since the average length of term served was measurably greater in the twentieth century than in the nineteenth, I concluded that stability increased.

One of the more conventional methods of analysis developed and used by the practitioners of the 'new economic history' in the U.S. is that of the counterfactual conditional. To assess the importance of a particular variable, institution or policy one measures the relevant variables in the existing situation, then compares their values with those which would have existed if the given variable, institution or policy were removed or changed. This technique employs in historical research the same approach used in cost-benefit analysis to determine whether an electrification project should be undertaken, a road built or a tax enacted. In theory at least the economic historian can evaluate a restricted group of past events and decisions, using objective criteria not dissimilar from those used in economic planning.

This method has many weaknesses when applied to historical data.

[1] See Alvaro López Toro, *Análisis demográfico de los censos colombianos: 1951 y 1964* (Bogotá 1968), on recent censuses.

Introduction

Since the counterfactual world (which one invents to compare to the real one) by definition does not exist, there is no means of establishing beyond all doubt what it would be like. One can offer a likely description of such a world, but it would certainly be subject to challenge. The argument in Chapter 7 suggests that the opening up of trade after 1845 caused a fall in average per capita product. This argument implies that I know what the movement in average per capita product would have been without the opening of trade and can hence compare the real situation with the hypothetical other. Historians have used this method on some occasions at least; the prophets of the new economic history have only sought to rationalize the procedure and give it quantitative dimensions.[1] Certainly there is the danger that the hypothetical world may be so different from the real one that one's credibility is sorely tested. But by adhering to the principle of replicability and by emphasizing the quantitative dimensions of the comparisons I offer the opportunity to challenge the conclusions of my analysis.

The method of the counterfactual conditional is especially important to my effort to measure the costs and benefits of Colombian railways. The benefits must be estimated as the difference in the country's transport bill with and without railways. The importance one attributes to the railways depends on the extent to which they lowered transport costs and permitted total traffic to grow. Ideally, one should have at hand data on the price elasticity of demand for transport services which would permit one to estimate the level of traffic without the cost-reducing innovation of the railway. That information is not available but has been estimated, and the elasticities used appear to conform well to *a priori* estimates of their values. In short, the internal consistency of the analysis of the impact of the railways lends support to the general conclusion that the Colombian railways were as important to that country's development as were the railways of North America to the United States.[2]

This work is by no means restricted to formal analysis of quantitative data. In many cases I have attempted to mix together techniques of

[1] For arguments in favor of this method see Alfred Conrad and John R. Meyer, *The Economics of Slavery and Other Studies in Econometric History* (Chicago 1964), particularly the first essay therein, 'Economic Theory, Statistical Inference, and Economic History', pp. 3–30. Other literature on the methodology of the new economic history is discussed below in Chapter 10. A recent summary with applications to American economic history appears in the recent text by Douglass C. North, *Growth and Welfare in the American Past* (Englewood Cliffs, New Jersey 1966), esp. pp. 12–14.

[2] The use of theory to measure variables for which data is not available is discussed in the general volume on American economic history, *New Views on American Economic Development* (ed. Ralph Andreano, Cambridge, Mass. 1965).

Introduction

quantitative and qualitative analysis. This mixing appears in my comparison of the developmental impact of coffee and tobacco; of the tendency toward persistent disequilibrium in the balance of trade; the role of the ideology of *laissez-faire* in the late nineteenth century, and in the evaluation of growing interdependence between economic activities in the stage of transition. The nature of the questions examined precludes formal and precise analysis or unambiguous evaluations of past events. In dealing with Latin America one cannot help depending very substantially on the methods of the old economic history as well as the new.

THE LESSONS

Does Colombia's economic history support any particular theories of economic development? The reader will find his own answers to the question in the course of his reading of the following chapters. For myself I have drawn several general conclusions which might usefully be presented here:

(1) A period of economic decline preceded the period of transition to economic growth in Colombia. There was also a redistribution of income from poor to rich during the period of economic decline. The following might prove to be a fruitful hypothesis for further research: the same factors that caused the decline produced the seeds of discontent that brought about the reversal of that decline. In the phase of transition from a pre-modern to modern economy decline and development may be intimately linked together.[1] I have offered some further thoughts on that question in the final chapter.

(2) The rapid expansion of the external sector, i.e. at a rate well above the growth of domestic production, is not likely to be neutral in any important respects. Its growth will alter the distribution of income; the development potential of various regions; the relative demand for products and services; the political, economic and social power of various groups. The conditions under which the new export is supplied to the world market will affect just how the local economy and society will be altered. The impact of the new imports will depend substantially on who is producing the competing home goods. Whatever the details, change will reach well beyond the confines of the export enclave except under very special circumstances.

[1] For brief observations on this question in the context of United States development 1800–40, and Britain during the Industrial Revolution, see Andreano, *New Views on American Economic Development*, pp. 19–22, and North, *Growth and Welfare in the American Past*, pp. 71–4.

(3) Although the course of events after 1850 shows the folly of a policy of *laissez-faire*, this finding is not a recommendation for autarchy. Other alternatives of balanced industrial and agricultural growth might have been pursued. But Colombians were constrained by a set of ideas of which we know only the outlines. Without further investigation of the intellectual history of the period it does not seem useful to suggest how they should have behaved.

(4) Export-led growth provides a satisfying 'mechanical' explanation of the transition to economic growth in Colombia. Nonetheless, the necessary increase in entrepreneurial initiative which permitted exports to expand rapidly requires its own explanation. My conclusion is that the transition to growth occurred because some Colombians (particularly the Antioqueños) wanted it to occur. The further analysis of their motivations lies outside the theme of this book.

PART ONE

THE ECONOMIC SETTING

CHAPTER 2

BOURBON AND REPUBLICAN POLICIES

1763–1845

The Bourbon reforms joined elements of an older mercantilism with a new colonial economic policy which achieved the first organized exploitation of the colony and the first phase of continuing economic change. The reforms, whatever their central purpose, resulted in the growing dissatisfaction of the criollo elite, the progressive alienation and subordination of the aboriginal population and growing tensions between colony and metropolis. One result was loss of support for monarchy in the second decade of the nineteenth century and finally an end to the colonial regime. Despite these political changes, however, many elements of an essentially exploitative colonial policy continued in the new state after independence. The continuity of economic policy and economic conditions leads me to treat the years 1763–1845 in a single chapter to de-emphasize the political change wrought by independence from Spain.

A change in the international payments position of Colombia did take place after 1825: the flow of resources in tax remittances to the Peninsula stopped after 1810, and the cost of foreign defense (expenditures in Peru

The economic setting

until the Battle of Ayacucho in 1824) and maintenance of a Colombian military force in Peru ended as well. The capital export implied by colonial policy and the foreign expenditures of the new republic on defense represented serious drains on the capital resources of colony and nation alike. It is the purpose of this chapter to describe the mechanism by which the colonial regime extracted the surplus generated in the colony and transferred it abroad to finance imperial ambitions. In the years after Independence formal exploitation gave way to a period of stagnation as political leaders wavered indecisively and failed to make internal improvements or economic policies conducive to development. Economic change continued at an imperceptible pace until the Reforms of 1850.

It has been argued that the colonial system of government, administration and economic organization was so implanted after some two and one-half centuries of rule in Colombia that it continued without substantial change well after the successful movement for independence.[1] This view is false, not because political independence altered economic policies but because colonial policies were themselves continually being revised from the beginning of the Bourbon period. 'The passing of Catalan autonomy in 1716 marks the real break between Habsburg and Bourbon Spain.'[2] Thus for roughly a century prior to the achievement of independence in South America, Bourbon kings chipped away at some traditional policies and strengthened or embellished others. As an example of the first kind of change, the Bourbons for their own reasons gradually reduced the protection accorded aboriginal populations by the Hapsburg kings. At the same time they gradually extended administrative authority of Crown officials vis-à-vis the criollo population. As Morse points out,

It was only under the 'enlightened' peninsular monarchies of the eighteenth century and the 'liberal' revolutionary regimes of the Napoleonic era that a status, 'colonial' in the modern sense, was adumbrated. The difference between Hapsburg rule, under which Spanish American institutions were established and Bourbon rule, which tried somewhat ineffectually to reform them, has been called the difference between absolutism and despotism.[3]

---

[1] This view is stated most strongly in Luis Nieto Arteta, *Economía y cultura en la historia de Colombia* (2nd ed., Bogotá 1962; first published 1942). Nieto is, however, summarizing a view current in the polemical and scholarly writing of nineteenth-century Liberals. For an analysis see Jaime Jaramillo Uribe, *El pensamiento colombiano en el siglo XIX* (Bogotá 1964).

[2] J. H. Elliott, *Imperial Spain, 1469–1716* (New York 1966), p. 371.

[3] The major general survey of Spanish imperial practice is that of John Horace Parry, *The Spanish Seaborne Empire* (New York 1966). A more imaginative examination of Spanish patrimonialism as a mode of administration is to be found in Richard M. Morse, 'The Heritage of Latin America', in Louis Hartz, ed., *The Founding of New Societies* (New York 1964), pp. 123–77, 322–3. The quotation is from p. 141.

Bourbon and republican policies

The early years of the republic in Colombia saw a continued evolution of policies which was started in the eighteenth century by the Bourbons. In the fields of colonial administration, tax policy, land policy, treatment of the aboriginal population, commercial contact with European powers, even the appropriate role of the Church and clergy in policymaking: in all these areas of governmental concern the Bourbon kings experimented and where they felt it necessary, altered traditional approaches, methods and policies. Republican governments continued the experimentation. While it is not true that independence brought no economic change to Colombia, neither is it true that one may discern in the policies followed in the years 1810–45 a momentous break with the past. The watershed of the eighteenth century is marked by the accession of Charles III in 1759, that of the nineteenth century by the Reforms of 1850. Independence stands between, a momentous event in the political dimension but of curiously little import in the process of economic change.[1]

COLONIAL POLICY

Already in 1739 the importance of the Audiencia of Santa Fe de Bogotá was recognized in the establishment of the Viceroyalty of Nueva Granada which was given administrative domain extending over the present territories of Venezuela, Colombia, Ecuador and Panama.[2] The administrative changes proved not to be so important as the economic changes to come in the 1760s. The reign of Charles III (1759–88) was marked by an acceleration in the institution of new fiscal, colonial and economic policies for the Spanish empire. It was during this period that the Spanish empire began to adopt the rationalizing principles of the Enlightenment in colonial administration.

How did the Bourbon policies affect the Viceroyalty of Nueva Granada? The area seems to have prospered in some respects; for example, population was on the increase. The population of what is now the Republic of

---

[1] For discussions of relevant periodizations in Latin American social history see Morse, 'The Heritage of Latin America', p. 165, and a note in the *Hispanic American Historical Review*, XLVII (1967), 318–19, reporting on 'New Approaches to Latin American Periodization: The Case for an Eighteenth-Century Watershed'.
   The insignificance of the impact of Independence on race relations is discussed by Magnus Mörner in *Race Mixture in the History of Latin America* (Boston 1967), pp. 91–109.
[2] A viceroyalty was first established in Santa Fe de Bogotá in 1717 on a temporary basis. In 1743 Venezuela was made independent of Bogotá, and Ecuador continued to be governed by a presidency at Quito. The important change, however, was that the whole territory of the northern Andes was made independent of the viceroyalty of Lima. See Parry, *The Spanish Seaborne Empire*, p. 288.

The economic setting

Colombia probably stood at some 940,000 in 1778.[1] A census conducted in that year counted 742,759 inhabitants in the viceroyalty, exclusive of those in the territory of Quito (now Ecuador).[2] However, the data are incomplete for the Pacific Coast area and Santander, since no figures are reported for what are known to have been populous provinces in those areas. In addition, mining areas and the eastern plains are not included yet must have had substantial populations. The population was probably growing by 1 to 1·5 per cent per annum. The viceroy-archbishop, Antonio Caballero y Góngora, estimated on the basis of incomplete evidence that population was growing 1·5 per cent per annum over the years 1778–88.[3]

Foreign trade was also expanding. Gold production and exports were increasing at a rate between 2 and 2·5 per cent per annum, i.e. somewhat more rapidly than the rate of population growth. This growth was achieved in part by greater freedom of trade within the empire and eventually with other European powers, particularly England.

Free trade within the Spanish empire, which ended the monopoly of Cádiz merchants, was established in 1778. Spain's military commitments in Europe prevented enforcement of trade restrictions; those which remained were completely eliminated in 1797 as the Spaniards finally recognized that they could no longer de jure control the trading relations of their colonies.

The native population of Colombia may never have been better off than in the middle years of the Bourbon period. Their numbers were increasing, all travelers of that time speak of the modest but adequate comfort of the population, and perhaps most important of all, there had been but a minor introduction of exogenous forces which could upset the ecological balance achieved between man and the land.[4]

Many new towns were being formed by Spanish immigrants, particularly in what is now the two Santanders, the area bordering Venezuela north of Bogotá. This same area produced one of the most important

[1] José Manuel Pérez Ayala, *Antonio Caballero y Góngora, Virrey y Arzobispo de Santa Fe* (Bogotá 1951), p. 393, Table A.

[2] Based on data from other censuses for areas not covered in the 1778 census data. I estimated the population for those areas and added them to the available regional figures to reach the total listed in the text.

[3] 'Relación del estado del Nuevo Reino de Granada que hace el Arzobispo Obispo de Córdoba á su sucesor el Excmo. Sr. D. Francisco Gil y Lemus – Año de 1789', *Relaciones de Mando* (ed. E. Posada and P. M. Ibáñez, Bogotá 1910), p. 242. Since the population of Antioquia grew by 20 per cent in that period, the viceroy judged that it could not have grown less than 16 per cent in other areas of the viceroyalty.

[4] See Luis Ospina Vásquez, *Industria y protección en Colombia, 1810–1930* (Medellín 1955), which presents estimates of real wages on several haciendas for scattered years in the eighteenth and nineteenth centuries.

Bourbon and republican policies

populist uprisings in the history of the Spanish empire. The townspeople of Socorro in 1781 marched on Bogotá to protest new Bourbon taxes (particularly the government's monopolization of the purchasing, processing and resale of tobacco) and their more rigid enforcement by viceregal authorities. The rebels marched as far as Zipaquirá, a small town some 30 kilometers north of Bogotá, gathering strength along the way. There they were met by the Archbishop of Bogotá who signed a list of 'Capitulations' promising to allay many of the grievances of the citizens. With that the rebel group disbanded to return to their homes. The capitulations were then rescinded and the leaders punished as insurrectionists. The Bourbon policy of increasing the profitability of the colony to the Crown was having its effects.

More than twenty years remained between the main period of Bourbon reforms and the first stirrings of a movement for greater autonomy (the demand for the *cabildo abierto* in Bogotá, 20 July 1810) for the colony. It was not a period of innovation although most of the changes introduced in the three previous decades continued to be enforced. At the end of the eighteenth century Colombia was still very much a traditional society with all that implies for the working of the economy. Most people produced little or nothing for exchange; there was little physical or social mobility; the effective market was limited by small local demand and high transport costs; the state played only an insignificant role in the economic life of the population.

Republican governments continued the task of altering colonial institutions and policies which had been begun by the Bourbons. In such matters as tax administration, regulation of trade, promotion of industry and agriculture, land policy, labor policy, public works, and other areas of political concern, early republican governments charted no new waters, explored no new frontiers. *Laissez-faire* became more strongly embedded in the minds of policymakers after Independence, but sources of revenue (the tobacco monopoly in particular) could not be given up by the central government.

The wars for independence served to strengthen the social and economic elites by giving them political power: 'The emancipation movement in Spanish America, anticipated by a great many crushed conspiracies, was above all the work of the criollo elite set in motion when the Napoleonic invasion of Spain had brought about a series of disruptive events.'[1] Certainly the principal beneficiaries of the change of political structure and personnel were members of that relatively small elite who monopolize public

---

[1] Mörner, *Race Mixture in the History of Latin América*, pp. 79–80.

The economic setting

office. They presided over the disposal of Crown lands in the new states and formulated economic policies which benefited themselves at the expense of the rural poor. They were able to make and enforce decisions affecting trade, land ownership and artisan activities. Perceiving these political effects of Independence, the popular classes were not favorable to the cause: it meant, in their eyes, a chance for further enrichment of the privileged.

This fact, poorly understood by both Hispanic historians and republicans, can be explained as a legitimate reaction of the people in the face of the frank efforts of the Criollo oligarchy, until the moment Simon Bolívar appeared, to reduce the emancipation movement to the level of a petty debate, destined to convert their commercial affairs into law and their interests into national policy.[1]

Independence gave the criollo aristocracy the administrative and political right to enact policies which would enhance their private interests; nonetheless, the governments after Independence sought first to establish the legitimacy of republican rule – a legitimacy clearly in jeopardy as the degree of open rebellion and breakup of Gran Colombia indicates – by minimizing actual changes from Spanish administrative and economic practice. The governments of Santander (1824–8, 1830–4) maintained the structure of Spanish government as well as its principal practices long after the Viceroyalty of Nueva Granada was whittled back to the size determined by the breaking off of the Captain-Generalcy of Caracas and the Audiencia of Quito.

TAX POLICY AND THE TRANSFER OF RESOURCES

If the aims of the Spanish state required a transfer of real resources to Spain from the colonies, then some mechanism had to be adopted for effecting such a transfer. Two problems had to be solved: (1) the extraction of a surplus from the local economy, and (2) the transformation of that surplus to some fungible form useful in Europe. The first problem was solved by a combination of new taxes and establishment of state monopolies; the second by assuring a net outflow of real resources through persistent deficits in the colonial trade balance.

The Bourbon reforms sought to rationalize and benefit from the production of tobacco in Nueva Granada.[2] The mercantilist side of the tobacco

---

[1] Indalecio Liévano, *Los grandes conflictos sociales y económicos de nuestra historia*, II (Bogotá n.d.), 98.

[2] One might advance the hypothesis that it was the low price and income elasticity of demand for products like tobacco, salt and liquor, which made them appealing for straight monopoly operation. With an inelastic demand, fairly high tax rates could be imposed on these products without greatly reducing their overall consumption.

policy shows up in the regulation of production and sale. In the colonial period and until 1845, there were no concerted efforts to make the tobacco industry an export activity; it was a state activity without prospects or intentions for rapid growth. Just under 20 per cent of total revenues in the viceroyalty were produced by the tobacco tax in the closing decades of Spanish rule.[1] It was the single most important source of revenue in the viceroyalty. The tax was levied in the form of a seniorage represented by the difference between the sale price as the finished product emerged from the tobacco factories owned by the state and the entry price of raw materials purchased at state-declared prices from growers.

The monopoly effected control of supply by designating only certain plots and farmers as eligible to grow tobacco. This provision limited the growing of tobacco and caused more protest than any other aspect of governmental monopoly. Whereas it had been grown freely in the river valleys of Santander and Boyacá prior to establishment of the monopoly in 1774, after that date tobacco growing was restricted to a few specified areas. Harrison notes that the monopoly policy from 1778 until 1845 was characterized by a gradual contraction of the legal growing area. This contraction was achieved, however, through the elimination of a growing number of municipios as legal areas for tobacco cultivation rather than a reduction in the absolute number of hectares planted. Over more than half a century production was increasingly concentrated in the Magdalena valley around Ambalema. The monopoly made a continual effort to restrict the area of production in Santander. By 1778 production was restricted to Zapatoca and the Rio de Oro valley.[2]

In contrast to the Hapsburg policy of allowing 'these and those kingdoms' to operate largely without reference to an international system, Bourbon policy was designed to promote economic development in the colonies as well as a larger flow of resources into the Spanish treasury. Perhaps more important than the new taxes established by the Bourbons, except in the cases of particular excises on tobacco, liquors and salt, was the new vigor with which old taxes were collected. A principal complaint of the Comuneros in 1781, for example, was that the tax laws were being much more vigorously enforced than previously. Moreover, the initial act of public

---

[1] Colombia, Ministerio de Hacienda y Crédito Público, *Memoria del Ministro de Hacienda, 1837* (Bogotá 1837), p. 20. Data presented by the Minister, Francisco Soto, compare revenue by types for 1801 and for an *año común* or average year between 1800 and 1810, with revenues for fiscal years between 1831 and 1836. Ministerial reports will hereafter be cited as *Memoria* or *Informe* with the year and ministry indicated.

[2] John P. Harrison, 'The Colombian Tobacco Industry from Government Monopoly to Free Trade, 1778–1876' (Ph.D. diss., University of California, Berkeley 1951), pp. 20–41.

The economic setting

opposition came in response to publication of an edict that a special surtax would be collected to support naval operations in the Antilles. The vigor with which Spanish authorities sought to extract the surplus from the colonies was clearly related in this case to power struggles with other imperial states.

The growing tax burden need not have occasioned difficulties in Nueva Granada had the revenues been spent locally. However, the net outflow of resources crippled the local economy. The effect was particularly severe in Santander where by-employments in tobacco cultivation had been destroyed by the Crown monopoly. The extension of the *alcabala* to cotton thread, which practically served as a medium of exchange in artisan towns, was particularly objectionable in Socorro and San Gil, two Santander towns where many textile artisans worked.[1] Even if a large share of total tax revenues was spent within the colony of local administration, there still was an outflow of resources and depression of economic opportunities in specific local areas. It should not be surprising that such an area also was the stage for rebellion.[2] The process by which tax revenues were extracted from certain towns and regions for support of the administration in Bogotá and Cartagena was analogous to that by which revenues in colonies are extracted for support of the metropolis.[3]

The transfer mechanism

A policy of sponsoring general economic growth can result in increased revenues for the crown overseas. Assume for example that the crown takes a constant share of total output; then as output increases, the crown's revenue increases. However, if growth occurs only in 'home' industries, and the demand for imports grows *pari passu* with output, then exports must grow at the same rate as total output just to maintain a balance in the balance of payments. Far from being satisfied with a mere balance in the balance of payments, however, a metropolis seeks a growing transfer of resources from the colony back to the metropolis. This transfer can occur at constant terms of trade when exports are equal to the sum of tax remittances and imports. If exports fall short of this goal, then imports may be reduced, and the terms of trade may move against the colony or some combination of those two changes may occur. In contrast to what

---

[1] See David P. Leonard, 'The Comunero Rebellion of New Granada in 1781' (Ph.D. diss., University of Michigan 1951), p. 78.

[2] The major analyses of the Comunero movement are reviewed in a paper by Eric Van Young, 'The Común of Socorro' (unpub. MS., Berkeley 1968).

[3] Rodolfo Stavenhagen, 'Seven Erroneous Theses about Latin America', *New University Thought*, IV (1966), 25–37.

might be expected for an underdeveloped country, the colony must become a capital exporter to effect the transfer of resources to the metropolis. This change requires substantial shifts in the use of resources from home to export activities. Moreover the expansion of imports will require a shift away from import substituting industries to home or export activities. To the degree that export expansion is matched by tax remittances abroad, there will be no impact of imported goods.

I would advance the hypothesis that the degree to which home industries, particularly those of artisans and cotton textiles, were injured in the colonial period was much less than that in the national period because the program of capital exports through tax transfers made necessary a smaller volume of imports, and hence less competition for the artisans. The absence of these international capital transfers after Independence shifted the total burden of reallocation of resources (from home to export industries) onto the import-competing producers in those areas. Whereas all colonists paid for capital exports to the degree to which they purchased goods being taxed by the Spanish king, in the post-Independence period the burdens of participation in international trade were shifted onto import-competing groups, i.e. the artisans.

Ospina Vásquez seems to hold a similar view (though not for the reasons expressed) when he writes:

The complex effect of the fiscal, economic and political measures, and of the social tendencies of that period [1810–30], was in the direction of greater socio-economic mobility, both vertical and horizontal.

This transformation placed the traditional industries in a state of crisis graver than any they had experienced in three centuries of Spanish policy.[1]

For the colonial period we can distinguish two effects of the substantial tax transfers made possible by Bourbon reforms in Nueva Granada: (1) capital exports (represented by an excess of exports over imports and the outflow of gold bullion in contraband) lowered the potential capital stock in the country and hence the potential level of per capita income and consumption: (2) imports (and competition for home producers) were kept at relatively low levels so that it was possible for artisan crafts to escape competition through the period of reform. The first of these effects was adverse for the local colonial economy; the second was more problematical. If one were to contend that elimination of inefficient local crafts was requisite to modernization and growth, then the lower potential impact of imports only served to slow down the process of modernization. If,

---

[1] Ospina Vásquez, *Industria y protección*, p. 131.

The economic setting

however, we recognize that in a backward economy transformation from one economic activity to another cannot be achieved smoothly and costlessly, then the tax transfers, by moderating the influence of potential foreign competition for artisans, probably eased the difficulties of making the transition to a more open economy.

If these two effects represented opposing impacts on the process of modernization and development, which was the more powerful, i.e. on balance was the policy of tax transfers beneficial or harmful? The answer must depend in part on the actual quantitative dimensions of the transfer about which one can only make some general inferences. There are no specific data available on the tax transfers for the colonial period; however, using estimates of gold production prepared by Vicente Restrepo,[1] we may prepare some rough calculations on production, minting, smuggling and direct transfers of gold to Spain in the eighteenth century. Restrepo, after an exhaustive review of official data and the views of earlier writers, estimates total gold production in the eighteenth century to have been Ps$205 million. There are no complete data on the temporal distribution of this output within the century except for partial data on minted gold for the Casas de Moneda of Bogotá and Popayán for the years 1753–1800. Using these data and assuming a slow growth of production from the beginning of the century yields the production curve in Figure 1. The total area under the curve is approximately Ps$205 million; the smaller block for the period 1753–1800 is gold actually minted in Bogotá and Popayán. Above that block is shown the putative contraband and other gold produced (and presumably exported) but not minted. Contemporary estimates of contraband ranged from a low of Ps$200,000 in 1789 according to Viceroy Ezpeleta to a high of Ps$2 million annually (period not specified) by Juan José d'Elhuyar. Humboldt's estimate of Ps$363,000 for the year 1800/1 tends to the conservative side. The calculations represented in Figure 1 suggest that the higher estimates are not impossible, if the assumptions underlying construction of that chart are correct.

Gold production was large enough to have facilitated the capital transfer to the Metropolis. The Restrepo data lend support to the hypothesis that the period of Bourbon reforms was one of substantial capital outflow for Colombia. This hypothesis helps solve the further problem of how an era of rapid economic development (which the period 1765–1800

---

[1] Vicente Restrepo, *Estudio sobre las minas de oro y plata de Colombia* (Bogotá 1952); originally published in 1884 with subsequent revisions. The 1952 edition was published as Number 7 in the Archivo de la Economía Nacional by the Banco de la República.

Bourbon and republican policies

undeniably was) can also be one of local depression. Total output was growing with some rapidity, but consumption could have been stagnant as the surplus was transferred from colony to metropolis.

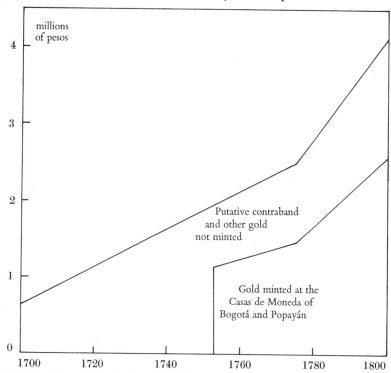

Figure 1 Putative production of gold, 1700–1800. *Source:* based on Restrepo, *Estudio sobre las minas de oro y plata*, pp. 196 ff.

The royal visitors after 1770 tried to expand export activities. The most notable activity to this end was that of the Oidor Juan Antonio Mon y Velarde, known subsequently as the Regenerator of Antioquia.[1] His efforts were directed principally at reviving mining activities of Antioquia and the Cauca Valley. His success is recorded in the growing physical volume of gold exports. Moreover, Mon y Velarde tried to rationalize agricultural production in the Antioqueño area by encouraging local farmers to replace imports from other sections of the country. Perhaps the

[1] The standard work is that by Dr Emilio Robledo, *Bosquejo biográfico del Señor Oidor Juan Antonio Mon y Velarde, Visitador de Antioquia, 1785–88* (2 vols., Bogotá 1954), which includes the principal documents of his 'visit' to Antioquia.

most lasting and important effect of Mon y Velarde's efforts in Antioquia was to establish a center of economic activity and influence outside of the capital. Antioquia became an independent entity, even receiving the right to have its own mint. Local groups in Antioquia challenged the traditional privilege of the merchant class in Bogotá by developing independent merchant, mining and industrial activities. The success of the Antioqueños will claim attention again in Chapter 8.

Bourbon policies in Colombia brought the advent of a truly export-oriented economy. It is not surprising that the Bourbons encouraged and stimulated export activities, for to fail to do so would have entailed an exchange risk and changes in the terms of trade as they began transferring the surplus from the colony to the Metropolis. Simply to extract the medium of exchange from the colony would have depressed local prices and made Spanish goods unsaleable in Nueva Granada. Moreover, massive depression would surely have resulted. Colombia had to be made more dependent on trade in order for mercantilist exploitation to be effective.

Trade and transfers

If we include the period of the Reconquest, more than forty years of Spanish rule in Colombia remained after the establishment of the free trade regulations of 1778. (Independence was not assured until the Battle of Boyacá in 1819.) In those four decades the total trade in visible exports and imports rose, though not as spectacularly as in other regions of Latin America. For the decade 1784–93 the port of Cartagena showed average annual imports of just under Ps$2 million annually, and exports of just over Ps$2 million. In the first decade of the nineteenth century imports seem to have fallen somewhat while exports were slightly higher. Available data are spotty and not all years are represented; contraband trade was substantial, and there is confusion in some reports as to whether the totals include values of trade for Guayaquil, which was administratively part of the Viceroyalty of Nueva Granada.[1]

Ospina Vásquez, after a careful review of the data, suggests that visible exports and imports were roughly equal for the two decades from 1790 to 1810. A comparison of his data with contemporary estimates which take contraband into account indicate that he underestimated total trade. Moreover, if his conclusion is correct, we must label the Bourbon reforms

---

[1] For a summary of data on colonial trade (1784–93) and the post-Independence period see Colombia, Ministerio de Gobierno, *Estadística general de la República de Colombia* (ed. Henrique Arboleda C., Bogotá 1905), pp. 224–7. On trade in other regions of Latin America see Parry, *The Spanish Seaborne Empire*, pp. 307–26.

a failure: if the successful improvement in tax revenues in this forty-year period could not be accompanied by a net transfer of these tax funds back to the metropolis, then the king in Spain gained nothing. Since it is hard to accept the conclusion that the Spanish policy was unsuccessful, we must look in a more complete statement of the balance of payments for that mechanism which made possible a transfer of funds.

Several possibilities for transfers existed: the most obvious was that of direct remittances to the king. Incomplete records of such transfers for New Spain include direct transfer of profits from the tobacco monopoly.[1]

Table 1 *Royal finances in Spanish America at the end of the eighteenth century* (millions of pesos).

Viceroyalty	Income	Expenditures	Net
Nueva España	20·0	14·0	6·0
Perú	4·0	3·0	1·0
Rio de la Plata	3·0	2·2	0·8
Nueva Granada	3·8	3·2	0·6
Total*a*	30·8	22·4	8·4

Source: Alexander von Humboldt, *Political Essay on the Kingdom of New Spain*, IV (4 vols, London 1811, trans. J. Black), 241 ff. The net calculated by me.

a These totals leave out of consideration those colonies which provided no net income to Spain.

It may be useful to cite here the estimates prepared by Humboldt of the state of royal finances near the end of the eighteenth century. There are no specific dates attached to the estimates in Table 1, but they show that the Spanish administration of the late eighteenth century was transferring funds out of the Americas and back to the Metropolis. The transfer was almost exactly balanced by the net exports of the American viceroyalties. The estimates of Humboldt on visible trade of the Americas at the end of the eighteenth century are presented in Table 2. They can be considered in comparison with data in Table 1. Colonial net exports of Ps$9·3 million

[1] A very complete study exists for viceregal finance in New Spain; see Fonseca and Urrutia, *Historia de la real hacienda* (6 vols., Mexico 1845). For Colombia one may cite Aníbal Galindo, *Historia económica i estadística de la hacienda nacional desde la colonia hasta nuestros días* (Bogotá 1874); Climaco Calderón, *Elementos de la hacienda publica* (Bogotá 1911), and Abel Cruz Santos, *Economía y hacienda pública* (Bogotá 1965), vol. xv in the *Historia estensa de Colombia* published by the Academia Colombiana de Historia.

is almost exactly compensated by the net transfer of Ps$8·4 million. These data tend to confirm for the colonies as a whole the picture I have been drawing for Colombia.

But for the Viceroyalty of Nueva Granada the Humboldt data are inconsistent with the hypothesis, for the net crown income of Ps$0·6 million should be compensated by a net export of roughly that amount. Since Humboldt's data instead show a negative commercial balance of Ps$0·7 million, they do not confirm the hypothesis presented here.

Table 2 *Balance of trade of Spanish American Viceroyalties at the end of the eighteenth century* (millions of pesos).

Viceroyalty	Exports	Imports	Balance (+ = exports; − = imports)
Cuba and Puerto Rico	9·0	11·0	−2·0
Nueva España and Guatemala	31·5	22·0	+9·5
Nueva Granada	5·0	5·7	−0·7
Venezuela	4·0	5·5	−1·5
Perú and Chile	12·0	11·5	+0·5
Buenos Aires	7·0	3·5	+3·5
Total	68·5	59·2	+9·3

Source: Humboldt, *Political Essay on the Kingdom of New Spain*, IV, 127–8. The balance was calculated by the author.

The exceptional position of Colombia as a gold exporter explains the discrepancy. Contraband gold exports were greater than the Ps$0·36 million estimated by Humboldt. The estimates in Figure 1 above show that Humboldt's estimate of contraband was too low. If contraband gold exports were Ps$1·2 million greater than Humboldt estimated, then total exports would have been (in Humboldt's figures) Ps$6·2 million and a positive commercial balance of Ps$0·5 million would have been recorded. This amount is quite close to the estimate of net colonial revenue from the viceroyalty indicated in Table 1, i.e. Ps$0·6 million. With plausible manipulations these data tend to confirm for Spanish America as a whole and the Viceroyalty of Nueva Granada in particular the hypothesis that positive commercial balances in the late eighteenth century were compensated by a flow of funds from America to Spain. It is only a short further step to argue that these flows represented an adverse capital movement for the colonies. Such movement was an essential part of the exploitative policy of the Bourbon monarchy.

The earmarking of revenues from the tobacco monopoly for shipment to Spain may have been one of the principal means of extracting the surplus from Nueva Granada as it was in New Spain. Tobacco was the principal source of revenue and was by itself nearly large enough to provide the surplus. The estimates of Francisco Soto in the *Memoria de Hacienda de 1837* for annual colonial revenues in the first decade of the nineteenth century place the total at about Ps$2·45 million of which Ps$0·47 million came from the tobacco monopoly. Data in the *Diccionario de Hacienda* of Canga Argüelles indicates an even higher net revenue from tobacco for the year 1808–9 of Ps$0·7 million.[1] Revenues of the tobacco monopoly thus account for the surplus transferred from the Viceroyalty of Nueva Granada back to Spain.

TRADE AND TARIFF POLICIES IN COLONY AND REPUBLIC

A review of tariff levels in the late colonial and early independence periods shows two things principally: (1) duties were in no case exceptionally high, and (2) there is very little difference in tariff levels in the colonial and early independence periods.

Imported goods paid several taxes in addition to the *derechos de aduana*. In some cases taxes were the same for domestic and imported goods, but in others, special surcharges were applied to imports or goods from other regions of the viceroyalty. Thus it is difficult to measure the overall level of protection for local industries. Table 3 summarizes briefly one analyst's estimate of the level of tariffs.[2] The range of duties applies principally to the major imports, namely cotton textiles of a fairly ordinary kind imported largely from England via Spain. Tariff levels of 30–45 per cent in the colonial period need not be regarded as especially high; however, when to these are added the high cost of transportation in the last part of the eighteenth century, it is clear that considerable protection was still accorded to domestic industry. More important than the restrictions offered by tariffs must have been the bureaucratic difficulties associated with trade within the Spanish empire. There seems little indication, for example,

---

[1] José Canga Argüelles, *Diccionario de Hacienda con aplicación a España*, II (2 vols., Madrid 1834), 521.

[2] See Ospina Vásquez, *Industria y protección*, p. 37.

that English textiles were spoiling the market for local artisans. An active artisan industry then existed in the viceroyalty, though principally located in Ecuador:

> Quito is the only province in South America that can be denominated a manufacturing country: hats, cotton stuffs, and coarse woolen cloths, are made there in such quantities, as to be sufficient not only for the consumption of the province, but to furnish a considerable article for exportation into other parts of Spanish America. I know not whether the uncommon industry of this province should be considered as the cause or effect of its populousness. But among the ostentatious inhabitants of the New World, the passion for everything that comes from Europe is so violent that I am told the manufactures of Quito are so much undervalued as to be on the decline.[1]

Table 3 *Estimates of tariff rates, 1780–1850*

Period	Rates (per cent)
1780–1820	30–40
1820s	30–45
1830–50	20–25

Source: Ospina Vásquez, *Industria y protección, passim.*

But despite European competition, artisan activities, particularly in woolen textiles and other specializations in which machine production developed slowly, continued to be important in the economy of Nueva Granada.

Tariff levels in the 1820s were not changed appreciably from those which prevailed in the late colonial period. The tariff law of 28 September 1821 established about a 20 per cent *ad valorem* tax on imports with variations between 15 and 35 per cent. Textiles, for example, paid 17·5 per cent. Imports of cacao, coffee, indigo, sugar and honey were strictly prohibited. Duties were 5 per cent higher for goods imported in foreign bottoms.[2] Subsequent changes slowly pushed the tariff rates higher.

Due to English insistence and influence duties were lowered somewhat

---

[1] William Robertson, *History of America*, II (London 1777), 498, note LXXIII.

[2] Galindo writes 'all legislative efforts from 1821 to 1846 were directed at (i) raising the cottage industry of Santander to the technical level of European factories by means of restrictive tariffs and (ii) nationalizing foreign ships by means of differential duties'. *Historia económica i estadística de la hacienda nacional*, p. 39.

in the 1830s. There remained the differential advantage for shipment in Colombian bottoms, but duties could hardly be regarded as more than a source of government financing, since little protection could be assured by a 20 to 25 per cent tariff.

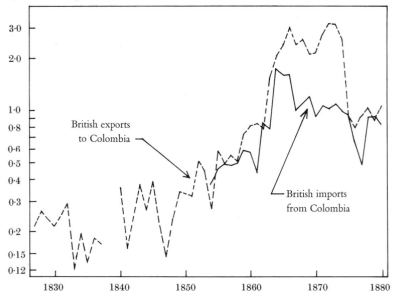

Figure 2 British trade with Colombia, 1827–80 (millions of pounds sterling). *Sources:* United Kingdom, Customs and Excise Department, *The Annual Statement of the Trade of the United Kingdom with Foreign Countries and British Possessions.* Found under 'Finance Accounts' in the *British Sessional Papers* prior to 1854 and from 1854 to 1920 in the papers under 'Annual Statement of Trade'.

Despite the lowering of duties, international trade did not grow until after 1845. For the years 1834–45 recorded average annual exports were just in excess of Ps$2·5 million. Total population had grown by about one-seventh, but exports were about the same as in the late eighteenth century. Lower duties, greater ease of shipping for British merchants, and the *laissez-faire* ambitions of the early Republican governments did not produce a substantial expansion in the total trade of the new country. British exports of cotton textiles to Latin America increased fivefold in the two decades 1820–40.[1] Despite the expansion of Latin American trade with Great Britain, there was no such expansion experienced in Colombia. Trade expansion awaited transport improvements and a viable export product.

[1] See E. J. Hobsbawm, *The Age of Revolution, 1789–1848* (New York 1962), p. 371.

The economic setting

Lower tariffs did not lead to trade expansion in the first quarter century of Republican governments.

The deficiencies in Colombian trade statistics can be partially adumbrated by the availability of U.S. statistics of trade with Colombia which begin in 1825, and British data for exports to Colombia beginning in 1827 and

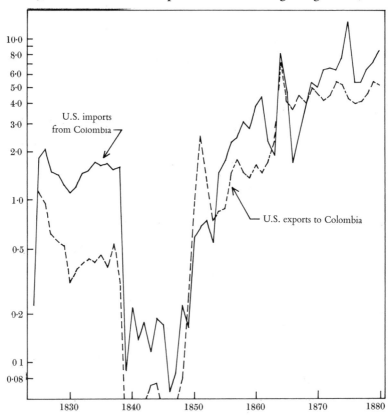

Figure 3 United States trade with Colombia, 1824–80 (millions of U.S. dollars). *Source:* United States of America, *The Commerce and Navigation of the United States*, various years; *Statistical Abstract of the United States*, various years.

imports from Colombia beginning in 1854. To be sure, these data will not together add up to total Colombian international trade, but they do give some quantitative evidence about main trends. (See Figures 2 and 3).

Colombian trade with the U.S. was active between 1825 and 1838, depressed from 1839 to 1847, brisk in the 1850s and at a high but fluctuating

Bourbon and republican policies

level from the mid-1860s to the late 1880s. The cyclical pattern indicates a rough doubling (with wide annual fluctuations) from 1830 to 1850, then a quintupling in the next score of years to a nineteenth-century peak in the early 1870s of around 3 million dollars annually. At about the same time U.S. exports to Colombia (including re-exports) reached levels of about $5 million or about one-third the value of British exports to Colombia. These data sustain the view that political independence did not in itself produce a substantial expansion in the international trade of the new country.

Table 4 *Comparison of U.S. and Colombian trade data, selected years, 1838–72* (current dollars and pesos).

Year	U.S. exports, including re-exports to Colombia (in thousands of dollars)	Colombian imports from U.S. (fiscal years) (in thousands of pesos)
1838	619	197
1839	65	228
1840	135	2
1841	110	131
1843	162	186
1854	937	344
1855	1,062	684
1856	1,611	302
1857	2,038	263
1858	1,689	406
1869	5,080	407
1870	4,792	484
1871	4,420	3,230
1872	4,677	557

Sources: United States of America, *The Commerce and Navigation of the United States* (Washington, various years); Nieto Arteta, *Economía y cultura*, pp. 343–6; República de Colombia, Ministerio de Hacienda, *Informe* (Bogotá, various years).

The deficiencies of Colombian trade data (already recognized in the ministerial reports of the period) are revealed clearly by a comparison of U.S. exports to Colombia and Colombian imports from the U.S. which should be approximately the same. But as the data in Table 4 indicate, there are wide discrepancies. The years shown are the only ones for which both Colombian and U.S. data are available. During the period covered the peso and dollar were approximately equal in value; nonetheless, Colombian data show only a fraction of the apparent trade recorded in U.S. statistics. Averaging those years in the three periods for which data can be grouped, we find Colombian as a percentage of U.S. returns to be: 1838–41, 60 per cent; 1854–8, 27 per cent; and 1869–72, 25 per cent. Part of the difference might be accounted for by fiscal *vs.* calendar year reporting; some part of U.S. re-exports may be recorded in Colombian returns as imports from third countries. However, these accounting errors should be more than offset by value added through normal costs, insurance and freight in the act of shipment. We may conclude that the Colombian data are deficient for the 1830s and 1840s and grossly deficient for the second half of the nineteenth century.

The real source of change in international trade came not from any local trade policies or even from endogenous developments within the former colonies; rather, as Parry has noted,

the remarkable growth in the productivity of mining, cattle raising and plantation agriculture in some parts of Spanish America in the later eighteenth century, the steady increase in the export trade of the Indies, reflected the growth in industrial productivity of northern Europe, and the demand there for raw materials, tropical crops and pastoral products, and the carrying capacity of European and merchant fleets.[1]

And if one looks to individual parts of the overall picture of increased productivity of manufacturing industry in western Europe, one will find particular improvements in the cotton textile industry.[2] The adoption of a host of new inventions and innovations in cotton textiles and ancillary activities produced an astounding decline in the export price of these goods. If, for example, we should place on a scale the cost of production of cotton textiles in 1779 at 100, by 1830 that cost had fallen to a mere 9, and by 1882 to roughly 5.[3] Lower manufacturing costs brought world markets into the sphere of Manchester. In those regions of the world which are now underdeveloped, industrial technology was not taken up until the latter part of the nineteenth century; local producers were at a tremendous disadvantage in their effort to meet the new foreign competition. The Industrial Revolution in England was a substantially more potent force

[1] Parry, *The Spanish Seaborne Empire*, p. 307.
[2] The standard source is *The Cambridge Economic History of Europe*, vol. vi (ed. H. J. Habakkuk and M. Postan) *The Industrial Revolutions and After* (Cambridge, England 1965); see especially Chapter V, 'Technological Change and Development in Western Europe, 1750–1914', by David Landes, pp. 274–601.
[3] These estimates were supplied to me by Robert Gallman, Department of Economics, University of North Carolina.

for economic change than had been the movement for independence or any new policies which may have been adopted by Republican governments in Colombia. As with a host of changes throughout the nineteenth century, exogenous forces were to be the main stimulus for change. If trade policies exhibited little change in the post-Independence period, fiscal policies, particularly taxation, showed even less. All the major forms of taxation and government monopolies were continued into the nineteenth century with the exception of the Indian tribute.[1] Were it not for the fact that several local interest groups within the colonies had applauded substantial changes in fiscal organization, we might not be surprised at the lack of change. However, beginning with the Comunero Revolt and even including a special report written by Antonio Nariño in 1797 criticizing fiscal organization, there was opposition to a number of taxes as anti-economic. Nariño wrote as follows: 'There is one type of tax contribution which is more burdensome because of the obstacles put in the way of the progress of the taxpayer than for the quantity of taxes which they yield for the treasury. Such in this kingdom are the local sales taxes and the monopolies of *aguardiente* and tobacco.'[2] Complaints against the monopoly system were common in the colonial period and continued into the 1840s. However, because no alternative sources of revenue presented themselves, no Republican government before 1850 was prepared to forego colonial taxes, however burdensome they might appear.

The state did not and could not play a substantial role in advancing the cause of economic growth. It was merely one of several competing organizations and institutions seeking to recruit the talent and funds of the Colombian population. Ideology and example were against an active state:

In this period, the miracles of economic liberalism, of free enterprise capitalism, were quite apparent. France had rapidly followed England in the path of industrial revolution. The United States, where the analogy to their own concerns always seemed strongest, had exploded to great power status in a veritable orgy of free enterprise. This earlier day 'theory of economic development' which the advanced nations were calling upon the underdeveloped world to imitate and repeat, was clear and compelling. And in fact, no alternative strategy was really available; it was still too early for there to be an 'Eastern' model as an option to the 'Western' technique of economic growth.[3]

---

[1] The tribute was first abandoned, then re-established. Final abolition came in 1832. For a review of this question I am indebted to an unpublished paper by Franklin Rothman, 'Abolition of the Tribute in New Granada' (Berkeley 1966).

[2] Antonio Nariño, 'Ensayo de un nuevo plan de administración del Virreinato de la Nueva Granada', in *Obras completas* (ed. José Maria Vergara y Vergara 1866), presented 16 November 1797; quoted in Nieto Arteta, *Economía y cultura*, p. 35.

[3] Charles Anderson, *Politics and Economic Change in Latin America* (Princeton 1967), pp. 29–30.

The economic setting

The government in Bogotá had one very substantial advantage over other institutions in the country: it was accorded legitimacy by the governments of Europe and North America and hence had access to outside funds. The legitimacy accorded it was ultimately earned; however for decades there was no real nation-state. The break-up of Gran Colombia in 1830 attested to a dearth of feeling for national solidarity.

In the republican period the main sources of revenue were still the tobacco monopoly and to a lesser extent import duties and minting charges. The source of central government revenue in the fiscal year beginning 1 September 1835 are perhaps indicative (see Table 5). If one regards minting

Table 5 *Central government revenue 1 September 1835 to 31 August 1836* (thousands of pesos).

		per cent
Tobacco (at the plant)	$375	33·5
Tobacco (at purchase)	25	2·2
Import duties	274	24·5
Mint at Chocó	31	2·8
Stamped paper	3	0·3
Minting charges	335	29·9
Miscellaneous	77	6·9
Total	$1,119	100·0

Source: Aníbal Galindo, *Historia económica i estadística de la hacienda nacional*, p. 42. Column sum differs from total due to rounding error.

charges as a kind of export tax, then virtually all revenue came from trade and the tobacco monopoly. The colonial government had relied on a variety of other imposts, but these were put into the hands of local and state governments, including tolls and imposts, duties on interregionally traded goods, and most importantly, the local liquor monopoly.

There was continuing ambivalence about the role of the central government. That ambivalence was a carryover from the two tendencies which marked Bourbon policy – on the one hand, a desire to shape economic growth to serve imperial ends, and on the other, a realization that a certain degree of local autonomy was essential to achieve any development at all.

The nation as an economic unit did not really exist; it was at odds with intense regionalism and the anti-nationalist spirit of the Catholic Church.

Bourbon and republican policies

The absense of a bureaucracy which could articulate a role for the state explains the confusion and indecision of Colombia's national government. The political leaders who moved in and out of office could not provide the continuity of bureaucratic apparatus essential to foster public order and entrepreneurial initiative. The ambivalence of the Spanish Enlightenment carried into the era of independence.

Despite this ambivalence the government did seek in limited ways to promote economic progress. Monopoly privileges were awarded to Colombian and foreign entrepreneurs who attempted to create modest industrial enterprises:

One Englishman contracted for the state salt farm. Another had the exclusive concession for rolling copper. A third formed a company to lease Bolivar's private estates, including silver. Two companies had pearl fishing concessions. Herring, Powles and Graham in addition to contracting a loan secured grants of land for mining and for emigrant colonies, and they maintained weekly newspapers at Bogotá and Caracas to advocate British interests.[1]

Governments of the 1830s and 1840s offered special privileges to Colombians who attempted local production of pottery, glass, linen, iron, paper and cotton textiles.[2] However, governments directed their greatest efforts and funds to the improvement of transportation and communications. Recalling that the Minister of the Interior could write in his report to the Constitutional Congress of 1823 that 'throughout the vast territory of the republic there is not a single carriage road ... ; all are bridle paths and very bad, particularly in the rainy season',[3] there was no chance of over-estimating the seriousness of this problem and its strength as a barrier to accelerated economic development.

Improvements in transportation were required on two fronts: water transport from the mouth of the Magdalena River to inland river ports was slow and costly; road transport from the river ports to highland population centers was in no better condition than on the arrival of the Spaniards in the sixteenth century. The main trunk of the Colombian transport system until the twentieth century was the Magdalena River, connecting the highlands with the Caribbean coast. Steamboats were used on the Magdalena as early as 1828, but they became common only in the second half of the century. Long dry seasons, low water and the rapids at Honda kept transport costs high. Twice a year rainfall becomes so slight that for several months at a time even the smallest boats cannot travel on the upper

---

[1] Leland H. Jenks, *Migration of British Capital to 1875* (New York, 1927), pp. 55–6.
[2] Ospina Vásquez, *Industria y protección*, pp. 175–80.
[3] *Reports of the Secretaries of State of the Republic of Colombia, First Constitutional Congress in the Year 1823* (London 1824), p. 78.

reaches of the river. Sand bars caused by soil erosion created formidable hazards; at the rapids all freight and passengers formerly had to leave one boat, make a twenty-kilometer portage by mule and then board another *champan* (the native canoe or pole-boat) or steamer. Before steamboat service was inaugurated the trip upstream from the coast to Bogotá took six weeks or more.[1]

By granting special monopoly privileges first to Elbers, then later to others, the Colombian government hoped to provide regular, cheap and rapid transportation on the river. At the time of the Congress of 1823, Vice-President Santander estimated the cost of river transportation at roughly 9·5 centavos per ton-kilometer.[2] Elbers was given monopoly rights of steam navigation on the river in exchange for his pledge to build a mule road from the river to Bogotá. Two of his boats were wrecked, however, and he was never fully successful in introducing the steamboat on the river. Competition from the *bogas*, or boatmen, who poled the boats up and down the river prevented the economic success of this technical innovation. It was only after the expansion of tobacco exports beginning in 1845 that regular steam navigation on the river was assured; even then, the bogas continued to pole up and down the river until the end of the nineteenth century. The costs of transport fell from the 9·5 centavos of Santander's period to 2–3 centavos per ton-kilometer after the introduction of steam on the river. Table 6 presents a series of data on transport rates over an extended period.

The early republican governments had little luck in encouraging improvements in road transportation. No carriage roads were built before 1850. A merchant traveling from the valley of Antioquia to the trading center of Popayán took two months to make the round trip. The situation had not changed perceptibly from the eighteenth century when 'most Antioqueño families, even those with moderate means, ate from wooden plates. Apparently the casualty rate of china brought over rugged roads was exceedingly high'.[3] Over some mountain passes and during the rainy

---

[1] See Robert L. Gilmore and John P. Harrison, 'Juan Bernardo Elbers and the Introduction of Steam Navigation on the Magdalena River', *HAHR*, xxviii (1948), 335–59.

[2] My calculation based on his estimate of the freight rate as ten to eleven pesos per carga of 250 lb. from the coast to Honda, a distance of some 1,000 kilometers. Santander's estimate is cited in John P. Harrison, 'Introduction to Steam Navigation on the Magdalena River' (M.A. thesis, University of California, Berkeley, 1948), p. 9.

At about the same time U.S. river rates were about 2 cents per ton-kilometer or less. They were substantially lower on the canals in subsequent decades. See George R. Taylor, *The Transportation Revolution* (New York 1951), esp. Chapter vii.

[3] Rodolfo E. Segovia, 'Crown Policy and the Precious Metals in New Granáda, 1760–1810' (M.A. thesis, University of California, Berkeley 1959), p. 19.

Bourbon and republican policies

Table 6 *Selected transport rates, overland and Magdalena River by route and type of transport, 1776–1949 (centavos per ton-kilometer).*

Date	Route	Human	Mule	Wagon	Rail	Upriver	Downriver
1776	Girón–Bogotá		10·7				
1786	Fusagasugá–Bogotá		13·0				
1882	Ibagué–Cauca Valley		64·0				
	Mompóx–Honda					9·52	
	Bogotá–Neiva		37·1				
	Neiva–Honda		3·94				
1823	Honda–Bogotá	39·7	24·8				
	General					9–16	1–4
1824	General					12–16	
1834	General					6·0	2·0
							4–6
1841–4	Ambalema–Santa Marta						5–5·5
1842	La Guama–San Antonio de Táchira		27·6				
1848	Bogotá–Honda		22·2				
	Honda–coast					2–6	3
1849	Tunja–Bogotá		14·6				
	Ambalema–Santa Marta						2·14
1840s	The Sabena de Bogotá		47·62				
1840s	Santa Marta–Honda					5·85	2·75
1850	Santa Marta–Honda					6·50	2·25
	Honda–coast					7	2–6
1853	Ambalema–Santa Marta						9·17
1854	Sabana de Bogotá				5·71		
	Honda–Bogotá		29·8				
1855	Honda–coast						8–9
	Santa Marta–Honda					6–7	
1856	Honda–Bogotá		39·7				
	General					7–10	
1857	General	25·0–					
		62·5					
	Bogotá–Guaduas		68·2				
	Guaduas–Honda		85·5				
	Barranquilla–Honda					14·5	12·9
	Honda–Bogotá	55·6	27·8–				
			49·6				
	Bogotá–San Gil		23·6				
	Zipaquira–Bogotá		18·8–				
			23·6				
	Santa Marta–Peñon de Conejo					5·60	2·80

cont.

Table 6 – (*cont.*)

Date	Route	Overland transport				River transport	
		Human	Mule	Wagon	Rail	Upriver	Down-river
1858	General	120·0	20·0	5·0			3·50^a
	Bogotá–La Mesa		13·8				
	Bogotá–Girardot		23·9				
	Bogotá–Neiva		23·1				
	Santa Marta–Conejo					4·80	3·60
1861	Honda–Bogotá		59·5				
1862	Girón–Zipaquirá		18·4				
1862–3	Honda–Bogotá		39·7–49·7				
1863	Barranquilla–Honda					6·0	
1864	La Mesa–Girardot		33·33				
	Girardot–Honda						16·0
	Honda–Santa Marta						5·56
	Barranquilla–Caracolí					4·70	
1865	Honda–Bogotá		32·2–54·6				
1866	Honda–Bogotá	63·5	34·7				
1867	Ambalema–Santa Marta						6·11
	Cúcuta–Maracaibo		38·94				
1868	Bogotá–Honda		36·08				
	Vélez–Barranquilla					6·55	
	Bucaramanga-Barranquilla					9·53	
	Honda–Bogotá	39·7	15·9				
1872	General		25·0	10·0			
	(Difficult places)		50·0				
1870s							5·5
1874	FC de Antioquia:						
	imports				17·05		
	exports				11·36		
	Coffee, tools, utensils				8·52^b		
1878	Bucaramanga-Barranquilla						12·57^c
	Cauca Railway				17·38		
1879	Barranquilla–Islitas						2·87^c
	Islitas–Medellín		64·17				
1880	Islitas–Medellín		58·33				
1890	FC de Cartagena				11·43		
1905	FC de La Dorada freight				20·0		
	Locally grown agric. prod.				15·0		
1914	Pto. Col.–Barran.				13·0		
	Barran.–La Dorada					1·58	
	La Dorada–Bogotá				17·68		
	Pto. Berrío–Cisneros						
	General Merchandise				20·0		

Table 6 – (cont.)

Date	Route	Overland transport				River transport	
		Human	Mule	Wagon	Rail	Upriver	Down-river
1920	FC de Santa Marta:						
	imports				8·0		
	local exports				4·0		
	FC de Girardot:						
	imports				28·1		
	local exports				15·0		
	FC de Antioquia:						
	local exports				15·0		
	food, const. mat.				10·0		
	Pto. Col.–Barran.				6·81		
	Barran.–La Dorada					1·26	
	FC de La Sabana				6·0		
1921	Girardot–Pto. Colom.						2·09c
	Bogotá–Pto. Colombia:						
	coffee						5·11c
	flour						6·62c
1928	Bucara.–Chuspas	80·0					
	Chuspas–Wilches				36·0		
1929	Medellín–Pto. Berrío				10·23		
	Berrío–Barranquilla						0·82
1932	Medellín–Berrío				10·92		
	Berrío–Barranquilla						0·74
1943	Medellín–Berrío				8·98		
	Berrío–Barranquilla						1·58
1949	General				6–10	4	2

Sources: see the Note on Sources. *a* An average of up and down river freightrates. *b* Special rate for coffee, utensils and tools. *c* Combined both overland and river transportation.

season on the road from the river ports to highland cities, even mules could not be used for transportation. Human carriers, called *tercios* because they carried approximately one-third of the 200–50 lb. carried by a mule, continued to be the only means of transportation in the wet season and the difficult mountain passes. It is said that one portly merchant who traveled in the highlands of Colombia in the nineteenth century would have been completely immobilized had the exceptionally strong Negro who carried him everywhere on his back been lost to service. Whatever the truth of the more exceptional cases, rates per ton-kilometer for human carriers were high (about six times as high as mule rates) and they were still required on even the principal trails until the second half of the nineteenth century. For a time the tercios even formed an effective interest group opposing improvements in the roads and trails, since they would immediately have been replaced by mules.

Failure of transportation improvement was matched by declining fortunes in export activities in the years after Independence. Gold declined from the late colonial period. Production was unusually high in the 1880s but did not again surpass the decade average of 160,000 ounces set in the years 1801–10 until the second decade of the twentieth century. And as the data in Table 7 indicate, output in the twentieth century, thanks to the use of more modern mining techniques and equipment, remained at a

Table 7 *Apparent production of gold in Colombia, 1537–1966.*

Period	Number of years	Value of production during period (millions of pesos)	Average annual production (millions of pesos)	Average annual production (thousands of fine ounces)
1537–1600	64	53	0·8	64
1601–1700	100	173	1·7	113
1701–1800	100	205	2·1	151
1801–10	10	31	3·1	160
1811–20	10	18	1·8	96
1821–35	15	36	2·4	103
1836–50	15	38	2·5	108
1851–60	10	22	2·2	113
1861–4	4	8	2·0	113
1865–9	5	12	2·3	113
1870–81	12	30	2·5	147
1882–4	3	8	2·8 ⎫	175
1885–6	2	5	2·4 ⎬	
1887–90	4	14	3·5	150
1891–1900	10			122
1901–10	10			135
1911–20	10			233
1921–5	5			203
1923–9	7			207
1930–9	10			350
1940–9	10			503
1950–9	10			396
1960–6	7			360

Sources: Restrepo, *Estudio sobre las minas de oro y plata*, p. 199; Cruz Santos, *Economía y Hacienda Publica*, p. 141; Banco de la República, *Informe anual*, pp. 190–1. See also the Note on Sources.

higher level than was ever achieved under the Spanish or early republic governments.

Gold, a high-value, low-bulk commodity, suffered less from the backwardness of the transport system than did other products. Until regular steam navigation was assured on the Magdalena River, transport costs for agricultural exports were prohibitively high. The mercantilist aims of export growth thus went unfulfilled. Moreover, since population was growing 1·5 per cent per annum, exports per capita were little higher in 1896 (near the start of the coffee boom) than they had been at the end of the colonial period. Internationalist policies, e.g. the trade treaty signed with England in 1825, could not themselves generate economic progress.

SOME TENTATIVE CONCLUSIONS

Until the reign of Charles III colonial policy was neither exploitative nor conducive to local economic growth. An exception to this general statement may lie in Spanish land policies but to that we devote a separate discussion.

An index of the success of the mercantilist policies of Charles III and his advisors would have to include two elements: (1) successful promotion of economic growth (particularly of exportable products) which would enlarge the taxable surplus, and (2) successful transfer of the fruits of growth back to Spain where they could serve the ends of the state. Growing output, tax revenues, exports and imports were compatible with constant per capita consumption. Moreover, the growing production of the colony could encourage a modest immigration and population increase even if per capita consumption was falling.

Growth in output almost certainly did occur in the last half century of Bourbon rule. Substantial transfers of the surplus generated by that growth were possible without price and income adjustments through the excess of exports over imports. Because the principal export product was gold (Colombia was the leader in gold production of the several Spanish colonies throughout the colonial period and produced one-quarter of world output in the eighteenth century), commodity conversion offered no difficulty to the Spanish authorities.

There were plenty of opportunities to transfer an export surplus. The calculations based on Restrepo's data support the view that substantial quantities of gold mined were never minted; a good share of this could have helped effect the transfer. If a complete balance of payments for Colombia for the period 1768–1820 could be prepared, it would show substantial capital outflow. The surplus earned by viceregal authorities and indicated in Table 1 presents a rough approximation to the probable annual outflow of capital.

Capital outflow persisted into the 1820s as Colombia participated in the destruction of Spanish viceregal power in Peru. All during this period there could persist a fairly high level of exports and production without a high level of imports which would have undermined artisan crafts in cotton and woolen textiles. Even when conditions approximating free trade were established in 1797, there was no flood of foreign goods which would have spoiled the markets of the artisans. In fact, neither tariff policies nor quantitative restrictions were to be as important as a continuing stream of cost reducing innovations in the English textile industry. Only with the expansion of agricultural exports – first tobacco and later coffee – could a significant inflow of imports be financed. The capital outflow engendered by the Bourbon policies reduced investment and the capital stock in the colony, but it spared local crafts from competition and preserved small manufacturing.

The events of the years 1763–1845 could have conjoined to bring momentous changes to colony and republic. Had the expansion of output been wholly expended in the area rather than partially drawn off to Spain; had imports expanded dramatically and destroyed artisan crafts; had the state moved successfully to expand international trade: the Colombia of 1845 would have been very different from the Nueva Granada of 1763. But events united to forestall any dramatic changes. Trade expanded – but slowly. The Bourbons exploited – but mildly. Policies changed – but haltingly. Population growth was slow; there was no radical reorganization of land tenure or the general distribution of wealth and income; international trade, despite great fluctuations, failed to become either an engine for growth or decline.

CHAPTER 3

CONTINUITIES IN AGRARIAN SOCIAL POLICY, 1760–1845

The historiography of Independence in Colombia has tended to emphasize political changes inherent in the turnover of elites – the ouster of Spanish officials, the political hegemony of a criollo elite already ensconsed in positions of economic power and social pre-eminence. Whatever the interpretive merits of this political emphasis – and it has been questioned[1] – it disguises much continuity in social policy, continuity which effectively links the period of Bourbon reforms and conservative domination of the Bogotá government until 1845 into a single social time-unit. An investigation of social policy in the years 1760–1845 reveals that continuity.

The most important aspects of social policy were those which treated of the disposition of agricultural resources. Land policies derived from two principal variants of the theory of property delineated on the one hand by the doctrine of Rousseau (and earlier Patristic and Biblical writers) that property rights emanate from the community's delegation of them to individuals and corporate entities, and on the other by those of Locke used to justify individual property rights unencumbered by residual claims of society. It has been suggested that Independence marked a shift from the doctrine of Rousseau to the doctrine of Locke; in fact, however, the change was gradual and continuous throughout the late Colonial and early National years. It is this gradual change which gives to the period the quality of continuity.

But land and property theory constituted but one congeries of social policy problems. Other continuities emerge in the analysis of the other main body of agricultural resources, the rural population and labor force. The social problem facing colonial and national governments might be stated thus; to what degree is the legal power of the state to be used to protect the Indian from exploitation by criollos and mestizos? Linked to this question was a more patently economic one: how best may we assure efficient regimes of production in agriculture? In the social calculus of that

---

[1] See Glen D. Dealy, 'Toward a Theory of Spanish American Government' (Ph.D. diss., University of California, Berkeley 1965), who emphasizes the broad participation of political figures in both colonial and independent governments.

era it appeared that protecting the Indian was counter-productive; and over the course of a whole century protection was gradually withdrawn. Colonial and early national governments were alike in a growing disdain for the resguardo de indios; also alike, they hesitated in spreading the dissolution of the institution. They recognized that more extreme forms of exploitation would follow the breaking up of the Indian communities. Enlightened colonial leaders and the few men of vision who made the revolution – most significantly Bolívar himself – sought in vain the simultaneous achievement of conflicting objectives – integration of the Indians (and negroes to a lesser extent) into a national society and protection of them from the exploitative criollo elite.[1] Indian participation in the larger society apparently required acceptance of exploitation; certainly the criollo elite was not prepared to accept competition in the limited local markets from Indian smallholders – if the elite could prevent it.

Land and labor policies during this period were more closely tied together by a basic economic condition of New Granada, viz., the low population density. Even at the end of the period under consideration only about two per cent of the cultivable cropland was being used. Land was thus freely available for the cost of burning it off. Free land implies that only limited differential rents accrue to land; land prices in the first half of the nineteenth century confirm that rents were in fact low.[2] The criollo elite could not rely on rental income alone unless the location and quality of their estates were superior, in which case they would receive differential rental income. But even in that favorable circumstance the basic availabilities of labor and land would produce reasonably good wages, limited of course by the productive capabilities of labor with a backward technology. Without artificial restraints of any kind a large share of agricultural product would accrue to labor, a small share to land and the rentier class.

This observation could not have been missed by the criollo elite. They realized that their well-being required exploitation of Indian labor. On a local level exploitation could be achieved by monopolizing local labor demand and paying wages below the putative marginal revenue product of labor.[3] But such behaviour may drive workers away to frontiers where land is available and it is not necessary to work for niggardly wages. The criollo elite learned quickly that a 'safety-belt' had to be drawn around the laboring population to cut them off from free land. Land and labor

---

[1] See Liévano, *Los grandes conflictos*.
[2] See Chapter 6 below.
[3] Exploitation here has the same empirical content and theoretical meaning as was breathed into it by Joan Robinson in the *Economics of Imperfect Competition* (London 1934).

policy evolved to assure a controlled market for these two resources in agriculture. Changes occurred with Independence to be sure; but change away from a social policy of protection to one of exploitation *preceded* Independence. And unremitting exploitation was too much for the conservatives who ruled until mid-century. Continuities in social policy reside in the evolutionary character of change.

In succeeding sections of this chapter I sketch out the origins of the resguardo and the social policy of protection. There follows an extended discussion of the evolution of policies presented in the several paragraphs above in theoretical outline. Finally, some general comments evaluate the coincidence of model and reality.

THE RESGUARDO DE INDIOS

The social policies of the late eighteenth and early nineteenth centuries cannot be understood outside of their relationship to the most significant historical social fact of conquest – the decimation and subsequent recovery of the Indian (later mestizo) population. Current estimates place the indigenous population of Latin America above 100 million on the eve of the Spanish conquest; the total population (including whites, negroes and mestizos) had fallen to some 12 million by 1650.[1] This general population decline has been studied in detail only for New Spain; however, Juan Friede found a similar decline for one Indian group (Los Quimbayas) in Central Colombia. The number of tribute paying Indians fell from 15,000 in 1539 to under 100 at the end of the 1620s.[2] These data apply only to one group, but if they reflect the demographic change experienced in other parts of Colombia, then there must have been a general disaster for the native population. Spanish policy from the end of the sixteenth century onward was designed to prevent a continuation of this unhappy phenomenon.

The government seems first to have acted to stem population decline in 1595. That year marks the first in which Indian communities were given title to land and in which severe limitations on the use of native

---

[1] The pre-conquest estimates are in hot dispute among demographers, historians and anthropologists. For a review of the debate and literature see Woodrow Borah, 'The Historical Demography of Aboriginal and Colonial Latin America: An Attempt at Perspective'. The more traditional estimate of 13·4 million for all the Americas appears in Angel Rosenblat, *La población indígena y el mestizaje en América*, II (Buenos Aires 1954), 102.

[2] Juan Friede, *Los Quimbayas bajo la dominación española* (Bogotá 1963), p. 253. The rates of decline of this group seem to parallel the timing and extent of decline observed by Borah and Cook for Central Mexico.

The economic setting

labor were instituted. Fals Borda writes in reviewing this new period of concern for the Indian:

This was a period of triumph of the royal patron over the local power of the enco-menderos ... From a serf-like status such as he had possessed in the preceding years, the Indian was lifted to the position of a lessee of the Spanish king. The revision of titles ordered by King Philip in 1591 according to the first *Cédula del Pardo* upset the two-layer pyramid (the conquerers and the conquered) which had been formed during the years of initial occupation. Moreover, such royal orders definitely cur-tailed the use of native labor.[1]

The land grants were not given in fee simple tenure but they do seem to have limited the infringement of white settlers on Indian lands. This policy of legal recognizance of Indian land rights continued until about 1642 as more and more resguardos were granted.[2] But after that date the claims of the Indian communities came more and more into conflict with the white population.

Although the period for formation of the resguardos came to an end in 1642, they continued without major pressure on them as an institution until the last half of the eighteenth century. During that long period the white population sought not to change the legal basis of communal land tenure but rather to lure the communal Indians away from their lands for work on the haciendas.

In highland areas populated by the Chibchas (the area around Bogotá) direct enslavement disappeared near the end of the sixteenth century to be replaced by a system of obligatory wage labor on white landholdings:

In like manner, Spanish and white hacendados were assumed to have the right to obtain that labor. Thus, in addition to obligatory work in the government mines (to which we have referred, and which ceased in 1729), and to grants of labor in public work projects (which were prolonged in the form of subsidiary personal labor long after emancipation was obtained from Spain) there was forced Indian labor in behalf of the white hacendados, 'white' having here a cultural connotation. It was a matter of forced labor, but paid for by those who also benefited from it in compliance with a public tax, which was wont to be presented as an equitable remuneration.

[1] Orlando Fals Borda, 'Indian Congregations in the New Kingdom of Granada: Land Tenure Aspects, 1595–1850', *The Americas*, XIII (1957), 331–51. The quotation is from p. 333.

[2] The term resguardo is usually translated to English as reservation lands, to have a meaning not unlike the reservations on which Indians of the North American plains were placed as a result of the westward movement of the American frontier. However, it could also mean *reserved lands*, i.e. lands specifically set aside for Indian use and beyond the claims of white settlers or encomenderos. Since the Indians seem initially to have been given good lands, the process did not have the exploitative and negative connotations North Americans may associate with reservations.

Without being the sole source of manual labor for the haciendas, this forced agreement ('concierto') represented undoubtedly a very important, indeed, an essential contribution to the economy of the whites in much of the eastern belt.[1]

The justification for such a system is presented in the *Relación* del Presidente de la Audiencia del Nuevo Reino de Granada, Don Antonio Manso, prepared in 1729: 'It is good for those who serve, because there does not reside in the Indians the desire to *have*; if we were to leave them at liberty, none would work voluntarily.'[2] Operation of the landholdings of the white population required Indian labor; thus the Spanish authorities sought to provide it, at the same time assuring that the rights and ability of the Indians to farm their own lands not be infringed too greatly. If there had to be exploitation, at least it should be regulated. But as Fals Borda points out,

Such a system, however, slowly degenerated, as it reverted into the seignorial arrangement to which it was leading: there were natives who, after being allocated to a farm, stayed there, practically as serfs, for an indefinite period of time. When landlords offered plots on which such Indians could settle (thus securing a dependable and steady labor force) and cash wages, the germ of the present system of resident laborers, with a tint of feudalism, was quick to gain strength.[3]

The protection provided by the Hapsburgs could not extend much beyond the establishment of legal restraints on the white population. The Indians were not the legal equals of the white colonists nor did Spanish justice try to make them so. The system was destined to be exploitative. Nonetheless, Ospina Vásquez, after study of accounts of some haciendas in the area around Bogotá, concludes that 'the remuneration of the *concertados* was relatively high, if one takes into account payments in kind'.[4] The payments in kind implied a level of consumption of principal foodstuffs much higher than that enjoyed in the mid-1950s (or even today) by the peasants of the Eastern highlands.

The system of concierto gradually sapped the Indian communities of population and partisans of the resguardo system. Thus it appeared that as community members moved away for permanent residence on the *haciendas*, *resguardo* lands were not being fully utilized. Moreover, in some cases there must have been continuing population decline even through the

[1] Ospina Vásquez, *Industria y protección*, p. 14.
[2] *Relaciones de mando*, p. 8.
[3] Fals Borda, 'Indian Congregations', p. 340.
[4] Ospina Vásquez, *Industria y protección*, p. 15. Forced labor (*la mita agrícola*) came to an end around 1740 in Chibcha areas, later in the South. But the free concertado continued into the nineteenth century during harvests and peak labor demands. Indians involved in this work may have provided the class of vagabonds who distressed the authorities by their idleness.

seventeenth and early eighteenth centuries exacerbating the empty appearance of some resguardos. Since these communal lands could not be alienated by the community, the *hacendados* were unable to gain control of the lands directly. Instead, new Spanish immigrants to highland Colombia moved onto the reservation lands and rented them from the Indians. This system was made possible in part by the departure of the Indians for work on the haciendas, in part by continuing population decline on some of the reservations.

BOURBON REFORMS

The process of demographic replacement, racial mixture of the population and decline of the resguardo appears to have been evolving slowly in the late seventeenth and into the eighteenth century. In that setting the administrative reforms of Charles III (1759-88) came to follow rather than lead rural social change. It was in those years that Spanish officials first recognized the results of the slow evolution of tenure patterns which were so at variance with the legal prescriptions for the use of Indian lands. The newly appointed *visitador*, Don Andrés Berdugo y Oquendo, 'found that the Indians had been renting their land to whites, leaving only a small portion of the resguardo to themselves. Not only were the whites occupying much of the land but some of them were living, illegally of course, in the pueblo itself.'[1] The Indians rented lands to the *chapetones* (newly arrived Spanish immigrants) and turned their own efforts to labor for nearby haciendas. This practice would be reasonable enough if in fact the Spaniards were more skilled agriculturalists than the Indians. These were, it should be noted, not latifundistas, holders of *mercedes* or encomiendas of Indians granted in the first century after Conquest: rather, these were members of an incipient class of immigrant family farmers often ignored by writers on land tenure in Colombia.[2] Fals Borda writes that the pressure on Indian lands, 'in contrast to general belief, originated not with the latifundistas and hacendados but with a new and numerous class of smallholders identified by Viceroy Manuel Guirior as members of a "middle class"'.[3] Ospina Vásquez after reviewing a number of studies of the history of haciendas in eastern Colombia and the actual state of the Spanish colonists concludes that vast wealth was not characteristic of them.

[1] Fals Borda, 'Indian Congregations', p. 342.
[2] Robert Beyer, for example, fails in his historical review of land tenure in Colombia even to mention such a group, speaking as do most writers of minifundistas and latifundistas. See his 'Land Distribution and Tenure in Colombia', *Journal of Inter-American Studies*, III (1961), 281–90.
[3] Orlando Fals Borda, *El hombre y la tierra en Boyacá* (Bogotá 1957), p. 84.

Agrarian social policy, 1760–1845

It appears that the *vecinos* – the Spaniards – were not a few large landholders. They were numerous in almost all the towns and parishes and very poor in general. The comfortable class, important and influential, was not that of the landowners, but rather that of the functionaries and merchants. (It is still a state of things which prevails in present-day Colombia.) There were a few large absentee landowners, very commonly religious orders. It does not appear that the latifundia was extending itself in a very conspicuous manner. In certain regions of the hot country it occupied an important share of the land. It was a question mainly of cattle estates, and more rarely of sugar cane and cacao plantations.[1]

If this new breed of Spanish colonist did bring with them the prospect of changed and improved agricultural techniques, these either disappeared or were assimilated in the cultural and racial potpourri of highland Colombia. Neither kulaks nor yeomanry nor rich peasant remain to give evidence of a smallholder agricultural class.

Both Fals Borda and Ots Capdequí would date the beginning of a new phase in the history of land tenure with the year 1754. Ots goes so far as to publish the whole of the lengthy *Real Cédula de 15 de Octubre* and comments on it as follows: 'In our judgment, the transcribed Royal Instruction also might well be considered as an attempt by the Spanish state at a true agrarian reform in America. Its scope is no less than the cited *Real Cédula* of 1591 was for its time.'[2] Though the order was promulgated in 1754, the first evidence of the sale of land (made possible by the elimination of resguardos which lacked clear titles) under this new ruling appears in November of 1759.[3] And apparently little concrete action was taken in enforcing new patterns of tenure and eliminating the supposedly inefficient Indian communal lands.

There are good reasons to pick a somewhat later year as a date of transition. Liévano suggests that a judgment by the Juez de Realengos in 1777 and the Cédula sent in response to it by Charles III to Viceroy Flórez dated at San Ildefonso 2 August 1780 marks a clear break with the older policy of protection for Indian land rights. Charles III wrote:

---

[1] Ospina Vásquez, *Industria y protección*, pp. 12–13.

[2] José Mariá Ots Capdequí, *Nuevos aspectos del siglo XVIII español en América* (Bogotá 1946), p. 250. The text of the Cédula appears on pp. 245–50.

[3] Ots, *Nuevos aspectos del siglo XVIII*, pp. 252–4, summarizes the results of a report on land sales prepared in December of 1775. There were thirteen land sales in the years 1759 through 1763; only three more in the next seven years, and eleven in the years 1771–4. This report covered only a part of the viceroyalty; it would appear nonetheless that little activity was carried out under this particular piece of legislation, compared with the wholesale abolition of resguardos in 1777 and 1778. One may even surmise that the land policies developed in the late 1770s (and even the writing of the report here cited) were engendered by the failure of the earlier law to bring changes in land tenure rapidly enough for the authorities.

The economic setting

I have resolved in accord with the counsel of the stated *Juez de Realengos*, and that of my Royal Audiencia, that in all the Viceroyalty owners of crown lands should not be bothered when presently they are in possession and enjoy them either by virtue of their corresponding sales titles, compact with my royal patrimony, private contract, or whatever other contract which might remove suspicion of usurpation, or should they be obliged to sell or rent their lands against their volition.[1]

Although this royal order might appear at first glance to support Indian claims to their resguardo lands, they in fact rarely had clear titles or the royal order which established the resguardo. Their lack of title had previously been ignored; from that moment the Indians were to learn to fear the system of written contracts designed by the whites for white benefit.

Liévano interprets the king's statement as full support for a system of fee simple tenure with no limitations on the right to property reserved by the state. He cites a Supreme Court decision of 1942 in support of his view:

The Juez de Realengos demanded, for the first time in the life of the colony, so it seems, the dominance of Roman rules of ownership and property, according to which the owner was free to do with his possessions whatever he felt like. The socialist criterion present in Spanish legislation for the Indies, which held sway for more than two centuries, encountered in the concept of the Juez de Realengos its first obstacle for the realization of the ends of which it had been tirelessly in pursuit since the age of the discovery and Conquest of America.[2]

The decision of Charles III recorded in the Cédula was fully in accord with the decision of the Juez de Realengos. Thus it altered sharply the basis for land ownership from that of a social function to a private right.[3] And because the new emphasis on the *private* right did not refer to the prebends of communal holdings, the Indian was left doubly without legal recourse.

[1] Quoted in Liévano, *Los grandes conflictos*, II, 215.
[2] Cited in Liévano, *Los grandes conflictos*, II, 213.
[3] In contrast the current Constitution of Colombia establishes the primacy o f the social over the private interest in property. Article 30 reads as follows:

Private property and other rights acquired by just title by natural or juridical persons are guaranteed, in accordance with civil law, and may not be disavowed or injured by later laws. When the application of a law enacted for reasons of public benefit or social interests results in a conflict of the rights of private persons with the necessity recognized by the same law, the private interest must give way to the public or social interest.

Property is a social function that implies obligations.

Expropriation may be undertaken, for reasons of public benefit or social interest defined by the Legislature, by means of a judicial decision and with previous indemnification.

Nevertheless, the Legislature, for reasons of justice, may determine the cases in which there is not ground for indemnification, by a favorable vote of an absolute majority of the members of each Chamber.

Cited in Seymour W. Wurfel, *Foreign Enterprise in Colombia. Laws and Policies* (Chapel Hill 1965), p. 364.

Agrarian social policy, 1760–1845

Viceroy Don Manuel Guirior had already taken on himself the obligation of regulating and rearranging conditions of tenure for the Indians which must have had the benefit of the white population largely in mind:

The promotion and settlement of the population is also a matter pertaining to the Government. The population, although it continues to augment itself naturally and is supplemented by those who are born in and come from Europe, still lacks a reasonable order which would promote its enlightenment and this defect goes back to conquest of the kingdom, when the places inhabited by the Spanish (meaning all those who were not Indians) were few, and the majority of middle class people lived dispersed over the countryside on the boundaries and in the vicinity of Indian towns, taking advantage of the latter's reservation lands and whatever small piece of land their miserable existence allowed them, without being able to comply with the laws which required their segregation nor avoid the damages which such a relationship caused. The result of all this was the sorry state of the towns, their lack of fiscal administration and the serious difficulty of administering justice. All this could in large part be remedied with favorable consequences if the *visita del Distrito*, which the King has charged to the *Fiscal protector don Francisco Antonio Moreno y Escandón* in order to suppress and unify the defective *corregimientos* and enumerated Indians, is put into effect along with regulated demarcations and salaried *Corregidores* with the full scope of jurisdiction which the laws provide for and charged with the collection of tributes. This measure, although difficult and overdue, may produce advantageous effects in substance and with regard to the promotion of the agriculture of the Indians, the separation of people of color, apportioning of parishes and unification of towns, so that I intend not to change the dispositions which have that purpose in mind; and if they are not able to be evacuated before my departure, I do not doubt that your majesty will uphold this measure with all the protection that so useful an enterprise as foreshadowed by your Majesty in the *real cédula de 3 de Agosto* of that year demands.[1]

One would err, however, when considering the history of land policy in this period, in being overly concerned with legal changes. What must be emphasized is that the growing Spanish population and the expansion of the urban population (Bogotá was probably growing in population at between 1 and 2 per cent per annum from the late eighteenth to the mid-nineteenth century) increased the demand for foodstuffs. The derived demand for well-located land was consequently pushed up, so that Indian lands near urban centers increasingly looked more appealing. The colonials thus got the state to institute a policy which would move the Indians off the best lands and make them available for consolidation with the haciendas. Moreover, with the bunching of the Indians together the returns to labor on the resguardos would decline and more Indians would willingly seek wage labor on the haciendas of the criollos. Juan Friede writes that the appearance of rural wage labor:

[1] *Relaciones de mando*, pp. 149–50.

is something which was achieved only in the eighteenth century, when, because of a scarcity of land and oppressive colonial taxes, together with the general impoverishment of the residual Indian populations of America, the Indian had to work for wages in order to subsist. The consistent policy of impoverishing the native population in order to force it to work has been utilized and is generally utilized in the colonial system. In a not dissimilar manner nowadays, as he was forced to work in Egypt and India, so the African Negro is forced to work in British and French colonies.[1]

A more recent analysis of a similar phenomenon has been provided for Zambia. The native Africans, far from failing to take advantage of new market opportunities, increased maize production. Notice the response of the colonials who, we may presume, were not especially different from the Spaniards of highland Colombia in the eighteenth century:

Rather than welcoming this response, the government viewed it with concern. By this time the number of European farmers was sufficiently large to exercise a dominating influence on agricultural policy, and obviously, these farmers were not interested in lowering the price of agricultural products to the mines. Instead, they wanted sufficient land for further expansion and high prices for their output. As a means of attaining their land objective, in 1928 native reserves were established in the railway area and the process of moving Africans into these areas was begun. The effects of the measure were to lessen existing African market competition, and, more important, by reserving for European settlement a strip extending in most areas about 20 miles on each side of the railway, to limit severely potential African competition in commercial markets.[2]

The human situation is too similar for there to have been other than similar responses: the powerful will, where they can, also get rich. And where they are not efficient, the power of the state will be brought to bear. Again citing the case of Zambia, we can see the likely policy response of a dominant white government:

If the weakness of European agriculture was recognized, so also was the growth potential of African maize production. In his 1931 report, the Director of Agriculture justified the lack of systematic agricultural assistance to Africans in the railway belt with the following remark: 'If the whole of this market were taken by the native (as it might well be, with the exception of a very few commodities, should deliberate attempts be made to foster the production of crops for this purpose) the European population would be rapidly driven off the land, and it is hard to see how the individual native would greatly be benefited, for his share of the proceeds would be infinitesimal.' The absurdity of this argument merely attests to the fears of the European farmer.[3]

[1] Juan Friede, *El indio en lucha por la tierra*; cited in Liévano, *Los grandes conflictos*, II, 210.
[2] Robert E. Baldwin, *Economic Development and Export Growth: A Study of Northern Rhodesia, 1920–1960* (Berkeley 1966), p. 150.
[3] Baldwin, *Economic Development and Export Growth*, p. 151.

Agrarian social policy, 1760–1845

It is the almost sudden removal of Crown protection of the resguardo as a legal institution which makes the Colombian situation distinctive. Removal of that protection was essential to the designs of the criollo elite seeking to control the best agricultural land and the wealth and income associated therewith in a growing economy. The policy of the Enlightenment (aimed at restoring some lost *laissez-faire*) only gave *carte-blanche* to a landed elite.

The principal objectives of the government of Charles III no longer included social justice for the Indian. All administrative efforts were bent to the gradual rationalization of colonial policy; what this meant in practice was that more and more tax monies were to pass from the American colonies to the Metropolis. The proper approach in pursuit of this aim seemed to be rationalization of the land tenure scheme. But since *de facto* occupance of Indian lands reached back to the end of the seventeenth century, and since the royal officials could observe the direction of change in tenure conditions, they saw themselves as only helping to speed up an inevitable process. During 1777 and 1778 the viceregal government arranged for the sale and disposal of all or part of the nineteen resguardos in Boyacá;[1] such a rate of turnover in land occupance can hardly be regarded as merely helping along an inevitable process. As the lands were sold, Indians were forced to leave and take up unoccupied space on other resguardos. The protest sent by the Indians of the resguardo of Betéitiva to the Viceroy on 12 July 1779 describes the results:

About two years ago Don José Campuzano commanded us to leave with all speed the lands which we possessed in said (Betéitiva) and Tutuzá and to move with our families and belongings to the pueblo of Duitama where we were to receive sufficient land. We pleaded with him all we could ... but he paid no attention. On the contrary, he said that if we did not obey his commands he would order our houses and huts to be burned. Therefore, we obeyed and walked to Duitama under the greatest difficulties, with so many hardships that we have no words to describe ... how we reached Duitama after two days of traveling with our women and more than sixty children, our cattle, and other animals. And when we arrived at Duitama, our only shelters were the trees and the eaves of the houses of the Duitama Indians ... We stayed, but until the present no land has been assigned to us, for which reasons we live like renters (*arrendados*), on the verge of perishing. ... The greatest (of our afflictions) is the ill treatment that we received from the Indians of Duitama.[2]

Thus the late 1770s marks an acceleration in the white assault on Indian land privileges established early in the seventeenth century. But control of land also implied control of the principal complementary resources,

[1] Fals Borda, 'Indian Congregations', p. 343.
[2] Cited in Fals Borda, 'Indian Congregations', pp. 346–7; also (without references) in Liévano, *Los grandes conflictos*, II, 289–90.

The economic setting

the labor of the indigenous population. An unintended result of Spanish policy was the growth of a floating rural population seeking employment on the haciendas when possible but more usually increasing the population of vagabonds.

One finds evidence of official concern with vagabondage in many areas of Latin America during this period. Mario Góngora has studied the problem in Chile and considered its temporal and social origins.[1] No comparable studies of this phenomenon have been carried out for Colombia. However, in several areas of the country the problem was just beginning to appear. For example, Juan Friede writes as follows in summarizing his review of the late colonial period in the Colombian Massif (Cauca and Nariño):

Summarizing these data we can say the following: in the last days of the Colony we find the Indian resguardos of the Colombian Massif greatly weakened by their century-long fight, with varying degrees of success, against the white, Spanish, and criollo colonizer. Many Indians, the unsubdued as much as those who belong to reductions, abandon their resguardos and towns and wander through the region living as day laborers, miserably exploited. ... They do not have refuge in either property, land or shelter. It is a true rural proletariat. The colonial authorities try in vain to prevent vagrancy with laws and ordinances. The resguardo itself begins gradually to decay. Traditional communal ties are weakened. Forced by precarious economic conditions, paucity of land, excessive taxes, various Indian families let loose of the main support of the community, and try to establish their own individual means of subsistence.[2]

The breaking up of the resguardos in that part of the country was bringing to the rural labor market a substantial increase in labor supply. As mentioned earlier forced labor (presumably only necessary in conditions of labor scarcity) was given up around 1740. We may suppose that the white landowners publicly deplored vagabondage but privately profited from it, since rural wages could not rise under such conditions. During any period of labor scarcity, as for example at harvest time, vagabonds could be rounded up and forced to work because of their violations of vagrancy laws. Moreover, the acceptance of Roman law implied in the Cédula Real of 2 August 1780 could have established a system of fee simple tenure. Land could thereafter be held out of productive use merely to assure that it not be taken up by the floating indigenous population for subsistence farming. In a land-surplus economy land had to be withheld from the

---

[1] Mario Góngora, 'Vagabundaje y sociedad fronteriza en Chile. Siglos XVI a XVIII', Publication No. 2, *Cuadernos del Centro de Estudios Socio-económicos* (Facultad de Ciencias Económicas, Universidad de Chile, Santiago, 1966).

[2] Friede, *El indio en lucha por la tierra* (Bogotá 1944), p. 97.

Indians in order for them to accept labor on criollo haciendas. Vagabondage was a result of the establishment of tenure rights unencumbered by social obligations to utilize the land. If land had not been held out of production, the vagabonds (and Indian laborers as well) would have settled down to subsistence production which generated no production surplus which could be exploited by the criollos.

It is difficult to accept Friede's assertion that population pressure in the late eighteenth century was lowering the per capita product of the land. It is much more likely that vast expanses of usable land were kept out of the hands of the Indians, the better to force them to labor on the haciendas. The discussion and concern about vagrancy can then be seen as a complement to a social policy designed to force the Indians to accept wage labor.

But vagabondage was not exclusive to Indian areas. The report of the Royal Visitor to Antioquia in 1789 is filled with references to the 'idleness' of the people.[1] Although the Spanish term for vagrancy (*vagancia*) is not used, idleness (*ociosidad*) is common. There were few Indians in Antioquia and apparently none on reservation lands. Thus the idleness spoken of there must have derived from other sources. Góngora shows in his study of Chilean social history that both poor Spaniard and Indian were forced into marginal status in the society.[2] His analysis suggests that the victims of the new social policies introduced by Charles III extended beyond the indigenous population to include the lower strata of Spaniards, criollos and mestizos. Since there is no *a priori* reasoning which would suggest that a 'liberal' policy must promote social mobility and the improvement of the life-chances of the middle strata, we need not deny the possibility that the principal victims of Bourbon policy were not Indians alone but a whole chromatic range of the poor of the viceroyalty.

The area of Santander was notable for its prosperity and well-being in the middle of the eighteenth century. It was a 'pull' area for Spanish immigrants. It was the area which produced in the Comunero rebellion opposition to Crown policies. Yet in the second half of the nineteenth century it was in undeniable decline. In this area at least the 'liberal' policies seem to have served the interest of the rich as against the poor and modest-of-means. Perhaps these lines were even more firmly drawn than those between Spaniard, criollo, mestizo, *pardo* and Indian.[3]

---

[1] See Emilio Robledo, *Bosquejo biográfico del Señor Oidor Juan Antonio Mon y Velarde, Visitador de Antioquia, 1785–88* (2 vols., Bogotá 1954).

[2] Góngora, 'Vagabundaje y sociedad fronteriza', *passim*.

[3] For a comparison with Mexico see François Chevalier, 'Conservateurs et liberaux aux Mexique', in Arturo Arnéiz y Freg and Claude Bataillon eds., *La intervención francesa y el imperio de Maximiliano* (Mexico 1965).

The economic setting

In Antioquia, however, the 'idlers' of the 1780s found an outlet for unspent energies in the southern frontier. The high birth rate in the area combined with free land brought a steady population shift along the temperate slopes of the central cordillera. Some of the first new towns were formed at the very end of the colonial period; the migratory movement gathered strength in the nineteenth and early twentieth centuries.[1] The aim of Bourbon social policy was elimination of inefficient communal holdings. The administrators of that policy in the years 1777 to 1808 probably thought that such an approach would ensure the desired growth of a class of smallholders who would promote economic progress and technical improvements. Why did the policy fail? Why did lands pass from communal holdings to large haciendas? The answer may lie in the changing theory of property which supported the attack on the resguardo.

We have already suggested that the land policies, though initiated and promulgated by Spanish authorities, were encouraged by the criollo upper class. Yet the combined forces of these elites only accelerated somewhat the change in land tenure; the resguardo was only slowly eliminated from various areas of the country. For example, in Boyacá a number of important resguardos were eliminated only in the years 1834 to 1840.[2] The areas to the north of Boyacá seem to have been in the hands of white settlers already in the mid-1850s. The provinces of Socorro, Girón, Pamplona, Vélez and others reveal by their Spanish names and origins the domination of Spanish population there. Moreover, the Comunero rebellion, which originated there in 1781, was almost purely a white colonist movement against the colonial government.

There were no significant Indian components in the area from the late eighteenth century onward.[3] Similarly, Antioquia had fewer than 5 per cent Indian population on the eve of Independence.[4] The resguardo remained strong into the twentieth century only in the south of the country. There, limited growth of the white and mestizo population plus some ties to the older Incaic traditions combined to produce a more stable communal setting for the resguardo system. Although the elites stood to gain from elimination of the resguardo, they could bring about its demise

---

[1] The Antioqueño story must in some respects be treated separately from other areas. See James J. Parsons, *Antioqueño Colonization in Western Colombia* (Berkeley 1949).

[2] See Fals Borda, 'Indian Congregations', p. 350.

[3] See Friede, *El indio en lucha por la tierra*, pp. 100–2, which examines briefly the insignificant role of the indigenous population in both the Comunero rebellion of 1781 and the movement for independence in the second decade of the nineteenth century.

[4] See Parsons, *Antioqueño Colonization in Western Colombia*, p. 4.

only where their numbers were strongest – around Bogotá, the administrative center of colonial government, and Spanish towns in Antioquia, Santander, and those scattered through more populous Indian territories. It took but 66 days in the rush of revolutionary zeal for the criollo Republican government to set in motion the legal process of eliminating the remaining Indian reservations. On 24 September 1810, the junta opened its formal attack on the traditional Indian system of land tenure. Under the guise of promoting individual rights the resguardo was denied legal sanction in the Republican period: the resguardos were to be divided among community members and the land was henceforth to be treated as individual private property (thus giving rise to the term *repartimiento* or partitioning of the land). The decree of 5 July 1820 gave the Indian his independence from the reservation; 'Thus', writes Juan Friede, 'the Indian problem in the Republic became one of the life or death of the reservation.'[1] Where the Indians held together and tried to retain ownership of their lands (as they did in southern Colombia), they were kept under constant legal pressure to sell by nearby haciendas.

The impact of criollo policies as formulated by the new republican governments varied in the several regions of the country. Reviewing the situation in Boyacá, Fals Borda concludes as follows:

> By 1810 the population of Boyacá had largely become a great community of mestizos. Most of the mountain localities had been by that time converted into *parroquias* regardless of whether they were inhabited by Indians, mestizos or whites. Therefore it seems that the government's decision to finish the resguardos altogether was more realistic than it has heretofore been considered.[2]

The contrast with the opinion set forth by Friede, who was studying the south, is clear. The most balanced view would have to take into account the fact that the initial legal enactments made little difference to land tenure arrangements. The actual breaking up of common lands and their distribution to tribute-paying Indians was delayed until 1832; still the Indians were prohibited from selling their landed share for ten years; but not until the Liberal government of José Hilario López enacted the Reforms of 1850 did the Indians – as other Colombian citizens – hold this land in fee simple with full rights of alienation. Thus many aspects of tenancy in all regions were to await two developments which came only in the second half of the nineteenth century: (1) expansion of trade in agriculture exports and textile imports; and (2) population growth which would depress the land-man ratio to create the problem of the minifundio.

---

[1] Friede, *El indio en lucha por la tierra*, p. 106.
[2] Fals Borda, 'Indian Congregations', p. 349.

The economic setting

Although the criollos moved slowly in their actual encroachment on Indian land, they were quick to seize other advantages presented by independence from Spain. One result of the military struggle, the first of many civil wars in Colombia, was the departure of Spanish loyalists for the Peninsula. Their lands were returned to the national patrimony, then put up as backing for bonds sold in support of the military effort for independence. It is impossible to establish the quantitative significance of that land redistribution. Although the 1963 report of INCORA, Colombia's agrarian reform agency established in 1961, refers to Republican seizure of Spanish Loyalists' lands in 1819 as 'the first agrarian reform',[1] most of these lands ended up in the hands of large landowners. It is true that the newly independent government did make illegal the system of entail (*mayorazgo*) thought to generate excessively large holdings.[2] Whatever the real effects of entail, its legal proscription did not stop formation of large holdings or bring about their disintegration. Aníbal Galindo writes that between 1820 and 1874 some 3·3 million hectares of government lands were distributed and that 'no more than 100,000 hectares have been ceded to occupants and cultivators of the land'.[3] The financially solvent criollos who brought about the revolution thus benefited from their control of the Republican government by acquiring the former Crown lands at bargain prices: lands which had sold for 20 to 30 pesos per hectare at the end of the Colonial period were ceded to bondholders or sold to finance the war for 1 or 2 pesos.[4]

Three categories of land came under the purview of the new republican governments: Crown lands (*baldíos*, known during the colonial epoch as *realengos*), which had never been alienated from the public domain during the colonial period; Loyalist lands which reverted to the national patrimony, and resguardos which had always been regarded as leaseholds of the Indians still in possession of the Crown. On the eve of Independence

---

[1] Instituto Colombiano de Reforma Agraria, *Segundo año de reforma agraria – 1963* (Bogotá 1964), p. 18.

[2] Most writers comment on this legal change, some suggesting it is important (Nieto Arteta, *Economía y cultura*, pp. 156–7), others that it was insignificant. Since many large holdings actually got their start during this period, the latter view seems more realistic.

[3] Aníbal Galindo, *Estudios económicos i fiscales* (Bogotá 1880), p. 259. Legislation and other material surrounding the alienation and sale of public lands, 1833–56, is reviewed in an annex to the *Memoria de hacienda, 1873* (Bogotá 1873), pp. lxxxiv–lxxxix, written by Aquileo Parra.

[4] As reported in lectures by Indalecio Liévano Aguirre at the Universidad de los Andes, spring 1963. Francisco de Paula Santander was granted the extensive Territorio Vásquez for his wartime efforts, and his colleague, Vincente Azuero, received the Carare concession for his good works. The area constituted a substantial proportion of what are now the Departments of Santander and Norte de Santander.

the first category of lands probably remained as valueless as they had been throughout the colonial period. It was only in the second half of the century that lowland areas came into economic use; and only after the gradual eradication of tropical diseases beginning in the 1920s could such areas support concerted economic activity. Some mountainous areas and the vast eastern plains (*llanos orientales*) will perhaps never be occupied. The mere change of political regime can hardly have made much difference in the disposition or personal profit associated with most of the baldíos.

Loyalist lands were probably limited in extent. We may assume that Spanish loyalists were limited to the upper echelons of the colonial bureaucracy and some few settlers recently come to the viceroyalty from Spain. Since one aim of Spanish administrative policy was to shift around personnel in order that they should not become too alienated with local points of view and local interests, it seems unlikely that these officials had great landholdings. Moreover, it is generally agreed that the colonial officials held high social status completely incommensurate with their economic circumstances which were inferior to the wealthiest criollo merchants, miners and landowners.[1] Thus the benefits to be gained from expropriation of Loyalist lands must have been limited.

It was to the Indian lands that the criollos looked for the windfall they hoped to derive from the acquisition of power. Two favorable results could flow from the final destruction of the resguardo: (1) land could pass out of the hands of the Indian community and into those of some nearby hacendado, and (2) labor would presumably be freed for temporary or permanent work for the same hacienda. It is here that one would expect to see the most strenuous efforts for 'land reform' to be exerted.

In fact, however, there was lengthy delay in prosecuting the attack on the resguardo. Legally abolished in 1810, it lived beyond the Reforms of 1850 well into the twentieth century in some areas.[2] Why was the attack on the resguardo so feeble? It seems strange that the institution should hang on until the 1940s. One can conclude several things. First, the Indian was clearly not a simple-minded victim of criollo malevolence and greed. He stood his ground well in many places. Second, the institution itself must have inherent qualities making it technically and economically

---

[1] For both evidence and views on this matter see *The Origins of the Latin American Revolutions, 1808–25* (ed. R. A. Humphreys and J. Lynch, New York 1966).

[2] There were still some eighty-eight resguardos covering 70,000 hectares in the Department of Nariño in 1928. Since that area accounts for 2.2 per cent of the department's territory, the continuing importance of the resguardo is undeniable. The resguardos probably accounted for well over 10 per cent of land in use. See Ospina Vásquez, *Industria y protección*, p. 19.

feasible. The Indians easily adapted to the growing Spanish and mestizo population and leased lands to them – whether for communal or individual profit would be most interesting to know. Third, the value of the land held by resguardos must have been substantial to generate so much concern, litigation and mutual distrust. This conclusion can hardly be surprising since the population growth (both urban and rural) experienced from the mid-eighteenth century onward would have driven up the value of well-located land if no land-saving new technologies came along.

But aside from these limited conclusions there is little that can definitely be said about the rise and decline of the resguardo with respect to its implications for the distribution and growth of income, or for changing social status within Colombia. This most important of institutions, though much studied from the legal point of view, remains with much of the rest of Colombian rural history, unknown.

SUMMARY

One is drawn to the conclusion that the period 1760–1845 makes a natural unit for continuities in social policy. In comparison with changes generated by exogenous forces in the second half of the nineteenth century the pace of change was slow.

Despite the Bourbon reforms and the gradual encroachment of the criollo elites on the disadvantaged, after Independence conditions of land tenure and land use changed only slowly. It was most rapid where conditions of domestic and foreign demand made the tension between potential and actual gain too great for the ruling class to resist. Leadership passed in the years 1845–85 to the Radical Liberals (*Gólgotas* as they were called) who presided over an acceleration in the pace of change. With the added factor of the disamortization of Church lands in 1861[1] there was an increase in land sales, land prices and the gradual polarization of farm units into latifundia and minifundia.

In few places had rapid agrarian change and polarization begun before the middle of the nineteenth century. But this fact cannot deny importance to the Bourbon social policies of the eighteenth century or the accumulative aspiration of the criollo elite in the early nineteenth. The social policies enunciated during this long epoch of slow change were to have substantial consequences for the pace and direction of change after 1845. For that reason they deserve attention.

[1] See pp. 72–3, 127–9.

PART TWO

THE LIBERAL PERIOD

CHAPTER 4

THE POLITICS AND ECONOMICS OF COLONIAL REFORM, 1845-85

Interpretation of the years 1845-85 in Colombian history has followed two lines of argument: one view common among the intelligentsia of that day was that the policies of nineteenth-century liberalism were the required medicine for turning a backward Indian country into a modern nation.[1] This opinion is sustained in the work of Nieto Arteta,[2] Fals Borda[3] and other historians of this century. Whatever the social costs of reform in the uprooting of indigenous peoples and disruption of traditional modes of living, they were regarded by these observers as the necessary prelude to economic and social progress. Fals Borda is not sanguine about the impact of events in the second half of the nineteenth century on the lives of the rural poor, but he attributes their problems to the co-optation of the reforming Radicals by the seignorial order which they attempted to subvert.

---

[1] For a review of the contents of the Reforms of 1850 by one of the young reformers see Aníbal Galindo, *Historia económica i estadística de la hacienda nacional* (Bogotá 1874), pp. 50, 93 ff.

[2] Nieto Arteta, *Economía y cultura.*

[3] Orlando Fals Borda, *La subversion en Colombia* (Bogotá 1967). This work has been revised and translated as *Subversion and Social Change in Colombia* (New York 1969).

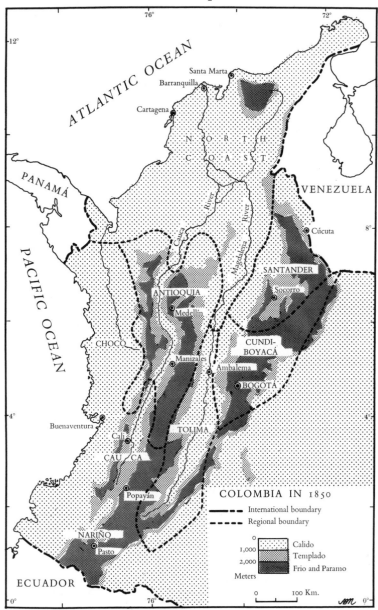

1   Colombia in 1850: topography and major regions. *Source:* Banco de la República, *Atlas de Economía Colombia* (Bogotá 1960).

Colonial reform, 1845–85

The present realities of Colombia have their foundation in this nineteenth-century synthesis, when a significant socioeconomic advancement was gained. This advancement was brought about on the basis of the partial disintegration of the seigniorial order from which there remained only those values and norms required by innovations in the political (representative democracy, nationalism), commercial (*laissez-faire*) and technological (mechanistic counter-values) realms. In this way the caste system was weakened to allow the emergence of a new type of peasantry and a new money-trade aristocracy. The two-party, open class political system of today was also created during this period as a result of acute local conflicts.[1]

Fals Borda's own research on the changing economic and social condition of the rural poor make it most difficult to accept the view that this was a constructive period.[2]

An alternative and pessimistic view of the Reforms of 1850 has been presented by two distinct groups: first, by the 'nativists' writing in the 1940s to show the disastrous consequences of these policies for Indian communal life and hence for the indigenous rural population;[3] and second by economic historians who held that the period 1850–90 was one of economic stagnation and decline, resulting in large part from errors in policy decision.[4]

The nativist group had been able to show the difficulties of particular Indian groups and their disappearance as identifiable cultural entities; however, the reformers of the nineteenth century had held the disappearance of such traits as an objective of their policy so that the nativist findings, even when accompanied by evidence of the difficulties of adjustment to the breaking up of reservations, could not of themselves undermine an essentially optimistic view of the reforms.

Ospina Vásquez was particularly concerned with the lack of industrial development during that period as well as the gradual decline of artisan industries due to foreign competition. He brought to bear more general evidence of declining real wages in agriculture (although his data are

---

[1] Fals Borda, *Subversion and Social Change*, p. 94.

[2] See, for example, *Campesinos de los Andes* (Bogotá 1961), pp. 23–5; *Hombre y tierra en Boyacá* (Bogotá 1957), pp. 98–102, and 'Indian Congregations', pp. 331–51.

[3] Publications of the Instituto Indigenista de Colombia of that decade deal with a wide range of Indian problems. The early study by Juan Friede, *El indio en lucha por la tierra*, has already been cited. Antonio García was leader of the Instituto and published a number of articles of interest.

[4] In effect, the only economic historian writing on this period was Luis Ospina Vásquez in *Industria y protección*. The reforms have been interpreted in pessimistic terms in the writings of Indalecio Liévano Aguirre, *Rafael Núñez* (Bogotá 1944), and *El proceso de Mosquera ante el senado* (Bogotá 1967). A critique of Liévano's work appears in Jorge Orlando Melo, 'Los estudios históricos en Colombia: Situación actual y tendencias predominantes', *U.N.*, *Revista de la Dirección de Divulgación Cultural*, II (Universidad Nacional de Colombia, 1969), 37–9.

subject to many criticisms) and showed stagnation in artisan industry and failure to develop manufacturing before 1890.

Still the picture was not complete. Advocates of reform argued that workers could shift from inefficient agrarian and import-competing activities into the export sector. As some activities declined, others would prosper to make the country on balance better off. The process of economic development always entails the shifting of resources and income from some groups and regions to others. Some groups suffer in the process, but that is not in itself evidence of overall decline even though it may indicate a trend toward a more unequal distribution of income. To show a downward trend in levels of living for artisans and rural wage workers in the highlands is not sufficient to prove stagnation or decline in the country as a whole. Thus in this and the following three chapters I have had to bring together a much broader range of data than either the nativists or the economic historians to evaluate the secular trend in total and personal welfare. Only when the gains of those groups who benefited from trade and other policy changes are matched against the losses of other groups can one assess the net effect. I make a case in Chapter 7 for the pessimists who hold that the Reforms of 1850 had disastrous economic consequences.

The deficiency in policy decisions was a principal cause of stagnation and decline. For that reason this chapter is devoted to the genesis and unfolding of government policy on four crucial issues in the period 1845–85. Elite groups were able to implement government decisions which served their own interests to the detriment of others. Because the elites controlled political decisions, they could affect the path of economic change and the distribution of income. The decisions they made on economic policy were not coincidental with the general welfare of the country. The economic history of this period thus requires a 'political' explanation.

ISSUES IN COLOMBIAN POLITICS

Four principal issues presented themselves during this period and had lasting significance for the growth path of the economy. They include the treatment of commercial policy, particularly levels of duties on imported manufactures; public land policy; the question of federalism or centralism in public administration, and finally the role to be accorded the Church in national life. To some extent these issues divided along major party lines between Liberals and Conservatives; but over the period 1845–85, the issues were much too important not to reveal lines of interest group rivalries and class conflict which transcended party lines and produced intra-party conflict. Perhaps if one felt sanguine about the directions and the results of these policies, no lengthy analysis would seem appropriate; but if political decisions made voluntarily produced a period of economic decline, a careful reading of the politics is in order.

Nineteenth-century Colombia had only one important issue of external economic policy, the tariff. There was no need for a policy on foreign investment since it hardly existed. Immigration policy provided no heated debate since few immigrants came or talked of coming. Exchange controls, export taxes, capital repatriation requirements had to await the serious crises of the Great Depression to become affairs of the state. A single issue – how much should the duty be – could be used to sum up Colombian commercial policy. That issue was enough to cause serious divisions among interested parties.

The second major issue for consideration was really a series of separate but related questions about the disposition of the major natural resource at the community's disposal – land. Much of the legal manipulation which went into the land laws of this period dealt only with lands unsuitable for agriculture in any form. The great extent of *tierras baldías*, government owned lands, is to be explained as much by their lack of utility as by under-population or lack of capital for land purchase in the nineteenth century. Legislation affecting government lands was probably less important than the treatment of Indian resguardos and Church lands (the so-called *manos muertas*). These were more likely to have qualities that made them worth owning.[1] Government lands became important during the several unusual 'booms' in export products which were gathered in low wastelands rather than produced by any agricultural production cycle. Concessions were given out for the gathering of cinchona bark and for indigo: once the export boom was over concessions usually reverted to the government and the lands to waste.

A microcosm of this process occurred when capital was diverted into the cinchona trade in the 1850s. Secretary of Finance José María Plata was severely criticized for practically giving away lands to private speculators. In 1855 the Sainte Rose Cie. of Paris obtained a concession of more than

---

[1] An exceptional case was that of Territorio Vásquez, 'which included two immense ele-emosynary holdings of the Church called Guaguiquí and Terán, sold to Lucrecio Salcedo and José María Peralta in 1865 and 1866.
  'These immense haciendas, which included almost all the area between Santander and Cundinamarca in the Eastern cordillera down to the Magdalena River, were bought later by the Texas Petroleum Company. Then as now the lands were occupied by *colonos*, i.e. inhabitants without legal title.' See Fals Borda, *El hombre y la tierra en Boyacá*, p. 101. This vast territory was probably of no use until oil was discovered. One may doubt that it even provided many masses for the souls in Purgatory.

thirty million hectares, and David Castello got a half a million hectares in a choice cinchona region near Neiva. Grants of from 1,600 to 8,000 hectares were not uncommon. But as it turned out the speculators did not profit from the concessions of 1855. The cinchona market collapsed, and they allowed contracts to lapse and concessions to return to public lands.[1]

Lands of sustained importance were those located around the several urban centers and in areas peculiarly adapted to production for export. And these were in general lands already occupied by owners in fee simple, by religious groups or by communal Indian organizations. Because the state held residual claims to Indian lands and asserted claims to *tierras en manos muertas* the disposition of these lands came to provide a series of political issues in the second half of the nineteenth century.

The question of public administration (federalism *vs.* centralism) dominated political commentary from the time of Bolívar's assumption of dictatorial powers in 1828 until the War of a Thousand Days (1899–1902). One would err, however, in attributing any persuasive political ideology to those espousing either centralist or autonomist views. The position which any particular political figure held on this issue seems more closely related in Colombia (as indeed in other parts of Latin America) to the range of personal control which that figure thought he could muster in the face of rivals. Colombia had no political leader after Santander in the 1830s who could enforce centralism until Rafael Núñez was able to force adoption of the Constitution of 1886. The experiments with federalism – particularly in the years 1863–80 – left the Government of Colombia weak and irrelevant to any planning for economic development. Even the functions of night watchman were largely turned over to regional governments! The weakening of the national government made articulation of a conscious development policy impossible.

Attitudes toward the Roman Catholic Church and its rightful role in Colombian society may seem rather far from the range of economic policy. But policies respecting Church lands were not developed independently of a total attitude about the Church. The Church was under attack from 1861 until 1885; during that time much of the land in the hands of the Church was expropriated and re-sold to private owners. Various valuations have been placed on the Church properties, Ps\$24 million being the highest estimate and somewhere around Ps\$15 million being the lowest.[2]

---

[1] The case is discussed briefly in the *Memorias de Hacienda for 1858 and 1860*, pp. 9–10, 46–7, respectively. For a general review see Safford, 'Commerce and enterprise', pp. 277–8.

[2] See Juan Pablo Restrepo, *La iglesia y el estado en Colombia* (London 1885), pp. 415–16; and Felipe Pérez, *Geografía general, física y política de los Estados Unidos de Colombia*, I (Bogotá

Another estimate concluded that the value of the expropriated holdings was equal to about five times the national budget of that period.[1] One of the leading authorities of the time, Juan Pablo Restrepo, in his *La iglesia y el estado en Colombia*, claimed that opponents of the Church overestimated the wealth of its possessions, and for that reason in part, the most frequently cited objectives of the expropriations were not fulfilled. Those were: (1) to pay the national debt and to establish public credit on a sounder basis; (2) to put into commercial circulation property and capital which were frozen; (3) to damage the Conservatives politically; and (4) to damage permanently the monastic societies and 'to end the cult'. Moreover, legislation forbade the further accumulation of lands.[2] There remained other outstanding issues, particularly control of the educational system, which continued to surround the Church in Colombia, but these need not be considered here.

These then were the issues which separated Colombians in the years between 1845 and 1885 and which, in the course of their resolution or postponement, influenced the possibilities of economic progress or decline. Only the tariff was a narrowly economic issue; the others, by producing divisions and divisiveness in the country, made the putting off of solutions to economic problems the only feasible response. The Reforms of 1850 produced the wrong answers to many questions of economic policy and led to a long delay in providing any answer at all to many more. Safford summarizes the results of 'reform' in the following terms:

The shock of the Liberal innovations deepened political divisions in Colombian society, and played an important part in provoking the frequent civil wars of the period. Church power was clearly at issue in the brief civil war of 1851. Decentralization, involving an attack on the federal army's budget, and very existence, was a factor in the Melo coup of 1854. Both federal autonomy and church power were involved in the conflict of 1859 through 1863. The free trade tendency after 1847 fostered the alienation of Bogotá's artisans; their hostility toward the upper, merchant-capitalist class led not only to the coup and civil war of 1854, but also to recurring fears of class revolution through the 1860s. These internecine struggles obviously

---

1883), 266. The value of lands actually appropriated by the government was placed officially at Ps$11·1 million. See Academia colombiana de Historia, *Historia extensa de Colombia*, vol. *xv*, Book I, p. 488. Some data is published in *Memoria del Tesoro, 1868* (Bogotá 1868), pp. 74–9.

[1] Guillermo Hernandez Rodrigues, *De los Chibchas a la colonia y a la república* (Universidad Nacional de Colombia, Sección de Extensión Cultural, Bogotá 1949), p. 185.

[2] In support of the agrarian reform program, Church leaders recently agreed to give all remaining lands, except those for Church buildings, convents, monasteries and the like, to INCORA for distribution to the landless. It was widely noted that the Church had almost no lands to give. See the *New York Times* (14 July 1967), p. 2.

played an important role in undermining development. Labor was killed and at the very least forced to interrupt its work. Immigrants were discouraged from coming to New Granada. In time of war, moneylenders called in their loans and credit was paralyzed. Capitalists sent their money abroad for safekeeping, on occasion going with it to reside permanently in England or France or Spain. The resulting scarcity of capital sent interest rates up. The high cost of capital discouraged new private enterprise. Beginning in 1855, and with increasing strength after 1864, a counter-current to the basic Liberal dogma set in, and government initiative in development was sought. But the government could not act. Civil wars constantly undermined its credit. It could not secure the capital needed to develop communications, to expand education, or to establish a national bank.[1]

The combination of self-serving private interests and the lack of state power sufficient to curb violence produced political conditions inimical to economic development. Without solution to the 'political' problems, economic progress was impossible.

INTEREST GROUPS IN COLOMBIAN POLITICS

There were four groups which together made up the spectrum of interests and participants, either vocal or subdued, in the politics of reform after 1845:[2] (1) the elites, (2) urban middle groups, (3) the rural peasantry and (4) communal Indians. These four groups contained within them sub-groups which often differed on matters of policy. The elites can be divided into four subgroups: merchants, landowners, clerics and politicians. These subgroups overlapped, but each had an internal consistency with respect to social origins, economic interests and political attitudes and affiliations. Urban middle groups included artisans and petty bureaucrats as distinct subgroups. Often, one of the subgroups, among either elites or middle groups, had a strong interest in one issue yet cared little about others, e.g. artisans and petty bureaucrats shared an interest in the tariff question, yet the former cared little about public administration, and neither were greatly concerned with land tenure questions.

The other two groups are less easy to differentiate, but the peasantry was distinguished from communal Indians by their greater involvement in a market economy and the degree to which they were influenced by the decisions of the elites. The communal Indians were in some respects an undifferentiated mass engaged only in subsistence activities. Their

---

[1] Safford, 'Commerce and Enterprise', pp. 406–7.
[2] For a more elaborate typology of political participants in Latin America see George Blanksten, 'Political Groups in Latin America', *American Political Science Review*, XIII (March 1959), 106–27. My more limited list is meant only to include groups interested in the economic issues.

concerns did not go much beyond public policy toward reservation lands. Since that issue was crucial to their continuing existence as communities, their interest in it and reactions to it were important. While outlining the composition of these groups and their subcategories I will also try to analyze their positions on the several issues of importance here.

Merchants, first of the elites to be considered here, were the principal proponents of free trade and a federal system of government. They have generally been identified with the Liberal Party and its radical wing (*Gólgotas*) in the period 1848–80. Some have held that this group cannot really be distinguished from landowners or other elites. Yet their interest in tariff policy, an interest not shared with landowners in the highlands, does differentiate them for our purposes. The Samper brothers, Salvador Camacho Roldán and Aníbal Galindo did combine interest in trade and commerce with export-oriented agriculture. They were also politicians. Nonetheless, they are best identified as merchants and free traders, advocates of a policy which was never supported by conservative landowners whose interests did not extend beyond local markets.

The landowning elite were the owners of highland haciendas who did not seek expanding external trade. They were largely satisfied with the possibilities of urban markets for highland crops grown on their lands. They sought no changes in relationship with their clients or with the rural system of power, *caciquismo*. The landowning elites were non-innovative highland groups who not only did not seek change but actively opposed it.

A very different landowning group appeared in the lowlands. They were agricultural innovators who opened new lands and tried their luck and skill in export markets for primary products. One example was Francisco Montoya, an Antioqueño who became the major owner of tobacco lands in the Magdalena Valley. He was a true innovator – different from the highland hacendados. He and others like him favored free trade and were often closely linked to the merchant group.

Perhaps the most consistent allies of this landowning elite were the clerical personnel of the Roman Catholic Church. They supported the interests of old families in the highlands because those families favored the stability and system of power of which the Church was a part. In highland areas the priest made important community decisions. His authority was unquestioned by the rural poor.

In the 1850s the Church was under attack from the Radicals. The Jesuits were expelled in 1850 by a Liberal government. The spectre of an anti-religious Vendée became a reality (or so it seemed) when the Constitution of 1863 established religious freedom and hence the possible growth of non-Roman churches, and also forced the expropriation of Church lands. Thus the hierarchy found itself in league with other opponents of change against the Liberal reformers.

Politicians constituted a separable elite group. They were drawn largely from those trained in the professions, particularly law. They established liaison with other elite groups and served as the intermediaries articulating the interests of others. Their positions on the tariff and federalism depended less on commitment arrived at through careful study than on the prospects for personal gain. Despite the supposed cohesion of the Liberal and Conservative parties after 1848, there were spectacular cases of party switching and factionalism within parties. No consistent approach to the issues came from the professional politicians. They manipulated the apparatus of government for their own ends. Consider for example the myriad changes in the tariff between 1850 and 1880. These changes cannot be explained by reference to the changing interests of other groups; rather, tariff changes are explained by the politicians' manipulation of commercial policy to curry favor with other groups. In the course of these manipulations the politicians came to be differentiated from other elite groups. Along with the petty bureaucracy they began to see a strong government as the source of employment and power.

The elites were small in number when compared to lower social strata. On all issues that required popular voting, even when the franchise was extended only to property owners, other groups became politically important. Artisans were numerically important. Silversmiths, weavers, tailors, tanners, furnituremakers, and many other trades were represented in the largest towns and had limited influence. They favored a protective tariff since many of the artisans (particularly those in textiles, leatherworking and furnituremaking) were in direct competition with foreign products. For historical reasons most of the artisans specializing in woolen textiles were located in the smaller towns of Boyacá and Santander; they were less susceptible to foreign competition than were workers of cotton goods. They were as a consequence unlikely to join in protests against free trade. Divisions within the artisan class prevented action to oppose the low tariff in the years from 1854 to 1880. Moreover, the divisions between urban and rural artisans worked against the formation of an interest group strong enough to enforce its demands.[1]

The petty bureaucracy was the only group which had a direct interest

---

[1] The opposition of Mexican textile producers to foreign competition in the first half of the nineteenth century is discussed in Robert A. Potash, *El Banco de Avío de México, 1821–1846* (Mexico 1959).

in the establishment of a centralized political system: it could provide them with employment and power. But they were too weak and too few in the third quarter of the nineteenth century to create such a system. Through that period, however, they were to grow and provide the stabilizing force after 1885 which made possible growth of a centralized system. They were concerned with the tariff, since it was the main source of central government revenue, and the form of public administrations.

The largest group numerically was the rural peasantry. Its style of life and dependence on the city differentiated it from the remaining communal Indians by a tie to the market system.

The peasants' foothold on the land had been slipping since the 1770s. The rate of change accelerated markedly after the Reforms of 1850. The size of holdings became polarized between the very large units and minifundia. More and more of the peasants found themselves to be either landless and renting occupants (*aparceros*) of land owned by absentee urban dwellers or victims of a system of inheritance which encouraged fragmentation and inefficient divisions of holdings. Yet these changes were so slow that the peasants never managed to articulate an opposition to public land policy. They were manipulated by an elite coalition of landowners, clerics and rural *caciques* (politicians). Their interests were rarely considered in the disposition of the issues which dominated Colombian politics.

More isolated than the rural peasants were communal Indians. It is difficult to establish their numbers for any period while the resguardo system still thrived. Many of the supposed occupants of reservation lands had left their communities for other employment on the growing haciendas in the lowlands and in cities. Despite these defectors from the reservation system the share of Colombia's total population still in the tutelage of this patrimonial arrangement must have been large. In 1850 perhaps a third of Colombia's population lived as communal Indians with practically no economic or social ties to mestizo and white Colombia.[1] Despite numerical importance they were easily exploited by elite groups.

The elites were able to form coalitions against weaker groups. Although politicians had little direct interest in land policy, they helped landowners establish legal conditions antithetic to the interests of peasants and communal Indians. Occasionally, intra-elite coalitions were opposed by an elite group's support of lower-class interests, as when the clerics supported local communities of peasants and Indians in their disputes with the

---

[1] This percentage is no more than a guess. Rosenblat, *La población indígena y el mestizaje en América* (Buenos Aires 1954), fac. p. 36, puts the Indian population in 1825 at 35 per cent of the total.

landowners and government. Only the merchants risked a direct struggle with other elites. With the support of an ex-Conservative general and former president, Mosquera, they attacked the Church and its wealth. Since the clerics found strong support among other elite groups, that attack did not undermine the essential functions and power of the Church.

An analysis of intra-elite struggles is too narrow to encompass the broad picture of economic change. Too much of Colombia's political history has been written within the narrow perspective of the elites. At the same time, Marxist class analysis is inadequate because of the inter-class coalitions along party lines and between specific elite patrons and their clients. Some combination of class and interest-group analysis is required to explain the formation of policies out of the struggle over issues. The next section examines the role of classes and interests in making policies.

FROM ISSUES TO POLICIES

The tariff

The tariff was important to four groups among those listed: the merchants, who favored free trade; the politicians, who sought revenue from the tariff but were so influenced by the ideology of *laissez-faire* as to oppose its implementation as a protective device; the artisans, who wanted protection; and the petty bureaucrats, who saw the tariff as the only means of supporting the administrative operations of the state. The limited range of groups influenced by the level of the tariff explains why it created little interest. As Bushnell writes, 'the tariff issue, which has often been a cause of dissension in Colombia as elsewhere in Latin America, has seldom loomed quite large enough in Colombian party struggles to become a main center of attraction'.[1] The tariff divided the Liberals. The party split after the election of José Hilario López in 1849 on the general issue of reform into the Moderates (*Draconianos*) and the Radicals (*Gólgotas*). The Radicals favored elimination of tariff duties and establishment of complete free trade. They were drawn from and represented the merchant group. The moderates, although no less imbued with an ideology of free trade, favored a slower course toward tariff reduction. Moreover, they saw the tariff as a revenue-producing agent rather than a means of protection. The Conservatives, who only began to recognize themselves as a party around 1848, took a position generally opposing high tariffs.

[1] David Bushnell, 'Two Stages in Colombian Tariff Policy: The Radical Era and the Return to Protection (1861–1885)', *Inter-American Economic Affairs*, IX(4): 3–23 (Spring 1965), p. 3.

Colonial reform, 1845–85

The tariff issue inflamed partisan interests in 1853. In the election of that year General José María Obando succeeded López and with Radical support sought to reduce duties. The Sociedad Democrática de los Artesanos led by Ambrosio López opposed the government of Obando and supported a successful military coup in 1854 by General José María Melo. (Ambrosio López, first leader of the Artisan Society of Bogotá, was the grandfather of Alfonso López, first of the populist leaders in twentieth-century Colombia.) But their political power was insufficient to maintain Melo in the presidency. A coalition of Radicals and Conservatives combined with disaffected moderates brought down the Melo government.[1]

With tariffs low and exports high there was a spectacular growth of imports, many of them in direct competition with local handicrafts. Imports did not rise because the tariff fell (it actually rose slightly between 1851 and 1859); nonetheless this was the issue around which interest-group lines were drawn. And the loss of the artisans is recorded in the growth of imports if not in the failure to enforce a protective duty.

Tariffs were not cut in the 1850s. Table 8 presents the estimate of Ospina Vásquez of the level of the tariff on one principal import from the late 1840s to the 1880s. A wide range of imports was subject to duties; the category *domésticas* was representative of cheap textiles which accounted for a large share of total imports. The difficulty of estimating tariff levels was increased after the tariff decree of 16 October 1861, when fixed duties per kilo of gross weight were instituted. In 1895 there were 15 separate duty rates in effect, no fewer than 9 of them applying to various manufactured cotton goods, 10 to linens and 5 to woolens. Moreover, duties were levied on the weight of the whole package, including coverings, box, etc., making the calculation of the rate on the goods themselves even more complicated.[2] Following Camacho Roldán, Bushnell suggests that the tariff on domésticas in 1870 was about 60 per cent. The *de facto* tariffs set by Radicals in the 1860s and 70s may have been significantly lower than those which had been imposed in the 1850s despite the apparent failure to alter legal duty rather significantly. I return to this question in Chapter 7. In any case, 'The mere fact that Colombian duties began to rise in the mid-seventies was often less important than the decline in the basic price of many European manufactures that marked the last quarter of the century.'[3]

---

[1] The government of Melo did not offer the promised benefits of a higher tariff. Melo deceived the artisans to gain support for his rise to the presidency. Once in power he sloughed off their requests. Miguel Urrutia M., *Historia del sindicalismo en Colombia* (Bogotá 1969), pp. 33–73.
[2] See *Bureau of the American Republics Bulletin*, 'Colombia, Trade for the Year 1895', IV (July 1896), 768. [3] Bushnell, 'Two Stages in Colombian Tariff Policy', p. 8.

The liberal period

Within any given duty class the gross weight levies weighed more heavily on low-value, bulky products, i.e. more heavily on *domésticas* than on printed cottons. As a result the tariff was at once highly regressive and minimally protective for producers of low-value textiles, cheap furniture and leather goods within Colombia. But local duties, state taxes and transport costs were probably greater in value than the tariffs; the tariff itself provided only part of the protection for domestic producers. The Liberal rhetoric of the years 1861–80 favored free trade; yet legal duties remained high throughout this score of years. But as will be shown in Chapter 7 in a quantitative analysis of government revenues accrued from tariffs, the protection accorded home industry reached a low ebb in the 1860s and 1870s.

Table 8   *Tariff on 'domésticas', 1849–1905.*

Year	Duty (per cent)
1849	51
1851	60
1857	57
1859	88
1869	77[a]
1870	76
1877	58
1879	43[b]
1883	110
1890	45
1905	60

Source: Ospina Vásquez, *Industria y protección*, pp. 223, 224, 258, 306, 307, 333.
[a] Crude linen. Estimates for domésticas not given.
[b] Ospina cautions that this figure may be too low.

The tariff issue was dead as a source of overt class conflict early in 1854, for the artisans were never again able to muster strength to protect their economic interests. In the decades after 1850 the principal imported products, accounting for 60–70 per cent of the total, were cotton textiles.[1] No more than a quarter of total consumption was supplied from abroad

[1] Ospina Vásquez, *Industria y protección*, pp. 214, 263.

in the mid-1850s,[1] but by 1890 the position was reversed and 70 per cent of cotton textiles consumed were imported.[2] The changing balance of domestic and foreign production is a good indicator of the powerlessness of the artisan class to prevent the incursion of foreign goods. Although artisans could in theory shift out of import-competing activities and into export or other domestic activities, the options did not open up significantly until coffee cultivation began in earnest after 1890. From the demise of Melo until century's end artisans were in trouble. Dependence on foreign sources for manufactures and the need to export primary products led to a changing balance of agricultural and industrial activities. There was no longer protection for domestic handicrafts which might distract the inhabitants from extractive and agricultural occupations.

The days were long past when President Santander proudly wore cottons and woolens spun and woven on Colombian soil. Handicrafts fared well in the years up to 1850. The relative prosperity of artisan regions in Boyacá and Santander was described by Manuel Ancízar in *Peregrinación de Alpha*.[3] His account was based on travels in 1850–1. Artisan activities then provided an important supplement to agricultural income. Education was backward in many of the artisan districts (Velez, for example), the inhabitants were poor and often dirty, but compared to other areas of the country conditions did not seem too bad. But after 1850 imported manufactures forced down prices and undercut domestic producers. Writing in 1861 Miguel Samper observed that artisans – particularly tailors, shoemakers and leather workers – were suffering most of all citizens in the pervasive poverty of Bogotá.[4] According to data presented in the Census of 1870, some 22 per cent of the labor force (including women) worked in

---

[1] This estimate was arrived at as follows: Rafael Núñez estimated in the *Memoria de hacienda* of 1856 that although registered imports of textiles were only Ps$1·8 million, actual imports probably totaled at least Ps$5–6 million. This estimate may have been substantially correct. Our data presented in Table 12 placed total imports for 1856 at $9·4 million. However, that year was the highest of the 1850s and may have been unusual. Since domestic production could be estimated at no less than Ps$20 million, imports were some 25 per cent or less of a total of Ps$26 million consumed.

[2] See Ospina Vásquez, *Industria y protección*, p. 320. This calculation is based on estimates of textile production in Santander presented in Francisco Javier Vergara y Velasco, *Nueva geografía de Colombia. Introducción y tomo 1* (Bogotá 1892–1901), Introduction, p. DCCXIV. He puts local production at Ps$6·5 million, imports at Ps$15 million for a total of Ps$21·5 million.

My more comprehensive estimates for production, imports and consumption of all importables in Table 21 indicate that 55 per cent of the consumption of importables was supplied by imports in 1890.

[3] Manuel Ancízar, *Peregrinación de Alpha* (reprinted, Bogotá 1956), pp. 92–3, 104–6, 16.

[4] Miguel Samper, 'La miseria en Bogotá', *Escritos político-económicos*, 1 (3 vols., Bogotá 1925), 7–102, esp. pp. 89–102.

artisan activities; thus a major portion of the Colombian population suffered as they lost their markets to imports.

Declining artisan income depressed the level of aggregate income. The depression was not restricted to artisans alone. The negative effect of foreign competition was spread among the semi-rural peasantry: (1) because cottage industry was supplementary to rural farming income, families simply began to depend more on agriculture; (2) some male artisans were forced out of their traditional occupations and into agricultural activities – competing with the rural peasantry for the use of land and driving down the average return to labor in farming. In this way the adverse effects of foreign competition were 'socialized' among the poorer classes. Catastrophe was averted by the sharing of losses. Because of that sharing the artisans were not sufficiently radicalized to make effective protest. Hence policies directly at odds with the interests of more than one-fifth of the Colombian labor force remained in force without effective, organized opposition.

It was not only traditional handicrafts which suffered from lack of protection. 'Little remained of the modern industries which had operated in the previous period [1830–45]', writes Ospina Vásquez, 'and very little new activity was undertaken.'[1] The country was given over to dependence on trade and agriculture.

The 1860s saw no changes in the picture of industrial development. 'Medellín appeared to be the most stubborn resister to industrialization. In 1865 there was scarcely a cacao mill and an ice house in addition to the usual cottage industries ...'[2] In the 1870s a gunpowder factory began operations in Bogotá, Chaves founded a large-scale chocolate plant, and gas lighting was installed in the city of Bogotá. There seems to have been no substantial change in other industrial activities, except that the iron works at Pacho was forced to suspend operations for several years.[3] The china and fabric industries were continuing a long-run decline. Manufacturing development had to await the end of Radical experimentation.

Land policy

The abolition of resguardos was of crucial significance to the politics of colonial reform. The communal Indians were the most directly affected. They were induced to sell their land and in subsequent years joined the landless rural proletariat. Landowning elites were the principal beneficiaries.

---

[1] *Industria y protección*, p. 228.
[2] Ospina Vásquez, *Industria y protección*, p. 266.
[3] At that time the ironworks had a capacity of about 300 tons annually, not much greater than that of 40 years earlier.

They gained control of lands around their existing holdings and secured for themselves an easily available labor supply.

The motivation for change among the Radical Liberals was as follows. Reservation Indians seemed still to live outside the national economy and society. They were not participants in even local markets. They often failed to speak the national language. They certainly could not be adjudged citizens appropriate to a modern democracy. Moreover, in the late nineteenth century governments and countries were judged not by the rate of economic growth which they could achieve but by the character and quality of the institutions under which they lived. The resguardo system (and in fact most of the other institutions eliminated by the Reforms of 1850) was an outmoded institution inappropriate for Colombia's entrance into the era of progress. The private interests of the landowning elites coincided with the ideology of the Radical Liberals in opposing continuation of the resguardo as an institution. Some flavor of the ideology driving the Liberals is contained in the following eulogy written by Aquileo Parra to Mosquera about the importance of his first administration (1845–9):

It was not the freeing of a certain goverment industrial monopoly; nor the efficient and powerful impulses given to material improvements throughout the country; nor the perfecting of the monetary and accounting systems in the National Treasury; no, it was none of these, nor all of them combined; it was something more transcendental and singular: it was the fact of beginning, as you did, a truly national program.[1]

It was exactly the changes which Parra, a Radical throughout his political career, rejected which appealed to the landowners and politicians. The development of a 'truly national policy' appealed more to ideologues than to 'interests'.

The clerics were less than enthusiastic about the abolition. The Church historically supported indigenous institutional arrangements. Moreover, the clerics were to find changing land policy making its attack on Church privilege in 1861.

Unable to make an effective attack on the spiritual power of the Church the Radical Liberals instead attacked its temporal power. The means of attack was establishment of the policy of disamortization – the expropriation of property held by religious and other corporate groups. The English cognate of the Spanich *desamortización* harks back to an archaic meaning. To amortize literally meant 'to put in the hands of the dead' or more

---

[1] From a letter of Parra to Mosquera in the early 1860s and reprinted in *Memorias de Aquileo Parra, Presidente de Colombia 1876 a 1878* (Comprenden de 1825 a 1876), (Bogotá 1912) p. 439.

broadly to grant inalienable property rights to a perpetually surviving organization. Thus to disamortize meant to take out of the hands of the dead or to free property from the condition of inalienability. Pious donors placed liens on income-producing property specifying that said income be used, among other reasons, to secure release of the dead man's soul from Purgatory or otherwise guarantee expiation for the sins of his life. A common format was the provision of income for a priest who would in turn say masses for the deceased. Alternatively, bequests were made to Church corporate bodies to carry on instructional programs, operate hospitals and conduct similar charitable works.

The practice in Spanish America differed in important respects from bequests typically received under English law by educational and religious corporations. Under English law the recipient of a bequest gains clear and unambiguous title to property. There can thus be no disagreement with other claimants on the underlying base of income-creating wealth. But in Spanish America it was only specified that out of a body of income-producing wealth a certain annual payment should be made, the amount usually stated as equal to 6 per cent of the total wealth (or the share therein which the benefactor wished to devote to the stated purpose). The recipient did not come to own the assets directly. There was no limit set on the period for which the payments were to be made. Not surprisingly the heirs to estates who retained *de facto* control but had to continue paying the holders of liens on their estates at times found the payments onerous. Moreover, when economic conditions were depressed it became impossible (or at the least inconvenient) to pay even the modest 6 per cent which the underlying assets were supposed to be earning. Not surprisingly there came a call for reform.

But an element of even greater immediate importance to a policy of disamortization was the proximate impoverishment of the public treasury by war or profligate spending. The first great disamortization in Catholic countries occurred during the French Revolution; others followed in the nineteenth century in Spain, Mexico and other countries. The Radicals thus followed an existing tradition.

The politics of disamortization had some complex twists and turns. General Mosquera, who had presided over the Colombian government from 1845 to 1849, was distressed by 1859 at the turn towards conservatism and federalism. Perhaps these two *isms* should have been distinguishable; in that period, however, as in many others in Colombian history, there was occurring a coalition of right and left against the center. The Radical Liberals and Conservatives had united against the Center Liberals (*Draco-*

nianos) to elect Mariano Ospina in 1857 and had in turn pushed even further the decentralization of government. Mosquera had become in the 1850s an advocate of a stronger central government and decided in 1859 to oppose the Ospina government with military force. He was successful by 1861 and began then to write a program reforming the Constitution of 1857. In that same year, he pronounced against the holdings of Church lands. His decree of 9 September 1861 said in part:

All rural and urban property, rights, shares, capital, usufructs, services, and other goods which are owned or administered as property or which belong to civil or ecclesiastical corporations and educational establishments in the territory of the United States of Colombia are judged to be property of the nation for the value corresponding to the net income which that land presently produces or pays, calculating that return at 6 per cent annually.[1]

This seizure of lands in 'dead hands' was an emulation of the Liberal reform instituted by Juarez and Lerdo de Tejada in Mexico in 1857.

Mosquera had hoped by this act to bring lands out of the hands of the Church and into those of agricultural smallholders. In fact, the land was bought and held in large units by the landowning elite, merchant speculators and politicians. The rural poor went unrepresented in the planning of Mosquera's disamortization. The tenure changes which actually occurred were very different from those envisioned by Mosquera in 1861. What began as reform ended in the aggrandizement of the speculators and the overthrow of Mosquera when he protested.[2]

In the 1860s the coalition of Radicals and Conservatives continued to work to the benefit of the landowners since they gained control of the disamortized lands. The Radicals were less satisfied. The Liberal intelligentsia began to write of the reforms in critical terms. They were most critical of the failure of land policy to create a rural middle class or to solve the problems of the foreign debt. (Confiscated lands were to be exchanged for outstanding public bonds.) Rafael Núñez, who spent much of the 1860s and 70s traveling in Europe, led the movement away from Radical policies in the 1880s. The resguardo was gone, the Church was no longer a major landowner and public lands had been distributed to private owners. But the results were completely unlike the utopian dream of the Liberals. By that time it was too late to reverse the dominant position of the landowning elite. They were already preparing their vast estates for the shift from cultivation of the soil to stockraising – an enterprise

---

[1] Quoted in Liévano, *El proceso de Mosquera*, p. 51.
[2] Liévano, *El proceso de Mosquera*, pp. 66-7. For a critique of disamortization see Restrepo, *La iglesia i el Estado*, pp. 375-419.

eminently suited to their own tastes and abilities but directly counter to the general interests. That subject will occupy us in Chapter 6.

Public administration

The issue which most animated political debate was the centralist–federalist struggle. A strong state was not at issue since all the elite groups espoused the principles of *laissez-faire* in government. Lines were drawn between those who saw their own power and interests better served by state governments and those who succeeded in gaining control of the national government in Bogotá. In this epoch the advocates of federalism had more on their side. Two kinds of limitations were set on the central government as a result of the Reforms of 1850: reduction of revenues and severe checks on the legal functions of the state. Elimination of the tobacco monopoly cut back on a major source of revenue. At the same time various taxes which had been gathered by the colonial Spanish government and by the government in Bogotá which succeeded it were given over to the states and provinces. The most important of these was the tax on production of liquors. Dispersion of revenues was the first and necessary step in weakening the central government. National government revenues fell by 47 per cent between 1849 and 1851.[1]

The government in Bogotá was unable to fulfill many of the functions which it had previously accepted. These included the provision of infrastructure for communications and transport. Although a railroad was built across the Isthmus of Panama during the regime of Mosquera, no further action was taken on the construction of railways until 1869. This delay may be explained partly by lack of demand for rail services but it must also be related to the continuing rivalry between states and the federal government for responsibility in construction and the granting of concessions. The national government retained responsibility for building an inter-oceanic highway, but construction of such a formidable addition to the transport system was not feasible in that era. The national government was to be responsible for any construction which served at least three states. In practice, however, internal improvements sponsored by the national government were rare in the nineteenth century.

The period 1863–80 was one of Liberal hegemony; it was also a period of continual civil disputes, regional uprisings and political conflict. Innumerable local disputes were settled by force of arms. In 1867 Mosquera, serving his third term as president, was deposed and tried by the Senate for supposed dictatorial activities. In the years 1876–7 Conservatives carried

[1] *Memoria de Hacienda, 1859* (Bogotá 1859), Appendix Tables 4 and 5.

on a protracted revolt against President Aquileo Parra for supposed fraudulent accession to office due to manipulated ballots. The Radical Liberals sought to enforce a hard-line liberalism which engendered the opposition of other elite groups. The political disturbances, both on regional and national levels, were military struggles between elite groups and only rarely was class conflict involved.

The weakness of the state made nearly impossible the establishment of public order. The legal size of the army was smaller than in neighboring Ecuador and Peru. The actual size of the army is reported at just under 5,000 in 1842; the legal size of the military was cut to only 800 in 1854. Only 511 soldiers were on duty in the national government's military establishment in 1858.[1] Limitations on the military force available to the central government served to increase regional autonomy. In the 1860s the Radical–Conservative coalition introduced measures to limit even further the power of Mosquera by reducing the military to little more than a palace guard.[2] There was little safeguard against petty local uprisings. Some authorities indicate that they caused considerable damage to property. Safford writes, for example,

Industrial enterprisers (as well as agricultural ones) were frequently disrupted by civil war. Whenever war occurred, industrial entrepreneurs could be certain their workers would be recruited. War also constricted the radius of consumption to the areas not already held by rebel armies. And it caused general impoverishment, thus greatly weakening the consumer base. Wars also drained away capital – through flight to Europe, or through loans to the government, voluntary or forced. ... In any case, the undermining of government credit in wartime raised interest rates, making the establishment of new enterprises even more difficult.[3]

But the loss of life due to civil conflict was certainly more important than the damage to real property.

In Table 9 I have brought together from disparate sources estimates of the level of conflict and hostilities in Colombia, by decades, from 1810 to 1960. Except for the period of the movement for independence and the decade of the 1950s marked by *la violencia*, the late nineteenth century was the most violent in the country's history. Thousands of lives were lost, perhaps more than contemporary accounts have acknowledged. No

---

[1] James L. Payne, *Patterns of Conflict in Colombia* (New Haven 1968), p. 120. Payne gives both legal size of the military and the actual number of men under arms. The legal size was reduced from 5,000 to 800 in roughly the same period. Only 12·5 per cent of the national budget was spent through the War Department, 1856–60. See *Memoria de Hacienda 1861* (Bogotá 1861), Table 15.
[2] See Liévano, *El proceso de Mosquera*.
[3] Safford, 'Commerce and Enterprise', p. 178.

The liberal period

decade passed without months of protracted and bitter fighting. Below in Chapter 7 I attempt a quantitative estimate of the impact of civil conflict on Colombian welfare. Here it only need be mentioned that the failure to establish a viable system of government which could assure public order entailed a great cost and long-felt burden on the Colombian people.

Table 9 *Level of hostilities in Colombia, 1810–1960.*

Decade beginning January	Reported or estimated deaths in hostilities	Casualties of military action not included in col. 2	Military and political executions	Duration of conflict in months	Greatest number of Colombian troops in decade
(1)	(2)	(3)	(4)	(5)	(6)
1810	10,200	7,300	800	62	3,600 (1814)[a]
1820	5,800	5,000	270	63	6,000 (1827)[a]
1830	2,200	30	17	10	6,000 (1832)[a]
1840	7,100	—	18	25	7,100 (1842)[a]
1850	4,000	—	—	14	11,000 (1854)[a]
1860	6,000	—	26	38	9,000 (1861)[b]
1870	9,000	—	—	13	24,000 (1877)[b]
1880	3,000	—	—	10	—
1890	2,000	—	—	11	10,000 (1896)[a]
1900	100,000	—	—	37	29,000 (1900)[b]
1910	—	—	—	—	—
1920	—	—	—	—	—
1930	—	—	—	—	—
1940	—	—	—	—	—
1950	100,000–200,000	—	—	99	20,000–30,000

Sources: see the Note on Sources.
[a] Including only government and patriot troops.
[b] Both sides counted.

The excesses of *laissez-faire* contained in the Reforms of 1850 were exacerbated in subsequent reorganizations. Each of the three constitutions (1854, 1858 and 1863) of this era bested its predecessor in the degree of autonomy permitted the regions and their governments. In 1870 state and local governments managed to take in more revenue than the national government.[1] The goal of creating a strong national state for the purpose of economic development was the antithesis of the policies actually adopted.

[1] *Memoria de hacienda, 1870* (Bogotá 1871), p. xvii. The national government received 46·7 per cent of revenues; states, 30·3 per cent and local government, 23·0 per cent.

Colonial reform, 1845–85

Role of the Church

Landowning elites and clerics joined to protect their rural interests. However, in the anticlerical atmosphere of the nineteenth century the Church faced a changing role in society. As the Enlightenment provided one kind of attack on the Church in the eighteenth century, Scientism and Liberalism provided yet another in the nineteenth. The Radical Liberals led the reform movement; they were most interested in changing the role of the Church in education. However, the means of attacking the Church which came easiest to hand was in the seizure of Church lands. Thus the disamortization laws of 1861 were as much an attack on Church power as an issue of land policy. It was thus possible to achieve a coalition of Radicals opposing the Church and landowners interested in gaining control of Church lands.

The attack on the Church was one of the most divisive acts of the period. Several groups could agree to take action in 1861 and 1863 to expropriate Church holdings; they could not agree on the disposition of those lands or on the future role of the Church. Much of the civil strife of the era can be related to continuing disputes about that role. In the words of Jaramillo Uribe:

> The most important [revolutions] were the political revolution and the religious revolution, because they broke the only bond of unity existing between the members of the new nation: the Catholic religion; they despoiled the interests of the only ruling group with political experience, enlightenment and a sense of direction on social issues: the clergy. On a people with venerable Catholic traditions, the prosecutors of the Independence and the legislators of all the constitutional assemblies which followed that movement wished to impose Anglo-Saxon institutions and a Protestant religion, based on the idea of free choice and the religious neutrality of the state, and an education contrary to their beliefs and sentiments. This disequilibrium between new institutions and old traditions was the cause of the social unrest in which Colombia lived for the first half century of independence.[1]

Whereas Radicals and Conservatives could join on some issues, particularly their opposition to any effort to establish a strong government in Bogotá, they could not agree on the role of the Church. Conservative strongholds in Antioquia and Cauca were in open conflict with Bogotá on this matter. The issue of church and state relations was not laid to rest until Núñez signed a concordat with the Pope in 1886. Yet even then the conflict could not be ended and continues to the present day.

The foregoing discussion of interest groups and political issues is summarized in Table 10. The positions of the groups on issues is only indicated

[1] Jaime Jaramillo Uribe, *El pensamiento colombiano en el siglo XIX* (Bogotá 1964), p. 271.

in those cases in which the group had a direct interest. For example, neither artisans nor petty bureaucrats had strong views on land policy since they were not directly affected. Only four groups (out of eight included) had a direct interest in the tariff; that was the issue, moreover, which was the least inflammatory. The question of public administration was of concern to five groups, all of them from among the upper strata of Colombian society. The positions of politicians on the issue of public administration were mixed, as I have suggested, because personal opportunity varied with access to the levers of power. A politician switched from federalist to centralist when he seized the chance to control the central government. Ambivalence and the pursuit of opportunity on this issue was a primary cause of civil conflict.

Table 10   *A schematic of Colombian groups and issues, 1845–85.*

	Groups	Tariff	Public administration	Land policy	Disamortization of Church lands
			Issues		
I	Elites				
	A Merchants	Low	Federalist	Reformers	Favored
	B Landowners		Federalist	Reformers	Mixed
	C Clerics			Mixed	Opposed
	D Politicians	High	Mixed	Reformers	Favored
II	Urban middle groups				
	A Artisans	High	Centralist		
	B Petty bureaucrats	High	Centralist		Favored
III	Rural groups				
	A Peasantry			Anti-reform	Opposed
	B Indians			Anti-reform	Opposed

Public land policy divided Colombians along lines of the reformers and those opposed to reform. More than other issues it was drawn along class lines. Elite groups imposed policies; deprived groups opposed them without much success. The issue of disamortization captured the attention of seven of the groups indicated in Table 10. Like the issue of public land policy it involved something of a division along class lines with the exception that the clerics, an elite group, found themselves standing against other elites. The attitudes of Conservative landowners were mixed on the issue because of their profound Catholicism. As I will indicate in Chapter 6 there is still too little known about who exactly obtained Church lands (Liberals or Conservatives) to judge which elite groups scored the greatest gains from disamortization. We do know that the rural poor were the losers.

The number of groups involved in each issue conforms roughly to the amount of dissent which the issue actually caused in Colombian life. The tariff, despite its importance to the artisans, was not the cause of physical conflict except on one occasion. The question of public administration involved the next lowest number of groups, but it was entirely a concern of the upper strata. Their disagreements and ambivalence on the question led them to wage lengthy battles in pressing their claims. Land policies and disamortization captured the attention of more Colombians – and divided them along class and interest-group lines more thoroughly – than did any other issues in the second half of the nineteenth century. Perhaps because those issues followed class lines, and because the rural poor had little access to weapons of war, they were resolved in favor of the elites without the civil conflict which marked the centralist–federalist struggle. Extended civil war was only possible when the elites fought among themselves. On issues of class conflict they were able to stand together against the deprived classes.

THE FAILURE OF POLITICS

Between 1845 and 1885 politics failed to serve the general interest. The census refers to the era as *'La época de las guerras civiles'*. Government lacked consistency and direction as first one group, then another, seized power to serve its narrow private interests. There was no conscious effort to assess and carry out the goals and aspirations of Colombian society. The problem lay in a lack of effective and stable leadership.

When one considers the fate of Mosquera's reform of Church land ownership one sees the hopelessness with which the bureaucracy regarded any long-term program. Lands which were to be distributed to small holders between 1863 and 1866 went almost completely to the landowning elites. When Mosquera in 1866 sought to undermine the titles to land of all those who had gained any holdings as a result of the disamortization, the Radical–Conservative coalition effectively blocked him. At about the same time, i.e. in 1867, this group which controlled congress submitted a new law on public order which read in part, 'When in any state an uprising occurs with the purpose of overthrowing the government or to organize another government, the Government of the Union must observe the strictest neutrality between the belligerent groups.'[1]

---

[1] Liévano, *El proceso de Mosquera*, p. 71.

The liberal period

Table 11   *Colombian heads of state 1819–1966.*

Year and month of accession	Months in office	Name	Post	Party
1819		General Simón Bolívar	President	
		General Francisco de Paula Santander	Vice-President	
1830 Mar.	3	General Domingo Caicedo	President of Council of State	
1830 June	3	Dr Joaquín Mosquera	President	
1830 Sept.	8	General Rafael Urdaneta	Dictator by coup	
1831 May	6	General Domingo Caicedo	Vice-President	
1831 Nov.	4	General José M. Obando	Vice-President	
1832 Mar.	7	Dr José Ignacio Márquez	Vice-President	
1832 Oct.	54	General Francisco de Paula Santander	President	
1837 Apr.	49	Dr José Ignacio Márquez	President	
1841 May	2	General Pedro Alcántara de Herrán	President	
1841 July	4	Dr Juan de D. Aranzazu	President of Council of State	
1841 Oct.	7	General Domingo Caicedo	Vice-President	
1842 May	3	General Pedro Alcántara de Herrán	President	
1842 Aug.	3	General Domingo Caicedo	Vice-President	
1842 Nov.	30	General Pedro Alcántara de Herrán	President	
1845 Apr.	24	General Tomás Cipriano de Mosquera	President	
1847 Apr.	8	Dr Rufino Cuervo	Vice-President	Cons.
1847 Dec.	16	General Tomás Cipriano de Mosquera	President	Cons.
1849 Apr.	30	General José Hilario López	President	Liberal
1851 Oct.	3	Dr José de Obaldía	Vice-President	Liberal
1852 Jan.	15	General José Hilario López	President	Liberal
1853 Apr.	12	General José Mariá Obando	President	Liberal
1854 Apr.	7	General José Mariá Melo	Dictator by coup	Draconiano (Lib. fac.)
1854 Apr.	4	General Tomás Herrera	Designate, govt. in exile	Liberal
1854 Aug.	8	Dr José de Obaldía	Vice-Pres., govt. in exile	Liberal
1855 Apr.	24	Dr Manuel María Mallarino	Vice-President	Cons.
1857 Apr.	48	Dr Mariano Ospina R.	President	Cons.
1861 Apr.	3	Dr Bartolomé Calvo	Attorney General	
1861 July	19	General Tomás Cipriano de Mosquera	Revolutionary victor	Liberal
1863 Feb.	3	Revolutionary Junta (during Rionegro Convention)		
1863 May	11	General Tomás Cipriano de Mosquera	President	Liberal
1864 Apr.	25	Dr Manuel Murillo Toro	President	Liberal
1866 May	12	General Tomás Cipriano de Mosquera	President	Liberal

Colonial reform, 1845–85

Table 11 – (cont.)

1867 May	11	General Santos Acosta	Designate by coup	Liberal
1868 Apr.	24	General Santos Gutiérrez	President	Liberal
1870 Apr.	24	General Eustorgio Salazar	President	Liberal
1872 Apr.	24	Dr Manuel Murillo Toro	President	Liberal
1874 Apr.	24	Dr Santiago Pérez	President	Liberal
1876 Apr.	13	Dr Aquileo Parra	President	Liberal
1877 May	4	General Sergio Camargo	Designate	Liberal
1877 Aug.	8	Dr Aquileo Parra	President	Liberal
1878 Apr.	24	General Julián Trujillo	President	Liberal
1880 Apr.	24	Dr Rafael Núñez	President	Liberal
1882 Apr.	9	Dr Fco. Javier Zaldúa (died in office)	President	Liberal
1882 Dec.	16	Dr and General José Eusebio Otálora	Designate	Liberal
1884 Apr.	4	General Ezequiel Hurtado	Designate	Liberal
1884 Aug.	20	Dr Rafael Núñez	President	Cons.
1886 Apr.	9	General José M. Campo Serrano	Designate	Cons.
1887 Jan.	5	General Eliseo Payán	Vice-President	Cons.
1887 June	14	Dr Rafael Núñez	President	Cons.
1888 Aug.	48	Dr Carlos Holguín	Designate	Cons.
1892 Aug.	72	Dr Miguel Antonio Caro	Vice-President	Cons.
1898 Aug.	3	Don José Manuel Morroquín	Vice-President	Cons.
1898 Nov.	21	Dr Manuel Antonio Sanclemente	President	Cons.
1900 July	49	Don José Manuel Marroquín	Coup	Cons.
1904 Aug.	59	General Rafael Reyes	President	Cons.
1909 Aug.	12	General Ramón González Valencia	Designate	Cons.
1910 Aug.	48	Dr Carlos E. Restrepo	President	Cons.
1914 Aug.	48	Dr José Vicente Concha	President	Cons.
1918 Aug.	39	Don Marco Fidel Suárez	President	Cons.
1921 Nov.	9	General Jorge Holguín	Designate	Cons.
1922 Aug.	48	General y Doctor Pedro Nel Ospina	President	Cons.
1926 Aug.	48	Dr Miguel Abadía Méndez	President	Cons.
1930 Aug.	48	Dr Enrique Olaya Herrera	President	Liberal
1934 Aug.	48	Dr Alfonso López	President	Liberal
1938 Aug.	48	Dr Eduardo Santos	President	Liberal
1942 Aug.	36	Dr Alfonso López	President (renamed)	Liberal
1945 Aug.	12	Dr Alberto Lleras Camargo	President	Liberal
1946 Aug.	48	Dr Mariano Ospina Pérez	President	Cons.
1950 Aug.	16	Dr Laureano Gómez	President	Cons.
1951 Nov.	19	Dr Roberto Urdaneta Arbeláez	President	Cons.
1953 June	47	Teniente-General Gustavo Rojas Pinilla	Dictator by coup	
1957 May	15	Junta Militar	Coup	
1958 Aug.	48	Dr Alberto Lleras Camargo	President	Liberal
1962 Aug.	48	Dr Guillermo León Valencia	President	Cons.
1966 Aug.	48	Dr Carlos Lleras Restrepo	President	Liberal

Sources: Monsalve M. Manuel, *Colombia posesiones presidenciales 1810–1954* (Bogotá 1954); Mendoza Vélez, Jorge de, *Gobernantes de Colombia (500 años de historia)* (Bogotá 1957); Henao y Arrubla, *History of Colombia.*

The liberal period

One can show with a simple statistical test how changing stability in the Colombian government has altered the chances for politics to establish clear priorities and goals for Colombian society. In Table 11 I present a listing of Colombian heads of state with the year and month of accession and period of tenure in office. Only those whose period of tenure was at least three months have been included; thus special appointees named during foreign visits of the head of state are not shown. I wished to test whether there was any trend toward full completion of the legal term of office. The average period in office did rise significantly over time: It was 14·0 months per term in the years 1830 to 1863; 16·1, 1863–84 when the legal term was 24 months; 34·0, 1884–1966; and slightly higher, 37·8 months, in the years of the present century. A t-test indicates that for the whole of the nineteenth century the average term in office was significantly shorter than the expected full term, but that for the twentieth century the average length of term was not significantly different at the 0·05 level of significance from the expected 48-month term. This analysis shows that the Colombian political system, as it came in reality to conform somewhat more to the prescribed norms for presidential service and succession, could more effectively plan long-term policy and carry out the decisions of elected officials.

In the years before 1884 the average president was in office little more than a year at a time. Any long-term plans – internal improvements in transportation, communications or education, for example – were almost impossible to effect under such conditions of flux. The Constitution of 1863 which provided for only a 24–month term without immediate succession exacerbated the tendency for power, authority and decisionmaking to be dispersed and unorganized. Although the average length of term rose slightly in the period 1863–84 over that of the previous period, the expectation of the period in power was shorter and hence long-term planning even less successful.

Petty bureaucrats made up the most important force favoring a strong government, consistent policy and long-term programs. Yet they were too few in number to keep the machinery running. With each change in party new occupants for office arrived with little in the way of plans for action.

Upon the establishment of representative government and the abolition of privileges, every citizen could aspire to enter the bureaucracy. The government was the focus of attention, (first) because preparation for other technical activities was non-existent, and (second) because commerce, industry and agriculture had received a negative stigma during the centuries of slavery. . . . Now that the prestige of the Spanish monarchy was gone and political opportunities were open to all, especially for the members of the dominant criollo class, conditions were right for the free reign of ambition and for the beginning of dissension among the (criollos), dissension which would affect the whole society.[1]

Moreover, with little prospect of continuation in power for more than a few years, and with the clear prospect that any program undertaken would be abandoned by the following government, there seemed to be little advantage in pressing reform.

The lack of direction reflects an unwillingness of bureaucrats and politicians – in themselves often able men – to establish any direction for the government. Knowing their term was limited they hesitated to build strength which might be turned against them by those who succeeded them in office. The state did not even provide the minimum of public order which could have made individual initiative feasible and profitable. Emphasis was on the short run and narrowly conceived personal advantage. Politics failed to turn private vices into public benefits.

The Reforms of 1850 were designed to restructure the political system along the lines of a *laissez-faire* utopia. They failed. The post-1850 political system eliminated various colonial and traditional proscriptions against the exploitation of the rural poor. The freedom which the reforms provided was the freedom to exploit existing inequalities and monopolies of power for the benefit of the elites. Before 1850 the landowners could not easily gain access to communal Indian lands or to Indian labor. Before 1861 lands in mortmain were available to peasant lessees of the Church at what were very favorable rates of interest and share-cropping. Before 1820 effective occupance was requisite to claims on land. The reforms, by legalizing, indeed encouraging, a redistribution of landed property, led directly to a reinforcement of the monopoly position already held by the large landowners.

In the name of social change and progress the reformers expanded trade (to the detriment of the artisan class), eliminated the resguardo (to put the rural poor at the mercy of the landowning elite), decentralized government (to leave the society with no means of preserving public order), and attacked the Church (to divide society and exacerbate civil conflict). These results stem directly from the Reform and the reformers – not from their co-optation or from the reaction of the years 1854–61.[2] A major part of the Reform and subsequent events – the expansion of trade and limitation of the central government's taxing powers – were directed at

---

[1] Jaramillo Uribe, *El pensamiento colombiano*, p. 271.
[2] Cf. Fals Borda, *Subversion and Social Change*, pp. 86–92.

serving the interests of those who authored the Reform, viz., the Radical Liberals and their constituency among the merchants and exporters. Another side of the reform involved the removal of proscriptions on exploitation of the rural poor. Hence the reforms involved a kind of log rolling in which the interests of several elites were served in the total package. Such log rolling is an essential technique of an effective political system so long as all relevant interests are included in the distribution of *quid pro quo*'s. But in 1850 the vast majority of Colombians participated in no way whatsoever in the formation of the reform program. The reforms – not surprisingly – were antithetical to their interests. The elites managed to assist each other in programs of exploitation of the unrepresented poor.

That exploitation was most direct and obvious in the growing concentration of land in the hands of the landowning elite. It was also apparent in the growth of the marginal or floating population in the eastern highlands. But exploitation was not so obvious in the gradual expansion of trade and Colombia's growing dependence on merchants and foreign manufactures. The merchants and exporters seemed in fact to be in the vanguard leading Colombia into a new era of progress.[1] It is only when one can measure the costs to displaced artisans and the risks of dependence on trade by a backward country that one can begin to assess the exploitation occasioned by the reform movement. In the following chapters I will bring together the information required to make that assessment.

---

[1] Even Fals Borda seems to hold this view. 'A compromise was reached between the vestigial elements of the subversion and those of tradition. They moved forward together toward a "modern" state with democracy, liberty and *laissez faire* as the new valued goals for economic and social development.' (*Subversion and Social Change*, p. 93.)

CHAPTER 5

TRADE EXPANSION UNDER THE
LIBERAL REFORMS, 1845-85

In the preceding chapter I outlined the economic issues and political maneu-vering which produced the Reforms of 1850 and a long period of political liberalism in Colombia. Here we are concerned with a statistical analysis of the effects of policies instituted on the course of international trade. The Liberal reforms were introduced specifically to increase the flow of inter-national commerce, thus to tie the country to the network of world trade. It was assumed that Colombia would produce agricultural products for export in exchange for the manufactures of Great Britain and the several North Atlantic countries which in this period became exporters of manu-factures. The Radical Liberals were prepared to accept the inevitable reallocation of resources: displacement of inefficient artisans was the price of new employment opportunities in export activities. The theory of comparative advantage seemed to promise benefits on balance from pursuit of such a policy.

The theory of international trade as developed in England and imported into Colombia painted a rosy picture of the gains which all nations might realize by trading. Particularly beneficial, it was thought, was the trade between those colder, northern nations which had developed skill in manufacturing and the tropical countries which could offer spices and other exotic wares in return for manufactures.[1] Florentino González, finance minister in the Mosquera regime, brought back this view from his visit in England. He argued before the Chamber of Deputies that

in a country rich in mines and agricultural products that can feed a large and profit-able export trade, the laws must not favor the development of industries which distract the inhabitants from extractive and agricultural occupations from which they will realize the greatest advantage. ... We must offer Europe raw materials and open our ports to manufactures to facilitate trade and the advantages it brings, and to provide to the consumer, at low prices, the products of manufacturing industry.[2]

[1] Richard B. Sheridan has suggested in a recent article that 'the expansion of Europe was in large measure motivated by a desire to achieve what may be termed a temperate-tropical balance, or a complementary economic relationship based on the products of different climatic zones...' 'Temperate and Tropical: Aspects of European Penetration into Tropical Regions', *Caribbean Studies*, III (1963), 3-21.
[2] Quoted in Liévano, *Rafael Núñez*, p. 52.

The liberal period

With the expansion of tobacco exports from under Ps$200,000 annually in the early 1840s to well over Ps$5 million in most years between 1850 and 1875, the economy grew more dependent on foreign trade. As a consequence success in export ventures was requisite to success in economic development.

But export expansion was hampered by foreign competition and technical supply difficulties with a number of export crops. Due to the fall in demand in Germany and the opening up of alternative supply sources in Java the tobacco period ended abruptly in 1875. Cotton was of but brief importance as an export product during the American Civil War. Indigo had a short boom in the 1870s which was ended by foreign competition; a leaf disease spread devastation among the cacao crop in the late 1870s. Quinine was an important export in the early 1880s until the introduction of synthetics. Sugar, rubber and vanilla passed through even briefer export cycles.[1]

Nor did exports keep up with the demand for imports, though the deficient Colombian trade statistics do not always reveal the unfavorable trade balance. Beyer notes that 'from the year 1876 to 1880, for example, every commentator in the country knew that Colombia was being drained of her specie to compensate for her insufficient exports, and yet export–import official data show a constantly favorable balance of trade'.[2] Though Colombia willingly became dependent on foreign trade, the nation was unable to expand the value and volume of exports rapidly enough. The value of exports increased by more than 18 per cent per annum during the early part of this period, but the trend line for the years 1866–85 shows no growth whatever. Until coffee cultivation and export came to play a significant role in the last decade of the century, the export sector did not even keep pace with population growth.

The country and its population were not so prepared for change as were the Radical Liberals. This group was not able to force a rapid rate of change of life style on an essentially backward society. It proved easy to induce new patterns of consumption, nearly impossible to introduce new methods of production. Thus after the period of rapid growth of tobacco

[1] On Colombia's troubled export history in the nineteenth century see Nieto Arteta, *Economía y cultura*, pp. 241–92. Harrison, 'The Colombian Tobacco Industry', summarizes the history of that product. Robert C. Beyer, 'The Colombian Coffee Industry: Origins and Major Trends 1740–1940' (Ph.D. diss., University of Minnesota 1947) reviews the causes of other products' failures. Export data are summarized in Banco de la República, *Informe anual del Gerente*, 1 July 1960 – 31 December 1962 (Bogotá n.d.), Part II, Table 127, p. 201.

[2] Beyer, 'The Colombian Coffee Industry', p. 348.

Trade expansion, 1845–85

Table 12 *Estimated commercial balance of Colombia (1845–85)* (millions of current U.S. dollars).

Year	Exports (f.o.b.) Merchandise	Gold	Total	Imports (c.i.f.)	Commercial Balance	Accumulated Balance
1845	2·6	1·3	3·9	3·5	0·4	0·4
1846	2·0	0·6	2·6	2·0	0·6	1·0
1847	2·0	0·6	2·6	1·4	1·2	2·2
1848	1·4	0·4	1·8	2·3	− 0·5	1·7
1849	1·0	0·3	1·3	3·3	− 2·0	− 0·3
1850	3·9	1·2	5·1	5·0	0·1	− 0·2
1851	4·6	1·4	6·0	8·0	− 2·0	− 2·2
1852	5·0	1·5	6·5	7·0	− 0·5	− 2·7
1853	3·7	1·1	4·8	5·4	− 0·6	− 3·3
1854	5·5	1·6	7·1	4·0	3·1	− 0·2
1855	5·1	0·5	5·6	5·9	− 0·3	− 0·5
1856	5·6	1·6	7·2	9·4	− 2·2	− 2·7
1857	7·1	1·9	9·0	8·0	1·0	− 1·7
1858	9·1	0·7	9·8	7·2	2·6	0·9
1859	9·2	0·1	9·3	8·3	1·0	1·9
1860	10·8	1·0	11·8	10·2	1·6	3·5
1861	10·9	1·0	11·9	9·9	2·0	5·5
1862	10·5	1·0	11·5	10·2	1·3	6·8
1863	9·5	0·9	10·4	17·9	− 7·5	− 0·7
1864	22·6	2·1	24·7	25·5	− 0·8	− 1·5
1865	16·9	1·2	18·1	23·6	− 5·5	− 7·0
1866	15·1	1·4	16·5	27·8	−11·3	−18·3
1867	12·0	0·6	12·6	23·2	−10·6	−28·9
1868	14·7	2·4	17·1	24·6	− 7·5	−36·4
1869	17·6	2·7	20·3	24·1	− 3·8	−40·2
1870	15·4	2·2	17·6	23·8	− 6·2	−46·4
1871	15·8	2·1	17·9	24·8	− 6·9	−53·3
1872	19·8	1·7	21·5	30·0	− 8·5	−61·8
1873	15·3	2·7	18·0	39·0	−21·0	−82·8
1874	20·4	3·1	23·5	33·6	−10·1	−92·9
1875	28·9	3·2	32·1	17·8	14·3	−78·6
1876	14·5	3·3	17·8	21·9	− 4·1	−82·7
1877	12·7	1·8	14·5	19·9	− 5·4	−88·1
1878	16·2	3·7	19·9	22·5	− 2·6	−90·7
1879	18·3	3·6	21·9	26·0	− 4·1	−94·8
1880	19·4	3·0	22·4	23·5	− 1·1	−95·9
1881	20·7	3·1	23·8	26·5	− 2·7	−98·6
1882	17·8	3·4	21·2	26·9	− 5·7	−104·3
1883	14·6	3·2	17·8	27·0	− 9·2	−113·5
1884	10·6	2·8	13·4	25·3	−11·9	−125·4
1885	7·3	2·9	10·2	16·1	− 5·9	−131·3

Sources: 1845–53: Estimated from Colombian and United States data; 1854–85: Estimated from Colombian, United States and British data.

For a full discussion of sources and methodology see the Working Papers of the Sub-committee on Historical Statistics and the accompanying text.

exports ended in the late 1850s, the import growth rate produced strong negative external balances and downward pressure on domestic prices and incomes. The policy of free trade failed in this period, not for lack of intuitive appeal or logical consistency (within its own narrow framework of analysis), but due to the inability of a backward society and economy to adapt itself rapidly to the vagaries of change.

The nature of the material presented in this chapter precludes the kind of exciting narrative which the reader has enjoyed up to this point. A large part of the discussion must perforce be devoted to the sources and methods used in arriving at data in Table 12. Colombian statistics on international trade are gravely deficient in all years prior to 1905. In this chapter statistics are largely (though not entirely) based on official statistics of the United States and Great Britain and their trade with Colombia. Before 1854 Colombian exports to Britain are not available in the British returns; nonetheless, we have been able to make export estimates by the use of U.S. data. Where possible, we have also used in our estimating techniques the returns on Colombian tobacco imports in the years 1850–70 into the German ports of Bremen and Hamburg.[1] This additional data is important because the German ports were the principal market, and tobacco was in some years the principal export product.

The next section is devoted to an analysis of the effects of persistent deficits on domestic income. Even with the substantial exports of mined gold Colombia was in deficit on current account in most years after 1865. While in some circumstances such deficits point to the healthy development of a young creditor country, the meager inflow of direct foreign investment, the currency depreciation after 1870 and the general slowness of development point to pathological rather than healthy change. This result seems to stem not from the growth of trade itself – whatever its unsettling effects may be – but from the failure of exports to grow rapidly enough to keep up with import demand. We will also have reason to consider some errors in commercial policy, particularly in the years 1864–74. We end the chapter with a comparison of the two problems – excessive imports in the years from 1864 to 1874 and deficient export expansion from 1876 through 1890 and beyond.

COLOMBIAN TRADE DATA

Scholars who have in the past explored the economic history of Colombia have had to do so with inaccurate and misleading statistical data. The

[1] These data were initially solicited and published by Salvador Camacho Roldán in his *Notas de viaje* (Bogotá 1898), p. 198.

wiser among them restricted their observations to qualitative evaluations of policy and avoided using these data as a basis for accepting or rejecting explanatory hypotheses. Ospina Vásquez presents a few statistical tables in *Industria y protección*, but for illustrative rather than analytical purposes. Understatement of imports in Colombian data makes them unusable for balance of payments analysis, calculation of capital movements or the timing of flows of direct investment.[1]

The introduction of other-country data now makes possible quantitative study of these problems. The data in Table 12 are based largely on the published trade statistics of the United States and Great Britain. The lengthy procedure by which we arrived at the estimates in Table 12 cannot be described in full here.[2] In general, however, the estimates depend crucially on two assumptions: (1) that the U.S. and British data are essentially correct estimates of their trade with Colombia (and hence Colombia's trade with them) and (2) the percentage distribution of Colombian trade as given in Colombian official statistics with those countries, even though based on a smaller 'sample' of total trade, is essentially the same as for total actual trade. Thus if in 1849 U.S. imports from Colombia (Colombian exports to the U.S.), corrected downward 20 per cent to eliminate costs, insurance and freight from the Colombian port, were listed as $0·25 million, and if according to Colombian figures one-quarter of Colombian exports went to the U.S., then we estimate total exports as $1·0 million.

A somewhat more complicated procedure was used for the estimation of imports. Assumption (2) above seemed unwarranted and when applied to the data yielded extremely high values for imports. Therefore, a technique was devised of simply marking up the U.S. and British data by a reasonable percentage.

The estimates of gold exports are perhaps the least reliable series. Mining was a scattered enterprise as placers were located in a number of rivers, and large-scale deepshaft mining was limited in extent. Thus it must have been quite easy to export gold without its being recorded. Only the fact that there were no significant tax levies on the production and export of gold makes these estimates credible. The ambiguous treatment of gold in the U.S. and British balance of payments made use of their data

---

[1] Some of the methodology and design of work in this chapter was informed by the study of British balance of payments and terms of trade in the nineteenth century by Albert Imlah, *Economic Elements in the Pax Britannica* (Cambridge, Mass. 1958). It is not possible in a work on the foreign trade of Colombia to match Imlah's work in wealth of detail nor in the power of consistency checks with independent estimates of capital stocks which are foreign-held or located.

[2] See *Estadísticas históricas de Colombia*, ed. Miguel Urrutia (Bogotá, to appear).

impossible. Since gold was during the nineteenth century a currently produced and exported product I have treated it as part of merchandise exports throughout the period although the ease with which it could be either exported or added to the domestic money supply might argue for special treatment. The treatment of gold followed here is essentially the same as that currently in use for countries which are producers and net exporters of the metal.

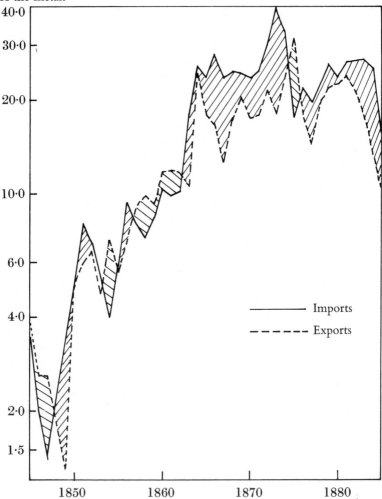

Figure 4 Colombia: imports and exports, 1845–85 (millions of current U.S. dollars). (Based on Table 12.)

Trade expansion, 1845–85

Estimates of Colombia's commercial balance and accumulated balance (columns 5 and 6 in Table 12) are derived from the previous columns. It has not yet been possible to undertake a thorough study of the other elements in the balance of payments. One would err in presuming that the accumulated balance at the end of the period ($131·3 million) is equivalent to net foreign investment in Colombia.[1] Too many items are left out of the current account transactions; moreover, independent estimates of direct foreign investments and the foreign holdings of government debt do not come up to $100 million even in 1914.[2] Our figures do however serve to emphasize the persistence of commercial deficits in the second half of this period.

Over the first half of this period Colombia experienced a rapid growth of total trade without any obvious balance of payments problem. Exports and imports grew rapidly from the late 1840s through the 50s and into the 60s, but there was a rough balance of trade throughout those years. There was no apparent need to restrict the growth of imports or to encourage the growth of exports. The price and income mechanisms which would cause depression if persistent deficits were to occur were not called into play until later decades. The volume and value of trade was probably not much greater than it had been at the beginning of the nineteenth century. Both exports and imports were apparently under $10 million until the end of the 1850s.

Over nearly a score of years no maladjustments showed up in Colombia's international commercial dealings. For the first time the country was integrated into the network of trade, and the process proved not to be unusually painful. Consider, for example, that in the interval 1845–60 the value of exports grew by some $8 million. Using conservative assumptions about labor productivity one may reason that fewer than 40,000 rural workers were required to shift out of subsistence farming and into production of an export product (in this case tobacco).[3] And, as will be shown in

---

[1] In his study of the U.S. balance of payments, 1790–1860, Douglas North did not use such a residual in attempting to estimate the flows of direct investment and the capital stock owned abroad at selected intervals. Our data does not include any estimates of service income from shipping, immigrant remittances or several other elements which could be important in determining the aggregate current account balance. Cf. Douglas North, 'The United States Balance of Payments, 1790–1860', *Trends in the American Economy in the Nineteenth Century* (Princeton 1960).

[2] See Table 24, p. 204 below, for an estimate of direct foreign investment in 1914. See also United Nations Department of Economic and Social Affairs, *Foreign Capital in Latin America* (New York 1955), pp. 68–73.

[3] The lowest of three estimates of rural wages in the 1880s is 30 cents per day or about $100 per annum. If the value of output per worker were just double that (about $200 per worker), 40,000 additional workers would have been required to produce the observed increment

Chapter 6, the increment in land used for export agriculture was small relative to the total area of the country. Although the rate of expansion of trade was rapid, its importance was still small relative to the size (measured by labor force or land area) of the country. This aspect of the growing dependence on trade is best illustrated in Table 13 which presents the value of exports and imports per capita over the years 1845–85.

Table 13 *Average annual per capita imports and exports, quinquennial periods, 1855–99* (current U.S. dollars).

Period	Per capita imports	Per capita exports
1845–9	1·20	1·10
1850–4	1·60	1·60
1855–9	3·40	3·60
1860–4	5·50	6·10
1865–9	10·70	7·30
1870–4	12·20	8·00
1875–9	8·00	8·40
1880–4	8·80	6·70
1885–9	6·90	4·00
1890–4	6·10	4·90
1895–9	4·90	4·10

Sources: Population data based on censuses and interpolations; trade data from Tables 12 and 26.

Since Colombian population reached a total of 2 million in 1851, and perhaps 2·2 million in 1857, we may estimate average annual per capita imports in the quinquennium 1855–9 at US$3·40. The subsequent growth of imports per capita in the nineteenth century as shown in Table 13 provides a comparative framework demonstrating the relative unimportance of foreign trade in the first half-century of independence. Per capita imports were more than three times their 1855–9 level in the decade 1865–74, and the levels reached in the former period already represented a

---

in output. Some estimates of wages are much higher: perhaps as few as 10,000 workers changed their occupation. In any case the absolute changes became much greater after 1864. On wage estimates see Great Britain *Diplomatic and Consular Reports* Dickson to the Marquis of Salisbury, 18 October 1888, no. 446, p. 18, and U.S. *Consular Reports*, Dawson and Esmond, 28 May, 23 August, 1884.

doubling over those of the 1840s. Imports per capita reached their peak in the quinquennium 1870–4 (an average of $12.20), then fell steadily to the end of the century low of $4.90. By that time, however, lower prices for imports make comparisons over half a century tenuous.[1] Exports per capita exhibit a similar rise and decline, reaching a peak in the quinquennium 1875–9, but at a level substantially below the peak for imports per capita.

Colombia was by 1870 substantially more dependent on trade than it had been a score of years earlier. The absolute value of imports increased by $15 million in the decade of the 1860s. Assuming that among artisans annual wages were $150, i.e. 50 per cent greater than in agriculture, but that the value of output per worker was also $150 since no other factor of production was required, the increment in imports could have replaced the labor of 100,000 local artisans in that decade alone.[2] From the point of view of the reallocation of labor as a result of trade expansion, the problem was reserved until the 1860s and after.

This rough timetable for economic decline in artisan areas agrees in general terms with the qualitative statements one can glean from contemporary observers. The Chorographic Commission appointed by Mosquera visited the artisan towns of Santander in the early 1850s. The head of the Commission, Agustín Codazzi, wrote that 'misery and want were unknown among the people'.[3] In areas of hat-making and cotton textiles an image of 'moderate abundance' prevailed; in areas dominated by woolen textiles the observer – Manuel Ancízar, another member of the Commission – was given the impression of stagnation rather than regression.[4] Even as late as 1875, the *Anuario estadístico* referred to the Department of Santander as 'one of the most prosperous in the Union'.[5] But the days of prosperity had passed by the late 1870s. In 1882 the Government of Santander collected Ps$485,468 and spent Ps$789,748, resulting in the largest deficit of any of the Colombian states.[6] By 1897 the artisans of Socorro were barely eking out an existence because of competition from British and American goods.[7] At the time of the Census of 1912 some 7 per cent of

---

[1] If Imlah's index of British export prices is used to achieve some semblance of comparability over this period the resulting per capita imports are as follows: 1855–9, $3.20; 1870–4, $8.65; 1855–9, $7.94; 1895–9, $6.10. As expected such adjustments reduce the size of oscillations in per capita imports, but the growing dependence on trade is still clear.

[2] Estimates of artisan wages are found in U.S. *Consular Reports*, 1884, cited above.

[3] *Jeografía física i política de las providencias de la Nueva Granada*, II (Bogotá 1959), 25.

[4] Manuel Ancízar, *Peregrinación de Alpha* (Bogotá 1914), *passim*.

[5] Felipe Pérez, *Geografía general de los Estados Unidos de Colombia* (Bogotá 1883), p. 162.

[6] Pérez, *Geografía general*, p. 204.

[7] Ospina Vásquez, *Industria y protección* p. 320.

Santander's labor force remained in artisan activities, a dramatic decline from 20 or perhaps 25 per cent in 1870.[1] The timing and rate of decline of artisan activities in the Santander region was clearly related to the timing of trade expansion.

The expansion of imports was most painfully felt among the artisans in the textile towns of Santander and Boyacá. However, the problem facing this large and heterogeneous group was compounded for the country as a whole because of the marked retardation in trade (and decline on a per capita basis) experienced from the middle 1860s onward. Had exports continued to grow at the 18 per cent per annum experienced in the score of years between 1845 and 1865, the problem of the artisans and of the gradually dispossessed peasantry might have been ameliorated in general prosperity. As it was, retardation in trade only tended to compound the effects of dislocation.

The phenomenon of retardation is illustrated by comparing trends of exports and imports for the whole period 1845–85 and for two sub-periods. Over the period as a whole exports and imports grew at average annual cumulative rates of 5·0 and 6·4 per cent respectively. For the first sub-period, 1845–64, exports and imports grew rapidly (exports, 18 per cent; imports, 21 per cent). There was a tendency for imports to increase more rapidly than exports in the first period, but there was not yet evidence of persistent imbalance. In contrast, the second sub-period is marked by a structural change in import demand indicated by the sharply higher beginning point of the trend line for 1866 when compared with the ending point of the earlier trend line in 1864. By the beginning of the second sub-period imports reached such high levels relative to exports, and the commercial balance was so adverse, that the secular movement of imports had to be downward, despite continuing growth of demand. The heart of the problem lay in the stagnation of exports, which failed to show any trend of growth over the years 1866–85. Imports actually declined in value, a striking reversal of the rapid growth of the first period. The failure of per capita exports to keep pace with import demand proved to be a principal source of economic difficulty, particularly in the last quarter of the century, and may have generated some of the internal dissension that kept Colombians at war with each other through much of that period.

[1] See *Censo general de la República de Colombia* (Bogotá 1912), pp. 239, 256; Francisco Javier y Velasco, *Nueva geografía de Colombia* (Bogotá 1892), p. DCLXIV; *Anuario estadístico, 1875*; and McGreevey, 'Economic Development of Colombia', Table V-A. Vergara estimated the artisan share in the 1870 labor force at 18·5 per cent; using the same census data I estimated 26·6 per cent.

Trade expansion, 1845–85

DEFICITS AND ADJUSTMENTS

Data in Tables 12 and 13 are relevant to a number of specific macro-economic problems in this period. Table 12 brings out most clearly the problem of persistent deficit in the balance of payments. Data on the merchandise trade balance point to especially large deficits in the years 1863–74 and 1882–97 (the latter years not included in this chapter). A persistent excess of imports is typical of a developing country which is importing capital; however, persistent deficit in goods was not matched by capital imports. Clandestine export of gold and specie, minuscule immigration and some income from shipping services made up the trade deficit. The required magnitudes for export of gold and specie are so large as to point to a severely deflationary situation after 1863. Alejo Morales writes in the *Memoria de hacienda* for 1867 as follows: 'The absence of currency in internal trade is such that very soon we will return to a barter system, not unlike that used by primitive peoples before the invention of money, if we continue paying in species for the export deficit in relation to what we import and consume within the country.'[1] Through the normal price mechanisms the trade deficit produced substantial gold outflows and limitations on the potential growth of the money supply under gold standard rules. That events pointed in this direction is indicated by yet another Finance Minister's report (Luis Carlos Rico) for 1879: 'The exportation of gold and silver is alarming and if it were to continue at the rates experienced in the last fiscal year, without the occurrence of an economic change . . . , it will be the cause of grave difficulties for industry, trade and the Government.'[2]

The smaller potential money supply should then have depressed the average domestic price level – a change which in classical theory should encourage exports, discourage imports and achieve external balance. In fact, however, the 'modern' alternative to deflation – the issuance of paper currency – was resorted to; thus the adjustment mechanism came to include exchange rate devaluation. As the data in Table 14 show, Colombian currency, tied to gold until 1880, remained stable. Bank emissions from 1870 onward helped solve the liquidity problem for local commerce without producing *de facto* devaluation;[3] the establishment of a national bank in 1880, and the extension of its privileges to include unlimited note issue in 1886 led to the inflation in the last decade of the

---

[1] Cited in Torres Garcia, *Historia de la moneda en Colombia*, p. 177.
[2] Cited in Torres Garcia, *Historia de la moneda en Colombia*, p. 182.
[3] See *Banco de Bogotá, 1870–1960*, ed. Oliverio Perry, n.d.

century.[1] But even in the early 1880s there was considerable depreciation in the value of the peso which was in turn the result of an expanded paper money supply and government deficits. Already in the 1880s Colombians were opting for an inflationary 'solution' to the problem of the balance of payments and government deficit.

Table 14   *Colombia: exchange rates, 1845–85* (cents per U.S. dollar).

	Rate of exchange	
Year	Medellín	Bogotá
1845–73	0·980	0·965
1874	0·965	0·965
1875	0·962	0·965
1876	0·933	0·965
1877	0·962	0·965
1878	0·947	0·965
1879	0·962	0·965
1880	0·903	0·836
1881	0·904	0·823
1882	0·856	0·823
1883	0·794	0·812
1884	0·796	0·806
1885	0·769	0·795

Sources: Medellín, Alejandro López, *Estadística de Antioquia* (Medellín 1914), p. 161; Bogotá, Torres Garcia, *Historia de la moneda en Colombia, passim.*

Another kind of adjustment mechanism was put to work during this period by the trade deficit. The lack of data which would permit its quantitative estimation is no reason to ignore it. Income which would have been generated by local production of imported goods was lost as payments went abroad. These losses were of course multiplied in the diminished demand for local products which would not have moved in international trade. In this way incomes throughout the society were depressed – though obviously not equally for all Colombians. Lower domestic incomes should help reduce the demand for imports and bring about external balance. But before balance is achieved the required downward reductions in income may be great -- they will be particularly great in a backward

[1] See Carlos Martínez Silva, *Las emisiones clandestinas del Banco Nacional* (Bogotá 1937), pp. 55–121, a special report of an investigating committee of the Cámera de Representantes, 14 November 1894.

society with low price elasticities of demand for imports, i.e. in a situation in which price adjustments do not automatically and rapidly lead to external balance. In Colombia the first-round income adjustments were centered in artisan groups who lost markets to imported cloth. We suggested above that the expansion of imports could in one decade have reduced artisan employment by 100,000. Their lower income then affected their purchases of local products; in this second-round adjustment incomes were particularly depressed in the artisan areas of Santander, Boyacá and Nariño. The slower rate of population growth in these areas may be taken as an aggregate indicator of local stagnation in the economy. For example, the rate of population growth in Santander fell from an average of 1·3 per cent per annum over the interval 1843–70 to 0·6 per cent per annum, 1870–1905. The growth-rate was 87 per cent of the national average in the first period, 58 per cent in the second. These data confirm the impact of imports on artisan areas. Other artisan regions experienced similar stagnation.[1]

Stagnation was not exclusive to artisan areas; the cities were growing slowly as well, especially when compared to the rates of growth typical of the twentieth century. In the years from 1851 to 1870 secondary cities actually grew as fast as Bogotá and the ports. (See Table 15.) This is surprising because the growth of trade should have expanded opportunities in primary cities and led to the concentration of population in a few places.[2] In the next intercensal period, 1870–1912, the capital, port cities and other cities grew at approximately the same rates. Contrary to expectations, trade expansion did not produce unusually rapid growth for the ports.[3] Growing dependence on trade, even its increased volume and value, did not bestow the benefits of rapid urbanization. Quite the contrary: by inhibiting manufacturing development in the cities it prevented Colombia from enjoying the economies of scale and innovational possibilities associated with urbanization and industrialization.

One may surmise that the slow growth of cities resulted from a bias in the structure of trade which minimized urban occupations within Colombia

---

[1] Growth-rates are based on census data for the years 1843, 1870 and 1905.

[2] Port cities include Barranquilla, Cúcuta and Santa Marta for this calculation. Cartagena could not be included for lack of reliable population estimates for censuses prior to 1912.

[3] Ospina Vásquez who did not have quantitative data at his disposal writes of the coastal port cities that 'With the increase in international trade beginning in 1850 the absolute and relative economic importance of the port cities increased.' (*Industria y protección*, p. 249.) This view, to which one might easily be led, is not confirmed by comparing rates of urban population growth.

Table 15 Population of nineteen major municipios, 1793–1964.

Municipio	1793	1800	1825	1843	1851	1864	1870	1884	1905	1912	1918	1928	1938	1951	1964
Bogotá	17,725	24,464	—	40,086	29,649	—	40,833	95,761	100,000	121,257	143,994	235,421	330,312	648,324	1,697,311
Medellín	—	5,000	5,000	(9,000)	13,755	—	29,765	37,237	54,916	71,004	79,146	120,044	168,266	358,189	772,887
Cali	6,548	—	—	—	11,848	—	12,743	—	30,740	27,747	45,525	122,847	101,038	284,186	637,929
Barranquilla	—	—	—	—	6,114	—	(11,595)	—	40,115	48,907	64,543	139,974	152,348	279,627	498,301
Bucaramanga	—	—	—	5,851	10,008	10,707	11,255	—	20,314	19,735	24,919	44,083	51,283	112,252	229,748
Cartagena	—	—	18,000	—	9,896	—	(8,603)	—	9,681	36,632	51,382	92,491	84,937	128,877	242,085
Manizales	—	—	—	—	2,809	—	10,562	14,603	24,656	34,720	43,203	81,091	86,027	126,201	221,916
Pereira	—	—	—	—	—	—	633	—	19,036	18,428	24,735	50,699	60,492	115,342	188,365
Cúcuta	—	—	—	—	5,741	—	9,266	—	15,312	20,364	29,400	49,279	57,248	95,150	175,336
Ibagué	—	—	—	—	7,162	—	10,346	—	24,566	24,693	30,255	56,333	61,447	98,695	163,661
Palmira	—	—	—	—	1,055	—	12,390	—	26,406	24,312	27,032	39,951	44,788	80,957	140,889
Armenia	—	—	—	—	—	—	—	—	9,632	13,720	17,406	33,368	50,838	78,380	137,222
Montería	—	—	—	—	2,039	—	(3,151)	—	4,542	21,251	23,268	36,581	64,192	77,057	126,329
Ciénaga	—	—	—	—	5,078	—	7,127	—	14,610	14,610	24,708	45,428	47,333	56,854	113,143
Pasto	—	—	—	—	8,136	—	10,049	—	30,835	27,760	29,035	43,162	49,644	81,103	112,876
Santa Marta	—	—	—	—	4,340	—	5,472	—	9,568	8,348	18,040	30,942	33,245	47,354	104,471
Popayán	—	—	—	—	7,010	—	8,485	—	28,448	18,724	20,235	31,829	30,038	44,408	76,568
Tunja	—	—	—	—	5,022	—	5,471	—	8,407	8,971	10,680	19,064	20,236	27,402	68,905
Neiva	—	—	—	—	7,719	—	8,332	—	18,333	21,852	25,185	29,988	34,294	50,494	89,790

Sources: National censuses and certain other sources discussed in the Note on Sources. Figures in parentheses are for years near to but other than those indicated.

while maximizing them among Colombia's trading partners. Colombia exported rural products: gold from scattered mining operations, tobacco from the lowland plantations. The country received urban products: cotton goods from Manchester and Boston. This bias added one more dimension to growing dependence on foreign trade.

PERSISTENT DISEQUILIBRIUM

At the most fundamental level the balance of payments problem stemmed from insufficient growth of exports. But of equal importance were the shorter periods of excess importation of foreign goods. Imports and the negative commercial balance were unusually high in the years 1863–74. Perhaps the most intellectually satisfying 'curve' which could describe the import time series would be a set of three straight lines, each with approximately the same slope and fitting the years 1845–62, 1864–74 and 1875–85. (The year 1863 was one of 'transition' to a higher level of imports.) In each period imports grew at about the same rate; the middle period is simply one at which a different relationship between population, income and imports was established, but at which the rates of growth of these variables remained as it had been in the previous period, and was to be in the following decade. The distinction and analysis are important. They point to a structural shift of import conditions as the cause of excess imports. Excessive imports seems not to have been due to a change in consumer tastes. The combination of tariff reforms, easier permission for importation and related 'structural' reforms produced the eleven-year boom in imports. Because data on this import boom had not previously been available (Colombian data indicate imports of under Ps$5 million annually in this period), it has not been analyzed. The excessive imports prevented orderly economic growth. The government policies which allowed the disequilibrium of the 1860s were a basic cause of economic instability. Those policies must bear a considerable share of the responsibility for the trade deficit and its adverse impact on the domestic economy.

The secular trend of export growth was deficient when compared to import demand over the period as a whole; however, the deficiency lies largely in the years after 1865. Were a trend line calculated for the years 1845–74 (even leaving aside the boom of 1875), exports would have been exceeding imports by a substantial margin after the downward structural readjustment of imports came in 1875.

The years of relative success in exports prior to 1875 were based largely on tobacco. The most typical explanation for the difficulty in exporting

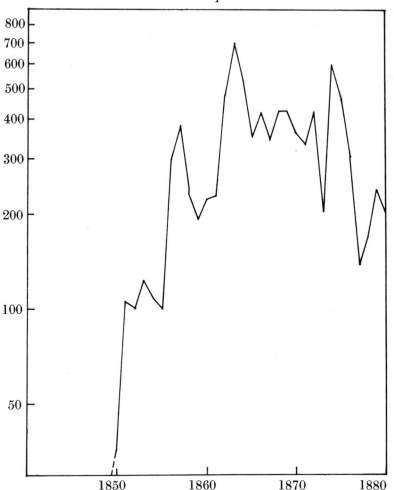

Figure 5 Value of exports of tobacco in index number form, 1850–80 (1852 = 100).
Sources: see text.

is that low-cost production began in Java in 1875 and drove Colombian leaf tobacco out of the German market.[1] The growth of tobacco exports is shown in detail in Figure 5. The curve there presented is based on several sources, principally the compilation by Camacho Roldán mentioned

[1] See Harrison, 'The Evolution of the Colombian Tobacco Industry, to 1875', *Hispanic American Historical Review*, XXXII (1952), 163–74.

earlier. The data available on price and quantity exported were put into index form with the year 1852 = 100. The price and quantity indices were multiplied to produce a measure of the value of tobacco exports, as shown in Figure 5. Despite the potential deficiencies of this statistical technique over the years of mutual coverage the series here presented coincides well with that prepared by Camacho Roldán.[1]

The cyclical movement of tobacco exports parallels that of total exports – a finding not too surprising in light of the dominant position of that crop in the total. The unusually high total for 1863, the same year in which the 'structural change' in imports led to new high levels of imports, suggests that the high earnings of that unusual year led the Colombians to believe they could sustain more importation than was in fact possible. In other words, when good times and a liberal trade philosophy were brought together in that year with the obvious advantage to merchants in the import business, new patterns of importation were inculcated which were to last for more than a decade – long after such patterns could be sustained by export prospects.

The close link between tobacco producers and the merchant importers provided the right situation for an import boom once the catalyst of an export boom was added. However, once new high levels of imports began it was difficult to hold them back in line with the real possibilities of exportation. In the 1950s such a phenomenon came to be referred to as the 'international demonstration effect'.[2] In Colombia of the 1860s the problem was probably less one of consumption standards and propensities than of the politics of forcing an interest group (the merchants) to accept government measures designed to achieve external balance. For more than a decade no firm support for such action was taken; the fact is perhaps sufficient commentary on the economic and political power wielded by the merchants during that period.

Tobacco exports did continue (and are even today an important though minor export product), suggesting that greater efficiencies and quality control in production might have supported continuing growth past 1875. Exploration of the conditions of production in tobacco cultivation will reveal some of the problems inherent in the industry as it existed in Colombia which would eventually have brought a crisis. In this as in other activities domestic conditions provided the efficient cause of external disequilibrium.

---

[1] See Colombia, Ministerio de Gobierno, *Estadística general de la República de Colombia* (ed. Henrique Arboleda C., Bogotá 1905), pp. 188–9. These data are probably based on the Camacho Roldán compilations though no source note is provided.

[2] The term is most often attributed to Ragnar Nurske. See his *Problems of Capital Formation in Underdeveloped Countries* (Oxford 1958), pp. 58 ff.

The liberal period

SUMMARY

Colombia's problems in international trade during the years 1845–85 can usefully be broken into two groups and periods: the problems of excessive imports in the years 1864–74, and the problem of deficient exports in the years 1875–85 (and onward into the early 1890s). The 'import problem' almost certainly relates to explicit government policy. Further, the apparent tie to an inflated, temporary level of export earnings generated in 1863 must be emphasized. The conjunction of adoption of a new constitution and unusually high exports seems to have been the necessary and sufficient cause for the structural shift of import demand. It is less clear what events caused the downward shift of demand eleven years later. There was no devaluation.[1] Devaluation through note issue, i.e. via an increase in the supply of paper money, did not occur on a large scale until the 1880s. Moreover, 1875 was a year of exceptionally high exports: from the experience in 1863–4 one might have been led to expect further acceleration on that account in the demand for imports.

Unfortunately, this perplexing problem is not dealt with in detail in any of the qualitative literature on economic and financial events in that epoch. Nieto Arteta provides a brief analysis of the period as he attempts to date turning points in economic cycles in the second half of the nineteenth century.[2] According to him the years 1870–4 were ones of prosperity for Colombia; however, the problems generated by the worldwide Panic of 1873 took their toll in Colombia in the next few years:

The fall in the price of export products – tobacco, cinchona bark and indigo – is explained by the competition presented by products from colonial areas. Moreover, the general crisis which came around 1873 halted the normal rhythm of growth of the world economy. It was natural that the general decline in prices would press down on the prices of our export products.[3]

Unfortunately, Nieto Arteta provides an explanation of events which did not occur. Problems with exports belong to the years 1876 and after. He does refer to the 'crisis of 1875' (p. 369) and its supposed causal relation to the civil war of 1876–7 but provides no analysis of the problem. The most valuable commentary on the period apparently came from Camacho Roldán in 1881:

---

[1] Total exports of the United States and Great Britain fell by about 7 per cent from 1874 to 1875; there was no apparent great fall in potential importables from Colombia's two leading trading partners.

[2] See Nieto Arteta, *Economía y cultura*, p. 363–70.

[3] Nieto Arteta, *Economía y cultura*, p. 369.

Trade expansion, 1845-85

We are passing through a true crisis, the intensity of which we have not formerly perceived since it has come by degrees, and because our patriarchal customs, on the one hand, and our limited use of capital markets and the general slowness of business on the other, diminish the violence of the great industrial crashes which from time to time one sees in the United States and Europe. The civil war of 1876, especially, restricted from that time on sources of credit, paralyzed business and drowned in the terrible noise of civil war the commercial crisis which began at that time.[1]

It would appear for lack of any substantial explanation of the adjustment of imports between 1874 and 1875 that unusual restrictions on credit made it difficult for merchants in Colombia to buy goods abroad. In this view the 'structural adjustment' would apparently have been achieved through commercial mechanisms in ways that did not become known to contemporary observers. Ospina Vásquez does speak of special emissions of paper money in 1875 by the banks;[2] it is conceivable that such emissions proved unacceptable as payments to European merchants and that Colombian imports were reduced as a consequence. Yet even more interesting than explanations which we might develop for the change from 1874 to 1875 is the succeeding permanence of imports at the new low levels in subsequent years. The value of imports did not again reach those of the years 1864-74 in the nineteenth century.[3] Thus the downward shift of import demand which occurred in 1874-5 proved to be relatively permanent. As such, it antedated by half a decade the efforts of Rafael Núñez to institute a policy of protection for home industry. In this as in other matters significant economic change does not seem to have coincided with political change.

Perhaps not surprisingly the crisis in exports is better explained in the literature. The civil war of 1876 brought direct damage to export activities as the value of exports fell by 50 per cent between 1875 and 1876. A low point was reached in 1877 followed by four boom years (1878-81), then a fall to a new low level in 1885. The export data used by previous analysis derive principally from the annual reports of the Minister of Finance. For this period the data are reasonably in agreement with those in Table 12 drawn from the statistical sources of Colombia's trading partners. The

---

[1] Salvador Camacho Roldán, 'Nuestra situación industrial', *La union* (September 1881); reprinted in *Escritos varios* (Bogotá 1892), pp. 665-74.

[2] Ospina Vásquez, *Industria y protección*, p. 235.

[3] The price of Colombian imports was of course falling from 1873 to the end of the century. The terms of trade between Colombian coffee (as distinguished from total exports) and imports was improving from 1880 through 1893. Since the import values given in Table 12 are in current dollars, price adjustments for imports have not been made. On import values and terms of trade see Albert Imlah, *Economic Elements in the Pax Britannica* (Cambridge, Mass. 1958), pp. 94-101, and William McGreevey, 'The Economic Development of Colombia', Appendix Table II-G, 'Colombia. Net Barter terms of Trade, Indices of Coffee Prices and Import Prices, 1881-1961'; see especially the source note.

relatively good quality of export data (since exports were not subject to duties) and poor quality of import data may explain why previous analyses have provided clear and meaningful interpretations of those phenomena restricted to a study of the situation in exports, and poor interpretations of imports and the balance of trade. Previously available data (as in the work of Ospina Vásquez and Nieto Arteta) suggest a rough balance in the current account and all that implies for domestic stability. Data presented here suggest a dramatic imbalance of such proportions as to be the underlying cause for the climate of social unrest and prolonged depression. Previous analysts could only watch the course of development of the *export* economy in quantitative terms: little wonder that they differed in their interpretations of its implications for the rest of the economy which remained enshrouded in statistical darkness.

CHAPTER 6

LIBERALISM AND AGRARIAN CHANGE,
1845–90

A previous chapter was devoted to a discussion of the intellectual and legal preparation for a phase of increasing concentration of ownership of land, for the establishment of new landed elites and strengthening of old ones, and for the creation of a large, mobile and socially marginal rural proletariat which would replace the sedentary resguardo Indian. In the years which include the Reforms of 1850, the disamortization of Church lands in 1861 and the return to a centralist, republican constitution in 1886, the earlier preparation was worked out in its fullest manifestations. In this chapter I discuss and try to depict the effects of the Liberal reforms on the economic well-being of the rural population. The Liberals used the political power they enjoyed in the years 1845–80 to enhance their personal control of national wealth and income; since land and its improvements proved to be the most important generator of income and the largest single item in an inventory of national wealth, control there was both natural and essential. The results of their efforts are detailed in this chapter. In contrast to earlier writings I will bring to bear quantitative information on the change of landownership to support the dual contention (1) that much land changed hands and (2) that ownership became more concentrated. Succeeding sections draw out the implications.

LAND PRICES AND LAND USE

The first administration of Mosquera marked the passing of the control of the nation to the Liberals and their decision to follow the concept of free trade.[1] The economic depression of the 1840s made it abundantly clear that Colombia's domestic economic potential was relatively limited. In 1847 the government contracted with the firm of Montoya, Saenz y Cia. to take control of the monopoly for the production of tobacco. This decision reflected a turning point in Colombian agrarian history and was

---

[1] The ascent of Liberalism may be more accurately dated with the accession of Florentino González to the Ministry of Finance in 1847. Mosquera was not himself identified with the Liberals. See J. Leon Helguera, 'The First Mosquera Administration in New Granada, 1845-1849' (Ph.D. diss., The University of North Carolina, 1958).

based on an understanding that a private concern probably would have easier access to scarce capital and credit than the government and hence could promote expansion and growth of the tobacco industry more quickly and more efficiently. It was under the regime of Montoya that tobacco became the principal export product of Colombia. The Magdalena Valley around Ambalema was turned into an area of brisk economic activity as in a few short years tobacco production for export reached the unprecedented level of 5 million kilos, steamboats plied the river with regularity and Colombia came to be inexorably tied to the network of trade.

It was a dominant assumption of the Liberals that such dependence was the path of salvation for the economy. Aquileo Parra found that the stagnation, lack of credit and weak agricultural production in Vélez

is not for lack of buyers for the valuable agricultural products, nor because of scarce labor, nor because of high wages, nor because of sterile land, nor for lack of transport for advantageously exporting its products, but rather because they do not want to produce anything beyond what is consumed locally; and with this kind of production, if a few farmers, in exceptional circumstances, are able to accumulate some capital, most farmers are only able to meet their subsistence needs.[1]

The Liberals expected that the economy would be much improved producing for the external market rather than for internal consumption. Colombian writings of the time are filled with accounts of the potentials of production for European markets.

The new emphasis on an export crop, tobacco, also reflected a belief that it would encourage the growth of a class of middle-sized farmers.[2] Until the middle of the nineteenth century Colombian landowners had failed to produce a major export crop. This failure is explained by two conditions which affected Colombia's prospects as an agricultural exporter: (1) transport costs were high so that no bulky commodity could hope to move in trade and (2) Colombian agriculture in the highlands (where a vast majority of the rural population was located) tended to duplicate rather than complement the agricultural systems of the industrializing countries. For these reasons there was no basis on which to build an export economy and system of trade with the North Atlantic countries. It was only when improved transport and population movement into the Magdalena Valley made production there possible that a basis for trade was established. Thus, only after mid-century did Colombia become an exporter of products of the soil. Gold and silver dominated Colombian

---

[1] Aquileo Parra, *Memorias de Aquileo Parra*, Presidente de Colombia de 1867 a 1878 (Comprenden de 1825 a 1876) (Bogotá 1912), p. 504.

[2] See Frank Safford, 'Commerce and Enterprise in Central Colombia', p. 207.

exports; the most non-metals had contributed was 17 per cent of exports in the years 1840–4. This picture changed after 1850 as tobacco became the dominant export product. The growth of agricultural products in export activities was but one aspect of changing land use after 1845. This phenomenon of growth was located largely in lowland river valleys and based on clearance of previously unused land. Highland areas also experienced changing land use and land values. Cattle raising was stimulated by the cultivation of artificial grasses and the importation of new breeds of cattle.[1] The introduction of barbed wire in the 1870s made possible semi-intensive cattle raising, for it became possible to shut off cultivated fields where feed grains and grasses could be grown. According to Ospina Vásquez, 'the extension of cattle raising ... was the principal dynamic element in our agricultural and economic evolution from the end of the colonial period until the big expansion in coffee production'.[2] These technical improvements probably came late in this period, however. In Argentina the major technical improvements in meat production (barbed wire, new feed grains and grasses, refrigeration) did not take place until after 1875.[3] The introduction of ruddy wheat and improved breeds of potatoes – staples of the highland Colombian diet – were other important technical improvements in agriculture. These general indications of growing demand for land can best be judged by a more detailed review of specific local conditions as they relate to long-term changes in the use, ownership and price of agricultural land.

There seems little ground for doubting that in Colombia as a whole land increased in value during the course of the nineteenth century, particularly after the expansion of tobacco exports. The mere fact of population growth will explain much of the improvement in land prices. However, there are no aggregate data on farm income, and land sales data are too few in number to make possible a detailed picture of long-term changes in land values. For those statistics we do possess the extreme regionalism of Colombia makes their assessment difficult. Land values were affected by time, space and accessibility. Despite these problems data on land sales prices (Table 16) indicate enough about the dominant trends to permit a few generalizations.

Five observations on land values prior to the 1840s and nine observations for the years 1841–65 are included in Table 16. The simple averages

---

[1] The most common artificial grass, Pará, could only be grown at altitudes up to 1000 m., that is, in *tierra caliente*. See Parsons, *Antioqueño Colonization*, p. 24.

[2] Luis Ospina Vásquez, *Plan agrícola* (Medellín 1963), p. 32.

[3] For a summary see Sanford Mosk, 'Latin America and the World Economy, 1850–1914', *Inter-American Economic Affairs*, II (1948), 53–82, esp. p. 70.

of the two groups are $3·56 and $31·37. The conclusion that land values increased almost tenfold in a quarter of a century is not warranted because the second period's sample is heavily weighted by land in tobacco cultivation and located along principal traffic arteries. The presumption of increased land values is confirmed although the magnitude of the increase must remain in doubt.

Land located in the area of export crop cultivation experienced the greatest gains in value. In the Magdalena area land prices rose tenfold during the peak tobacco period from 1850 to 1865. The Bunch hacienda of 14,429

Table 16 *Estimated land values, various areas and years, 1822–74.*

Year	Price in current pesos per hectare	Remarks
1822–3	2·50	Interior, wastelands
	5·00	Coast, wastelands
1826	1·85	
1829–40	6·80	
1835	1·65	Minimum price
1841–50	9·50	
1850	12·40	Ambalema–Magdalena Valley
1851–61	20·00	
1851	98·80	Along road from Bogotá to Facatativá
1853	3·45	Near Pacho ironworks
1855	0·17	Giveaway
1857	1·00	
1863	37·00	Land values inflated in 1860s
1865	100·00	Ambalema–Magdalena Valley, tobacco land, inflated
1869–75	0·30–0·40	San Martín, baldíos
1870	0·25–0·30	Giveaway
1871	60	Tierras altas, propiedad territorial
Ave. value for uncultivated	10–15	Tierras templadas de la falda de la cordillera, territorial
or partially cultivated land	6–10	Los climas cálidos de las vegas del Magdalena, del Fusagasugá y otros, territorial
	30–50	Tierras calientes, pastos artificiales
Cultivated lands	70–100	Tierras calientes, caña de azúcar
valuated	100–200	Tierras calientes, cacao y café
according to	300	Tierras calientes, planteras
crop	500–600	Tierras calientes, tierras de tabaco, populated area at height of tobacco boom
	6–10	Tierras vírgenes
1874	13·30	La cuchilla de Gallegos near Carare

Sources: see the Note on Sources.

fanegadas had originally been purchased for $30,000 and was on the market around 1854 for $100,000.[1] The Canada Company was established in 1826. It acquired lands at less than a peso per acre.[2] From 1829 to 1861 the sale value of its lands increased from less than 3 pesos per acre to more than 8 pesos per acre. During that time it sold over 2 million acres of land for almost 10 million pesos. In 1861 it still possessed over 4,000 farms which were selling at a maximum of 15 pesos per acre.[3]

The more detailed data prepared for 1871 by Salvador Camacho Roldán for land values of various locations, qualities and uses tends to confirm the hypothesis of increasing land values. Lowland areas which came more and more into use after 1845 were of higher value than highlands or areas in a middle altitude. Land used for production of export products (tobacco in particular) was of higher value than that of land used for domestically consumed goods (sugar, pasture lands).

The increase in land values was due largely to the success achieved in the production of certain export products which enjoyed brisk and growing demand in Europe. Without foreign demand land values would presumably not have risen.

There is little information currently available on the changing value of land; investigations into local and regional rural history will eventually bring new data to light from notarial archives and the records of private haciendas. For that reason I must restrict my conclusions to two: (1) land values rose in general from the first to the second-half of the nineteenth century; (2) the rise of land values was caused by growing demand for agricultural exports from the lowlands.

There is still less information available on land use. Table 17 does present estimates of cultivated land and its division by use between subsistence cropping, production for urban markets and production for export. Because of the great variation in land-use intensity in stockraising, it proved impossible to estimate land in use for grazing.

The estimates were built up from the components of final demand. The records of international commerce (including those of Colombia's trading partners, Great Britain, the United States, France and Germany) provide

---

[1] Ramón Guerra Azuola, 'Apuntamientos de viaje', *Boletín de historia y antigüedades*, IV (1906), 69–70.

[2] As late as 1873 government lands were still being sold at uniform prices without regard to their actual values. In the legal literature 'The Colombian fanega (or fanegada) of 1·50 acres was used until the 1850s in delimiting adjudications, after which they were made in hectares (2·47 acres) ... The caudra, used by cattlemen, is comparable to the fanega.' (Parsons, *Antioqueño Colonization*, p. 197.)

[3] J. D. Powles, *New Granada: Its Internal Resources* (London 1861), pp. 78–9.

The liberal period

data on the quantity of agricultural products exported. From contemporary sources we estimated the cultivated area required for a given volume of the exported product. The estimation of hectares devoted to export production proved to be the easiest component of demand to estimate.

Area devoted to urban and rural consumption was estimated by multiplying population in the two groups by 0·16 hectares. A justification for this procedure is contained in the appendix to this chapter.

Table 17 *Estimated cropland by final demand 1837–1960* (thousands of hectares).

Year	For urban consumption (1)	For rural consumption (2)	For export (3)	Total cropland (4)	Per cent of total arable land (5)
1837	16	318	17	351	2·3
1857	25	338	11	374	2·5
1870	33	350	31	414	2·8
1910	92	689	139	920	6·2
1925	152	925	395	1,471	9·9
1938	244	1,148	403	1,795	12·1
1951	446	1,402	616	2,464	16·6
1960	741	1,712	589	3,042	20·6

Sources: see appendix to this chapter for sources and methods used.

Expansion of the derived demand for export-productive land raised the price of that land. The new income generated by higher rents in turn increased the demand for other agricultural products and stimulated price increases in land usable for supplying urban demand as well as that generated in the export-producing areas. These effects were reversed once export growth ceased. The gradual extension of the cultivated area of Colombia was accomplished primarily by the growth of external demand for exports and secondarily by the growth of urban markets. Between 1837 and 1910 cropland in use to satisfy export demand increased at the rate of about 3 per cent per annum, whereas land in use for domestic needs expanded only about 1·2 per cent per annum.[1] Rural population growth extended the area of subsistence cropping, but that extension produced little incentive for economic change. Only a tiny fraction of total arable land in the country (less than 3 per cent in 1870) was being tilled. There was no land scarcity which might have prompted agricultural innovations.

[1] Estimates in Table 17, columns 1 and 2, depend on an assumed constancy of the ratio of population to cropland in use.

Liberalism and agrarian change, 1845–90

The abolition of resguardos

Changing land use and the changing price and value of land were accompanied by significant political events which brought large blocs of land onto the market for quick sale. The first of these events was the 'final' abolition of resguardos by an act of 22 June 1850. Although the Indian was not initially free to sell his lands, state legislatures had been authorized to dispose of certain resguardos by Law 3 of June 1848. Leading Liberal intellectuals supported proprietary individuation. Commenting on the romantic liberalism of 1850 Hernán Jaramillo Ocampo has written:

> The Liberals' agrarian revolution in 1850 tended to seek democratization of the rural properties by absolutely negative means, abolishing red tape and obstacles, rather than providing positive protection to the farmers. Throughout its history, the country has abandoned its agricultural profile, its pastoral structure, and its real economic orientation. Politics were manipulated from the city, for the city and by the city – the countryside remained at the margin of national life.[1]

The acts stemming from the Liberalism of 1850 were a reflection of a re-emergence of paternalism with a new twist, namely an attempt to 'civilize' the Indian by folding him into the body politic of the nation. This ideology overlooked the fact that Indian landownership was communal, not individual; by persuading Indians to be individual landowners as an alternative to living on the resguardo lands, Liberalism opened the door to the Indian to sell his birthright to landgrabbers and speculators for money which could be used for immediate consumption.

The authorization to sell the resguardos was a formal recognition of the fact that many Indians had been illegally leasing and selling their lands for decades. The law of 1850 meant, in the words of Salvador Camacho Roldán, that

> they [the Indians] immediately sold out their lands to the city bosses at ridiculously low prices. The Indians were converted into day-laborers, with salaries of 10 cents a day; food became scarce, agricultural land was converted to pasture for cattle, and the rest of the indigenous race, the former owners of these regions for centuries, dispersed in search of better wages in the hot lowlands, where their sad conditions have not improved.[2]

Lands which were previously cultivated intensively now became the domain of cattle, and the extension of stockraising became the principal

[1] Hernán Jaramillo Ocampo, *Exegisis de nuestra economía agraria* (editorial Zapata, Manizales, 1940), p. 7.
[2] Quoted in Carlos Mario Londoño, *Economía agraria colombiana* (Madrid 1965), p. 14.

catalyst in the evolution of agriculture until the 1890s. 'This is how, in the region of Chocontá, it became possible to form haciendas like *Las Julias* composed largely of lots which had belonged to the Indians and which were sold at ridiculous prices during the nineteenth century.'[1] General Posada Gutierrez observed in 1865, 'Having declared them citizens, we have prostrated them.'[2] And in 1856 José Manuel Groot wrote: 'When the Law has left them to their own means, intending to make them free men, it has made them into slaves of misery.'[3]

Thus the Indians left in search of work elsewhere or remained as landless peasants to work on the hacienda. Isaac Holton found evidence of decline throughout the Cauca Valley: 'a very Eden by nature is filled with hunger and poverty from Popayán to Antioquia'.[4] Guerra Azuola has left a description of the degradation of the Indians he saw near Bogotá in 1881:

My companions were depressed to find no remains of the Indian generations which had passed and which are still seen in other areas, with clear indications of their enlightenment and riches. Certainly we had seen Indians after our departure from Bogotá, grouped in towns, and spread out over the land we passed; but these resembled not the ancient inhabitants of the land: their degradation has increased, because of the systems applied here. The Indians of our time are little different from beasts of burden.[5]

Those Indians who remained on the land – as many did in Nariño, Cauca and parts of Boyacá – introduced a pathologic fragmentation of land holdings. Not only did the average size of landholdings among Indians and mestizos decline but also each farmer had numerous small, scattered and inefficient patches which he attempted to cultivate – in a most uneconomical fashion.[6] This fragmentation – a result of original pressures from Spanish agriculturalists in the eighteenth century, a haphazard policy of rescinding legal recognition of communal holdings, and Indian failure to develop a custom of primogeniture or equivalent means of consolidating holdings – is the historical basis for the present problems of the minifundista

---

[1] Orlando Fals Borda, 'Los orígenes del problema de la tierra en Chocontá, Colombia', *Boletín de historia y antigüedades* (1954), p. 49.

[2] Joaquín Posada Gutierrez, *Memorias histórico-políticas del General Joaquín Posada Gutierrez*, IV (Impr. Nacional, Bogotá 1929), 126.

[3] Quoted in Fals Borda, 'Los orígenes del problema de la tierra en Chocontá', p. 49.

[4] Holton, *New Granada, Twenty Months in the Andes*, p. 498.

[5] Guerra Azuola, 'Apuntamientos de viaje', p. 421.

[6] Very similar conditions are mentioned for England in the eighteenth century (Paul Mantoux, *The Industrial Revolution in the Eighteenth Century* (revised edition, New York 1961), p. 143); and Mexico (Oscar Lewis, *Life in a Mexican Village: Tepoztlán Restudied* (Urbana, Ill. 1963), p. 120), and Colombia (Orlando Fals Borda, *El hombre y la tierra en Boyacá*, pp. 118–37) in the nineteenth and twentieth.

Liberalism and agrarian change, 1845–90

in Colombia, the landed peasant proprietor who owns almost nothing and scarcely makes a subsistence living.

The fact that parcelization began in the interior and had most success *vis-à-vis* the Indian communities which were most involved in the market economy, suggests that economic conditions were much more important than juridical ones. Increased fragmentation was the rule even in cases where government decisions were clearly meant to favor the Indian community. In one case 42 per cent of former resguardo lands were used for building a school and in payment for community improvements thought desirable by the provincial government.[1] This left the individual Indians with little land for private cultivation.

The cases of Cauca and Nariño illustrate that the Indians were better off where colonial traditions were strong and where the Indian himself was never an easily exploited asset. Governmental decisions failed to have the expected results in areas which were backward economically and isolated geographically from the main sources of change. With the exception of Law 90 of 1859 which recognized communal holdings (*el régimen comunal*) as the natural and permanent state of the resguardos in the Department of Cauca, and the Decree of 30 January 1863, which conceded lands to the towns of Pitayó and Jambaló in Cauca, there was no legislation of a positive manner to protect the Indian communities from the wider economic and social forces at work in the society at large.[2] In the words of Antonio García:

> The division of resguardos in the interior states, using the words of the federalist period, did not represent a multiplication of individual properties in the hands of the traditional *comuneros*, but rather an act of substitution of the great haciendas for the Indian properties ... the results of which ... were that the real Indian policies ... were not enacted within the judicial framework, but outside of it.[3]

But despite policies designed to bring on the universal demise of the resguardo it hung on where isolation and the social resilience instilled by earlier traditions would permit. Not unexpectedly these same areas are today among the most backward and resistant to change.

Parcelization and fragmentation, though apparently inefficient to the casual observer, offer distinct advantages to the *minifundista*.[4] Most important among these advantages is the hedge provided against a calamitous

[1] Antonio García, *Legislación indigenista en Colombia, introducción crítica y recopilación* (Ediciones Especiales del Instituto Indigenista Interamericano, Mexico, 1952), pp. 26–7.
[2] See Alvaro Gaitán Suarez, 'Acción indigenista en América ... métodos y resultados en Colombia', XXXV Congreso Internacional de Americanistas, pp. 315 ff.
[3] García, *Legislación indigenista en Colombia*, p. 12.
[4] Fals Borda, *El hombre y la tierra en Boyacá*, pp. 123–4.

loss due to unfavorable weather. By holding parcels at several altitude levels, with varying soil conditions and other special advantages, the minifundista pays a price in lower efficiency as a form of insurance against the loss which might befall a single plot.

In a majority of cases the fragmentation of land had its roots in inefficient farming operations, due as much to the lack of capital as a congeries of unfavorable physical factors and legal enactments. Therefore, the beginnings of subdivision might have been somewhat accidental. This may help explain why there seems to have been little protest on the part of the Indians other than in the courts, although a more thorough investigation of local sources may yet disclose that Indian opposition to Republican laws was widespread. One exception was the Indian revolt in Tierradentro in 1861 and Indian participation in the Mosquera revolution of those years. And an alternative explanation to the survival of the resguardos in Cauca might be that the Indians of Pitayó and Jambaló participated in the revolutions against the large landholders in that state.[1]

Where local circumstances permitted parcelization, once the process began it was irreversible. If decisions by the Liberals could have halted or reversed the process, they were not forthcoming, because the whole period under discussion, in fact, knew but one law pertaining to Indian lands, repeated with minor variations from 1821 to the agrarian law of 1891. From approximately that date abstentionist theories of public law were in agreement with Church authorities and once again gave the Church a measure of vigilance over Indian communities. In the words of Antonio García, from that time forward:

All the Indian policies were carried out not with laws but by means of 'agreements' with the Church; or to be more exact, the Indian policies acquire the exclusive character of an ecclesiastic activity. It is not an agreement between the Church and the State, but rather the total absence of State intervention regarding the treatment of the Indian peoples.[2]

For several decades before mid-century resguardos had been gradually broken up or abandoned by Indian communities. By 1850 only the most viable units remained as communal lands. With the last defense of communal ownership removed there came a swift alienation of Indian lands in all areas except the south of the country. An observation by Miguel Samper is quoted in nearly every work on the economic and social history of Colombia: it is worth repeating once again here. 'The poor Indians were induced to sell their little plots, in which each had his own house, enjoyed

---

[1] See Antonio García, *Legislación indigenista en Colombia*, p. 26.
[2] García, *Legislación indigenista en Colombia*, p. 43.

a certain independence and found a secure basis for subsistence living. In a few short years all that property was concentrated in a few hands, the Indian became a tenant [and] the land was used for grazing cattle.'[1]

Thus some of the more desirable land in highland areas quickly passed out of the hands of smallholders and into concentrated ownership.[2] The greater physical mobility of the rural population induced by employment opportunities in the lowlands made traditional communal ownership less feasible than it once had been. Communal Indians left the resguardos and failed to contribute to communal needs. In most parts of Colombia the resguardo was in decay for reasons of its own impracticality. However, the legal changes attacked both viable and non-viable resguardos. As such, they so accelerated the process of transition from archaic forms of land tenure to modern ones, that the Indians were deluged and drowned in change.

Church lands

The process of accumulation of land in Church hands is probably as old as Spanish occupance of Colombia. The custom of willing land titles to the Church and its several Orders has resulted in the accumulation of a large share of the good farm land in the hands of religious organizations.[3] In other cases liens (usually called censos) were placed against the earnings of farms to pay for masses or to support some member of the clergy. In the eighteenth century Church organizations possessed the largest pool of liquid capital available and hence became moneylenders to agricultural estates. Through the accumulation of mortgages the Church acquired an even greater stake in landed property. The persuasive power associated with control of the destiny of many sharecroppers or lessees must certainly have added to the prestige and social control enjoyed by the parish priest. He in turn must often have taken the opportunity of suggesting to major landholders that they too might help cleanse their souls by giving lands to the Church in exchange for masses.[4]

[1] Miguel Samper, *Escritos político-económicos*.

[2] Stockraising, particularly of cattle, is almost wholly an activity of large agricultural units in Colombia. In 1960, 85 per cent of all pasture land was held by *explotaciones agropecuarias* 50 hectares or greater in size. See T. Lynn Smith, *Colombia* (Gainesville 1967), p. 57.

[3] For a discussion of the role of one Order see Germán Colmenares, *Las haciendas de los jesuítas en el nuevo reino de Granada* (Bogotá 1969).

[4] The accumulation of Church lands and their moneylending operations are discussed by Arnold Bauer, 'The Chilean Rural Society, 1830–80' (Ph.D. diss., University of California, Berkeley 1970); Michael Costeloe, *Church Wealth in Mexico* (Cambridge 1967); and J. Ignacio Méndez, 'Colonial Survivals in Panama: Public Administration and the Censo' (Ph.D. diss., University of California, Berkeley 1970).

The liberal period

Perhaps typical of the process of accumulation is the example given by Holton of the Hacienda de la Paila in the Cauca Valley near Cartago:

The hacienda extends from Las Canas River to the River Murillo, which formerly bounded the provinces of Antioquia and Popayán. The width there is seven miles, the length, from Cauca to the summit of the Quindio, may be 30 miles, and the whole can not contain less than 500 square miles, and may well be a thousand. During the good old regime of tyranny ... two hundred years ago a dying Sanmartin bequeathed this property to the souls in Purgatory, and, until lately, it has been in dead hands, 'manos muertas'. Republicanism might protest against the arrangement, but it would be a sacrilege to change it. The work should be undone in some way, that society may not be blocked up till the end of time by a superstitious provision in a will of the 17th century. So, too, thinks the democratic – ultra-democratic – government of New Granada. Hence the law for abolishing mayorazgos, and the law for redeeming capellanias and other perpetual charges – censos they are called.[1]

Mosquera's revolutionary pronouncement expropriating Church lands in 1861 was already discussed in Chapter 4. That such measures against the Church were difficult to carry out was indicated by the necessity of another measure against it in 1877. Law 8 of 19 March of that year declared 'cancelled all nominal rent belonging to churches, patronages, chaplaincies and in general all religious and ecclesiastical entities, whatever class or denomination they may be'.[2] And problems with the Church continued to plague administrations throughout the century. If the Liberals were not able to dispose of former Church lands in a manner which would have aided the small farmer this was because the expropriated land was purchased by owners of large estates rather than being divided up among the small property owners or the landless. This was a fact which stemmed both from government intention and policy and from the continued power of the Church in terms of the pressure it exerted against purchase of what it considered to be its rightful property. As Guerra Azuola remarks in his *Lecciones de Legislación fiscal*:

The properties inappropriately called 'manos muertas' (church lands), which earlier were bought and sold freely, passed into the hands of the land speculators to such a degree that they did not enter the market except under extraordinary pressure, since public opinion would not stand for the land speculation which would result from their public sale ... Nineteen years have gone by, and conscience, or instinct, prohibits the open sale of these properties. ... On the other hand, these properties remain even more stagnant than before, from the people's point of view. The innumerable small farms that were called 'muertas' used to be rented at extremely low prices, within reach of the poorer classes, that is, the masses; today, however, only the few rich can afford to rent these lands, and the poor people have had to take

---

[1] Holton, *New Granada. Twenty Months in the Andes*, pp. 418–19.
[2] Juan Pablo Restrepo, *La iglesia y el estado* p. 414.

refuge in ill-built barracks and shanties, where hundreds of individuals, who could be useful members of society, live in agony and die in horrendous abandon.[1]

Thus not only did the government fail to redistribute Church holdings because they were too costly and because there was too much pressure put to bear against buying them, but those that did sell eventually failed to bring into the treasury the money that was supposed to underwrite economic development and payment of debts. A contemporary historian, Eduardo Rodríguez Piñeres, commented that 'the disamortized lands were sold in auctions, and paid for with public debts. This paper had such a high discount rate, that in reality the lands were sold for one-tenth, or even one-twentieth of the value.'[2] Miguel Samper agreed: the government bonds issued in 1861 kept decreasing in value and were eventually sold at about 10 per cent of their original value. 'In spite of the hopes held for the disamortization, the transactions carried out were akin to those involving the devil and his dealings with human beings, who, seduced into accepting gold, see their profits turn to dust.'[3]

Thus the nature of Church 'bienes', the difficulties encountered in trying to dispose of them, the paper bonds with which transactions were made, and the fact that the disamortization was undertaken more as a tactical measure in a political dispute than as a fiscal measure all added up to mitigate any favorable results, either to the economy or to political stability. That the men of the Liberal generation of 1850 were slow and hesitant politicians and not bold revolutionaries is nowhere more clear than in the fact that they did not take direct measures against the latifundio, but indirect ones. As Nieto Arteta puts it, 'the liberal theoreticians limited themselves to the suppression of the "confessional latifundio" – that is, the Church lands – but retreated before the lay latifundio'.[4]

Government lands (baldíos)

The main unit of colonization in Colombia was and is the family. In 1843 the Executive authorized the concession of 100 fanegadas of *baldíos* (government lands) to each family which would reside in territories designated by the Government. A law of 17 June 1844, conceded baldíos to families that would settle in Casanare. The territory of Caquetá was

---

[1] Quoted in Juan Pablo Restrepo, *La iglesia y el estado*, pp. 415–16.
[2] Quoted in Academia Colombiana de Historia, *Historia extensa*, XV, I, p. 45.
[3] Quoted in *Historia extensa*, XV, I, p. 44. The same ideas appear in *Memoria del Tesoro, 1874* (Bogotá 1874), pp. 50–1, along with data on the meager revenues from the disamortization. Less than 5 per cent of *censos* redeemed by purchase from the state were paid for with cash; the rest was with depreciated bonds.
[4] Nieto Arteta, *Economía y cultura*, p. 167.

created in 1845, and soon after a law passed on 12 May authorized the Supreme Executive to adjudicate up to 150 fanegadas of baldíos to each family living there after that date. Although previous laws more or less implicitly contained clauses calling for the reversion of lands that were not worked, the definitive expression of this provision was not written until 7 May 1845 which, in effect, recognized that cultivation of lands was impractical where adequate access to transportation was not available. This law provided for the concession of up to 60 fanegadas of baldíos on the borders of national roads.[1] Although the laws seemed to favor smallholders and the family farm, most public lands went to the landowning elites.

Independence brought land to many of the revolutionary leaders and kept land in the hands of the already established Colombians. 'The Caycedo family, the Marquez, the Lozanos, and other eminent families continued being owners of vast haciendas inherited from their Spanish ancestors.'[2] Santander himself acquired a hacienda near Zipaquirá and a house in Bogotá, right after winning the battle of Boyacá. He eventually became a bonafide *latifundista* as he was awarded the vast Territorio Vásquez. The main problem of land tenure in Colombia – excessive concentration – was not one which was primarily handed down by the colonial government but arose in the redistribution of political power and income in the decades after independence. When Antioqueños turned to new frontiers for agriculture in the 1840s they found that:

The territory was appropriated.

And not by the conquistadores or their descendants, protected by titles given under the precepts of Roman law.

Not by the Indians, our grandfathers, whom fortune maintained dispersed in remote jungles, waiting, trembling for the order to continue walking.

Not by the heroes in the labor conflicts . . .

To reward service in the War of Independence, and the following conflicts until the year 1843, the government issued a considerable number of documents which gave territorial concessions, in what numbers it was never easy to determine.

These documents, given over to commerce and valued at extremely low prices, gave rise to immense land grants of uncultivated territories which remained sequestered from labor.[3]

Since there was no enforced provision for effective occupance of lands in Colombia until late in the nineteenth century it was possible for indi-

---

[1] Mardonio Salazar, *Proceso histórico de la propiedad en Colombia, 1810–1930* (Editorial A.B.C., Bogotá 1948), p. 297.

[2] Fals Borda, 'Los orígenes del problema de la tierra en Chocontá', p. 48.

[3] Alvaro Restrepo Euse, *Historia de Antioquia* (Medellín 1903), pp. 170–1.

viduals to buy up huge expanses of government owned lands. Even with the best policies, as when public lands were granted to settlers in Antioquia and with strict stipulations that such grants were conditional on their effective use, there was no effective mechanism of enforcement. The grants read: 'The establishment of new parishes on good lands contributes directly to the public welfare, giving value to the land which it did not have before and at the same time facilitating the support of a growing number of families who have no lands or occupations to secure the necessities of life ... '[1] The results of such a policy depended on local conditions. In Antioquia, where most of the land was virgin and only nominally held by grantees of the Spanish crown, no displacement of native population resulted. In other areas Indian communities were liquidated and labor supplies manipulated by new owners.[2]

Criollo control of open lands in Colombia was designed to head off colonization and to make land acquisition legally difficult. Land policies thus were aimed at discouraging the flight of the labor force from poorly-paid sharecropping and rural labor. The *Código Fiscal* of 1873 made the acquisition of public lands by individuals of modest means even more difficult than acquisition had been under a law of 1868 which required heavy initial land survey expenses. Land prices were set at a minimum of 50 centavos per hectare and were acquired through the purchase of '*bonos territoriales*' rather than auctioned publicly. An attempt to diminish the importance of that Código was made under the leadership of Camacho Roldán with the passage of Law 61 of 24 June 1874. It provided that *ganaderos* who had some form of property on their land whereby they could prove that they were not nomadic would have their lands declared inalienable and could acquire more land. Property rights of those who had worked more than 30 hectares for at least five years were also recognized. Restrepo Echavarría pointed out at the time that Law 61 of 1874 'will remain on paper without causing the slightest practical change'. His judgment was confirmed.[3]

Three categories of landowners gave up possession and use of land in the second half of the nineteenth century: Indian communities, the Church and the national government. It is impossible to estimate the total of all

---

[1] Parsons, *Antioqueño Colonization*, p. 83.

[2] See Robert C. Murphy, 'Racial Succession in the Colombian Chocó', *Geographical Review* (1939) pp. 461–71.

[3] Emiliano Restrepo Echavarría, *Una excursión al Territorio de San Martín en diciembre de 1869* (Bogotá 1955), p. 214. See Guillermo Fonnegra Sierra, *Los fundamentos de la ley sobre regimén de tierras* (Medellín 1930), and Carlos Mario Londoño, *Economía agraria colombiana*, pp. 16–17.

The liberal period

lands which went out of the hands of these owners and into the hands of others except to say that by any measure it was substantial. Highland areas saw the gradual disappearance of the resguardo through repartimiento, the acquisition of Church lands by Liberals in power and the slow expansion of cultivated areas. Lowland areas saw the gradual occupation of government lands as stockraising spread into those zones.

Nearly everywhere the turnover in land ownership favored the concentration in fewer and fewer hands. Never was the principle of land to the tiller, presumably at the heart of the Liberal program, so little honored in reality.

REAL WAGES AND STOCKRAISING

In contrast to a static view of traditional society, nineteenth-century Colombia exhibited a succession of tenure changes of unparalleled magnitude and importance. Not only was there rapid turnover in land ownership, but the social composition of landowners changed as well. The passage of land out of communal tenure to large haciendas; from mortmain to rural stockraising and from public lands to fee simple tenure: all these changes had far-reaching social implications.

Table 18 *Purchasing power in alternative wage-goods of one year's labor in agriculture, 1727–1962* (kilos).

	1727	1768	1791	1848	1892	1962
Corn	3,833	2,516	2,156	3,125	1,168	1,929
Meat	1,917	1,006	1,006	833	416	304
Flour	1,333	1,312	1,565	694	463	868
Potatoes	5,110	4,472	5,030	3,125	1,786	2,713

Source: Luis Ospina Vásquez, *Industria y protección*, p. 429. Figures for 1962 based on DANE, *Anuario general de estadística, 1962* (Bogotá 1964), pp. 700–16. The 1962 figures are not necessarily comparable with those for earlier years.

Among the most immediate of these changes was the apparent secular decline in the real wages of rural workers. As the data in Table 18 indicate, the purchasing power of a year's labor declined dramatically in the second-half of the nineteenth century. These data are based on a sample of only six highland haciendas and these may not be representative. It is almost certain that wages in lowland areas did not move so adversely. However, even if several observers may argue about the specific magnitude of the decline, the downward direction seems confirmed. As an experiment I made computations similar to those of Ospina Vásquez for the year 1962. They indicate a level of real wages (in terms of the same wage-goods) higher than that of 1892 but lower than 1848. The long-term slack demand for labor and the painfully slow growth of rural productivity together explain the slow growth of real wages since the end of the nineteenth century. Of more interest is the secular decline in the previous half a century.

A less apparent and immeasurable implication of the redistribution of landownership was the concentration of rental income into the hands of a small group. Such rents consisted not only of the unearned increment accruing to the land but also any rental income which may have previously accrued to the unusual natural abilities of the general working population. The apparent decline in real wages may be taken to indicate that up to 1850 there was accruing to the rural laborer a substantial increment above the need for subsistence. (Otherwise, real wages could not have fallen so much during a period of continuing rural population growth.) If an increment was obtained by the laboring group, then a roughly equivalent differential must have been received by independent smallholders and Indian communal farmers. (One need not assume perfect mobility of workers out of smallholding and into a rural proletariat to hold that marginally affected workers would shift back and forth to tend to equalize returns in the two closely related occupations.) Once ownership was concentrated, the landowner could capture not only the rental income of land but also any increment above subsistence which accrued to labor. This last was achieved partly by the exercise of traditional ties to the land but most importantly by action taken to appropriate all available land and keep it out of the reach of rural laborers.[1] Since communal Indians probably did not foresee the implications of their losing a claim to rents of scarcity associated with their own labor, they accepted with only limited opposition the breaking up and sale of communal lands.

One serious problem in the agrarian history of this period cannot be

---

[1] In a country where land is freely available only minimal Ricardian differential rents will accrue to the ownership of land. Insofar as the Colombian situation in the nineteenth century approximated the Ricardian picture, rents were small. Yet it proved politically possible to capture other rental income normally accruing to labor (in this Ricardian situation the 'scarce' factor) simply by declaring unoccupied land to be unavailable. Here lies the importance, first of consolidating political power in the hands of an elite, and second eliminating the notion of property as a 'social function' or limited right based on effective use.

overlooked here, since analysis of that problem is an essential step to explaining a series of related facts. Ospina Vásquez has written about the impressive expansion of stockraising (see above page 119) and contemporary observers also remarked on the replacement of subsistence smallholders by grazing cattle. One is led to look for changing conditions of

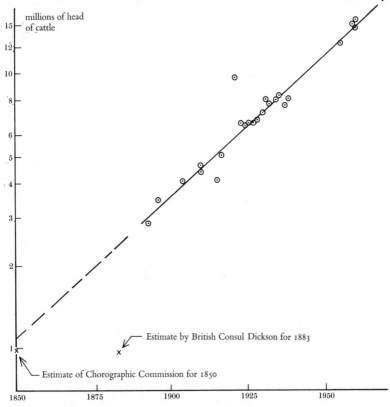

Figure 6 Estimated cattle population of Colombia, 1850–1963. *Source:* see text.

demand which would stimulate this changing land use. There was fairly substantial growth of the physical volume of hides exported, but that growth was not sufficient to explain any great expansion of grazing lands. The demand in cities also was not growing fast enough to explain the presumed rapid change in land use. Data from disparate sources suggest, moreover, that aggregate growth in stockraising may have been illusory (see Figure 6).

Liberalism and agrarian change, 1845-90

There had been no formal and successful census of agriculture in Colombia before the one conducted in 1960; thus any enumeration of the population of cattle (and other farm animals) before that date is based to a greater or lesser extent on guesswork. The estimates presented in Figure 6 do, with some notable exceptions, fit fairly well a linear function (in logarithms) which indicates a constant annual rate of increase over more than a century of about 2·5 per cent.[1] The principal problem presented by these data is the deviation observed for 1883. According to the British consul who prepared the data the enumerations he gives are based on the latest official returns in 1883; he goes on to add, however, that 'the number are certainly underestimated in some cases, owing to deficiencies in the returns from certain districts'.[2] The basic material underlying the British estimate was published in 1881.[3] A letter asking for the cattle population of each municipio was sent out 30 October 1880; about a quarter of the municipios of Antioquia replied; only 10 per cent of those on the north coast and other areas. The materials available could be used to estimate the total cattle population based on the available 'sample', but that calculation was not made either officially or by the British Consul who offered the limited data as totals.

Both the 1850 and 1883 data are probably too low, i.e. below the actual cattle population for those years. If the expansion of stockraising had been 'normal' between 1850 and 1883, the population of cattle would have been about two and one-quarter million rather than the 950,000 indicated by Dickson and the official returns.

Nonetheless, the Dickson estimate – even if it is too low – conforms to the hypothesis of declining agricultural output over the years 1845-85. Even if the actual 1883 cattle population were twice that indicated by the Dickson figures, it would still lie well below the secular trend. In contrast to qualitative assessments, the quantitative data point to an actual decline or stagnation in the population of livestock for the country as a whole. This aggregate picture conceals the absolute growth of some

[1] The 21 data points between 1893 and 1963 were used for fitting the function which was then extrapolated backward to 1850. The equation of relationship is

$$\log C = 1·0371 + 0·0103t$$

and the coefficient of correlation is 0·93, significant at the 0·1 level. Some 86 per cent of the cattle population's growth is explained simply by the passage of time. This analysis would indicate that the estimate for 1850 is not much below the backward extrapolation of the secular trend, but that the estimate for 1883 is far below that trend.

[2] Great Britain, Diplomatic and Consular Reports, No. 446; W. J. Dickson, *Report on the Agriculture of Colombia*, pp. 5–6.

[3] *Memoria de Fomento, 1880* (Bogotá 1881), Part III, Informe del Comisario Nacional de Agricultura, pp. 147-270.

The liberal period

regions (Antioquia and most probably the north coast) and precipitate decline of others (Boyacá, Cundinamarca and Santander). In those populated highlands agrarian change was not simply a matter of replacing population by stock; there must actually have been a declining intensity of land use and some tendency for land to fall into disuse. The depression of rural wage rates was a result of a decline in aggregate labor demand in the region. The apparent decline in capital invested in agriculture (the best analogue of which is the cattle population) is then one more element in the picture of secular depression in the eastern highlands.

This reasoning may appear to contradict the data presented in Table 17. Data included there indicate an expansion of cropland for domestic consumption in the nineteenth century at about 1·2 per cent per annum. However, underlying the construction of those data is the assumption that cropland per capita remained constant – an assumption which is reasonable if per capita product is constant or growing but certainly questionable if per capita product is on the decline. There remains of course the unanswered question as to whether the decline in the eastern highlands could successfully have been compensated by growth in the west and north coast. In those areas the livestock population grew and presumably carried upward with it other indices pointing toward moderate improvement. Those regions had easiest access to foreign markets for hides; the limitation of the local market which must have plagued the eastern highlands at that time proved to be no barrier.

The changing regional distribution of population complemented the changing location of stockraising. The north coast and Antioquia together increased their share of the total Colombian population from 22·3 per cent in 1851 to 25·7 per cent in 1870 and 36·4 per cent in 1912. Still, the population of cattlemen identified in the 1870 census placed only a quarter in the areas of Antioquia and the departments of the north coast with over 57 per cent in the three eastern departments of Boyacá, Cundinamarca and Santander.[1] One can make only rough guesses about the geographical distribution of the cattle population, but it would appear that about one-fifth were on the north coast and Antioquia in 1850 and over 35 per cent by 1883.[2] In contrast, the share of the above-named eastern departments declined from nearly half to slightly more than a

[1] *Anuario estadístico, 1875.*

[2] See La Comisión Corográfica. *Jeografía física i política de las provincias de la Nueva Granada* (Bogotá 1856, 1957); Felipe Pérez, *Jeografía de las provincias del norte de la Nueva Granada* (Bogotá 1862), vol. 1; R. S. Pereira, *Les Etats-Unis de Colombia, Précis d'Histoire et la Géographie Physique, Politique et Commerciale* (Paris 1883); W. J. Dickson, *Report on Agriculture in Colombia*, p. 5.

quarter of the cattle population over the same period. In the redistribution of the herds, highland herdsmen would have found themselves either unemployed or facing a move into the west – particularly the north coast lowlands.

Contemporary observers correctly emphasized two phenomena in the decades between 1850 and 1890: first, that the economic well-being of the Indian population was in decline and second, that stockraising was growing in importance – in the west. They erred, however, in seeing an uncomplicated direct relationship between the two. There was no simple process of the substitution of stockraising for subsistence farming since to a considerable extent Indian labor and capital in the hands of hacendados were complementary rather than competing resources. General depression, where it occurred, carried downward with it Indian and hacendado alike. No doubt the already poor Indians got the worst of the secular depression in the eastern highlands, but the landowners of the areas apparently also suffered, if the decline in the population of cattle and other stock is an accurate indicator.

The growth of cattle and other stockraising was a phenomenon of the Antioqueño area and the plains and lower valleys, the Sinú region for example. Already in the decades before coffee was to become the principal export crop of the Antioqueño region, the locus of development and growth was squarely there. But in contrast to the twentieth century, growth there was not rapid enough to overcome the bleak picture of depression in the East.

CONCLUSIONS

The Radical Liberals were primarily interested in making over Colombian society in the image of the progressive European states which led the world in industrialization, democratic institutions and social equality. By increasing individual freedom they thought they would necessarily produce the desired social and economic results. Nowhere did this policy fail so miserably as in the changing picture of agrarian well-being.

It is undoubtedly true that benefits accrued to Colombian agriculturalists as a result of free-trade policies. It was, however, only a small portion of the rural population which benefited. Increases in land values associated with tobacco and other export crops prior to coffee were concentrated in the lowlands which were at the same time coming under the increasing domination of speculators and latifundistas. Only rarely were smallholders the beneficiaries of free trade.

Liberal policies do not seem to have accelerated the conversion of land use from subsistence or near-subsistence cropping to production for market. Indians were only slowly turned into peasants, and peasants only slowly made more responsive to urban markets and urban demand. Since the Radical Liberals were concerned to foster the dissolution of traditional, anti-modern institutions such as the resguardo, their concern was clearly with speeding up the rate at which rural peoples could be integrated into a national community. Expansion of international trade was in their view the key to internal integration. They failed to see that their objectives could have been better served by the selective protection of urban artisan activities, the preservation of well-located land for small farmers and the gradual integration of subsistence Indians into this rural–urban symbiosis. A policy of agricultural exportation could then have been a source of an important increment to the rate of economic growth rather than the sole leading sector within the economy. And because that leading sector had only limited impact on the growth potential of the domestic economy through demand for labor and home products, the spread effects of growth in exports were probably less than the growth that would have been generated by an urbanization–industrialization policy. As it was the rate of growth of population of the nineteen major cities in the years 1851–1905 (2–2.5 per cent per annum) was not much greater than the population of the country as a whole (1.2–1.5 per cent per annum), indicating a very slow migration from rural to urban areas.

During the last quarter of the nineteenth century when railroad building began, the improvements in the transport system exacerbated the regionalism of the country by improving each region's tie to the external market while roads for internal travel went into decay.[1] Since it was the potential internal market rather than the external market in which many smallholders and potential peasants could aspire to compete, the advent of free trade was at best irrelevant to them and at worst undermined their chances to move out of subsistence and into market production.

Not unexpectedly, it was only the larger landholders who could participate effectively in production for the foreign market. The scale requirements for export production effectively closed out smallholders. Although smallholder tobacco growing had been practiced in Santander

---

[1] A geographical study of internal trade at the end of the eighteenth century indicated brisk exchange between Eastern textile towns, Western mining areas and grazing and croplands in between. (Robert C. West, *Colonial Placer Mining in Colombia* (Baton Rouge 1952), pp. 120–1). Much of this trade seems to have disappeared toward the end of the nineteenth century. (Ospina Vásquez, *Industria y protección, passim*. The decline in internal trade is one of this author's principal concerns in evaluating the effects of free trade.)

Liberalism and agrarian change, 1845–90

and some other regions since early in the eighteenth century, these areas failed to participate in the tobacco export market which was controlled first by a state monopoly, then by a handful of commercial agents and land speculators. The technical conditions of production and marketing precluded development of a yeoman class so long as tropical agriculture aimed at a foreign market was the leading sector. Only local agricultural development directed at growing urban markets could have created the conditions for such a class. Urbanization was, however, being undercut by the expansion of imports which replaced local manufacturing activity. In this period the social and economic aims of the Liberals were in conflict: the social aim of creating a rural–urban middle class participating in national politics could not be achieved if the economic aim of expanded exports was achieved. Expanded exports implied expanded imports and a declining propensity for urbanization, industrialization and a market-oriented agriculture. By the end of the 1880s it was clear that no middle class had been formed. But even more disheartening, it was clear that the supposed gains were illusory. Foreign demand for tropical exports was too erratic to permit regular economic growth, as witness the series of disasters in tobacco, quinine bark and cotton.

The Radical Liberals knew that their objectives of creating democratic institutions, economic progress and social equality required first and foremost the growth of a substantial class of rural smallholders. Whether given the conditions of Colombia in 1850 such a goal could have been reached by 1885 is an essential question. I am inclined to believe it could. Smallholders had gotten a start in the eighteenth century only to be quashed by new Bourbon attitudes and the policies of the criollo elites in the first decades after Independence (see Chapter 3); and coffee was in the twentieth century to be in many areas of the country a smallholder operation with functional characteristics not unlike those which the Liberals sought. Thus under roughly similar conditions a rural middle class was gaining ground against the joint problems of minifundia and latifundia in the eighteenth and twentieth centuries; there is little reason to believe that it was impossible in the nineteenth. The difficulty seems to lie in the policy errors committed and the social and economic decisions taken.

Unfortunately, all policy measures taken between 1845 and 1885 were essentially negative. That is, they eliminated one restraint or another which presumably was holding back individuals from reaching their full potential. Virtually no positive actions were taken to insure that the course of social change would follow the prescribed path. Nor was there any heed to the fact that removal of particular restraints might actually (in a 'second-best world'[1]) lead to a movement away from rather than towards the desired state. The abolition of the resguardo as a legal entity in 1850 certainly increased the freedom of all individual Indians and should in a perfect world (i.e. one without other prior restraints) have made them all better off. In fact, however, the rapid sale of Indian lands brought little but harm to most Indians. For as the restraints on Indian sale were cast away so too were the restraints on criollo purchase. And once the Indians were landless (though they individually could not have predicted it), they had to offer themselves at lower and lower wages to the new owners of the land. In a less than perfect world a simple increase in freedom does not necessarily yield an increasing well-being.

A cynic might argue that economic progress and social equality were never the real aims of the Radical Liberals: self-aggrandizement alone might be thought to explain much of their agrarian policy. Yet the sadness with which the leading Liberal intellectuals viewed their work (I refer to the later writings of Camacho Roldán and the Sampers) tends to confirm the view that they meant well but knew not what they wrought. Certainly there were Liberals who gained much in wealth and power from the policies of those years, and much of the civil disorder of that period seems more to be a struggle over spoils than over high principles. But all that aside one need not be a cynic to explain Liberal policy and Liberal behaviour.

There was in the late nineteenth century no positive program for the kind of agrarian reform in which the Liberals were engaged. There was no thought of implanting colonists and smallholders on the land with requisite credit, implements and technical advice. In eliminating communal lands and lands in mortmain, in distributing freely lands still in the public domain they acted on the best advice of men of liberal persuasion in the developed North Atlantic area. Their failure was in trying to apply advice appropriate to a homogenous, Indian-free country to a country marked by segmented societies. In some respects the difference between the two is little more than that between self-interest and greed. By whichever name we call the motivating force for man's economic activities do we define our own attitude about the implications of encouraging free choice. Attitudes aside, however, it is clear that the new

---

[1] The theory of the 'second-best' refers to a body of analysis which has grown up in international economics and the economics of welfare to refer to the implications of change attendant on a policy decision in a less than perfect world. The example in the text may give some flavor of the kind of problem with which this theory deals.

opportunities opened to the criollo elite as a result of the Liberal policies led them to undermine any chance of reaching the stated goals of economic progress and social equality. Only a very different set of policies could have led to attainment of that goal.

In a recent essay Claudio Veliz suggests that the whole period of liberalism should be viewed as an aberration (though admittedly a long enduring one) from the true character of Spanish American policies and ideology.

> The Latin American institutional tradition includes neither nonconformity nor those fundamental political – as distinct from social – features of feudalism which determined the relations between central and peripheral power; its history has been dominated by paternalistic centralism with the qualified exception of the hundred years after 1830. ... Once the prosperity of the nineteenth century came to an end, and with it the artificially-sustained liberalism and radicalism of its dominant urban groups, Latin America started slowly to find its way back into its own cultural main stream.[1]

This kind of view – essentially correct – points to the Liberal period in Colombia as an age of aberrant, legislated *laissez-faire* based on imitative social theory and policymaking. As we have shown in this chapter agrarian problems of that age were a result of the conscious policies of that era and not of inexorable forces beyond human control.

APPENDIX

ESTIMATING LAND USE: A METHODOLOGICAL NOTE

A crucial problem in economic development is that of the gradual transfer of resources out of traditional activities and into the growing modern sector. This transfer process is usually discussed in terms of the transfer of labor out of agriculture and into manufacturing.[2] An equally interesting process, and one which has temporal precedence in the scenario of development, is that of the transfer of physical resources from use in the 'subsistence', nonmonetary sector of the economy to production

---

[1] Claudio Veliz (ed.), *The Politics of Conformity in Latin America* (New York 1967), pp. 13, 14.
[2] See, for example, W. Arthur Lewis, 'Economic Development with Unlimited Supplies of Labor', *The Manchester School* (1954), and the elaborations of the Lewis model in Fei and Ranis, *Development of the Labor Surplus Economy* (Homewood, Ill. 1964).

for market. This process usually includes the growth of urban markets and their demand for foodstuffs (and hence the derived demand for land itself) plus the growth of agricultural export markets which also create a derived demand for land and help pull it out of use for subsistence agriculture and into a national and world market.

This brief note discusses one technique of estimating the use of cropland in Colombia over the years 1837–1964. We have distinguished land use by three types: (1) export products; (2) urban consumption and (3) subsistence or rural consumption. With these land use estimates we are able to determine the timing and extent of the transfer of resources out of traditional activities and into modern uses.

Before the 1950s, no more than educated guesses were made regarding the amount of cultivated land in Colombia. A census of coffee production (*censo cafetero*) was carried out in 1932 by the Federación Nacional de Cafeteros,[1] and the Ministry of Agriculture has from time to time made calculations based on aggregate production and yield estimates.[2] Several agricultural samples were made during the 1950s, but since the universe was unknown sampling techniques left the results subject to wide margins of error. In 1960, however, a full census was taken. The first results published[3] only provided data on land tenancy rather than crops and yields. The land tenure problem has been analyzed exhaustively.[4] But changing land use has yet to be analyzed statistically.

In attempting to trace the broad statistical outlines of agriculture in the last century and a half we must have recourse to indirect calculations. The two longest series of statistics at our disposal are for population and foreign trade. The volume of agricultural products exported can be related to surface under cultivation given estimates of yields per unit of land and losses in transit, spoilage, and processing. Moreover, if there is a fairly consistent relationship between population size, its urban–rural distribution, and agricultural exploitation, census data will give us a

---

[1] FNC, 'Censo cafetero levantado en 1932', *Boletín de estadística* (Bogotá 1933), Boletín Extraordinario no. 5.

[2] DANE, *Anuario general de estadística*, for 1932 and 1938 (title and publishing agency varies); Colombia: Ministerio de Agricultura y Ganadería, 'Economía agropecuaria de Colombia', División de Economía Rural (Bogotá 1949–53); Guillermo Palacio del Valle, *Desarrollo agrícola de Colombia, 1940–1952*, Ministerio de Agricultura (Bogotá 1953); Cathryn H. Wylie, 'The Agriculture of Colombia', *Foreign Agriculture Bulletin # 1*, U.S. Department of Agriculture (Washington, D.C. 1942).

[3] Departamento Administrativo Nacional de Estadística, *Censo agropecuario de 1960* (Bogotá 1964).

[4] See T. Lynn Smith, *Colombia* (Gainesville 1967), and Comité Interamericano de Desenvolvimiento Agrcrla. *Tenencia de la tierra y desarrollo socioeconómico del secttor agrícola* (Washington D.C. 1966) among others.

rough approximation of how much land was cultivated in the past. Appropriate adjustment for international trade in foodstuffs must of course be made.

Agricultural production for the domestic market in Colombia did not suffer the extreme fluctuations which beset the export sector. The high proportion of subsistence farmers in the total rural population has always lent a measure of stability to demand which was lacking in the market for export agriculture. The *campesino* family is at once producer and consumer of most farm output. These circumstances lead one to expect a fairly constant numerical relationship between population and cropland.

The data and estimates on per capita availabilities of cropland (excluding pasture and land devoted to export production) tend to confirm the foregoing propositions. The earliest reasonable estimates on aggregate cropland were made during 1937–38 and published in the *Anuarios* of those years. Rough calculations render per capita availabilities of cropland of 0·155 hectares.[1] As a consistency check on these early estimates, we calculated the per capita derived demand for land, using a cost of living sample of 1936.[2] Dividing annual per capita consumption of major food items by estimated yields, we derived a figure of 0·16 hectares, with a 95 per cent confidence interval between 0·15 and 0·17.[3] Since this latter estimate was based on urban consumption, it appears that urban and rural demands for land are not significantly different.

Computing derived demand and availabilities data from later years gives similar results. Using a method similar to the one described above for urban derived demand for land, applied to a consumer survey conducted in 1953, we were able to arrive at a figure of 0·16 hectares per

---

[1] Wylie, 'The Agriculture of Colombia', p. 146. Acreage in major crops, minus coffee and bananas, was 3,325,000, or 1·35 million hectares. Population in 1938 was 8·7 million.

[2] Paul Hermberg, 'El costo de la vida de la clase obrera en Bogotá', *Anales de economía y estadística*, Contraloría General de la República de Colombia, I: 1 (1938). The sample included 225 blue-collar families.

[3] Paul Hermberg, 'El costo de la vida', p. 29 and *passim*. Frijoles, habas, garbanzos and lentajes all grouped as 'frijoles'. Bread, cuchuco and pastas halved to obtain wheat equivalents. Tobacco, cotton and plátano were our own estimates based on per capita availabilities. Yield estimates were from E C L A *Study*, p. 170. We took the lowest estimates and arbitrarily reduced them about 20 per cent to take into account losses from spoilage and processing, and to encompass less important crops not enumerated. For imports divided by total availabilities, see E C L A *Study*. Essentially the calculation was the same as in the 1936 case, except that we were able to use an average weighted urban diet utilizing data from all seven cities. We used current yield estimates from E C L A *Study*, Table 127, and a 'farm-to-table' ratio derived from net foodstuffs availabilities calculation (Table 104), to give farm equivalents of quantities consumed in cities.

capita.[1] National per capita availabilities apparently did not change significantly either: ECLA found that, 'In 1953 *per capita* availabilities [based on an agricultural sample] of cultivated land stood ... at only 0·17 hectares when coffee was excluded from the aggregate.'[2] As mentioned above the preliminary results of the agricultural census of 1960 reported only detailed data on tenancy, but by using our figures for export acreage (see text below) we calculated per capita availabilities of cropland for domestic consumption at 0·188 hectares.[3] Several consumer surveys were conducted in the early 1960s but those to which we have access are not appropriate for deriving demand for cropland due to biases in the samples.[4]

There is no data upon which to determine if there occurred movements in per capita availabilities of cropland for internal consumption prior to 1936, but secondary sources seem to negate this possibility. Mechanization and commercial agriculture are essentially post-World War II phenomena. Although ECLA notes new investment in agriculture during the period 1925–9, this was primarily in the export sector.[5] The major thrust of the public investment program of the 1920s was in transportation and was meant to service the export sector, not agriculture for domestic markets. This latter sector, which Berry calls non-commercialized, is still 'a very large segment of the agricultural population [and it] retains its traditional methods, along with its small plots of land and low amount of capital ... '[6] These traditional functions of agriculture

[1] Colombia, DANE, 'Memoria de las Encuestas,' *Economía y Estadística*, No. 85 (Bogotá 1958), and ECLA *Study*. The calculation was the same as in the 1936 case except for use of an average weighted urban diet utilizing data from sample surveys for seven cities. Current yield estimates from ECLA *Study*, Table 127, and a farm-to-table ratio derived from net foodstuffs availabilities (Table 104) were used to give farm equivalents of quantities consumed in cities.

[2] ECLA *Study*, p. 161.

[3] Colombia: DANE *Directorio Nacional de Explotaciones Agropecuarias (censo agropecuario), 1960, Resumen Nacional* (Bogotá 1962). Population extrapolated between the 1951 and 1964 censuses was 15,333,006.

[4] See *Nutritional Survey* May–August 1960, a report by the Interdepartmental Committee on Nutrition for National Defense, December 1961 and *Colombian Import Demand for Selected Agricultural Commodities 1965 and 1975*, Centro de Estudios sobre Desarrollo Económico, Universidad de los Andes (Bogotá 1964), pp. 85–8.

[5] ECLA *Study*, p. 152. Actually, investment in agriculture during the period 1925–36 increased only one half of one per cent more than the increase in investment throughout the economy. (ECLA *Study*, 'Statistical Appendix,' Table 6.)

[6] R. Albert Berry, 'An Introduction to the Key Issues in Colombian Agriculture' (mimeo) p. 4. A similar observation may be found in Henao and Arrubla, *History of Colombia*, p. 535: 'Considerable improvements were made also in the raising of livestock and the cultivation of coffee, but most other phases of agriculture continued to be followed with the same old indifference to scientific methods.' Refers to the first quarter of this century.

are inherited from the nineteenth century, and it is doubtful that prior to 1936 any radical changes in diet or farm production occurred which would have significantly altered the amount of land required to give sustenance to a given number of people.

For purposes of analysis, we have used two population series. One is population living in nineteen major cities (Table 15), which we have termed urban. The other is rural population, which here is total population minus urban population as defined above. For more recent times we can attribute a greater degree of mechanization and commercialization to that sector supplying urban markets, but to what extent this is true for nineteenth-century agriculture is unknown. We might speculate that even then those areas close to cities would be the most likely to receive new technologies from Europe and the United States, and to respond to the possibilities of supplying urban markets.

Table 17 presents our estimates of cropland devoted to three different markets, exterior, interior urban, and interior rural, at selected points in time throughout the past century and a half. Cropland for rural and urban markets has been estimated by multiplying the corresponding population data by 0·16 hectares. The series on area cultivated for export was obtained by simply dividing export tonnage by yield per unit figures.

CHAPTER 7

THE ANATOMY OF ECONOMIC DECLINE IN NINETEENTH-CENTURY COLOMBIA

The preceding three chapters have dealt with three facets of the economic difficulties in which Colombia found itself in the second half of the nineteenth century: those three facets might be distinguished by typological characteristics – political, economic and social – or by their sectoral manifestations – domestic policymaking, the role of the external sector and secular trends in agriculture. It is the purpose of this chapter to draw together the details from preceding chapters and attempt a more complete anatomy of economic decline in the second half of the nineteenth century. More than in previous chapters I will attempt here a quantitative assessment of the set of liberal policies informed by the ideology of *laissez-faire*.

This chapter relates trade, land and institutional policies to some disturbing facts: (1) income apparently declined for significant groups of the Colombian population in the second half of the nineteenth century; (2) land tenure and land use problems arose which are only now in process of solution; (3) artisan handicraft production declined in the second half of the century; and (4) civil conflict and loss of life were exacerbated by ideological conflict between Liberals and Conservatives.

The quantitative investigation presented in this chapter shows that the institution of 'liberal' land and trade policies caused a reversal in the slow growth of Colombia's economy. Since it is just the opposite expectation we have from traditional economic theory, this case deserves careful analysis so that we may determine why the expectation of improvement with *laissez-faire* failed to materialize.

The description of economic decline requires at least the rudiments of a causal analysis. In the first section, I deal with two general problems in economic theory as they affect the Colombian situation – the problem of evaluating the gains (or losses) from the opening up of trade, and the more general problems inherent in the theory of 'second-best', that branch of welfare economics used to analyze policy changes in nonoptimal situations. These problems deserve analysis because Colombia's participation in international trade as a result of the Liberal reforms did not lead to impressive welfare gains; one must analyze how the welfare gains came to be more than offset by the losses. The two bodies of theory mentioned provide the most useful clues to historical analysis.

In the second section of this chapter I will sum up the case for the view that substantial and general economic decline did occur in Colombia over half a century. This decline can be attributed only in part to adverse and fortuitous circumstances; it must be explained by a congeries of human error in the making of government decisions.

THEORY AND THE DECLINE

Trade and welfare

A nation will not necessarily be better off to trade than not to trade. Some investigations indicate that after one or two centuries of international exchange, some nations on the periphery of the world economy were relatively worse off in 1960 than they were in 1860. 'The inequality of the distribution of the world income increased considerably during the last century. . . . The 25 per cent of the world population that lived in the lowest income areas of the world in 1860 earned 12·5 per cent of the world income, against 3·2 per cent in 1960.'[1] The aggregate international comparisons of Zimmerman indicate that the poorest countries have become better off in absolute terms but not in relative terms, i.e. when compared to the industrial countries. This finding would seem to indicate that the benefits of trade have been unequally shared between the advanced and the backward countries. The explanation for the inability to gain from trade has increasingly emphasized the lack of reallocative ability, i.e. the failure to shift resources with the vicissitudes of changing price relationships and international demand.[2] Even the export sectors themselves have often not been a source of dynamism in underdeveloped countries: 'The failure of the mines and plantations to become the "leading sector" in the underdeveloped countries was due, not to their producing primary exports as such, but to their cheap labour policy which has perpetuated the pattern of low wages and low productivity.'[3] Handicrafts, which had to compete with industrial imports from the

[1] L. J. Zimmerman, *Poor Lands, Rich Lands: The Widening Gap* (New York 1965), p. 38.
[2] The literature of this subject is large and growing; the principal articles are included in Caves and Johnson (eds.), *Readings in International Economics* (Homewood, Ill. 1968). The analysis used here was in part suggested by S. Burenstam Linder, *An Essay on Trade and Transformation* (Stockholm 1961). See also C. P. Kindleberger, *Foreign Trade and the National Economy* (New Haven 1962), pp. 99–115.
[3] Hla Myint, *The Economics of the Developing Countries* (New York 1964), p. 64.

North Atlantic area, declined in the underdeveloped world. 'In India the decline of traditional indigenous manufacturing, under the competition of foreign industry and, later, of some domestic large-scale industry, compelled large numbers of artisans and craftsmen to turn to the land. ... Even if India did not become progressively ruralized, this does not deny the fact of economic stagnation or, at best, "static expansion."'[1] This consideration of the general difficulties of adjustment faced by underdeveloped countries since the great expansion in international trade in the nineteenth century leads us to a theoretical investigation of the beginnings of foreign trade and the rigidities in Colombia which may have prevented realization of the possible gains from trading.

The model

A fully articulated model of change resulting from the opening up of trade would have to consider the following:

(1) In the pre-trade situation population and aggregate income are growing at a modest rate; per capita income is low and stable but lies above the level of subsistence.

(2) Within certain limits the rate of population growth is a positive function of the level of income, i.e. as per capita income rises the rate of population growth will increase.

(3) Land is an important factor in the production of exports as well as in the agrarian subsistence sector: more intensive use of land can only be effected at the cost of diminishing returns to labor.

(4) Shifting of productive factors from one major economic use to another is costly and difficult.

(5) Whereas the pre-trade economy produces one composite good, after trade three distinct sectors emerge: the agrarian subsistence sector, the import-competing sector and the export-producing sector. Out of equilibrium sectors can have different factor returns and average income, as implied by (4) above.

In the pre-trade situation it is assumed that the country can be described by a single production function (v_a in Figure 7) which determines along with the population growth function (r) the level of per capita income

---

[1] Gunnar Myrdal, *Asian Drama*, I (New York 1968), 461–2. Myrdal, in his discussion of the decline of crafts, has moved away somewhat from an earlier position that India was progressively ruralized by the incursion of foreign textiles. Occupational data from the censuses of 1881 and 1931 show only that the industrial distribution of the Indian working force stood still, i.e. the share of industrial and artisan workers did not decline.

and a stable equilibrium growth rate of population, the capital stock and aggregate income.[1]

With the opening up of trade the single v_a function splits into three parts. The v_x function of the export sector will be raised since trade increases per capita income in that sector. The agrarian sector being initially unaffected by trade remains as before with per capita income y_a. The v_m function of the import-competing sector will be depressed as factor rewards have to be reduced so that products may be marketable in the face of foreign competition.

When trade begins, average incomes in the new export sector will rise above average income in the rest of the economy to induce the shifting of resources into production for export. Income will fall in the import-competing sector due to foreign competition. If resources could be shifted rapidly and easily out of the import-competing sector into the export-producing sector the opening up of trade would occasion no difficulties and might be an unmixed blessing. Barring this, however, assessment of the gains from trade requires that we balance off the sum of (a) consumption-reallocation gains for all sectors of the economy due to lower prices of imports *plus* (b) production-reallocation gains for those who have shifted into the export-producing sector *minus* (c) production-reallocation losses for those in the import-competing sector. If the losses are greater than the gains from the opening up of trade then the nation has been made worse off from trading.

At this level, however, the argument is purely one of comparative statics; dynamic implications come into play as well. Hagen's argument for protection is presented as a complement to the comparative statics framework.[2] He observes that wages are higher in manufacturing than in agriculture and that the opening of trade, which would drive workers out of manufacture (or prevent the growth of employment in manufacture), would lower average wages and hence income. A more recent empirical

[1] The model appears in this or similar form in a number of works. See R. R. Nelson, 'A Theory of the Low-Level Equilibrium Trap in Underdeveloped Countries', *American Economic Review*, XLVI (December 1956), 894–908; Everett E. Hagen, 'Population and Economic Growth', *AER*, XLIX (June 1959), 310–27; Harvey Leibenstein, *Economic Backwardness and Economic Growth* (New York 1957). An article by R. M. Solow, 'A Contribution to the Theory of Economic Growth', *Quarterly Journal of Economics*, LXX (February 1956), 65–94, emphasized certain characteristics of the v function in analyzing growth paths. The model here presented draws heavily on the analysis of S. B. Linder, *An Essay on Trade and Transformation*. All these models emphasize time rates of change of the important variables.

[2] E. E. Hagen, 'An Economic Justification for Protectionism', *Quarterly Journal of Economics*, LXXII (November 1959), 496–514.

observation is relevant as well to the argument: the level of average real income in cities of various sizes within the country is directly proportional to the size of the city. Policies which reduce the level of urbanization can

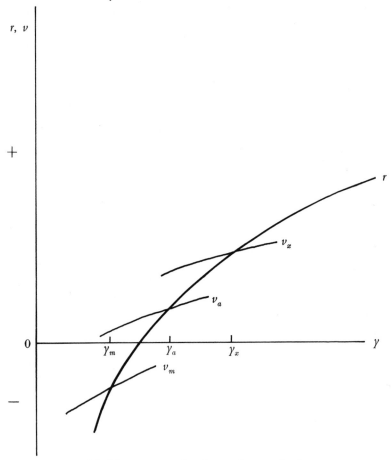

Figure 7   A model of the economy after the opening up of trade.

thus be expected to reduce average real incomes. Whether the losses from these changes, which become 'dynamic' when the element of infant industries is added, will offset the consumption and production gains is moot. However, the effects of actions taken must be judged not only in the immediate results but in the long-term implications for development.

Economic decline in nineteenth-century Colombia

One argument offered in defense of the nineteenth-century opening up of trade in the underdeveloped world is the following: 'The indigenous peoples of the underdeveloped countries took to export production on a voluntary basis and enjoyed a clear gain by being able to satisfy their developing wants for the new imported commodities.'[1] This argument is naïve. Identifiable interest groups made the policies which opened Colombia (and other countries as well) to foreign trade. Those groups made the decisions on the basis of their own self-interest. The degree to which any decisions were 'voluntary' was limited to those groups alone.

Insofar as the income distribution in traditional and new export activities is different, one could expect differences in the distribution of benefits associated with the opening up of trade. If the export activity takes place under technical conditions which give rise to low wages, high rents for land, and monopoly profits, the gains would be more concentrated in the hands of landowners and merchants. Not only the gains would be unequally distributed but inequality in general would be increased in the society. As we will show in a succeeding section, these conditions were roughly approximated in Colombia's tobacco export sector in the second half of the nineteenth century.

The theory of second best

In their article on the general theory of second best Lipsey and Lancaster introduced a powerful theorem as indicated in the following statement of it, proved mathematically later in their paper:

It is well known that the attainment of a Paretian optimum requires the simultaneous fulfillment of all the optimum conditions. The general theorem for the second best optimum states that if there is introduced into a general equilibrium system a constraint which prevents the attainment of one of the Paretian conditions, the other Paretian conditions, although still attainable, are, in general, no longer desirable. In other words, given that one of the Paretian optimum conditions cannot be fulfilled, then an optimum situation can be achieved only by departing from all the other Paretian conditions.[2]

---

[1] The problem of estimating the gains from the opening up of trade is investigated in Hla Myint, 'The "Classical Theory" of International Trade and the Underdeveloped Countries', *The Economic Journal*, LXVII (270, June 1958), reprinted in Caves and Johnson (eds.), *Readings in International Economics*, pp. 318–38. Myint is particularly concerned with a general case not unlike that of Colombia in which land is freely available and there exists surplus productive capacity because of the inefficiency of existing market mechanisms, poor transportation and communications, etc. The quotation is from p. 335.

[2] R. G. Lipsey and Kelvin Lancaster, 'The General Theory of Second Best', *Review of Economic Studies*, XXIV (1) no. 63 (1956–7), 11–31. The quotation is from p. 11.

A less technical description of Paretian conditions would refer to the simultaneous achievement of all the requirements for the model of perfect competition, i.e. the absence of monopolies, coercion, force, or other aspects of control over exchange or other persons. Lipsey and Lancaster prove that if these conditions of perfect competition are not met, there is no reason to believe *a priori* that a movement toward the greater achievement of them (not fully realized) will improve welfare.

In nineteenth-century Colombia it was naïvely believed that the elimination of any particular restraint on individual freedom and initiative was necessarily a good thing in terms of improving welfare. The previously stated theorem shows first that there is no *a priori* expectation of improved welfare from a movement toward more closely fulfilling the optimum conditions (of competition, free exchange in markets, etc.). Such a change *could* improve welfare, but such a result is far from certain. Second, the theorem proved that if initially none of the Paretian conditions are fulfilled, and then one of them is fulfilled, welfare could be diminished. The assertion of 'untrammeled' individual liberty, though it may have satisfied one of the Paretian optimum conditions, could as the second best theorem proves, have also spelled a decline in welfare.

A certain naïveté pervades the discussion of the economic effects of trade, illustrated in the following quotation:

At most, the case for protection rests on a 'second-best' argument; since there are divergences between marginal values and costs elsewhere in the economy, it can be held that a policy of protection is better than no policy whatsoever. But it would be even better to attack the divergences directly through policies designed to promote investment in the underdeveloped sector, increase the knowledge of market conditions, reduce the imperfections in factor markets, and create greater opportunities for technical substitutability of factors.[1]

If a country could attack the divergences mentioned, it would not at the same time have all the characteristics of an underdeveloped country. But even the recognition of these features still leaves veiled the political conditions which make possible a process of decision-making in no way adapted to the solution of social problems. The political system is rather geared to the purposes of a small elite.

The 'new' welfare economics developed in the late 1930s offered the compensation principle as a means of moving the study of economic welfare farther along in the evaluation of economic policies. Previously

[1] Gerald M. Meier, 'International Trade and International Inequality', *Oxford Economic Papers*, x: 3 (October 1958), 277–85; reprinted in Richard Weckstein (ed.), *Expansion of World Trade and the Growth of National Economies* (New York 1968). The quotation is from pp. 90–1.

it had been held that a policy change which can make at least one individual better off without making other individuals worse off could be judged to be one which improves community or total welfare. For practical purposes, however, one would like to move beyond the same restraints of this test: few policies can be guaranteed to make no one at all worse off, no matter how great the improvements in welfare for many individuals. The compensation principle holds that welfare is improved if the beneficiaries of a change could sufficiently compensate those who become worse off so that the latter groups would willingly accept the change. It is further asserted that compensation need not actually be made from gainers to losers – only that the necessary compensation be less than the total benefits.

It is not necessary that income will actually be redistributed so that everybody will in fact be better off; there will practically always be some individuals who are worse off than before. But it is sufficient that everybody *could* be better off. That is the definition of what is meant by saying that one situation is better and constitutes a larger national income than another.[1]

Haberler suggests in a footnote (added to the Caves and Johnson version) that there may be some objection to this criterion. He is aware of the problem of interpersonal comparisons and the conceptual difficulties associated with the 'as if' redistribution of income. Nonetheless, his static analysis, admirable in its clarity and insight, completely misses the dynamic issues which must concern an economic historian who cannot ignore the advantage of hindsight.

In the real situations with which our analysis must deal it is unrealistic to assume away coercion and the use of force in the making of policy or in determination of the distribution of income, status and power. The clearest evidence of force and coercion is revealed in the high level of physical violence in Colombia. The assumption of individual decision-making units exercising choice in terms only of the constraints offered by competitive markets is not even a caricature of Colombian reality. Given the extent of force, coercion and violence one can make no *ex post* evaluation of the type, 'they acted thus; therefore, it must have been in the general interest'. One cannot assume that any changes were evaluated with a view to national welfare improvement via the compensation principle. Coercion and force make a farce of the idea of compensation.

One would err in assuming that the size of total output alone is sufficient

---

[1] Gottfried Haberler, 'Some Problems in the Pure Theory of International Trade', *Economic Journal*, LX (238): 223–40 (June 1950); reprinted in Caves and Johnson, *Readings in International Economics*. The quotation is from p. 216.

measure of welfare. Although an ideal redistribution of income could always result in all-round improved welfare if the total were larger rather than smaller, no such redistributions occurred in nineteenth-century Colombia. Therefore, the compensation principle does not apply because over several score years the growing total income was not re-distributed through taxes or other measures. Concentrated political power made redistribution unnecessary for the beneficiaries.

The effects of income distribution

There are, moreover, the dynamic implications of the failure to achieve a more equal distribution of income. An unequally distributed and low per capita income may lead to a lower rate of saving than an equally distri-buted income. Once individual consumption levels pass the minimum for subsistence, consumption expenditures can be devoted to human resource development. Investment in education (regarded by the indi-vidual as a form of consumption expenditure) is only the most obvious resource-developing expenditure. Simple improvements in nutrition may be even more important at some consumption levels.

Passing beyond some income level, however, the consumer will wish to devote a share of income to a style of consumption which does not have resource-developing benefits. Luxury consumption may devour so much of the total surplus above subsistence needs as to make growth impossible.

Figure 8 illustrates the hypothesis that an unequal distribution of in-come makes development unlikely because of the small proportion of expenditures related to resource development. The cross-section of consumption–income relationships is indicated by the straight line C. It is shown with the standard assumption that income earners at low levels will tend to consume more than earned income. At any point on C above the $45°$ line consumption exceeds income. At higher levels of income there is an increment available for saving and investment. It is belief in the importance of this increment as a source of investable funds that has been used to justify an unequal distribution of income as a neces-sary condition of economic development.[1] But if development-related consumption is quantitatively important, then an income distribution with most income receivers in the middle income range would yield a greater potential for economic development. In figure 8 the curve $C^\star$

[1] See, for example, the article of Walter Galenson and Harvey Leibenstein, 'Investment Criteria, Productivity and Economic Development', *Quarterly Journal of Economics*, LXX (August 1955), 343–70.

represents the amount of expenditures on development-related consumption at various income levels. It is drawn to take into account two factors: (1) most expenditures of the very poor contribute simply to the maintenance of life; (2) expenditures of the wealthy are likely to be devoted to sumptuary living. This presentation assumes that it is principally middle-income earners who spend on self-education, medical care which improves labor efficiency and such other items which yield improvements in human capital.

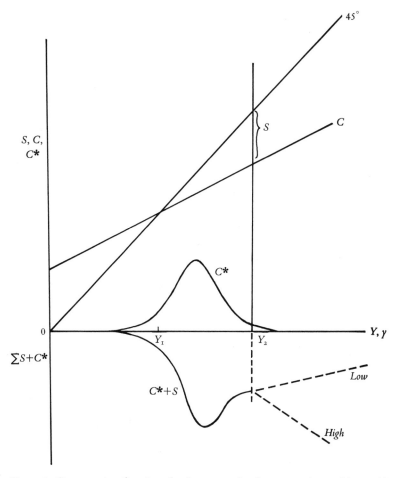

Figure 8 Consumption function, development-related consumption and investable funds: the relation to income distribution.

The bottom half of Figure 8 presents the sum of $C^\star$ and S up to the income level Y_2. The curve $C^\star + S$ leads to the following hypothesis: societies which have many income earners in the range between Y_1 and Y_2 have a larger potential investable fund (and hence greater potential for economic growth) than do societies with few income earners in that range.

To the right of Y_2 one finds high-income earners. As income rises there is a widening gap between direct consumption 'needs' and income; the gap produces the potential savings S. It is not possible to predict *a priori* whether these potential savings will be devoted to investment or luxury consumption – both possibilities are shown. If the high-income earners place a high priority on investing their savings, then a society with a few high-income earners, few in the middle range Y_1 and Y_2 and many with incomes below Y_1 may achieve more rapid growth by generating more investable funds than the society with mostly middle-income earners. Alternatively, should the wealthy set a low priority on investment, the result could be substantially inferior to the 'society of equality'.

Finally, this line of argument suggests a basic asymmetry in the relationship between growth or stagnation on the one hand and equality or inequality in income distribution on the other. It is brought out in the following two-way table:

	Growth	*Stagnation*
Equality	Yes	No
Inequality	Yes	Yes

Inequality in the distribution of income can produce either growth or stagnation; equality in the distribution of income produces only growth. This result emerges because of the underlying assumption of the model that middle-income earners will always devote a substantial amount $C^\star$ to the improvement of human capital and hence to productivity and growth.

The foregoing discussion emphasized some theories relevant to problems of development, distribution and welfare. These are intimately related elements in the economic decline of Colombia. It makes no sense to evaluate change merely in terms of total output and its growth or decline. One could not impute equality to a $100 decline in income for a lord and for a peasant: the one experiences minor discomfort, the other starvation. An unambiguous decline is not observed in Colombian economic history; if it were analysis would be trivial. What appears to occur is the transfer of $100 from peasant to lord: the peasant still starves but the lord is better off. Is Colombia better off or worse off? How will long-term

Economic decline in nineteenth-century Colombia

development prospects be affected by the redistribution? Difficult as they are, these questions cannot be ignored. It is time to put the theory to work.

SECTORAL IMPACT OF LAISSEZ-FAIRE

The export sector

The export sector experienced more substantial growth than any other sector of the economy in the years 1845–1900. The apparent highest sustained rates of growth for exports was around 5 per cent per annum achieved in the 1850s. But this growth rate was not sustained beyond the decade of tobacco expansion between 1847 and 1857. Two observations are pertinent: (1) the leading sector itself did not perform well beyond an initial spurt; (2) the failure to sustain the rate of expansion could relate to the technical character of the production process. It is with the production process in the tobacco region of Ambalema that the anatomy of decline must begin.

Ambalema is a small village on the Magdalena River. It became the market center for tobacco exports when Francisco Montoya established a commercial house there during the years in which his firm had taken over management of the government monopoly.[1] In the valley of the nearby Rio Recio volcanic ash had given properties to the soils which made it productive of a tobacco so high in quality that it came for a time to be the leading source of leaf for cigar wrappers in Germany. These same few hundred hectares produced in the 1850s over half of all Colombian foreign exchange.

Some 90 per cent of the Colombian tobacco which was sold in Bremen came from Ambalema. In the peak year 1857 about 326,000 *arrobas* were sold there. Assuming that each plant occupied one square meter, and given the prevailing yield of one arroba/100 plants in each of two annual crops, then about 1,600 hectares were under cultivation. Thus a tiny area which was easily monopolized was the key element in Colombia's export economy for a period of three decades.[2]

How was tobacco grown in the Ambalema region? An *aparcero*, a kind of share-cropper, did the actual cultivation, apparently without much supervision by the landlord or commercial house. Tobacco growing did

[1] See Harrison, 'The Colombian Tobacco Industry', p. 275.
[2] The estimates of production, yields and plantings are based on data in Harrison, 'The Colombian Tobacco Industry', pp. 265, 266, 360, 368 and 371. These data lead to the estimate of an average output of 800 kilos per hectare annually. Export data by crops are

157

not lend itself to large-scale managerial units. Medardo Rivas writes: 'The tobacco industry is more democratic than those of quinine, stock-raising, coffee, or indigo extraction: tobacco plants can only be cared for by a family which receives remunerative work for all its members. Family cultivation establishes intimate and indispensable relations between the proprietor, the capitalist and the cultivator.'[1] Successful plants require great care with the rhythm of development from seedlings through regular weeding, topping, selective leaf harvesting and the long process of curing. This process is rarely carried on in *managerial* units larger than the family plus a few extra hands. It is generally recognized that the tobacco plant is among the most delicate cultivated by man. Since Ambalema tobacco was sold for cigar wrappers, it required unusual care. Each leaf had to be cured to the proper degree of moistness lest it turn brittle and break in rolling or become moldy.

It is not clear whether the curing process was the duty of the aparcero or was assumed by the exporting agency. It seems likely that long racks of partially cured leaves were brought into the exporter's warehouse where temperature and moisture could better be controlled in the last stages of curing. The work of packing, itself a specialized and crucial task, was assumed by the exporter.

At this stage the product from many share-cropper plots was gathered together by the single exporting agency. Economies of scale missing in the growing process are evident and dramatic in the marketing. Even after the monopoly privilege was ended three Antioqueño companies were able to control more than two-thirds of tobacco exports.[2] The work of packing and shipping required practical control over the entire output of Ambalema tobacco in the early 1850s and subsequent decades. Fairly sizable shipments had to be brought together to fill a *champan* (pole boat) or later a river steamer. When it held the monopoly of tobacco export, the firm of Montoya, Sáenz y Cia. maintained commercial agents in Hamburg and Bremen to handle sales. They also maintained an office in Barranquilla to expedite the transfer of the hogsheads of tobacco from

---

summarized in Banco de la República, *XLIX y XLIII Informe anual del Gerente a la Junta Directiva*, Part II (Bogotá 1967), p. 189.

    For related estimates of production see Salvador Camacho Roldán, *Notas de viaje* (Bogotá 1898), p. 198, and Nieto Arteta, *Economía y cultura*, pp. 266–7. The data in the former were assembled from reports by consular officials in Bremen and Hamburg concerning imports of Colombian tobacco into those ports.

[1] Medardo Rivas, *Los trabajadores de tierra caliente* (Bogotá 1946), p. 137.
[2] See Miguel Samper, 'Ambalema', *El Neo-Granadino* (27 August 1852); cited in Safford, 'Significación de los Antioqueños', p. 66.

river steamer to ocean vessel. This was by no means a vast commercial enterprise on the scale of that created nearly a century later by the Federación de Cafeteros. But in that single firm and the oligopoly which succeeded it resided the scarcest resource in Colombia – skills of organization and marketing.

We have already seen in Chapter 6 that land was plentiful (though local scarcities and rents occurred) and labor, because of the institutional changes in landholding, was easily available. Entrepreneurial skill was the scarce factor of production. The ecology of the Ambalema region generated a certain specific scarcity of land because of the limited availability of alluvial soils which were the best for Ambalema leaf tobacco. It is hard to judge the significance of this scarcity since it was observed that as exports of Ambalema grew, the growing area spread out of the Rio Recio to less suitable lands. One would wish for data comparing the sharecropping arrangements on alluvial and non-alluvial soils. Such data would reveal whether ground-rents, concentrated in the hands of a small number of landowners, were a substantial share of the product of the Ambalema region. Some individuals amassed significant fortunes: 'There were more than a few men who, like don José L. Viana or don Pastor Lezama, had property income of more than one hundred thousand pesos annually.' [1] But this information alone reveals little about the distribution of the total product. In particular, we are not able to tell whether this property income was really the result of monopoly control of a scarce resource or the entrepreneurial skill of the individual.

The limited evidence available suggests that land ownership was not so important as entrepreneurial skill. The fortune which Montoya and his firm assembled in the management of the tobacco monopoly is best attributed not to landownership, or even monopoly control of marketing, but to personal organizational skill. The subsequent hiatus of the tobacco industry between 1875 and 1919, the latter year marking the formation of Coltabaco (Compañía Colombiana de Tabacos) may attest to the crucial role of that organizational skill.

According to Felipe Pérez, one of the principal causes for the declining quality of Colombian tobacco resulted from the fact that the cultivator was always forced to sell his tobacco to the landowner at a fixed price and thus was more concerned with its quantity than with its quality:

Among the important warnings made about the development and production of tobacco, that which appears most important is the counsel of free use-rights, i.e. the suppression of the abominable system employed by the proprietors of Ambalema

---

[1] Rivas, *Los trabajadores de tierra caliente*, p. 136.

which consists of conceding to share-croppers or small entrepreneurs land for the cultivation of tobacco, under the monstrous condition that they cannot sell it freely, but instead must turn it over at a low price to the proprietors. While the current price of leaf tobacco in Ambalema is between $3.20 and $3.80 the arroba, the share-cropper must sell his crop to the landowner at $2.40. From this flows various lamentable consequences for the cultivators and the general interests of the country.[1]

According to Pérez, landlords made their profits solely on the differential between the price they paid their tenants for tobacco and the price they got for it on the world market. John Harrison has pointed out that not only did the cultivator pay a 5 to 6 per cent rent but also paid an interest rate of about 3 per cent per month, or 10 per cent of the total crop, on various loans he might receive from the landlord.[2] Terms of repayment on loans varied widely. Some landlords required their tenants to buy all their essentials on the hacienda at extremely high prices. Harrison argues that the government abolition of the tobacco monopoly did little to change the lot of the cultivator:

The cultivators were kept on the land by a system of advances in kind, not money. The goods that they received were over-priced and interest up to 6 per cent per month kept them in a permanent condition of peonage. With this advantage the hacendados forced their agricultural laborers to sell tobacco at a fixed price to them only, precisely as the government previously had done. The differential, seldom less than 100 per cent, was in addition to the regular rent paid by the cultivator. As far as the man with the hoe was concerned, the hacendado had replaced the monopoly.[3]

What was true for tobacco seems to have been true with other crop systems and the land tenure arrangements associated with them. The hacienda of la Paila exported bulls, horses and hogs. 'Some of the tenants owe personal service for rent. ... The others pay a ground rent of from $1·60 to $3·20 per annum. All have their estancias, or fields in the forest. They contain from half an acre to two acres, ... but, as they work [them] only occasionally, it makes little difference.'[4] The cattle hacienda of Robert Haldane in the 1860s was bringing in eight dollars rent for every two acres. With 180 families working the land and many others trying to get on, the annual rent of the estate in the 1860s was greater than the price he originally paid for the entire estate twenty years earlier.[5]

---

[1] Quoted in Ignacio Gutierrez Ponce, *Vida de Don Ignacio Gutierrez y episodios históricos de su tiempo, 1806–1877*, I (London 1900), 437.

[2] Harrison, 'The Colombian Tobacco Industry', p. 320.

[3] John P. Harrison, 'The Evolution of the Colombian Tobacco Trade, to 1875', *HAHR*, XXXIV (May 1952), 172.

[4] Isaac F. Holton, *New Granada: Twenty Months in the Andes* (New York 1857), pp. 422–3.

[5] J. D. Powles, *New Granada: Its Internal Resources* (London 1863), pp. 152–3.

We do not have direct evidence on the distribution of the product in the tobacco export industry. There are suggestions in Harrison's dissertation and in *Los trabajadores de tierra caliente* that real wages were higher in the lowlands than in the highlands. 'One must also add that while the daily wages of artisans in Ambalema, Honda and all the tobacco growing regions were up to six pesos per day, wages in Bogotá were only slightly higher; and many articles which were cheap in Bogotá, cost ten times as much in the other regions because of difficulties in transport.'[1] This 'evidence' is contradictory. On the one hand there are indications that money wages were possibly higher in the lowlands; on the other that the cost of living may have been sufficiently different in the two areas to produce higher real wages in the highlands. However, the lowlands were largely unpopulated at the beginning of the tobacco boom, so that some wage differential would have had to exist to draw in labor. Returns to capital and entrepreneurial skill were also probably higher in the lowland export sector than in the highlands. Even without direct evidence it seems fair to assert that labor's *share* in the product of the export sector was probably less than in highland agriculture even though wages may have been higher. The apparent decline in wages in the tobacco zone after 1857 tends to confirm the view that a premium over the highland wage (if it existed at all) was only an initial inducement to migration and not an inherent characteristic of tobacco growing.

The implications of this income distribution are several. First, the substantial benefits flowing from the growth of tobacco exports were concentrated in the hands of a few entrepreneurs and landowners.[2] They in turn made a large share of their purchases outside the country so that the multiplied effects of export growth were small.

One reason for the limited impact on the highland economy was the continuing high cost of transportation from Ambalema to Bogotá in the highlands. Nearly all transportation improvements between 1845

[1] Rivas, *Los trabajadores de tierra caliente*, pp. 140-1.

[2] Two very different export economies may be worth mentioning in this regard. Only some 3 per cent of guano proceeds in the years 1840–80 went to the Chinese coolie laborers discussed in Levin's study of the Peruvian guano export economy. (See J. V. Levin, *The Export Economies*, pp. 88, 112.) The percentage is my estimate based as follows on Levin's figures: if coolies themselves got about $100 per annum and there were 5,000 working each year (Levin says 'a few thousand'), then over 40 years their total income was $20 million or 3 per cent of the $600 million in gross receipts from the industry.

The Braden Copper Company, first of the big producers in Chile, paid but 9 per cent of total sales in wages during the years 1920–5. (See Mamalakis and Reynolds, *Essays on the Chilean Economy*, pp. 363, 366.) Neither industry had extensive local processing activities which might have raised labor's share. Labor's share of gross receipts in tobacco growing may not have differed significantly from these two cases.

and 1895 improved lowland access to the sea without changing transport costs between lowlands and highlands. The economic distance between the highland and lowland was particularly widened with the advent of regular steamboat service on the Magdalena. Even without the luxury importers there was little chance for a firm tie between the export economy, a kind of home-grown enclave, and Colombia's highland where most of the population lived.

It is perhaps instructive to consider the most extreme example of economic distance between highland and lowland, that between Bogotá and Panama.[1] There was practically no interchange between the two even before completion of the Panama Railroad in 1855; after that date Panama came more and more to be a province unto itself. At the time of secession in 1903 there were no significant economic ties between the Isthmian province and the rest of the country. The swampy Darien region made an impenetrable block to connection by land which ocean transport never effectively overcame. Without significant economic ties it proved difficult to sustain political union. Secession was considered seriously in the 1820s and again in the 1840s. Panama was for all practical purposes an independent state between 1861 and 1885.

The export economy of tobacco did not draw Ambalema completely apart from the highlands because labor supply and the entrepreneurs came from and returned to the highlands. But the interchange of goods was limited and the domestic linkages of a technical nature were insignificant between highland and lowland economies. Highland artisans had for decades been producing textiles for trade with western and southern regions of Colombia, and there can be little doubt that the river valley population also participated in that trade.

The movement in transportation costs favored lowland trade with the outside world rather than the highlands. Table 19 presents a comparative analysis of freight rates on the river and overland from the river ports of Honda and Girardot to Bogotá. While the costs of river transportation apparently fell slightly as a result of regular availability of steamers after 1845, costs of overland freight movement increased about 50 per cent from one period to the next, i.e. prior to the opening of railroads. The relative attractiveness of trade with the highlands as compared to international commerce dwindled with the increasing relative costliness of highland goods delivered to the lowlands.

---

[1] An interesting study which deals in part with the relation between Panama and the highland is that of J. Ignacio Méndez, 'Colonial Survivals in Panama: Public Administration and the Censo' (Ph.D. diss., University of California, Berkeley 1970).

Economic decline in nineteenth-century Colombia

There can be no doubt of the great expansion of imports into Colombia; it is reasonable to assume that the first impacts were felt in areas – such as these lowlands – which were at a substantial economic distance from the highland centers. The contention of Medardo Rivas that the artisans of Bogotá derived their 'bread, work and life' from their markets in the lowlands seems at best an exaggeration. The expansion of imports between 1864 and 1875 must have left little or no market in lowland areas for interregional trade in artisan import-competing goods.

Table 19 *Average freight rates on the Magdalena River and overland to Bogotá from river ports, two periods, pre-1845, 1845–80* (centavos per ton-kilometer).

Period	River	Overland
Pre-1845	8.32	27.6
1845–80	6.42	41.6

Source: Table 6.

The tobacco export economy never generated sufficient demand for the creation of formal banking institutions. The first successful Colombian bank opened in 1871.[1] Although many of its founders were involved in the tobacco business either as landowners or exporters, they were primarily interested in financing imports and merchant inventories. Not until the period of coffee exports does one witness the growth of financial intermediaries which assisted and were called into existence by the export activity itself. Direct connection between exporting and importing was an obvious necessity given the primitive state of banking. Each commercial house had to handle for itself the acquisition and expenditure of foreign exchange. Thus it would be difficult to distinguish the profits earned in commercial activities from tobacco exporting itself.

Import activities were apparently much less risky than exporting. Importers of cotton textiles made large and steady profits in the years of tobacco exports. But Montoya, Sáenz y Cia. failed, and the Colombian Mining Association lost over a million pesos by the time it ceased operations in 1874.[2] Countless other losses were sustained by entrepreneurs

---

[1] See *Banco de Bogotá, trayectoria de una empresa de servicio, 1870–1960* (ed. Oliverio Perry, Bogotá 1960). This publication of some 273 pages contains much information of general interest about the bank's foundation and subsequent development.

[2] Vicente Restrepo, *Estudio sobre las minas*, pp. 135–7.

in minor tropical exports. In contrast import houses appear to have thrived throughout the period. Their success can be explained by the inexorable rise in imports through the 1870s. At the beginning of the twentieth century these same merchant houses provided the capital to start local cotton textile manufacture.[1] By that time the only large fortunes originating in exports which could be devoted to industrial development came from placer mining and coffee *fincas* in Antioquia. Even there, however, the principals had gained much of their wealth in the import trade.

For the merchant class the years 1845–90 brought wealth and new fortunes. It is impossible to determine just how large the merchant class was and how many were the people who benefited directly from the expansion of imports. The census of 1870 found 23,184 people who identified themselves as *comerciantes*.[2] This number must include thousands of clerical personnel as well as the leading merchants. But even the full figure constitutes less than one per cent of the total Colombian population in that period. Since the number of merchants was small, they probably retained much of the benefit of lower English costs of production as oligopoly profits. Merchants could effectively control supply because of the special skills and connections required to operate in the import trade. Since only a marginally lower selling price than prevailed for artisan textiles would be needed to shift buying habits, the profits of trade could continue for decades.

The artisan class

If the main beneficiaries of free trade were the merchant class, then the principal losers were the artisans. But the blow to the artisan class has gone largely unnoticed by economic historians. The abortive coup which brought Melo to power in 1854 was the last visible act of self-defense by the artisans. There is practically no record of labor protest in Colombia between 1854 and 1926 when the banana workers struck for improved working conditions. A recent labor history by Miguel Urrutia and a political history by James Payne discuss at length the Reforms of 1850 then skip almost directly to the 1930s in their historical analysis.[3]

An explanation for the dearth of artisan protest is not hard to find. Rural artisans were mostly women and children whose employment and

[1] See Enrique Echavarría, *Historia de los textiles en Antioquia* (Medellín 1943).
[2] Colombia, Oficina de estadística nacional, *Anuario estadístico de Colombia – 1875* (Bogotá, n.d.), pp. 22–8. Hereafter cited as *Anuario estadístico, 1875*.
[3] James L. Payne, *Patterns of Conflict in Colombia* (New Haven 1968); Miguel Urrutia M., *History of the Labor Movement in Colombia* (New Haven 1969).

Economic decline in nineteenth-century Colombia

income were supplements to male earnings in agriculture. The Census of 1870 listed a total of 305,824 artisans (exclusive of the Isthmus of Panama) of whom less than a third (92,347) were male. In Santander female artisans outnumbered males by more than five to one. Since that area concentrated on cotton textiles, these data strengthen the view that females made up the vast majority of artisans working with cloth, the principal artisan product facing import competition.[1] There must have been many male weavers, tanners and smiths, but in those activities in which home goods competed with imports, women and children predominated. Even a generation later in Medellin's textile mills women constituted the majority of all workers.[2] It was female artisans who in the latter half of the nineteenth century were most substantially affected by growing imports. Two things were happening to them: the price of textiles (and other imports) gradually eroded, and sales fell. Neither happened suddenly enough to provide a symbolic moment of disaster. And even if a symbol had been found (e.g. the arrival of a boatload of English textiles), female artisans were not likely to be active protestors.

The definitions of the labor force in the several Colombian censuses are so inconsistent as practically to forestall an analysis of the trends in the number of artisans after 1870.[3]

---

[1] *Anuario estadístico, 1875*, pp. 22-8.

[2] See República de Colombia, Ministerio de Hacienda, *Informe del Ministro de Hacienda, 1916* (Bogotá 1916), pp. xcvii and following. Women and children combined made up 79 per cent of the labor force in two major Antioqueño textile factories in 1915. For later periods see Fernando Gomez Martinez and Arturo Puerta, *Biografía económica de las industrias de Antioquia* (Medellín 1945), and Ospina Vásquez, *Industria y protección*, pp. 331, 341 and 409.

[3] The census of 1912 included 190,301 in the category, 'Artes, oficios y aprendices'. In 1918, 522, 321 were put in the group called 'Artes, oficios, Industria manufactura y fabril'. Some 527,246 were included in the more modern classification, 'Industrias de transformación', in 1938. The same term was used in the 1951 census, and 460,907 were placed in the category. In the superior classification system adopted for the census of 1964, the total of artisans and operatives was placed at 835,468. Women by this time constituted only 20 per cent of the total. But in comparing the censuses of 1951 and 1964, the general summary placed the number of workers in the 'Industrias de transformación' in 1964 at 655,961. An even fairer representation of the number of artisans is the number of workers in 'Industrias de transformación' who are also cross-classified in Table 38 of the census summary as artisans: that number is 536,153.

From this maze of data it seems most difficult to get an accurate estimate of the number of artisans for any point in time in the twentieth century. It is clear from analysis of recent censuses that the number of women included in these occupational and industrial classifications is declining – 34·1 per cent women in 'Industrias de transformación' in 1951, 27·3 per cent in 1964. Some 69·8 per cent of artisans listed in 1870 were female. This secular change seems reasonable since the cottage industries of the nineteenth century were by-employments supplementing agricultural labor.

The liberal period

The classifications were revised by ECLA to arrive at a more useful approximation of the distribution of the labor force. According to their estimates the population of artisans in manufacturing was 197,000 in 1925 and 224,000 in 1938.[1] There is no reason to believe these data are inconsistent with the censuses themselves; thus it seems fair enough to accept their data. They point to a decline by more than a third in the number of artisans between 1870 and 1925. The 1912 census figure (190,301 in the category 'artes, oficios y aprendices') is the only other one which fits into the quantitative dimensions sketched by the combination of the ECLA data and those of the 1870 census; moreover, it fits the other evidence suggesting fairly rapid expansion of local manufacturing after 1910, an expansion which would probably have increased artisan employment between 1912 and 1925. In short, the case seems strong for the absolute decline of artisan activities until the First World War as a result of the expansion of foreign competition.

The organization of artisan production was so primitive that there existed few formal or informal associations organized to protect artisan interests. There had not even developed the limited complexity of the putting-out system. Each household carried out the entire process of spinning, weaving and marketing. Santander was the only region of the country for which a detailed study of artisan crafts was undertaken in the nineteenth century, other than the data presented in census materials. Table 20 shows the number of shops by principal product in 1892 in that area. Textiles and clothing continued to dominate among artisan activities. Work with hard fibers – the Colombian *fique* which is extracted from the *agave* plant – must have been largely devoted to the fabrication of sacks for coffee. This activity constitutes one of the forms in which artisans shifted into the export activity without great disruption or difficulty. Tobacco exports appeared to offer no similar opportunities.

Virtually all the artisan activities must have been operated as one-man shops. For example, Camacho Roldán put the value of output of cotton textiles in Santander for the year 1887 at about $1 million.[2] Assuming that 5,000 establishments were devoted to that activity, then output per establishment would have been $200 in then current pesos, equivalent to perhaps U.S.$50 at the then prevailing rate of exchange. If the number of persons per establishment were even as high as two, the per worker product would have been too low to continue in business. Apparently, small shops were the rule. As a result the artisans could not organize

[1] ECLA *Study*, Statistical Appendix, p. 6, Table 5.
[2] *Notas de viaje*, p. 155.

166

themselves for opposition to free trade. They were too scattered – as it were, an uncongealed *lumpen proletariat.*

The rural quality which permeated spinning and weaving was probably less characteristic of other artisan trades. The silversmiths, who stood at the top of the status ladder of artisans, were ranged along Carrera Sexta just north of the cathedral and the Plaza Bolívar in Bogotá. They were organized as a guild. Unlike the female, rural textile workers they

Table 20 *Classification of artisan enterprises in Santander, by type of activity, 1892.*

Type of shop or principal product	Number	Per cent
Soft-fiber textiles	7,400	41·6
Hard-fiber textiles	5,000	27·9
Clothing and tailoring	1,725	9·6
Food, beverages and tobacco	1,002	5·7
Chemicals	6	0·0
Leatherworking (saddles, etc.)	150	0·8
Ironworking and other metals	277	1·5
Rubber goods	8	0·0
Pottery and tilemaking	582	3·3
Woodworking, carpentry	410	2·3
Soap and common candles	1,270	7·1
Printing and photography	28	0·2
Total	17,918	100·0

Source: compiled from Francisco Javier Vergara y Velasco, *Nueva Geografía de Colombia* (Bogotá 1892), p. DCCLXXXVI. I have re-grouped his detailed data into some semblance of modern categories. The data presented on pp. 319–20, by Ospina Vásquez, *Industria y protección*, and based on this source, are apparently incomplete.

had the organization which could have led opposition to Liberal policies between 1861 and 1880. It is perhaps a quirk of fate that the opening up of trade caused them no inconvenience since they worked silver, a product never to be counted among Colombian imports. So the silversmiths had no reason to oppose free trade. Already secure as the elite of the artisans, they became comfortably unconcerned with politics and social change. One cannot and need not conclude that the potential leadership of the artisan class was co-opted, as does Fals Borda.[1] Rather,

[1] Fals Borda, *La subversión en Colombia* (Bogotá 1967) suggests that legitimate protest has been consistently subverted in Colombia by the absorption of protest leaders into the elite.

the interests of that group diverged from the mass of rural spinners and weavers. No protest could be effective since urban artisans were less affected by the events which were harmful to the interests of the rural artisans.

One other factor deserves emphasis in considering this problem. The merchant class was almost completely separated from the spinners and weavers with respect to physical location. Most merchants were located in the capital and the several river and sea ports. The artisans were scattered through the rural highlands. There was probably little direct contact between the two groups; the primitive marketing arrangements of the artisans did not even require business contacts with merchants since they sold directly to consumers in local town markets. Certainly there were almost no kinship ties. These qualities of separation make it hard to imagine that merchants could care in any significant way about the artisans. Of course the barrier that existed between merchants and artisans is but one aspect of the several dualisms – rural–urban, leisure class–working class, patron–client – which characterized the system of stratification. Some dualisms imply mutual aid, but the merchant–artisan dualism was competitive. The lack of contact made it easy for the merchants to justify their *laissez-faire* policies in the face of artisan decline: either merchants were unaware of the growing misery of the artisans or they had little reason to care.[1]

The merchants had effective political power after 1854 which was only challenged by the coffee growers and nascent industrialists after 1890. But the interests of the artisans were not even then represented. Santander, which in 1870 counted over a quarter of its labor force in artisan activities, was dominated by the Liberal Party. The region provided one president for the country, Aquileo Parra, who held office from 1876 to 1878. He was a merchant and small landowner. The Liberal Party was the principal proponent of free trade; hence we must assume that the interests of the artisans, despite their numbers, were never really considered.[2]

Colombia's two-party system shut out artisan interests. The Conservative Party represented the interests of landowners and regions of the country (Antioquia and Valle del Cauca) where there were few artisans. The Radical Liberals had raised free trade and individualism almost to

[1] For an exceptional case of sympathetic treatment of the problems of artisans see Miguel Samper, 'La miseria en Bogotá' *Escritos político-económicos*, I (4 vols., Bogotá 1925), 7–134, especially pp. 89–102. His principal emphasis is on 'public peace, harmony between the working classes, and moral and industrial habits' (p. 102).

[2] A similar argument is offered by L. Nieto Arteta in *El café en la sociedad colombiana* (Bogotá 1958).

the position of a state religion, particularly in the sovereign state of Santander. The artisans could not turn to the Conservatives when they were abandoned by the Liberals. Two-party politics may have appeared to offer a form of competitive interest-group representation but in fact it alienated significant minorities from the electoral process. The result was civil conflict which broke out often in physical violence. Artisans were not alone in their non-participation in the formal political process: but with them more than others we can observe the failure of politics.

Lack of organization, physical location, differential impact of imports amongst artisan groups, and non-cohesive stratification patterns within the artisan class: the confluence of all these elements served to thwart or diminish artisan protest. Without effective protest from the artisans the political and commercial elites pursued policies consonant with their own narrowly conceived class interests.

The effects of trade

From this qualitative description of decline for the artisan class (a description not devoid of novelty in the study of Colombian history) one does not generate either a quantitatively satisfying appraisal or an explanation which ties into changes in other sectors of the economy. The event of interest is the imposition of free trade as government policy after 1850. Government policy is not revealed merely in the level of tariffs (as presented, for example, in Table 8). The government apparently never did, even in its most radical period, eliminate tariffs. Rather, some goods must have entered free of duty. The mechanics of this practice remain unclear. A possible explanation is the ruse of double invoicing. However, the Colombian tariff was levied as a fixed sum per unit of weight of the imported product, including the box, packing materials, etc. This procedure of levying the duty plus the fact that many rate categories were available at the discretion of the officers in the ports could lead to a *de facto* cut (or increase) in the real *ad valorem* rates with no changes in the legal rates. One can with a little imagination also reconstruct how customs officials' low salaries were supplemented. Whatever the mechanisms they made possible the extravaganza of imports between 1864 and 1875. Allowing them to function can be construed as an act of policymaking. The uncertain timing of these actions as opposed to the legal manipulation of tariff laws makes it difficult to be precise about the timing and extent of the *laissez-faire* policy.

One possible indicator of *de facto* policy change is government tariff revenues as a percentage of total imports by value. Table 8 above presents legal duty estimates for some principal products, all the rates being above 40 per cent. There was a vast discrepancy between these legal rates and the apparent rates actually paid. In the years 1850–9 the average apparent duty was 13·7 per cent of the value of imports. The percentage fell to only 5·9 per cent in the years 1862–72, then rose to 11·4 per cent, 1873–84. The percentage was particularly low in the 1860s. Although no official reductions in duties were made, the duty rate over that decade was only a third of what it had been in the 1850s. The growing discrepancy between legal and *de facto* rates leads one to conclude that some form of double invoicing was being used. The only alternative explanation would be a shift in the composition of imports with respect to duty rates. I know of no evidence supporting two such compositional shifts, one in the early 1860s and a second in the first half of the 1870s.[1]

The fall in *de facto* duties, and more importantly the decline in export prices for British textiles, reduced the market for local producers of importable goods. Domestic producers had available to them that part of the market which remained after imports are subtracted from total demand. The average of total imports in the years 1845–9 was U.S.$2·5 million. We may arbitrarily estimate that the total consumption of importables was U.S.$23 million in 1845. We may assume that the demand for importables expanded at the same rate as population, 1·5 per cent per annum. Thus we can present in column 1 of Table 24 estimates of the demand for importables, 1845–85.

Column 2 is based on Table 12. The residual market (*ex post*) for locally produced importables appears in column 3. This market is not an ideal measure of the total demand for home-produced importables, but in measuring what was presumptively sold by artisans it provides a reasonably sensitive index of artisan well-being.

This procedure reverses the usual assumption that price and sales of imports are set by the domestic market. It may be justified in part by the words of the British Consul in 1888. 'The price of the native fabrics is, therefore, apparently ruled entirely by that of imported goods of the same nature, but of greatly superior quality; the poor peoples who

---

[1] Percentages are calculated from tariff revenues in Aníbal Galindo, *Historia económica i estadística de la hacienda nacional*, Table 4, for the years 1850–72; Ministerio de Gobierno, *Estadística general de la República de Colombia*, p. 180, for 1873–84. For similar calculations based on official data see *Memoria de Hacienda 1883*, p. 17. My calculations based on value of imports in Table 12. Percentages are the simple averages of annual percentages over the indicated years. A simple *t*-test indicates that the rates for the 1850s differ significantly at the 0·01 level of significance from those for the years 1862–72.

chiefly buy native goods not realizing the more durable nature of the latter.'[1]

The data in Table 21 confirm the decline of the market for local artisans. The market was of the order of $20 million in the 1850s and declined to only $7·8 million in 1865. It did not again reach the levels of the 1850s until 1885. Since there were some 300,000 artisans in Colombia in 1870,

Table 21 *Demand for importables, actual imports and the residual market for artisan products, 1845–85.*

Year	Domestic consumption of importables (1)	Imports (2)	Local production of importables (3)
1845	23	3·5	19·5
1850	24·8	5·0	19·8
1855	26·7	5·9	20·8
1860	28·8	10·2	18·6
1865	31·4	23·6	7·8
1870	33·8	23·8	10·0
1875	36·5	17·8	18·7
1880	39·3	23·5	15·8
1885	42·3	16·1	26·2
1890	45·5	25·1	20·4

Source: column 1 – estimated (see text); column 2 – Table 12; column 3 – column 1 minus column 2.

these data lead to the conclusion that their average annual output was only about $33. By-employments in artisan activities which had to meet foreign competition thus could provide only a small part of family income. No census before 1870 provided a count of artisans; thus any estimate of average artisan output for earlier years could be at best an unsupported guess.

Direct gains and losses from trade, 1850–70

The merchant class and import-competing artisans were the two groups most affected by the opening up of trade. How can we balance their respective gains and losses to arrive at an estimate of the net effect of *laissez-faire* policies?

Since Colombia neither levied nor published detailed census data for the period between 1870 and 1905, it would not be possible to make a

[1] Great Britain, Diplomatic and Consular Reports, *Report for the Year 1888 on the Trade of Colombia*, Annual Series, no. 455, p. 11.

quantitative assessment of *laissez-faire* policies (prior to the expansion of coffee cultivation) for any date after 1870. Moreover, there is every reason to believe that the changes experienced in the score of years between 1850 and 1870 were exacerbated in the next three decades; hence, the findings relevant to that latter year only become magnified as a result of the stagnation of exports after 1875.

The direct gains from trade on the side of expanded export income can be estimated as simply the amount by which exports were larger in 1870 than they would have been if no growth in trade had taken place between 1850 and 1870. That amount is $11·5 million. The losses suffered by the artisans may be estimated as the difference between their actual sales in 1870 and the sales they would have realized if imports had constituted just one-fifth of the total sales of importable goods as they had in 1850. That difference for the year 1870 was $17·0 million. (These calculations are based on Table 21.) However, insofar as artisans entered alternative employment rather than simply becoming unemployed, the losses would be smaller. But since most artisan activities were by-employments to agriculture which may already have had a full supply of labor (at least in local, specific labor markets which the artisan women and children might conceivably enter), the opportunities were probably not very good for alternative employment. It would therefore appear justifiable to maintain the estimate of artisan losses at $17·0 million.

These amounts must have had opposite but not necessarily symmetrical effects on the rest of the domestic economy. For example, if the increased income from exports went to a substantial extent for luxury imports, then the impact on the local economy would have been slight. If expenditures did not 'leak out' of the local economy, then they must have had multiplied effects which pulled up the rest of the economy. The analysis presented earlier in this chapter about the likely uses of income increments by income earners at various levels, when added to evidence suggesting the riskiness of export ventures and hence the concentration of earnings in the hands of a few, argue in favor of the view that the leakages were substantial on the side of export gains. Hence, the multiplied effects of earnings in exports and trade were not extraordinarily high.

The cutback in artisan earnings, in contrast, probably had a large multiplied effect on the local economy since the decline in their income must have led to fewer local purchases with no foreign leakages.

Thus if one uses a multiplier of 1·5 for increased income from exports and trade, the benefits yielded were $17·3 million. The losses of artisans may be multiplied by 3 to yield a total of $51 million. On balance then –

and taking into account only the comparative statics and leaving aside dynamic questions – the direct net loss from the opening up of trade was about $34 million in 1870 as compared to an extrapolation of the relatively autarchic conditions of 1850.

After 1870 the decline in the growth-rate of exports and the disorder caused to the economy of Colombia by restrictions on the money supply were a substantial disbenefit to the nation. Up to 1870 both static and dynamic effects may have been favorable to trade expansion. But especially after 1875 the Colombian economy was no longer able to depend on the expansion of the export sector but instead suffered stagnation and instability. Yet a taste for foreign goods had been established so that balance of payments problems plagued the country from 1875 until 1910. The opening up of trade and the advent of *laissez-faire* were not in themselves bad for Colombia. It was the inability of the export sector to maintain its rapid expansion that permitted international trade itself to appear to be the guilty party.

The preceding analysis included only the multiplied effects of the expansion of exports and the decline of import-competing activities. These factors by no means encompass all the effects of trade. Others will be considered in the following section.

Before proceeding, however, it would be well to consider the distributional impact of the gains and losses just discussed. Assume for a moment that all the gains from trade are divided among the occupational groups in the 1870 census category of comerciantes. Then the average gain for individuals in that group was $496. In contrast, the losses averaged among all the artisans was $56.[1] Since the artisans were already poor, and in many cases the comerciantes were already rich, the expansion of trade had the effect of increasing the degree of inequality between these two groups.

Effects of laissez-faire *on the peasantry*

One can delineate five principal ways in which the rural population was affected by the advent of *laissez-faire* between 1845 and 1885. (1) Some people were drawn into work in the export sector or into market production for purchases by the export sector and its ancillary industries; (2) many benefited from the lower cost and improved quality of imported products; (3) some had their markets diminished as artisans went into unemployment, or else suffered from the increased competition of those

---

[1] Labor force figures from 1870 census previously cited. Gains and losses are directly estimated amounts prior to consideration of multiplied effects.

who left the production of importables in order to return to subsistence agricultural production; (4) some suffered from the extensive civil conflict between Liberals and Conservatives; (5) *laissez-faire* policies led to the diminution of demand for agricultural labor in the highlands because of the shift of stockraising from highlands to lowlands as Guinea and Pará grasses came into use, and the usurpation of flatlands in the river valleys by stockraising.

The group considered under the broad category of the peasantry probably made up three-quarters or more of the population. Thus, the 'net' effects on this group are quantitatively more important to know than the impact of the more easily identifiable traders and artisans.

But at the same time information is less easy to secure and the group less homogeneous than other classes. The peasantry of Antioquia began during this period the phased interplanting of corn, beans and coffee. The peasantry of Nariño stoically observed the collapse of their market for *jipijapa* hats and fought for the retention of communal forms of land tenure. In short, the impact of *laissez-faire* could not be uniform because of the variegated social scene on which policy and ideology were imposed.

(1) *Employment in the export sector.* The export sector and ancillary services probably employed no more than 35,000 workers in the peak year for the nineteenth century of 1875. If one doubles that number to account for employment in ancillary activities, then export-related employment at its peak would have used only 5 per cent of the labor force. Total employment generated in all other years was either much more poorly paid or required a reduced share of the labor force. The impact on the labor force was small indeed.[1]

But although few were directly affected as producers during this period, the effects on those few were substantial. The exporting regions were away from highland population centers so that people had to move to work. The expansion of exports facilitated internal physical mobility. The mobility broke down family ties and loosened somewhat the rigid local social structures. It brought Colombians from several regions into contact and conflict over land and its possession. It coincided temporally with creation of a floating population of beggars and vagrants who were then slowly leaving the Indian resguardos. Export expansion did generate internal social change. But the decline of exports after 1875 left some of the workers drawn into these activities in difficult straits.

[1] The estimate of labor force in export activities assumes average output per worker of about $1,000. This estimate is probably too low and hence total employment too high.

Economic decline in nineteenth-century Colombia

(2) *Lower import prices.* If few of the peasantry benefited from having work in the export sector, few also enjoyed the benefits of imported goods – at their peak (1870–4) per capita imports were only $12·20 per annum. At that time the population of 18 Colombian cities totaled just above 200,000. If the consumption of only half of total imports had been distributed equally among this urban population, then each urban resident would have received about $75 per annum of imported goods. This exercise serves to indicate that it was entirely possible that most imported goods remained among the urban population and did not spread out significantly to rural areas. Consequently, the benefits of lower costs would as well have been concentrated in the cities.[1]

(3) *Decline of local markets.* There is no direct way to determine how the decline in artisan income and employment affected the aggregate labor market or the demand for home products in the last half of the nineteenth century. But referring again to the Census of 1870 one may find in the number of vagrants and *reos rematados* or imprisoned criminals, a proxy for excess labor supply or unemployment. The largest numbers in these categories appear in the states of Santander and Boyacá. There were 15 vagrants and criminals per 1,000 population in Santander, 13 in Boyacá, 10 in Cundinamarca, 9 in Tolima, 2 in Cauca and Antioquia, and 1 in Bolívar and Magdalena.[2] The eastern highlands thus proved to have – by this measure at least – the most significant social problems of unemployment and crime.

These measures would seem to support the view that the pressure of change was being more strongly felt in the highland artisan areas than in either the western highlands or on the north coast. Whether the pressure was exercised directly through unemployment and low income of artisans or through their depression of local labor markets as they sought alternative work in agriculture must remain unanswered. And of course the derived effect on farmers who might otherwise have sold their produce to handicraft workers (were it not for foreign competition) cannot easily be determined.

(4) *Civil conflict.* The manifestation of the policy of *laissez-faire* through freer international trade was but one form in which nineteenth-century

---

[1] For city population see *Anuario estadístico, 1875*, pp. 28–45. The statistics for the state of Bolívar given in this source are not from the 1870 national census as the editor implies, but from an 1874 census conducted by state officials. See note in Oficina de estadística nacional, *Estadística de Colombia* (Bogotá 1875), p. 10. All other data derive from national censuses of 1870.

[2] *Anuario estadístico, 1875*.

liberalism appeared in Colombia. More fundamentally important was the conflict between Liberals and Conservatives which engendered not only heated debate but death and destruction. Most of the deaths due to hostilities in the years between 1830 and 1902 (the ending of the Thousand Days War) can be attributed to a struggle for power inflamed by unyielding ideology in the two opposing camps. Conservatives finally 'won' in the sense that they managed to rule politically from 1886 to 1930, but virtually all Colombians lost in the missed opportunity for cooperative development. Illustrious names appear among the more than 130,000 Colombians who died in 70 years of civil war, but the vast majority must have been poor peasants who little understood or cared about the ideologies or political ambitions of the elite.

The extreme violence of civil conflict was pointed out by one scholar in the following way. Accepting the estimate of deaths for the War of a Thousand Days, some 2·5 per cent of the total population was killed in 37 months of conflict between 1899 and 1902. In the Civil War of the United States slightly less than 2 per cent of the 1860 population lost their lives. 'The political differences which were the ostensible causes of civil strife were never great enough to account for the repeated bloodletting except by a people whose need aggression was almost uncontrollable.'[1] In one of several major conflicts more death and destruction was unleashed (on a proportional basis) than in the much better known American Civil War.

If all deaths on average occurred to males in their early twenties who had an average of 30 years remaining to work at the time of death, and if their average annual earnings were $300, and if that expected earning be discounted to the time of death at a rate of 3 per cent, then the total of losses due to death by violence can be put at $822 million. This large figure is of course analogous to an extant stock of capital and thus should not be compared to flow concepts such as national income and product. But even when discounted again for comparative purposes the figure proves to be large and important. The direct losses from internal warfare probably far outweigh any benefits which finally accrued from the hegemony of the Conservative Party. A less intransigent ideological stance among the opposing elites would certainly have benefited the mass of the population who bore the suffering and death of civil war.

(5) *Stockraising and the peasantry*. The formation of latifundia accelerated after Independence; it was a logical economic step to control the labor

---

[1] Hagen, *On the Theory of Social Change*, p. 379.

supply. Stockraising was perhaps the most skill-saving activity for large blocks of lands. The owner could visit his *finca* once a week to provide managerial direction, devoting the major part of his time to commercial or professional work.[1] The annual cycle of planting and harvesting on a large estate required more planning and risk than stockraising – thus the latifundista would properly regard the latter as the most efficient use of all the resources at his command.

The efficiency for management associated with stockraising is indicated in the low employment in the activity. At a time when the stock of cattle may be estimated to have been some 1·75 million (see Figure 6), the number of ganaderos or stockmen was 14,633.[2] Each cowboy or herdsman could care for about 120 cattle. Even a very large herd could thus be maintained without the problem of managing an unwieldy labor force.

Since stockraising was almost certain to be an appealing form of enterprise to the well-to-do merchant class, they needed only the opportunity to gain possession of land to carry out their business. Here the ideology of *laissez-faire* met the private interests of the merchants to deprive the Indian of his common lands, the Church of its holdings and the national government of remaining public lands.

Changing ownership was accomplished in a manner not unlike that of passage of the Dawes Act of 1887 in the United States which 'struck at tribal authority and organization by breaking up reservation land into small family or individual holdings, with the best of the land usually sold to the whites'.[3] According to one standard textbook on American economic history, 'The Dawes Act ... failed to solve the problem of the Indian, but it has been instrumental in opening much land to white settlers.'[4] Although it is dangerous always to assume that a direct relationship exists between the legislation passed by constituted authorities and actual behavior, in this case the changing law and ideology opened a floodgate to individual opportunity and exploitation.

Nearly all observers in the first half of the twentieth century have been impressed with the apparently inefficient use of land resources which placed pastoral activities in good bottom lands and crop cultivation by

[1] 'Even though the returns from pasturing are often very substantial, such use of the land is not the best possible. But the compensations appear to outweigh economic considerations in the minds of the owners of the large cattle haciendas. ... Even though the owner may live in a distant city and not supervise the operation closely, a good cattle ranch has nearly always enabled the owner to live very well.' IBRD, *Basis of a Development Program for Colombia* (Baltimore 1950), p. 63.

[2] *Anuario estadístico, 1875.*

[3] John M. Blum, et al., *The National Experience* (2nd ed., New York 1968), p. 418.

[4] Harold U. Faulkner, *American Economic History* (5th ed., New York 1943), p. 372.

minifundia on the less efficient slopes. Parcelization and fragmentation were apparently combined with appropriation of the best lands for the use of large landholders. With most valley lands in the hands of a few, the many searched wherever they could for additional land to farm. A major result has been the erosion of soils and not insignificantly the silting of rivers to an extent making fluvial navigation difficult and costly. Neither erosion nor silting are independent of the inexorable growth of rural population and the further push up the hillsides leading in its turn to soil erosion and land depletion.[1]

These external diseconomies of the system of land tenure engendered by the spread of pastoral activities and their usurpation of bottom lands must be considered in evaluating the state of Colombia's economy after 1850. The high cost of transportation alone, which was in part due to the uncertainty of river navigation, inhibited the spread of coffee cultivation and raised the delivered cost of imported goods. How can one estimate the cost of these externalities? No means is at hand. But a judgment of developments in the latter half of the nineteenth century cannot ignore them.

One might proceed as follows to estimate for the year 1870 the benefits and losses of the policies of *laissez-faire* experienced by the peasantry. These figures are only rough orders of magnitude. One must assume that some offsetting errors will improve the aggregate total as compared to the individual figures.

	Millions of dollars
(1) *Employment gains.* 10 per cent of the total value of exports. Assumes that income gains for export workers and ancillary workers together constituted that amount	$+1 \cdot 76$
(2) *Lower import prices.* Assume half of imports consumed in countryside; elasticity with respect to price equal to $-0 \cdot 6$; consumption of home goods would have been 10 million, consumption of imports was 12 million, price fell from $1 \cdot 50$ to 1,[2] then benefits are	$+5 \cdot 5$
(3) *Decline of local markets.* One-fifth of the decline in artisan income	$-3 \cdot 6$

---

[1] Cf. Fals Borda, *Campesinos de los Andes* (Bogotá 1961), p. 91.

[2] The 33 per cent fall in price may overstate the benefits. Imlah's data on the price trends of British exports indicate that cotton manufactures, woolen manufactures and other exports all rose in price between 1850 and 1870. However, there are no reliable data on the movement in local prices for importables in any market in Colombia during this period. For Imlah's data see *Economic Elements in the Pax Britannica*, Appendix Tables II, III and IV.

(4) *Civil conflict.* Losses through the civil conflict of 1876 considered at 10 per cent of the present discount value of lives lost in warfare, 1840–79. Future incomes discounted at 3 per cent   −16·13

(5) *Effects of stockraising.* Assume labor is offered at the constant wage of $150 per annum and that the demand for labor declines by 5 times the total number of ganaderos in 1870. Subtract earnings in subsistence agriculture at two-thirds of other agricultural employment   − 0·84

Net effects on the peasantry   −13·31

The foregoing crude estimates are at best an exercise in showing the rough orders of magnitude implied by one set of assumptions about the impact of trade, land and institutional policies on the mass of the rural population. It was the significant losses associated with civil conflict which led to the net loss indicated. In any case the sum appears to be small. For example, if the total income of that 80 per cent of Colombia's population which were rural was on the order of Ps$220 million, i.e. about Ps$100 per capita, then the loss indicated above was some 6 per cent of income, virtually all of it attributable to the seemingly endless civil conflict. Free trade itself would appear not to have overcome the effects of that conflict, nor to have had much impact on this group.

Sum of direct effects and effects on the peasantry

If the preceding figures deserve any consideration at all, then they lead to the following general assessment of the trade, land and institutional policies in the third quarter of the nineteenth century:

	Millions of dollars
(1) Direct benefits to the merchant class and related multiplied effects	+17·3
(2) Direct benefits to urban consumers of imports equal to direct benefits realized by peasant consumers as estimated above	+5·5
(3) Direct losses of the artisans and related multiplied effects	−51·0
(4) Indirect net losses of the peasantry	−13·3
(5) Net effects of the trade, land, and institutional policies of *laissez-faire*, comparing 1870 with an extrapolation of 1850 conditions	−41·5

These amounts taken together constitute a large share of total national product for the year 1870 – at least 10 and perhaps as much as 20 per cent.[1] In short, there occurred significant losses in quantitative terms which can be directly related to trade, land and institutional policies.

But even this substantial sum fails to consider the distributional effects of the shift of income away from the relatively poor artisans and into the hands of the relatively well-to-do merchants and urban residents. A normative position which would hold that a more equal distribution of income is better than a less equal one would lead to an even more negative interpretation of these changes, even on the purely static level. Consider further that the redistribution may have led to a lessened ability of Colombian society to transform itself when in the last quarter of the nineteenth century the vicissitudes of trade left the economy stagnant. The dynamic losses due to this income redistribution were perhaps even greater in magnitude than the static losses discussed in greater detail.

The stagnation of trade was a post-1870 phenomenon. The specific losses discussed above all relate to a period when total exports were growing at about 5 per cent per annum. Exports were increasing up to 1864 but stagnated after that date, even into the first decade of the twentieth century. (See Figures 4 and 11.) This stagnation caused adjustment problems of its own, particularly because the once dynamic export sector could no longer provide the impetus for change. The demand for imports did not easily conform to the slower growth of exports. Recurrent balance of payments crises and the scarcity of money then had a chance to work downward pressure on prices and incomes. The crisis came to a head in the 1890s when the terms of trade for coffee (by then Colombia's leading export) declined from a peak of 171 in 1893 to 73 in 1899, the year that civil war broke out. The buying power of Colombian coffee fell by nearly 40 per cent in the last year alone.[2]

The violence of the War of a Thousand Days, following as it did the local, sectional and country-wide conflicts of the nineteenth century, must itself be taken as an indicator of secular economic decline in Colombia. After the last great conflict of the nineteenth century Jorge Holguin attempted to estimate the direct costs to the Colombian treasury and nation attributable to the civil wars of the nineteenth century. He

---

[1] Using employment data from the 1870 census and labor productivity estimates for 1925 developed by CEPAL, I estimated product per capita in 1870 at about $150 in dollars of 1950 purchasing power. Total product would thus have been $405 million, a figure which I judge to be too high by one-third. A more reasonable assumption is that per capita product was $100.

[2] Terms of trade calculated on the basis of an index of coffee prices and import prices.

put the total cost as Ps$52 million as of 1903.[1] His measure is not comparable to the analysis used here, but it confirms that contemporaries were sensitive to the great costs of warfare.

The difficulties which Colombia faced in the late nineteenth century make all the more curious the successful period of development which began in the twentieth. To that happier story we turn in Chapter 8.

---

[1] Jorge Holguín, *Desde Cerca (Asuntos Colombianos)* (Paris 1908), p. 144. The details of his calculation are also in Urrutia, *Historia del sindicalismo en Colombia*, p. 77.

CHAPTER 8

ANTIOQUEÑO COLONIZATION AND
THE EXPANSION OF COFFEE

The programs of Colombia's nineteenth-century Liberals failed to achieve the goals of economic development and social improvement. A further hiatus plagued Conservative rule until well after the War of a Thousand Days. A quickening did occur in Colombia's development in the twentieth century, but it would appear to result not from a more active or intelligent government policy so much as independent changes in the economy and society.

These changes were not spread throughout the country but were specific to several major cities and the Antioqueño region. The degree to which the quickening of economic development can be specifically attributed to the Antioqueños has been a matter of controversy for some decades. The controversy is important because the several interpretations rest to some extent on contradictory theories of the process of economic development. Here it will be possible to explore some of these theories and test in a rough way their efficiency in explaining available data.

The period 1885–1930 presents a special analytical challenge. Not only does regular economic development seem to begin in these years, but a

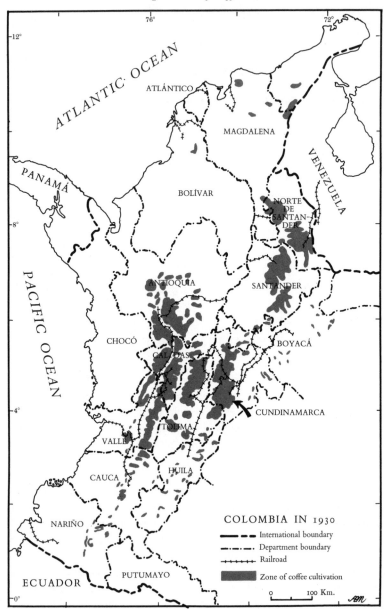

2 Colombia in 1930: departments, railways, zones of coffee cultivation. *Source:*
Federation of Coffee Growers, *Coffee Map of the Republic of Colombia* (Bogotá 1933).

major reversal from economic decline is achieved. The years after 1930 are marked by structural change in the economy (evidenced by internal migration and urbanization) and continuing growth through the mid-1950s. Yet the crucial transition to growth dates from the early decades of this century. It was based on mutually interdependent changes in Colombia's demography, export capacity, transportation system and industrial potential. It will be the purpose of this and following chapters to explore this period of transition and theories about how it happened.

INDIGENOUS DEVELOPMENT

It seemed at one time that there were two types of theories of Colombian economic development: one which accorded a special role to the Antioqueños, and one which did not. As the historical analysis has grown more sophisticated, however, types of theory have grown more disparate and rich in their demands for information. Nonetheless, the 'myth of the Antioqueños' remains as the necessary starting point in attempting to understand Colombian economic development.

A principal contributor to the myth of the Antioqueños, even though he wrote long after the myth had been established, is Everett E. Hagen.[1] 'The proximate answer to the question why growth began is because of the enterprise of the Antioqueños', writes Hagen.[2] He rejects the doctrine of 'peculiar barriers' which hold up the process of economic growth, noting in Colombia that foreign capital, foreign contacts and the infrastructure of transport were much less available to Antioquia than to other regions of Colombia. Yet industrial development got its start there. 'Thus growth began in spite of the supposed economic barriers', he writes, 'not because those barriers were removed.'[3] When attention is diverted from the external conditions of capital supply, foreign influence and the like to personality formation, one finds, in Hagen's view, striking differences between regions of Colombia which do provide an explanation of differential aptness for technological change and economic growth:

The successful economic innovators of Antioquia in 1957 were so different in personality structure from a group of equally prominent community leaders elsewhere in Colombia who were interviewed and studied that they may be thought of as a different breed of men. ... The incidence of creative personality is probably

---

[1] See 'The Transition in Colombia', *On the Theory of Social Change* (Homewood, Ill. 1962), pp. 353–84 and *passim*. The cited chapter has been translated and published in Colombia as *El cambio social en Colombia* (Bogotá 1965).

[2] Hagen, *On the Theory of Social Change*, p. 364.

[3] Hagen, *On the Theory of Social Change*, p. 363.

much higher among Antioqueños than elsewhere; ... this is an important cause of their greater entrepreneurial success.[1]

It should be noted that Hagen's TAT tests were given to upper-class males from Popayán, one of the most traditional cities of Colombia. The most important annual event in Popayán is the celebration in sacral fashion of Holy Week. (The arch-Catholicism of *Semana Santa* contrasts strikingly with the gaiety of *Carnaval* in Barranquilla.) Traditionalism and clerical dominance would seem to be enough to explain the differences Hagen observed. It would only be fair to note, however, that Antioquia (and Medellín) rank on most scales as among the more 'Catholic' regions of Colombia. Nonetheless, one is tempted to say, 'Of course *Paisas* and *Payaneses* are different. So are the businessmen of Chicago different from leading male citizens of Marietta, Ohio.' But Hagen was principally interested in throwing light on the Antioqueño personality and those characteristics of it which made them innovators.

The main condition which made the Antioqueño apt for innovation and entrepreneurial activity was 'status deprivation,' i.e. 'withdrawal from the Antioqueños of respect for their status in the society'.

Economically, throughout the colonial period and into the era of independence, they were looked upon as backward; ... The Antioqueños, however, did not think of themselves as inferior. Today they are as conscious of the attitudes of many other Colombians toward them as an outsider is, and they smart under them. Undoubtedly they did so in the nineteenth and eighteenth centuries. I suggest that this tension, by its effect on family environment, caused changes in personality (in needs, values, and world cognition) conducive to creativity. I suggest, too, that as these changes in personality proceeded, the Antioqueños sought restlessly to prove their worth and, in the world of the nineteenth and twentieth centuries, found what they sought in economic prowess.[2]

Thus the central theme of Hagen's theory of Colombian development is denial of expected status, the social changes which it caused and the movement into industrial activities occasioned by it. This theory either denies the importance of other causes or relegates them to the position of derivative effects of status deprivation.

Insofar as Luis Ospina Vásquez[3] has a theory of Colombian development, that theory is in accord with Hagen's general proposition that there was something different about the Antioqueños. As the title of his

---

[1] Hagen, *On the Theory of Social Change*, pp. 368–9.

[2] Hagen, *On the Theory of Social Change*, pp. 376, 377–8.

[3] His writings include *Industria y protección en Colombia, 1810–1930* (Medellín 1955); 'Perspectiva histórica de la economía colombiana', *Ciencias económicas* 6 (16): 5–32, May 1960; *Plan agrícola* (Medellín 1963). Ospina Vásquez, a wealthy landowner and member

book would indicate, Ospina Vásquez was concerned with the role of protection in promoting industrial development in Colombia. Thus he assembled a wealth of information on the industries which have developed, the history of tariffs and the apparent relations between the two. His theory of industrial development holds the tariff as a necessary condition of industry's existence, but he feels that commercial policy has not been decisive:

> In fact, free trade and protectionism have been equally disastrous for us – they have failed to alleviate our misery, and our backwardness has not diminished . . . Free trade failed to bring that great increase in the volume of international trade which might have gotten us a life of plenty, and protection brought forth no industries as had been hoped.[1]

Other factors were essential for the emergence from stagnation.

Ospina Vásquez considers the advent of economic development as more than a process of forming manufacturing establishments; the forerunners to the first large-scale plants near the end of the nineteenth century were the spread of the cattle hacienda and coffee cultivation. These particular economic activities, along with mining, provided important lumps of capital for the further extension of agriculture and the eventual shift to industry. Only at the end of the nineteenth century did the major fortunes of Medellín, first center of large-scale industry, turn their interest to manufacture. The fortunes, both large and small, were held by some hacendados, 'rich' peasants, comerciantes and some mining entrepreneurs.[2] Ospina Vásquez has put capital formation and entrepreneurship at the heart of his theory of Colombian industrial development. At the turn of the century in Medellín, industry

> was a small thing but an industrial future was visible, based on experience gained in mining activities which had helped develop a spirit of risk and innovation and ability to operate in joint associations. . . . Antioquia did not lack at that time for men of vision and boldness. In literature and in politics, Antioquia was living through a period of unusual brilliance.[3]

---

of one of Antioquia's most illustrious families (both his father and grandfather were Presidents of Colombia), has opted for a unique combination of scholarly pursuit and active interest in economic policy. Despite being independent financially he has served with the staff of 'planeación', Colombia's central planning bureau. His major work, *Industria y protección*, is evidence of a deep personal involvement in Colombian economic history and an unmatched command of the primary sources which provide information about Colombia's past. Ospina Vásquez was trained as an economist at the London School of Economics; thus his work shows none of the tendency toward lofty and undocumented generalizations which characterize the work of some Latin-American historians.

[1] Ospina Vásquez, *Industria y protección*, p. 440.
[2] Ospina Vásquez, *Industria y protección*, p. 447.
[3] Ospina Vásquez, *Industria y protección*, pp. 308–9.

The florescence in Antioquia was not confined to economic activities; a number of important literary works came out of the region at that time, Marco Fidel Suarez, poor son of a washwoman who rose to the presidency, reached the high point of his career and many other Antioqueños were rising to positions of importance on a national scale after a long period of relative backwardness on the national scene. There was in fact a general social emergence.

Ospina Vásquez offers a number of possible reasons for the switch into industry: entrepreneurial experience in mining, falling profit margins in commerce and some decline in the profitability of agricultural investment all played a role in fostering the implementation of industrial activities in Antioquia.[1] More importantly, however, he is not convinced that these factors explain enough: returns in agriculture were still high. 'The resolve to begin factory manufacture', writes Ospina Vásquez, 'is not easily explained "as a function" of purely economic motives.'[2] The alternatives remained attractive; thus Ospina Vásquez falls back finally on the peculiarity of the *modo de ser* of the first entrepreneurs.

Mining experience, particularly the experience with joint ventures, may have been important, but only some 40 per cent of all the gold mined in Colombia came from Antioquia. The main source had been Cauca with mine ownership centered in Popayán, the most traditional of all Colombian cities.[3] Gold mining in Antioquia was in some cases hard rock rather than placer and was consequently more complicated and possibly more capital using, particularly after 1850. But it would appear that the joint venture institution which had been established in Antioquia was the element which differentiated mining [there from other parts of Colombia.

A complete theory should provide not only an analysis of all the contributing factors which may be of interest to gain a balanced view; it should contain as well a notion of that crucial and to some extent immediate impulse which changed people's attitudes about the range of possibilities. Ospina Vásquez' book does provide a broad picture of important forces contributing to the change from decline (1850–90) to growth which emerges with coffee expansion and early industrialization. Yet he leaves a residue of doubt as to the completeness of his scheme. There is some illogical jump from the traditional agrarian society to the

---

[1] Ospina Vásquez, *Industria y protección*, p. 310.
[2] Ospina Vásquez, *Industria y protección*, p. 309.
[3] Rodolfo Segovia, 'Crown Policy and the Precious Metals in New Granada'. See also Vicente Restrepo, *Estudio sobre las minas de oro y de plata de Colombia* (Bogotá 1952).

one trying to industrialize. Ospina Vásquez is unable to explain this jump.

Moreover, the picture he presents fails to recognize growth taking place in other areas as well. Medellín's cotton textile industry was certainly ahead of other areas – Bogotá, Barranquilla and Cali in particular – but those areas developed in a different pattern with their main industrial activities linked to food processing for the domestic market. Though they lagged to some extent, one would be giving a false picture of the timing of industrial development to say that Medellín preceded other areas by many years. At the time of the 1945 census of industry the Antioqueño region led in the total value added by manufacture but the lead was not so great as to indicate unrivaled dominance. The balanced growth of cities since the early part of this century indicated that no premium attached to leadership which could prevent development in other locales.

The tie between the psychological-personality theory of Hagen and the rather more usual approach taken by Ospina Vásquez is clearly brought out in the following excerpt of a letter from Ospina Vásquez to this author:

I thought, when I read Hagen's book, that his explanation tied in rather well with the one I was setting forth (at least 'a medias palabras': my work was descriptive not theoretical). He had, of course, stated the case much more explicitly (he was not writing a book about the tariff: his avowed object was to explain why and how industrialization had got its first good start in Colombia). His explanation was rather sternly psychological, and I thought that was all to the good. He singled out for consideration as important factors, within his psychological frame, some of the factors I had found particularly significant. He went one step further than I did, an important step indeed: he elaborated on the psychology itself, and in a way I find rather convincing. I think he has some of the capacities of the novelist that I suggested (in the introduction to *Industria y protección*) should be, or could profitably be, applied to the case of Antioquia's industrialization. I am not quite certain that I would give *status deprivation* all the importance Hagen gives it. In any case, it is a very important factor. It was and still is. It is perhaps a modal form of the search for prestige which is a very important element in the psychological workings of promoters and pioneers; it may be the specific form which the craving for prestige takes, at the deep level, in the case of the Antioqueños. If this is the case, I think that Hagen has shown great insight, an amount of insight that is very rare indeed among economists. He would have brought out the peculiar cast in our modo de ser that elicited the not-quite-to-be-expected response to a certain set of circumstances, a response that is very difficult to explain if we suppose that it was worked out with paper and pencil, on a pesos and centavos basis only.

So he went further than I dared to go, but up to a point we had been going together. It was my idea to take the psychological data as given, as the basic data in the problem, and to work them up, along with the other ones, into a complicated ('money-powered') model. (I had broached the subject in the Introduction to *Industria y*

Expansion of coffee

protección and elsewhere in that book.) Hagen went in a different direction: he tried
to get to the 'cause' by delving into the psychological depths.[1]

Hagen and Ospina Vásquez are both within a great tradition in the
economics profession which attributes a special and decisive role to entrepreneurial initiative. Safford agrees with the general principle which
accords a special role to the Antioqueños, but suggests that no special
psychological theory is required to explain that role. In contrast to the
commonly held conception that Antioquia was one of the poorest
regions of the country, Safford sets out to show that it was perhaps the
richest because of its dominance of gold mining. He states, for example,
that Antioquia had but 8 per cent of the population and 40 per cent (or
more) of exports at the end of the colonial period.[2] Moreover, the
greater local supply of money yielded a wage, price and profit structure
which was conducive to the formation of large holdings of wealth which
could be and were used to finance agricultural and commercial enterprise
throughout the country.[3] It was thus the special opportunity presented
by gold and mining which gave Antioquia a superior opportunity for
development. In this view any special psychological explanations are
redundant. But Safford goes even further to dispute the assertion of
Hagen that status deprivation actually existed for the Antioqueños.

Doubtless there has existed in Colombia a stereotype of the Antioqueño as a social
being. But the Antioqueños were not the only regional group that carried a stereotype.
The Colombians during the Republican epoch invented distinctive, often contemptu-
ous caricatures of the inhabitants of the various provinces, the concept of the Antioqueño being far from the worst. ... The Antioqueño was painted as a type very
close to the stereotype of the *santandereano*: serious, healthy, simple, plain, frank; a
hard worker who fought with equal vigor. Medardo Rivas, who employed a gang
of Antioqueños in order to clear the mountain on his tobacco estate in Guataquisito,
described with surprise their titanic industry; with respect, their honesty and honor
in economic agreement; and with consternation, their consumption of brandy and
machete fights. Among Bogotano writers, the emphasis on the willingness to work
of the Antioqueño did not signify a scornful attitude. On the contrary, work had in
the nineteenth century a positive value, at least it was paid lip service. It is noted, for
example, that *laboriosidad* was one of the words of praise most utilized in the obituary
notices of the Bogotá press.[4]

Hagen might argue in response that *denial* of expected status requires that
it be expected and that the racial configurations of the *pastusos* and
caucanos were not of a kind to lead them to expect anything but derision

---

[1] Letter, dated at Suba, D. E., Colombia, 3 December 1964.
[2] Safford, 'Significación de los Antioqueños', p. 60.
[3] Safford, 'Significación de los Antioqueños', p. 63.
[4] Safford, 'Significación de los Antioqueños', pp. 56–7; notes omitted.

from criollos and others who identified with them. In contrast to those groups the Antioqueños expected deference and did not receive it. But unfortunately for Hagen's case one can (and Safford does) mount impressive literary evidence of the esteem in which Antioqueños were held in the middle of the nineteenth century by other Colombians. The status-deprivation hypothesis is placed in doubt because of the lack of firm evidence for deprivation.

Still, there remains the view that there was a unique role played by Antioqueños in Colombian development because of their domination of mining activities. Yet this view does not depend on noting anything more extraordinary about the Antioqueños than that they took advantage of their opportunities. And once they enjoyed superiority of wealth, not only did the differentials between Antioquia and other regions grow, but 'internal imperialism' by Antioqueño merchants and bankers became the means of equilibrating interregional income levels.[1] It was the natural act of a capital-rich area to strike out in search of opportunities throughout the country. This search must have appeared to some as an intrusion. It was in that climate, according to Safford, that the surreptitious accusation of Jewish ancestry for the Antioqueños got its start.[2] Thus Safford reverses Hagen's theory of causation to make the semitic myth an effect of economic success.

But Safford's argument itself depends on a questionable reconstruction of the past. He asserts Antioqueño economic leadership whereas other authorities emphasize the region's backwardness in the colonial period and early nineteenth century. Certainly mining ventures were important to the Antioqueños, but Safford and more recently Alvaro López have exaggerated their importance. Mining technology, for example, was not of the kind which would produce the side effects Hagen, Ospina Vásquez, Safford and López attribute to it. The placer mines were mostly small, scattered operations with the largest managed and funded by Englishmen.[3] Moreover, technological advance in mining seemed to depend not on innovation among indigenous entrepreneurs but on the skills of English engineers who came with English companies. Parsons mentions the Cornish or Antioqueño stamp mill and the 'Antioqueño table' as two

---

[1] The complementary movement of Antioqueño merchants and loans to Bogotá is analogous to complementary international factor movements which supposedly lead toward factor-price equalization.

[2] Safford, 'Significación de los Antioqueños', p. 67, holds that references to the semitic origins of Antioqueños were not current in Bogotá before the 1840s.

[3] See Rippy, 'The Peak of British Investment in Latin American Mines', *Inter-American Economic Affairs*, II: 1 (41–8), 1948.

principal elements in the production process which were developed by European mining engineers.[1] The first large mining syndicate, La Sociedad Zancudo, was founded in 1851, i.e. even after Montoya, Saenz y Cia. had taken over management of the tobacco monopoly. The marketing organization for the export monopoly took temporal precedence over the Zancudo group. It is not hard to imagine that it was a more complicated operation and hence proved in the end to provide a better example for subsequent industrial organization than did the mining syndicates. Certainly the riskiness of export activities in lowland agricultural products was no less than that for mining enterprises in the nineteenth century; the special role attached to mining may be attractive for a number of reasons, but I see little support for the view that such organizations alone provided the model for Antioqueño industrial organization after 1900. If for no other reason, the temporal break between indigenous mining enterprise in the middle of the nineteenth century and the establishment of large manufacturing plants for cotton textiles is altogether too great. It is broken, moreover, by a dramatic expansion of foreign investment in mining activities by British and North American engineers.

The technical character of mining could make it at once a highly profitable enterprise for a few lucky individuals and distinctly lacking in linkages which would promote development in ancillary activities. For example, although much of the machinery used in mining in the nineteenth century was made in Antioquia, there was never sufficient demand to induce the expansion of a metal products industry to grow beyond the simple machine-shop stage. Mining activities apparently employed 10 per cent of the Antioqueño labor force in 1870,[2] but the industry was still not large enough to induce industrial growth. Any reference to the large fortunes which were apparently based on mining in Antioquia must be tempered with a realization that such a risky venture must have entailed great losses as well. Certainly the few who were lucky and smart did find themselves in a position to invest and loan large sums throughout Colombia. They pursued portfolio diversification to reduce their risks and at the same time were moving capital away from where it was plentiful (Antioquia) to places where it was relatively scarce (Bogotá, the north coast).

Yet these observations far from prove that Antioquia was a rich province. All they show is that income and wealth were concentrated in a few

---

[1] Parsons, *Antioqueño Colonization*, p. 56.
[2] *Anuario estadístico*, 1875. Percentage calculated by author; area covered includes the Chocó. Parsons has noted that many workers in placer mining were women.

hands and were probably very unequally distributed. One might speculate that the southward movement of the Antioqueño frontier in the second half of the nineteenth century was partially a response to inequality and limited opportunity in the older mining areas. Safford counters this view by reference to data for the colonial period which he suggests indicate real wages in Antioqueño mining roughly two-thirds above highland agriculture.[1] If mining wages were that much above agricultural wages, it would certainly suggest greater general well-being in Antioquia than in other parts of Colombia. Moreover, the subsequent pre-eminence of Antioquia in per capita output might be thought to stem from an initial advantage in income level which only grew greater in absolute terms. But available data do not confirm Safford's generalization. The agricultural wages to which he refers were for 1727 rather than 1780.[2] Since agricultural wages rose in the eighteenth century, there may have been no real wage differential between eastern agricultural and Antioqueño mining. Data for the 1880s indicate a nominal wage differential in favor of mines, but since nearly all mining camps were isolated, costs of foodstuffs probably equalized real wages.[3]

One important set of qualifications must be considered before accepting the view that Antioquia was at least no better off in terms of levels of living than were other regions of the country. The region was achieving a much more rapid rate of population growth in the century 1780–1880 than were other Colombian regions. Before 1780 Antioquia was growing in population at about one per cent per annum, a rate not very different from the rest of the country. But in the period mentioned the rate of population growth rose to between 2·5 and 3 per cent per annum.[4] One might hold that this demographic upsurge is itself a sign of economic development. In contrast to that view, however, is one which refers to increasing evidence from other countries which indicates that the rate of population growth may accelerate well before economic development begins:

There is a suggestion (in the records of the United States before 1850, of Sweden before the 1880s, even of Great Britain before the 1820s) that the acceleration in

[1] Safford, 'Significación de los Antioqueños', p. 63.
[2] This observation may be confirmed by reference to Ospina Vásquez, *Industria y protección*, p. 15. The listed wage is, moreover, a minimum and not a maximum as Safford states. Elsewhere in his work Ospina Vásquez shows that agricultural wages rose between 1727 and the end of the eighteenth century so that Safford's wage differential is probably illusory.
[3] See Dawson, 'Labor in Colombia', *American Consular Reports*.
[4] The data and interpretations of them are discussed in Alvaro López T., 'Migración y cambio social en Antioquia durante el siglo diez y nueve', CEDE, Facultad de Economía, Universidad de los Andes, Monograph 25 (Bogotá, July 1968).

the rate of growth of population is initiated before that in growth of per capita income: the swarming of population, to use the demographers' term, is such that despite the technological changes the rise in total income can barely keep up with or only slightly exceeds the increase in numbers. It is only with some lag, as the high rate of population growth becomes stabilized or begins to decline and as the process of industrialization gets into full swing, that a significant increase in the rate of growth of per capita income is attained. ... It is, therefore, in this phase, that many 'secular' decisions are made that have a lasting effect on the rate, pattern, and characteristic of economic growth unfolded through the later decades.[1]

If events in Antioquia proceded in the same sequence as outlined above by Kuznets, then the upsurge of population may have been the necessary prelude to rapid economic change.

This point might not have required so much emphasis were it not for the inordinate role assigned to mining and its related activities as a stimulus to Antioqueño development.[2] It has been argued, I think without firm basis, that Antioquia was ahead of other areas as early as the eighteenth century (Safford) and certainly in 1880 (López). And it appears that much of the evidence adduced by these writers for early precedence in Antioquia is based on only two kinds of data – population growth rates above the national average and the expansion of gold output. If we may reasonably assign to the acceleration of population growth the role of predecessor to improvements in the level of living, then only the expansion of gold output remains as a significant indicator of early economic development. Recognizing however that the expansion of gold production was far from exclusive to the Antioqueño region there is less justification to regard these data as indicative of an acceleration in economic development or even as necessarily implying improvements (over other regions) in the level of living. As the data in Table 7 indicated earlier, Colombian gold production was, in the middle of the nineteenth century, below levels of output achieved in the eighteenth as well as the twentieth centuries. In the years 1801–10 average annual production was about 160,000 fine ounces; in the 1940s the average exceeded 500,000, but in the years between 1810 and 1885 the highest decade average achieved was under 150,000 fine ounces.[3] Certainly gold production continued to expand, and some interesting innovations in business organization and joint stock ownership ('the association of equals' to which Ospina Vásquez refers) can be attri-

---

[1] Simon Kuznets, *Economic Growth and Structure* (New York 1965), p. 21.

[2] I refer of course to the publications by Safford and Alvaro López which despite their great merits push the period of Antioqueño economic development farther back into the past than it belongs.

[3] See the brief discussion of data and sources above in Chapter 2. Over the years 1851–69 average annual output was 113,000 ounces.

buted to Antioqueño experience with mining. But neither the quantitative expansion nor qualitative changes indicate that the principal thrust of Antioqueño development occurred because of the mining experience or during the middle half of the nineteenth century, i.e. from roughly 1825 to 1875.

Despite the several arguments, offered and discussed here, it is difficult to credit the Antioqueños with a superior level of living at any time prior to 1885. Yet by 1953 Antioquia clearly ranked first among Colombian regions in per capita product.[1] The forward surge of the region and its people must then be a phenomenon of the period since 1885.

Parsons leads us to a different explanation of Colombian development. It is an explanation which still emphasizes the peculiar contribution of the Antioqueños but does so by reference to the special opportunity presented by coffee. The *cafe suave* bush found an ecological niche in Antioquia and the Antioqueños were there ready to take advantage of it. And, in Parsons' view Antioqueño experience with the southward movement of the frontier prepared them for new opportunities with coffee. Objective conditions encased the Antioqueños in a relationship with the land of which they could take good advantage. This is essentially a geographer's description of the events surrounding the transition of Antioquia from a backward to a relatively advanced region of Colombia.

There can be little doubt about the swiftness with which coffee came to Antioquia ... and to Colombia. When the railroad opened interior Brazil in 1852, coffee was not even on the horizon as an important Colombian export.[2] Strange as it may seem now, the coffee house was practically unknown in Colombia in 1850. Tea and chocolate were more common beverages.

The first date for which there exist estimates of Colombian coffee production is 1874. The total crop was about 114,000 sacks. In that year 90 per cent of the crop was grown in Santander. Table 22 shows dramatically how the center of gravity shifted from Santander to Antioquia thereafter. Production increased in Santander, Cundinamarca and Tolima but nowhere as fast as in the areas of Antioqueño colonization. Just prior to World War I the Antioqueño region was producing 35 per cent of Colombia's crop. In the decade after its opening in 1893 coffee exports via the Ferrocarril de Antioquia grew by more than 18 per cent

---

[1] See the report of the Misión economía y humanismo headed by Father Luis LeBret, which estimated per capita product for principal regions of the country in 1953.
[2] See Stanley Stein, *Vassouras* (Harvard 1957).

per annum.[1] Antioquia's share in Colombian coffee production reached 46·9 per cent by the time of the Coffee Census of 1932. By that time Santander's share had fallen to 12 per cent even though production had quadrupled since the 1870s.

From the point of view of economic and social change, the most important feature of the introduction of coffee as an export product was that it drew significant numbers of the population directly into the market. The older hacienda operations introduced only a small portion of the population into a money economy. Coffee production induced a shifting over from non-market to market orientations for thousands of peasant families. Smallholders dealt directly with urban buyers of coffee and sellers of consumer goods.

Table 22 *Colombia: production of coffee by regions, selected years, 1874–1956* (per cent distribution by regions).

Region	1874	1913	1932	1943	1953–6 (3-year ave.)
1. Bolívar, Atlántico	0·2	2·4	0·6	0·5	1·3
2. Antioquia, Caldas	2·2	35·4	46·9	48·9	49·2
3. Cauca, Nariño, Valle	1·7	7·8	12·4	16·7	16·5
4. Tolima, Huila	0·9	5·5	14·4	15·5	17·9
5. Cundinamarca, Boyacá	7·5	18·7	12·4	9·6	9·9
6. Santander	87·6	30·2	12·2	8·9	5·1
Other areas	—	—	1·0	—	—
Total	100·0	100·0	100·0	100·0	100·0
Thousands of 60-kilo sacks	114	1,085	3,453	5,177	5.944

Sources: see the Note on Sources.

There were some 150,000 coffee farms in Colombia in 1932 (the year of the first coffee census), most of which were under 10 hectares. In contrast to the organizational structure of coffee growing in Brazil or Central American countries (El Salvador for example) a large share of total coffee production as well as a large number of producing farms were smallholder peasant operations. The Lorenz curve in Figure 9 indicates visually the greater equality of coffee farm size in Colombia when compared to El Salvador. Although the data refer to the 1950s, the earliest year for which comparable data are available, the Colombian distribution would

[1] Alejandro López, *Estadística de Antioquia* (Medellín 1914), p. 150.

not have been more unequal in earlier decades. This difference in the organizational structure of coffee production is a major explanation for the favorable impact of coffee growing on Colombian development.

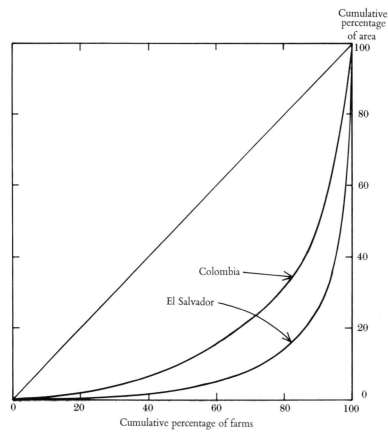

Figure 9 Lorenz curve comparing coffee farm and land distribution in Colombia and El Salvador, 1950s. *Source:* UN ECLA/FAO, *Coffee in Latin America. I. Colombia and El Salvador.*

The apparent average production per farm in 1932 was about 23 bags of 60 kilos per annum, an output requiring perhaps 0·6 to 0·8 hectares. Only a very small area was required for a significant output.[1]

[1] I assume each coffee bush requires 4 square meters of space and an average output per bush of 1·5 to 2 pounds of hulled beans. These assumptions were checked informally with J. J. Parsons.

Expansion of coffee

There were probably about 5,000 producing units which grew coffee in the mid-1870s, most of those located in the eastern highlands.[1] Assuming a rural family size of six (a conservative estimate) about 30,000 farm family members did at that time have some tie to the market through the sale of coffee and purchase of consumer goods with the money from coffee sales. A half-century later some 900,000 members of farm families were linked through coffee to the market. Since Colombia's rural population had reached some five million by 1932, the coffee-growing population made up about 18 per cent of the rural total. This percentage underestimates the number directly affected by the coffee-market tie since the larger farms (as well as many smaller ones) employed non-family members for certain agricultural tasks (cultivation and harvesting principally) and in some cases had a regular year-round labor force. We may estimate that in the half-century from the 1870s to the early 1930s a fifth to a quarter of Colombia's rural population was brought out of subsistence cultivation and into the market by coffee. No other substantive economic change in Colombian economic history can have been of such overriding social importance.[2]

The expansion of production was a necessary but not sufficient condition for great social impact. For example, if an equivalently large and rapid expansion of output had occurred in geographically marginal areas in which capital, labor and entrepreneurship were brought from abroad, then there may have been no substantial effects felt in Colombian society. Such a case was described at length in Levin's study of guano exports from Peru in the years 1840–80. Had expansion occurred, alternatively, in large-scale agricultural units then only a small proportion of the producing population would have established direct ties with the market. Management and entrepreneurial functions would have remained in the hands of a few who could act as filters between the rural labor force and urban markets. The social characteristics of such plantation and hacienda systems have been discussed at length; they appear rarely to induce continuing economic and social change, having instead the qualities of a rigid social structure and non-innovative managerial attitudes. Colombian

[1] The estimate of 5,000 farms assumed that average output per farm was 23 kilos, the same as in 1932. Since land and capital requirements for that output are modest, it seems at least possible that such an average farm size existed even at the early stages of coffee production in Santander.

[2] Oliver La Farge noted a similar change in Guatemalan coffee growing. He regarded the advent of coffee production and export as the most significant source of change in Mayan history. 'Maya Ethnology: The Sequence of Cultures', in *The Maya and Their Neighbors* (New York 1940), pp. 281–91.

coffee expansion contrasts radically with these other prototypes of export economies.

The first stirrings of modern industrial activity came on the heels of the expansion of exports of coffee from the Antioqueño region. The first large-scale textile mill began production in 1906 with 102 looms and 300 employees. By 1910 capacity had doubled, the plant was using about 300 horsepower of electricity generated by a nearby waterfall and employment had passed 500. Coltejer got under way in 1907; by 1915 this company, with assets valued at Ps$470,000, had 140 looms in operation and more than 150 employees. A third mill began production in 1913 with 120 employees and produced 15,000 yards of cloth per week. Seven other firms employed about 290 people in 1915 and operated about 150 looms. Just a decade after its inception Antioquia's cotton industry was the largest in the country.[1] In 1918 industrial investment and employment in the commercial district of Medellín were estimated at 3·19 million pesos and 6,000 employed, respectively. P. L. Bell, United States Trade Commissioner, who made this estimate, stated that 'recent developments in the increase of textile mills in Medellín and its district ... tend to put that city in first place as the manufacturing center of the country'.[2]

As incomes rose in the export sector with rapid expansion of coffee exports, the level of demand for industrial products rose. 'Hence', states the ECLA *Study*, 'it does not seem to have been by accident that the first industrial nucleus was formed in Antioquia. ... It was the principal coffee-producing centre, thereby receiving a major share of the benefits accruing from exports and possessing the greatest real possibilities of financing investment in the manufacturing sector'.[3] Particularly in the case of Antioquia's cotton textile industry does this line of reasoning seem important: as importing firms were faced with growing demand for imported textiles, they must have seen the budding opportunities for domestic production in large-scale plants. Moreover, they were financially prepared to undertake domestic production with available capital originating in the profits from trade.[4]

[1] See Ospina Vásquez, *Industria y protección*, pp. 340–1; *Informe del ministro de hacienda, 1916*, xcvii–cxiii; Enrique Echavarría, *Historia de los textiles en Antioquia* (Medellín 1943). The author was a nephew of the founder of Coltejer and played a role in the early growth of that firm.

[2] *Colombia: A Commercial and Industrial Handbook*, United States Department of Commerce, Bureau of Foreign and Domestic Commerce, Special Agents Series, no. 206 (Washington 1921), pp. 180, 235.   [3] ECLA *Study*, p. 252.

[4] Hirschman in his *Strategy of Economic Development* (New Haven 1957) p. 174, suggests that this kind of response is typical of less developed countries in the first spurt of industrialization.

Expansion of coffee

When one attempts to draw together the threads of causation for Antioquia's economic and industrial development, it appears that a fairly traditional explanation is in order. The rapid growth of a new export product raised income levels and generated new demands for imported and locally produced goods of all kinds. There were special opportunities for the production of cotton textiles because high transport costs tended to keep the local price of imports high; thus there was considerable encouragement to local production. When this factor was added to a protective tariff instituted in 1905, local manufacturing had a good chance to grow. Moreover, Antioquia lacked the entrenched artisan class of Santander and Cauca so that there was relatively little opposition to factory manufacture.

Capital and entrepreneurial skills were made available to the new industries directly from the export sector: the same family which began the first textile enterprise was headed by the owner of one of the largest coffee exporting and processing houses. This same individual ran one of the largest importing firms. With such a wide variety of economic enterprises held within one family, neither supply of capital nor of managerial skills proved to be bottlenecks preventing the expansion of manufacturing.

The theory put forward by Parsons seems in some respects the most tenable of those considered which emphasize the special contribution and role of the Antioqueños in Colombian economic development. Those which require some reference to psychological differences between the Antioqueños and other Colombians too often lack the data necessary for careful testing. Moreover, they contain in them the seeds of 'national character' theories which are probably not very fruitful for scientific investigations into the causes and nature of social and economic change.

Those theories which emphasize the nineteenth-century experience in mining are of considerable value in bringing to light the important premodern phase of Antioqueño development; however, they go too far in several cases in attempting to show that Antioquia was already in the nineteenth century ahead of other regions of Colombia, a state of affairs which practically no quantitative data tends to confirm.

But any theory of Colombian economic development must explain more than the Antioqueño colonization, the expansion of coffee growing on Antioqueño slopes and the emergence of cotton textile manufacture in Medellín. Recall that over half of Colombia's coffee production in 1932 took place outside Antioquia; and there were important manufacturing establishments in Barranquilla and Cali early in this century, not to speak of Bogotá. Although some of these enterprises were begun and managed by Antioqueños, many more were in the hands of other Colombians who were beginning their own indigenous industrial revolution. Still others were of course in the hands of foreign-born immigrants or even of foreign-owned corporations. These elements cannot obliterate the fact that industrial development (not to speak of economic activities in banking, commerce, retail trade, plantation agriculture and others) was begun before the 1930s by Colombians who were not Antioqueños. Any explication of Colombian economic development in the formative years between 1880 and 1930 must take these activities – their successes and failures – into account as well as the events in Antioquia.

THE EXTERNAL SECTOR

I suggested above that a garden-variety economic explanation could be offered for Antioqueño economic development: as much can be said for the general wave of improvement which initiated the modern phase of economic development in Colombia in general. The growth-rate of exports accelerated to over 11 per cent per annum for the decade 1910–19 and remained at nearly 8 per cent per annum between the cyclical peak years of 1920 and 1928. As Figure 10 illustrates, export growth rates for

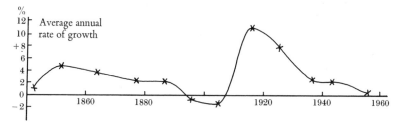

Figure 10 Colombia: rates of expansion of exports, 1834–1960.

the score of years between 1909 and 1928 were decidedly above those ever before or subsequently experienced on a sustained basis in Colombia. The specific data on which Figure 10 is based are presented for closer inspection in Table 23. Data used are all from Colombian sources and were originally prepared well in advance of the study of other-country data discussed elsewhere in this book. However, I have shown elsewhere that for the period considered there are not such substantial differences between Colombian export data and that revealed in the compilations of other countries as to vitiate the growth rate results recorded here. The differences between the rates of the years 1910–28 and those of earlier and later periods is too great to be hidden by any deficiencies in the data. Moreover, the growth-rates presented are between fairly distant peaks or troughs of data which have been smoothed by a weighted five-year moving average. Only during the earlier tobacco boom of the 1850s did growth-rates approach even 5 per cent over any extended period.

Table 23   *Rates of export expansion, selected periods, 1834–1960.*

Period	Cyclical position	Interval in years	Average annual rate of growth (per cent)
1834/8–42/5	—	7·5	0·6
1842/5–54/9	—	13	4·8
1854/9–69	—	13	3·9
1869–84	T–T	15	3·2
1880–90	P–P	10	2·4
1891–7/9	—	7	−0·5
1897–9–1907/9	—	10	−1·5
1910–19	T–T	9	11·4
1920–8	P–P	8	7·9
1930–40	T–T	10	2·7
1938–46	P–P	8	2·7
1946–53	P–P	7	1·7
1950/2–58/60	—	8	0·5

T–T: trough-to-trough of five-year weighted moving average.
P–P: peak-to-peak of five-year weighted moving average.

Sources: Colombia, Contraloria general de la República, *Anuario de comercio exterior*, various years, especially 1915; Banco de la República, *Informe anual*. Data and sources have been summarized as part of the *Historical Statistics of Colombia* project of the Conference on Latin American History.

These data show that the export expansion of the 1910–28 period was a singular event in the economic history of Colombia. Neither before nor since has a major sector of the economy been able to expand at such a rate, bringing with it a myriad of opportunities and changes throughout the domestic economy. According to estimates of ECLA in the years between 1925 and 1930 coffee exports constituted about 18 per cent of gross domestic product – a larger economic sector than manufacturing, government services or transportation.[1] In less than a score of years Colombia developed an export economy.

Although Colombia's export economy is a twentieth-century phenomenon, I would judge exports to have served the very nineteenth-century function of providing an engine of growth.[2] Whatever problems one may now associate with monoculture and dependence on a single crop, it is hard to imagine a more effective means for permitting rapid economic expansion than the rapid growth of an export sector such as coffee. It has become altogether too easy in the post-World War II era to blame the economic difficulties of Colombia (and other Third-World countries as well) on an 'unnatural' dependence on some particular agricultural export product. When Colombia was enjoying an expansion of the country's share of total world exports of coffee, few would have suggested that too much emphasis was being placed on the crop. Coffee brought with it an era of change. Its effects proved to be free of the vagaries of political change; it was a more powerful cause of development in Colombia than was any individual government policy or any private entrepreneurial decision. Of course in the years after 1930 the country had to face the problem of transforming its economy to take into account the fact that the market share was by then so large, and local costs were so high, that earlier high growth-rates could not be maintained any longer. In effect the coffee boom was over by 1930 as Colombia and the rest of the world's coffee producers (save the smaller producers of Central America and Africa) faced an inelastic world demand for their product. But the problems of the late 1950s and early 1960s could hardly have been anticipated in the 1920s when Colombia hitched its star to coffee and enjoyed the Dance of the Millions.[3]

The achievement of economic expansion was not entirely a Colombian phenomenon: to some extent foreign capital and immigrants participated in these events. But the limited ways in which such participation did occur must give some satisfaction to the more nationalistic Colombians.

[1] ECLA *Study*, Statistical Appendix, Tables 1, 14, 27.
[2] This last phrase is generally attributed to Sir Dennis Robertson who pointed out that when a local economy is considered in isolation the rate of growth of output of any sector (as well as the economy as a whole) is effectively limited by the natural rate of growth of population and the slow expansion of per capita consumption. It is only when greater demand elasticities can be achieved through international trade that very high growth-rates will be experienced by a local economy. English economic growth was in large part achieved by the rapid expansion of textile exports.
[3] This last phrase even worked its way into the subtitle of Vernon Lee Fluharty's study of Colombian politics. It has previously given title to one chapter in J. Fred Rippy's *The Capitalists and Colombia* (New York 1932).

Expansion of coffee

Total foreign capital in Colombia in 1914 (including both direct investments and external debt) may be estimated as about $60 million. If we assume a population of 5·2 million people, with per capita income of $100, and a capital-output ratio of 4·4:1, then the foreign component of the total capital stock was about 6 per cent.[1] Although this contribution may appear small, the proportions must have been even smaller

Table 24 *Total foreign direct investment in Colombia, by sector of investment, 1914* (millions of dollars).

Sector	Dollars
Transport	24
Mining	18
Agriculture	16
Miscellaneous	2
Total	60

Source: J. Fred Rippy, *Globe and Hemisphere*, p. 38.

three decades earlier. Perhaps half of the foreign capital was concentrated in transport facilities – mainly railroads. There was virtually no foreign investment in manufacturing; thus the earliest phase of industrial development was achieved almost completely without the assistance of foreign capital, requiring only the help of technicians who set up and operated the first mills for Colombian owners. Since investments in agriculture (bananas) and mining (placers) were physically in Colombia but far from population centers and generally unrelated to the domestic economy (banana plantations did use much labor on the north coast), even those investments were not decisive in the achievement of development.

A crucial event with political and economic dimensions occurred in 1922 with final ratification of the Thomson-Urrutia treaty. That agreement between the United States and Colombia provided that the U.S. expressed regrets over the secession of Panama, and Colombia in turn received a $25 million indemnity as compensation for any injustices

[1] The ECLA *Study*, pp. 29–30, using a different procedure, estimated the foreign-owned component of the capital stock at 5·9 per cent in 1925. Their data imply a capital-output ratio of 4·8.

occasioned by the U.S. role in the Panama incident of 1903. The Colombians in turn decided to devote this fund to internal improvements. The settlement, along with the report of the Kemmerer mission which recommended creation of the Banco de la República, so increased investor confidence in Colombia that the country was able, in the years between

Table 25   *Colombian loans floated on the New York market, 1920–8* (millions of dollars).

Period	Amount
1920–25	20·4
1926–28	215·4

Recipient of loans	
Central government	75·4
Agricultural mortgage bank	16·0
Departments	69·8
Municipalities	30·3
Private banks	21·9
Mining companies	1·5
Oil companies	20·8
Total	235·8

Sources: Adapted from J. Fred Rippy, *The Capitalists and Colombia* (New York 1939), pp. 156–9.

1922 and 1929, to sell more than $235 million in bonds and similar securities. National, departmental and municipal governments were all successful in their search for funds in Wall Street. Funds for internal improvement were made available on a scale unprecedented in Colombian history. As Table 25 indicates, most sales took place in the second half of the 1920s. This was just at the time that the import expansion was catching up with the export expansion and tending to produce constraints via the balance of trade on the development possibilities. The boom which might otherwise have been cut short in the years 1926 or 1927 was thus sustained until 1928 when the bond market collapse of late summer ended Colombia's Dance of the Millions.

Immigration was never of great importance during this period: no more than 100 or so migrants came to Colombia annually in the 1880s; about 200 in the 1890s and first decade of this century and perhaps 400 annually between 1908 and 1919.[1] During this same time-period some 50,000 Italians migrated to Brazil annually; Beyer writes that 'Immigration, although encouraged by acts of Congress and generally viewed as the nation's most pressing need, has been negligible. During the years 1887–1936 while Brazil admitted over 2,800,000 immigrants, only a handful of farmers came from abroad to settle the rugged frontiers of Colombia.'[2] In four decades Colombia received fewer than 10,000 migrants, a minute fraction of European migration to Latin America.[3]

Unlike the development of Brazil and the State of São Paulo in particular, there was practically no migration to Colombia which would have expanded the labor force and hence permitted a rapid growth of output based on cheap labor. Nonetheless, immigrants have played a significant role in the development of Colombia. A long-time director of the Banco de Bogotá was the German Guillermo Kopp Castello; he was responsible in part for the development of Cervecería Bavaria, presently the largest manufacturing firm in the country. The term *turco* referring broadly to Middle Easterners is no stranger to Colombia where many have succeeded in manufacturing and trade. Santiago Eder, scion of the family which has operated the country's largest sugar plantation since the late nineteenth century migrated to the Cauca Valley in the 1860s.[4] These scattered examples point to the importance of the foreign-born in Colombian economic development. But at the same time they cannot detract from the decisive role played in that development by native Colombians – not only Antioqueños but natives of other regions as well.

The expansion of international trade was more than a simple expansion

---

[1] These estimates are based on data computed from Walter Willcox (ed.), *International Migrations*, vol. I, *Statistics* (New York: National Bureau for Economic Research, 1929). Detailed references and computations of immigrants by country of origin are presented in Appendix Table I–C–1 of McGreevey, 'The Economic Development of Colombia'.

[2] Beyer, 'The Colombian Coffee Industry', p. 157. See also Franceschini, *L'Imigrazione Italiana Nell'America del Sud* (Rome 1908), pp. 131–5. Figures there given are for gross migration from Italian ports and do not include estimates for returning individuals or for those who have left the country of original destination.

[3] European migration to Latin America between 1800 and 1950 is said to have totaled some ten million: Italian, four million; Spanish, four million; Portuguese, two million. See Richard Robbins, 'Myth and Realities of International Migration into Latin America', *Annals of the American Academy*, 316: 102–110 (March 1958), p. 103.

[4] See Phanor Eder, *El fundador, Santiago M. Eder* (Bogotá 1959), p. 74. On German immigrants see Horacio Rodríguez Plata, *La inmigración alemana al estado soberano de Santander en el siglo XIX* (Bogotá 1968).

of the cultivated area devoted to coffee. Other products also participated in the expansion of Colombian exports – even from a date early in the twentieth century. The country's principal exports at five-year intervals since 1885 are shown in Table 26. Coffee's share has been rising almost steadily since it first took hold at the end of the nineteenth century. But oil has also been of sustained importance as have bananas.

Table 26 *Percentage distribution of principal exports from Colombia, 1874–9, 1955–9.*

Period	Coffee	Bananas	Petroleum	Precious metals	Hides	Other
1874–9	7	—	—	28	4	61
1905–9	39	4	—	21	8	28
1910–14	46	9	—	19	9	17
1915–19	54	6	—	16	12	12
1920–4	74	6	—	12	4	4
1925–9	69	6	17	5	3	—
1930–4	59	6	19	13	2	1
1935–9	54	5	20	17	2	2
1940–4	64	1	16	13	1	5
1945–9	73	2	15	5	1	4
1950–4	79	2	14	2	—	3
1955–9	78	4	14	1	—	3

Source: Banco de la República, *XXXVIII y XXXIX Informe anual del gerente de la junta directiva*, Part II, pp. 202, 203, 216.

The export of bananas and oil seems to me to deserve less attention than coffee largely because they failed to make the same kind of impact on the domestic economy. Bananas grow on Colombia's north coast and in a small area in the south of the country not too distant from the Pacific. Both operations were in the hands of foreigners who little concerned themselves with the domestic economy, seeking only to assure themselves of a ready supply of labor at low wages, and a minimum of interference with their operations. The United Fruit Company, for its banana planta-tions in the district south of Santa Marta, restored the port of that coastal town, and built a railroad with necessary spur lines in the banana zone to service their enterprise. The banana railroad was not good for any-thing else, ending some distance from the Magdalena River to which it would have had to connect if the route were to be of use to highland Colombia. *La Companía* as it is known to north-coast residents was an alien element to the local economy and society. It is no accident that the first major strike and labor violence in Colombia was directed against the policies of the company in the banana zone.[1] But if banana exports provided a major source of employment in the north-coast region, oil exports provided almost nothing at all. Few were employed, taxes were negligible and the substantial entries of export earnings were largely remittable to the foreign owners of the exporting companies. For each dollar of coffee exports there was generated immensely more in local activities than from a dollar of either banana or oil exports. It is for that reason that these two products play such a minor role in the economic history of Colombia.

These thoughts would suggest that a simple analysis of the merchandise balance of trade of Colombia in the years 1886–1930 is of limited value. Coffee may have been an important stimulant to development via the derived demand for other domestically produced products and the generation of useful linkages; but other exports were not equally useful in this respect. Consequently, aggregate trade data might fail to provide any useful information about the course of economic change. Some activities – oil production, for example – permitted profit remittances abroad (unrecorded in merchandise trade balances) to be automatically extracted from the total output and hence provide no buying power for imports. Such direct remittances could easily have been handled internally within the vertically integrated international corporation. An expansion of oil exports thus had no unequivocal impact on Colombia's balance of payments: perhaps the total supply of foreign exchange would be increased, perhaps not. But for the years before 1930 both agricultural and petroleum investments were still growing; consequently, growing exports probably meant growing availability of foreign exchange and a real impact on the balance of payments not offset by immediate profit remittances. A look at the balance of merchandise trade is then both useful and informative about the course of change in the complete balance of payments.

The persistent deficit in the balance of trade observed for the latter part of the period 1845–85 continued into the twentieth century and until 1909. Total trade declined precipitously as a result of the war of 1899–1902. The balance of trade did not turn substantially to the plus side until 1911, then remained favorable for most years until 1924. The latter half of the 1920s was marked by substantial capital imports devoted to public improvements in transportation and urban facilities. Even the

[1] On this incident in 1928 see J. Fred Rippy, *The Capitalists and Colombia*; and Miguel Urrutia, *History of the Labor Movement in Colombia* (New Haven 1969).

peak year for exports by value in 1928 was exceeded by the unusually high imports for that year. By the end of the 1920s Colombia was decidedly more of a trading nation than it had been two decades earlier.

The rapid expansion of exports made possible an equivalent expansion of imports for a full score of years between 1909 and 1928. The balance of payments thus proved to be no serious constraint on economic development. The accumulated balance is theoretically equivalent to net claims by foreigners against home resources less local claims against foreign resources. However, other estimates of the sum of direct private foreign investment and foreign-held debt differ substantially from the data presented in Table 27. For example, earlier in this chapter I estimated foreign investment at only $60 million for 1914, whereas the accumulated balance was $195·3 million. For the end of the 1920s ECLA put the value of foreign-held assets at $540 million in 1950 dollars – equivalent to $355 million in 1929 prices.[1] My figures would indicate that foreign assets were about $208·4 million at the end of 1929. The accumulated balance appears to overstate foreign-held assets in 1914 and understate them in 1929. The differences may be attributed to several factors. (1) My estimates of the accumulated balance which begin in 1845 may have a consistent bias toward overstating the deficits in the commercial balance. Service charges are consistently included in imports; however, no service earnings are included in exports. (2) The estimate for 1914 foreign investment may be too low. (3) The accumulated balance does not take into account changes in official reserves; these were increased substantially in the latter half of the 1920s.[2] (4) Estimates of trade, 1910–30, are based entirely on Colombian data; the official estimates may as in earlier years underestimate imports. Even though I have adjusted for costs, insurance and freight, under-reporting of imports will not have been captured in my data for those years. (5) The estimates of foreign investment for 1929 are based on estimates of the transfer of financial rather than real resources, i.e. the stated value of foreign-held debt (see Table 25) plus direct investment, rather than the market value of real assets. Evidence on the movement of relative prices in Colombia and the United States in the years 1925–34 suggests that the transfer of financial resources implicit in the sale of bond issues did not result in the full transfer of complementary real resources. While prices were falling slightly in the United States between 1925 and 1928, they rose by more than 20 per cent in Colombia. The financial transfer increased Colombia's money supply enough to raise prices. The

---

[1] Deflated by U.S. implicit GNP deflator. See *HSUS*, p. 139, Series F-5.
[2] See ECLA *Study*, Appendix, Table 10.

price increase indicates that the quantity of money was growing more rapidly than the available supply of goods. Since it was the time lag between bond sale and the purchase of real resources which determined the loss due to inflation, one would need more detailed information in order to estimate the value of real resources transferred. They were certainly less than the stated value of foreign-held debt.

Further analysis of the accumulated-balance series will be essential before one can attach much confidence to the figures. However, if one

Table 27 *Estimated commercial balance of Colombia, 1886–1930* (millions of current U.S. dollars).

Year	Exports, f.o.b.			Imports, c.i.f.	Commercial balance	Accumulated balance
	Merchandise	Gold	Total			
1886	8·9	3·2	12·1	20·9	− 8·8	−138·5
1887	11·7	3·4	15·1	25·8	−10·7	−149·2
1888	10·2	3·9	14·1	26·1	−12·0	−161·2
1889	9·2	3·8	13·0	21·7	− 8·7	−169·9
1890	12·2	4·0	16·2	25·1	− 8·9	−178·8
1891	18·2	4·8	23·0	24·1	− 1·1	−179·9
1892	9·7	4·7	14·4	19·8	− 5·4	−185·3
1893	11·0	5·0	16·0	20·6	− 4·6	−189·9
1894	10·3	4·6	14·9	16·3	− 1·4	−191·3
1895	10·5	2·9	13·4	17·8	− 4·4	−195·7
1896	13·0	3·7	16·7	22·9	− 6·2	−201·9
1897	12·0	4·0	16·0	22·3	− 6·3	−208·2
1898	13·1	3·8	16·9	16·2	0·7	−207·5
1899	12·8	2·4	15·2	13·7	1·5	−206·0
1900	9·1	1·4	10·5	9·0	1·5	−204·5
1901	9·3	1·4	10·7	15·7	− 5·0	−209·5
1902	8·1	1·2	9·3	12·5	− 3·2	−212·7
1903	10·5	1·6	12·1	18·3	− 6·2	−218·9
1904	16·6	2·6	19·2	22·4	− 3·2	−222·1
1905	12·9	1·7	14·6	15·0	− 0·4	−222·5
1906	13·7	2·8	16·5	16·7	− 0·2	−222·7
1907	13·2	2·9	16·1	17·8	− 1·7	−224·4
1908	12·0	3·7	15·7	17·4	− 1·7	−226·1
1909	14·4	2·8	17·2	16·9	0·3	−225·8
1910	14·416	3·371	17·787	17·385	+ 0·4	−225·4
1911	18·539	3·837	22·376	18·109	+ 4·3	−221·1
1912	25·579	6·643	32·332	23·965	+ 8·3	−212·8
1913	29·903	4·412	34·315	28·536	+ 5·8	−207·0
1914	26·403	6·230	32·633	20·979	+11·7	−195·3

Table 27 – (*cont.*)

1915	25·602	5·977	31·579	17·841	+13·7	−181·6
1916	30·610	5·397	36·007	29·660	+ 6·3	−175·3
1917	31·915	4·825	36·740	24·751	+12·0	−163·3
1918	34·895	2·549	37·444	21·783	+15·7	−147·6
1919	78·125	0·886	79·011	47·452	+31·6	−116·0
1920	64·418	6·600	71·018	113·566	−42·6	−158·6
1921	53·236	9·806	63·042	37·047	+26·0	−132·6
1922	46·843	5·888	52·731	46·989	+ 5·7	−126·9
1923	55·995	4·253	60·248	67·208	− 7·0	−133·9
1924	84·246	1·919	86·165	62·251	+23·9	−110·0
1925	83·214	1·610	84·824	97·203	−12·4	−122·4
1926	110·195	1·522	111·717	123·974	−12·3	−134·7
1927	107·622	1·377	108·999	139·166	−30·2	−164·9
1928	132·502	1·104	133·606	162·381	−28·8	−193·7
1929	121·677	5·195	126·872	141·541	−14·7	−208·4
1930	104·225	9·063	113·288	70·382	+42·9	−165·5

Sources: 1886–1909: Based on adjusted trade data of four Colombian trading partners – England, U.S.A., France, Germany – and Colombian official statistics; 1910–30: Controlaria General de la República, *Anuario de comercio exterior*, various years. Official data were adjusted where necessary to conform to standard concepts of exports f.o.b. and imports c.i.f.

recalls that the series represents merely the balance of visible trade and is neither a summary of the current account nor of the balance of payments, it should still prove useful.

At the beginning of the export expansion of 1909, per capita exports from Colombia amounted to about $3·87. At the same time Cuban exports per capita were about $61, and those of Mexico were about $8·50.[1] The lack of exports (demonstrated by these great differences between three countries proximate to the United States) was surely a barrier to early industrialization. Since industrialization and import substitution required the importation of foreign technology and equipment, such a low level of exports per capita made growth of manufacturing most difficult.

The international comparisons for 1913 developed by Alfred Maizels indicate that per capita imports of manufactures into Colombia were only about two-thirds those of Brazil, despite the fact that the latter country probably had a lower per capita income. By 1929 the comparison had

---

[1] All figures are in dollars of that year. Data for Colombia from sources herein cited; for Cuba: Dirección General de Estadística, *Comercio exterior, 1949–1950* (Havana 1951), p. 1, and Guerra y Sánchez et al., *Historia de la nación cubana*, IX (Havana 1952), 67; for Mexico: *Estadísticas económicas del Porfiriato* (El Colegio de México, Mexico 1960), pp. 152, 532; and Howard F. Cline, *The United States and Mexico* (Cambridge, Mass. 1965), p. 68.

changed dramatically. In that year Colombian imports of manufactures (of which a much larger percentage were by then capital goods) were a third higher on a per capita basis than those of Brazil.[1]

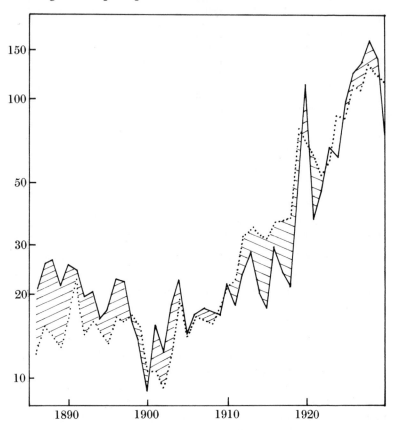

Figure 11 Colombia: imports and exports, 1886–1930 (millions of current dollars). Imports ———, Exports .....

At each stage of advance the scarcity of foreign exchange hindered further development. Those with access to foreign exchange through credits earned by the sale of exports had a clear advantage in the drive to industrialize. Exchange receipts earned in oil and bananas were controlled

[1] Alfred Maizels, *Industrial Growth and World Trade* (Cambridge, England 1963), Table A14, p. 443, A34, p. 463, E2, p. 533.

by foreign interests which had no interest in local manufacturing. Coffee alone provided the increment of exchange earnings which were to finance new equipment in cotton textiles and other manufacturing.

The limited advance of manufacturing in this period is indicated by the degree to which consumer goods output exceeded capital goods output. Hoffman suggests in *The Growth of Industrial Economies* that at most consumer goods output is five times as great as capital goods output in the first phases of industrialization.[1] From that point the ratio has fallen in all countries studied by Hoffman – in the most advanced to a $1:1$ relationship. The ratio was about $5.3:1$ in Colombia at the time of the 1953 industrial census.[2] For earlier years it was much higher – a sign of relative backwardness on Hoffman's international scaling.

In the mid-1920s only about 3 per cent of the active labor force was employed in modern manufacturing. Many of these workers were in small shops that were little different from artisan methods of production. That labor force produced about 7.5 per cent of gross product. The factory and its method had made little inroad in Colombia.[3]

The link between low per capita exports, a primitive industrial structure and general underdevelopment early in this century does not itself elicit special comment. The process by which these variables change is, however, of peculiar interest in trying to understand the mechanisms of economic growth. The Antioqueño case, with which we are most familiar through existing documentation, demonstrates that there was an intimate connection between export earnings and industrial investment. The timing of export expansion was attuned to the timing of industrial development.

(1) Imports of machinery on the Ferrocarril de Antioquia were about 32 tons per annum in the last five years of the nineteenth century but were over 520 tons per annum in the years 1909–13, the last for which I have data available in this form.[4] The availability of transport services which could bring machinery into the area at lower cost than pre-railway conditions encouraged industrialization. Since the growth of the railways of Colombia was closely correlated to the expansion of coffee exports

[1] Walther G. Hoffman, *The Growth of Industrial Economies* (trans. W. O. Henderson and W. H. Chaloner, Manchester 1958), p. 16.
[2] ECLA *Study*, pp. 264–74.
[3] Labor force and output estimates appear in the ECLA *Study*. Their investigations of manufacturing seem on inspection to be among the most exhaustive which they conducted on the Colombian economy. Thus the orders of magnitude presented here have a high probability of being correct.
[4] Alejandro López, *Estadística de Antioquia* (Medellín 1914), pp. 150–2.

Expansion of coffee

(as will be shown in Chapter 10), export expansion indirectly promoted industrial development through its demand for transport services.

(2) In a survey of industries in Medellín in 1922 a group of nine coffee processing plants employed about 1,400 workers. This branch of industry constituted the largest employer in manufacturing, exceeding textiles which were in second place with 815 workers. Although most employees in the coffee-threshing mills were women (95 per cent), the sex ratio was in the same direction in textile milling where 66 per cent of employees were women. Coffee processors constituted more than 40 per cent of the labor force recorded in the 1922 survey.[1] The quantitative importance of the export activity in creating a demand for processing activities makes an obvious connection between the two activities. Moreover, the urban labor force raised the volume of demand for industrial products.

(3) Exports expansion permitted a change in the composition of imports which made possible the import of capital goods to be used in manufacturing. For the years 1912–19 capital goods imports were on average 18·6 per cent of total imports; the share rose to 27·6 per cent in the 1920s.[2] Part of this increase must be attributed to the new availability of investment funds from bond sales used for the direct purchase of capital equipment; however, the capital goods share was rising even prior to the massive bond sales of 1926–8. Exports grew so rapidly in the score of years after 1910 that the demand for consumer imports was outstripped. Residual exchange earnings could then be used for machinery.

Antioquia, and by extension Colombia, began economic development through a process involving mutual interdependence between export expansion and manufacturing activity. The intervening variables of transport improvement, financial intermediaries and related processing activities were themselves important in the process. The degree to which the process was successful in each of the regions of Colombia was a function of the expansion of exports from that region and the preparation of that region to undergo the changes implied by industrialization. Antioquia maintained a position of leadership in part because of the superior system of education as well as the experience in entrepreneurial activities gained in nineteenth-century mining and export activities.

[1] *Anuario estadístico del Municipio de Medellín, relativo al año 1922* (Medellín 1923), pp. 96–121.

[2] McGreevey, 'The Economic Development of Colombia', Appendix Table II-E. Data on the structural composition of imports were put together from several sources including the ECLA *Study* and K. H. Wylie, *The Agriculture of Colombia* (Washington 1942), p. 159.

Antioqueño colonization

SUMMARY

By way of summary of a mass of information and ideas about Colombian economic development, it may be of interest here to present a beguilingly simple relationship:

$$\dot{D} = a + b\dot{X}$$

This relationship states simply that the rate of development is proportional to the rate of expansion of exports multiplied by a parameter b which can be allowed to vary with each particular export experience.

Any direct experience with quantitative data will indicate that this theory is difficult to support. The linear relationship implied cannot be confirmed by available data. Even if one permits substantial shifting of the parameters over time, the hypothesis cannot be confirmed empirically.

Nonetheless, as a general proposition guiding more detailed investigation it has considerable merit. For example, two works by A. J. Youngson build on and elaborate this hypothesis in comparative analyses of several areas of the world.[1] The intervention of many other variables is discussed in his work as the unique influences on a common process, that process driven and determined by the expansion of demand for exportable products. What makes that process central is that the market is suddenly expanded in size and continues to expand at rates far greater than any 'home' or local market can expand. Other features of the local economy, of the technology of the export activity, even of the local political and social milieu then enter to influence the direction in which the expanding export activity will carry the economy as a whole.

The most appealing feature of this approach is that it gives prominence to the exogenous variable which drives the whole system while permitting systematic consideration of the wealth of diversity in growth experiences. It can tell a tale of missed opportunities and analyze the strategies of the successful.

The problem of transition to growth in Colombia has been treated by most of the analysts discussed in this chapter as an autonomous change either in the psychology of the Antioqueños or the entrepreneurial skills of the merchant and elite groups of several major cities. These variables are excellent measures of the receptivity of the local economy and society to the possibilities for economic development. The perspicacity

---

[1] See A. J. Youngson, *The Possibilities of Economic Progress* (Cambridge, England 1959), and 'The Opening of New Territories', Chapter 3 in vol. VI of the Cambridge Economic History of Europe (Cambridge, England 1965), pp. 139–211.

of local elites, the willingness of Antioqueño merchants to invest in manufacturing and the prior experience of these groups in mining must all have played a role in the transition. But without the unprecedented expansion made possible by the growth of coffee exports to what would their efforts have come?

One kind of answer is offered in the following chapter. A comparison of the two export economies of tobacco and coffee offers some lessons for the study of Colombian economic development.

CHAPTER 9

AGRICULTURE, EXPORTS AND ECONOMIC DEVELOPMENT: A COLOMBIAN COUNTERPOINT

There were two noteworthy periods of export expansion in Colombian history based on two different export products – tobacco (1845–75) and coffee (1890–1930). The effects of these two periods of expansion were in many respects different for the overall development of the country. During the tobacco expansion income remained static or possibly fell for the mass of the population and was redistributed in favor of large landowners. During the coffee expansion, on the other hand, the first signs of economic development in the country became visible. Total welfare increased with coffee's expansion, declined with tobacco's.

This chapter provides a framework for the analysis of agricultural export expansion and attempts to show why it leads sometimes to growth, other times to stagnation. It includes a general theory of how natural and technical conditions may determine the scale and character of agricultural enterprises, the distribution of income, saving and import propensities and the chances for sustained economic growth. The second part presents a comparative analysis of tobacco and coffee in Colombia within the general framework. Some final comments are addressed to the prospects of extending this analysis to other cases. The argument concerning coffee and tobacco in Colombia depends on factual material presented elsewhere in this book, particularly in Chapters 4, 7 and 8. In this analysis I have tried to avoid simply repeating details available in those chapters.

This study draws its general perspective from the work of Fernando Ortiz, *Cuban Counterpoint*.[1] Ortiz compared the impact of sugar and tobacco on Cuban society. His approach involved a broad investigation into social, political and cultural elements associated with the two crops in Cuba and in other milieux as well. My approach is much narrower but the objective is the same: to provide as general an explanation as possible of how the mode of production determines many features of economic, social and political life.

[1] Fernando Ortiz, *Cuban Counterpoint: Tobacco and Sugar* (trans. Harriet de Onís, New York 1947).

Expansion of coffee

At the same time I will develop the analysis within the tradition of the literature on export economies. That literature emphasizes the impact of a rapidly growing export sector on the growth potential of the total economy. Some studies concentrate on the inherent instability of export markets, others on excessive dependence on decisions made by foreigners, many on the prospects for secular trends in terms of trade of primary products, and others on the relative 'development potential' of various products. As the analysis proceeds I will attempt to point out places of congruence and divergence in my analysis from principal works in that literature.

A MODEL OF AGRARIAN CHANGE

The purpose of a model is not to describe any given real situation. It is a tool used to improve the understanding and explanation of real situations. A good model generates hypotheses which can be tested against real situations. The failure of real situations to conform to the hypotheses generated by the model may signal either the inutility of the model or the fruitfulness of examining the source or cause of nonconformity. For example, a model which associates rates of migration with economic opportunity yields hypotheses about relative real wages and net population movements. When expected population movements differ from those observed, we could conclude either that no relation exists along the lines implied by the model, or that variables unaccounted for may have intervened to alter the expected result. If the second conclusion seems warranted, then one may begin analysis of intervening variables within the framework of the general model. Neither the model nor the hypothesis is discarded; it is altered to do its job better, viz., to aid in the understanding and explanation of real situations.

The model of agrarian change which I propose to consider is unlike any specific real situation. It involves the formulation of a relationship between the probability of the occurrence of economic development and two very generalized variables. The model is useful because it provides a means of taking into account many specialized features of real situations. It aids in putting the various strands of the web of causation into place.[1]

My hypothesis is the following: two conditions – one natural, one technical – determine the functional distribution of income, the savings

---

[1] The best brief statement of the requirements for a theory of development is that set out by Robert M. Solow in his critique of the Rostow theory of take-off. See W. W. Rostow (ed.), *The Economics of Take-off* (London 1963), pp. 468–74.

Agriculture, exports, economic development

rate, and in general terms the social and political structure of agricultural units and the regions or countries in which they exist. These conditions are:

(1) Land availability defined by the ratio of population to cultivable land for a given best crop.

(2) Technical conditions of production for that crop which determine the relative efficiency of small, medium or large farms which produce much, little or no surplus above the payment for factor inputs, and do or do not involve separation of the functions of entrepreneur and cultivator.

Table 28 *Conditions of production in agriculture, defined by size of production unit and availability of land.*

Size in hectares; productivity or surplus generated; division of functions	Land availability	
	Open frontier	Severely limited
Small: low productivity, no surplus; no division of function	Swidden Slash-and-Burn	Minifundio Share-cropping
Medium: surplus above subsistence; no division of function	Mid-western U.S. family farm	Strong incentive for rural–urban migration, shift to manufacture
Large: surplus above subsistence; division of entrepreneurial and cultivator functions	Livestock production; extensive cropping	Plantation agriculture

Consider six combinations of these conditions as in Table 28. Both conditions are continuous, neither is as unambiguous and easily definable as I would like. Physical acreage, surplus and ownership characteristics must be included in a meaningful definition of production unit *size*. For example, a modern truck-farm near a large city producing high-value vegetables could well be much larger in value of output than a vast stock-ranch far from any population center. Land availability in its turn cannot be independent of population density and the state of the arts. Until the steel plough made it possible to break prairie soil, the vast lands west of the 100° meridian in the United States were impenetrable to the farmer. The land was there, but it took the plough to make it 'available'.[1] In citing but two *determining* conditions I am trying to

[1] *See footnote [1] on p. 220.*

Expansion of coffee

summarize in useful fashion a much larger body of causal elements which lie, so to speak, behind the blackboard. The emphasis in this model is on the conditions of supply for the agricultural product. The earliest approaches to this problem in the development literature concentrated on conditions of demand for the agricultural export.[2] The alleged secular decline in terms of trade for primary products was a natural outgrowth of the concern with foreign demand.[3] The next step in that direction was the growing concern with dependence on the vagaries of foreign demand and foreign decisions.[4] But that whole discussion left aside the question of supply conditions, a set of problems simply referred to in the Latin American context as structural rigidities. For analysis of supply conditions one looks rather to other world areas. A paper by Mogens Boserup, for example, is based on European and Asian experience.[5] The work of William Nicholls and associates on Southern agriculture in the United States attests to the rigidity of agricultural systems not subject to competition from urban-based activities. Industrialization and urbanization appear to present the only exit from stagnation under some conditions of production in agriculture.[6]

[1] See on the role of the frontier and land availability in U.S. development, Frederick Jackson Turner, 'The Significance of the Frontier in American History', *Frontier and Section. Selected Essays of Frederick Jackson Turner* (Englewood Cliffs, New Jersey 1961), Chapter 3.
The recent text by Douglas North, *Growth and Welfare in the American Past* (Englewood Cliffs, New Jersey 1966), pp. 122–48, deals with the interaction of technology and land availability.

[2] See, for example, Henry Wallich, *Monetary Problems of an Export Economy* (Cambridge, Mass. 1950).

[3] The debate was begun by Raul Prebisch in a United Nations publication (Economic Commission for Latin America), *The Economic Development of Latin America and its Principal Problems* (Lake Success 1950). See also Paul T. Ellsworth, 'Terms of Trade Between Primary Producing and Industrial Countries', *Inter-American Economic Affairs*, x (1956), 47–65, and Theodore W. Schultz, 'Economic Prospects of Primary Products', in *Economic Development for Latin America* (ed. Howard Ellis, New York 1962), pp. 308–39. The empirical study undermining the Prebisch thesis was prepared by Charles P. Kindleberger, *The Terms of Trade, A European Case Study* (New York 1956).

[4] Two very different views on that problem in a Latin American context are offered by Osvaldo Sunkel, 'The Structural Background of Development Problems in Latin America', in *Latin America: Problems in Economic Development* (Charles T. Nisbet, ed.; New York 1969), pp. 3–37; and Andre Gunder Frank, *Capitalism and Economic Development in Latin America* (New York 1967).

[5] Mogens Boserup, 'Agrarian Structure and Take-off', *The Economics of Take-off* (ed. W. W. Rostow), pp. 201–24.

[6] William H. Nicholls, 'Industrialization, Factor Markets and Agricultural Development', *Journal of Political Economy*, LXIX (1961), 319–40; 'Research on Agriculture and Economic Development', *American Economic Review*, L (1960), 629–35; 'Southern Tradition and Regional Economic Progress', *Southern Economic Journal*, XXVI; reprinted, *Regional Development and Planning, A Reader* (ed. John Friedmann and William Alonso, Cambridge, Mass. 1964), pp. 462–73.

Agriculture, exports, economic development

Conditions of supply can even be a major determinant of the local structure of demand, particularly the demand for imports. Aggregate demand is the sum of individual demands for goods. Since individual demand depends on income and its distribution, and income distribution depends on factor prices which are in turn dependent upon prevailing techniques and factor supply, aggregate demand springs from the prevailing conditions of production. For example, the composition of imports will vary with the share of total income received by 'luxury importers'.[1] Even in the analysis of demand one returns to conditions of supply. Much of the following discussion is aimed at elucidating this point.[2]

In an extended work it would be worthwhile to draw out the argument relating each set of natural and technical conditions to particular forms of agricultural enterprise. However in this chapter I will consider only two types – the tobacco plantation as it appeared in the upper Magdalena River Valley, and smallholder coffee cultivation in highland Colombia. Thus I will confine my general remarks to these two ideal-types.

According to this model two conditions are neccessary for the existence of the plantation: technical economies of scale (which permit large units, surplus above subsistence, and division of function) and some natural scarcity of land. The plantation is distinguished from the livestock ranch or hacienda by the larger number of laborers per unit of land. Because in plantation agriculture the labor-land ratio is high, there is likely to be some surplus in the form of ground rent which may be used directly for consumption by the rentiers or might be diverted into some form of investment. The existence of rents due to land scarcity distinguishes plantation from hacienda. The failure of the hacienda as an economically viable institution probably lies in its inability to generate natural ground rents for reinvestment and reliance on costly systems of labor exploitation to support a would-be rentier class. Neither company store nor debt peonage, both costly institutions to the ruling group, are needed where population is densely settled and rents are naturally high. There are numerous historical cases in which land has been made artificially scarce by restricting access and holding it out of production. The labor–land ratio has often been successfully raised (thus giving rise to rents) by the importation of slave or indentured labor. The condition of land availability is

---

[1] On the concept of luxury importers see Levin, *The Export Economies*.
[2] An analysis of certain aspects of the effects of income expansion on international trade and adjustments which I found useful was Chapter IV of Harry Johnson's *Money, Trade and Economic Growth* (Cambridge, England 1962), pp. 75–98. The essay is followed by a bibliography of recent works dealing with trade and growth.

thus not strictly natural since it is in some wise subject to human decision.[1]

The plantation system concentrates the surplus in the hands of a few who, if past performance is a guide, are not likely to use its productivity within the economic region.[2] Colonially sponsored plantation systems have usually repatriated a large part of this surplus so that little domestic income generation resulted from substantial export expansion. And if investment was undertaken, it was limited to capacity expansion for more exports rather than balanced diversification to include new economic activities.[3] One is led to expect little ability to diversify holdings and branch out into productive new activities among domestic plantation owners. The tendency to plough back profits into an ongoing operation may be due to the superior profitability of the plantation; there may, however, be psychological blocks to diversification. It was Lord Keynes who wrote: 'If human nature felt no temptation to take a chance, no satisfaction (profit apart) in constructing a factory, a railway, a mine or a farm, there might not be much investment merely as a result of cold calculation.' The plantation system seems likely to produce risk-averters in the ranks of the owners and managers – one has only to bring to mind the image of the Southern cotton planter or the Brazilian sugar baron to find a basis in fact for this presumption. Experience suggests there is a small probability that the plantation system will provide the setting for sustained economic development.

In a different set of natural and technical conditions, our theory produces a different development outcome. If there are no scale economies which permit the growth of large agricultural units, then population growth in a region can lead to multiplication of family-farm enterprises which expand out over the existing landscape. (There may be physical characteristics of the land or of the best crop for that region which work against large agricultural organizations. Given production techniques also set limits on unit size though these limits may change substantially

---

[1] Cf. P. P. Courtenay, *Plantation Agriculture* (New York 1965).

[2] For a discussion of the import propensities associated with plantation systems see J. V. Levin, *The Export Economies*, pp. 170–85. For both empirical data and general analyses of the plantation in the Americas see Sidney W. Mintz, 'The Culture History of a Puerto Rican Sugar Cane Plantation', *Hispanic American Historical Review*, XXXIII (1953), 224–51; and 'The Plantation as a Socio-cultural Type', *Plantation Systems of the New World* (Pan American Union, Social Science Monographs, Washington 1959), pp. 42–9; and Mintz and Wolf, 'Haciendas and Plantations in Middle America and the Antilles', *Social and Economic Studies*, VI (1957), 380–412.

[3] Hla Myint, *The Economics of the Developing Countries* (New York 1964), pp. 53–68, discusses this problem in terms of a faulty 'low-wage' policy among plantation owners.

Agriculture, exports, economic development

over time.) In the early period of population growth under such conditions, there may be sufficient fertile land to provide some surplus above immediate needs of subsistence. Because production units are small, entrepreneurial opportunities remain within the reach of many more individuals than in the case of plantation agriculture. Many more people will face the responsibility of management, a condition which should raise the probability of effective problem solution and improve the prospects for technical and economic progress.[1] The most important investment of all, that in the capital improvement of personal skills with education and training, will be fostered. Not only will the oldest son be prepared for a life of independence and self-management, but all the sons and daughters must be prepared for a life in which each can look forward to self-determined choice of location and occupation. In other words, such a situation, typified by the American mid-western farm family in the nineteenth and early twentieth century, favors inputs into education and training for many more members of society than does that typified by large agricultural units.[2]

This argument applies *a fortiori* to medium-sized enterprises in a situation of limited land availability, for now skills and training will be devoted not only to furthering one's chances of success in agricultural activities but also to preparing youth for the new possibilities of an urban life. Market expansion and growing opportunities in non-agricultural employment will induce the shift of labor out of agriculture and into urban activities. The very limitation of agricultural expansion will in itself provide the push element in effecting this structural change in the economy.[3] Industrial development and the acceleration of industrial growth occur when conditions dictate medium-size production units without

[1] See the discussion of Robert E. Baldwin, 'Export Technology and Development from a Subsistence Level', *Economic Journal*, LXXIII (1963), 80–92. An earlier article by Baldwin, 'Patterns of Development in Newly Settled Regions', *Manchester School of Economics and Social Studies*, XXIV (May 1956), 161–79, and one by Douglass North, 'Location Theory and Regional Economic Growth', *Journal of Political Economy*, LXIII (June 1955), 243–58, are included in *Regional Development and Planning* (ed. Friedmann and Alonso). In some respects my argument derives from their reasoning although I have provided a more general formulation of supply conditions.

[2] Baldwin, in 'Patterns of Development in Newly Settled Regions', contrasts the flow of capital and labor into two regions with natural conditions offering radically different demand for skilled and unskilled labor as well as for capital with various characteristics. But just as these natural conditions will determine immigration of capital and labor, they will also influence the pattern of investment, education and skill development of the local population.

[3] At least two other authors have made similar points. In two of his articles, 'Location Theory and Regional Economic Growth', and 'Agriculture in Regional Economic Growth', *Journal of Farm Economics*, XLI (1959), 943–51, Douglass North discusses the American South,

rigid separation of cultivator and entrepreneurial functions, producing some surplus above the demands of subsistence, and limited possibilities of further agricultural development because of the costliness of extending the cultivated area.

The foregoing arguments relate essentially to likely economic behavior under different production systems. In themselves they would hardly be sufficient to convince many readers of the efficacy of the theory presented. However, the quality and character of status relationships and the roles of owners of resources (land) and those who have only their labor to sell will vary with conditions of production. Where land availability is limited and production units are large, we would expect to arise a highly stratified society with clear distinctions based on wealth and strong barriers against social mobility. These conditions exist in colonial settings in which class stratification may be enforced by color or race consciousness complementary to stratification by wealth. The plantation society when it is not broken asunder by absentee landlordism exhibits these and many correlate social qualities.

Contrary conditions lead to very different social stratification and mobility. Free land was a major determinant of American social conditions from the seventeenth through the nineteenth centuries. Habakkuk has brought out the importance of land availability in a telling comparison of agrarian conditions in Argentina and the United States:

The Argentine in the mid-nineteenth century devoted its land to pastoral farming, the most land-intensive, labour-saving form of agriculture. . . . The net result was that the floor set to the industrial wage by openings in agriculture was a low one. In the U.S.A., on the other hand, given the qualities of the land and market conditions, the most profitable form of agriculture was cereal production, and although it was conducted by the most labour-saving methods available, it was, from its very nature, much more labour-intensive than pastoral agriculture. In the New England colonies the character of the early settlement was, of course, favourable to the development of a community of small farmers, as opposed to a society like that of the Argentine dominated by great landowners. But the more strictly economic circumstances also ensured that agriculture was conducted by small farmers and that the benefits of high agriculture productivity accrued to them.[1]

He emphasizes the *prior* existence of two radically different social structures; however, the social structures did not *cause* patterns of land

---

the Pacific Northwest and wheat farming west of the Mississippi and contrasts the impulse to development resulting in these different cases.

More directly related to the historical relation of agriculture and industry is the study by H. J. Habakkuk, *American and British Technology in the Nineteenth Century, The Search for Labour-Saving Inventions* (Cambridge, England 1962), pp. 11–90.

[1] H. J. Habakkuk, *American and British Technology in the Nineteenth Century*, pp. 35–6.

ownership and distribution but were rather effects of the natural and technical conditions under discussion here.

Size of units will determine other aspects of relations between owners of land and suppliers of labor. Where production units are large, work must be carried out in concert. One may expect the growth of sanctions and special forms of social control to achieve efficient operations. Slavery, serfdom, debt peonage and the company store are among the more obvious consequences of the organizational demands of large units. Eric Williams was one of the earliest to suggest that racism had its origin as an ideology complementing exploitation on plantations. Social control was easier when the exploited class could also be identified as naturally inferior.[1] Such work arrangements can be outlawed by public social policy; opposition to them has informed every important social movement in Latin America in the past two centuries. But one can hardly deny that oppressive labor systems remain in many areas and would arise again where outlawed if given conditions were appropriate. Moreover, where natural conditions impede exploitative labor systems, i.e. whenever land is plentiful and labor is scarce, then one can expect dominant political and social groups to make land artificially scarce by restricting access to it and hence driving down money wages and raising land rents. Domar and others have suggested that this approach informed Czarist policy in the creation of serfdom in seventeenth-century Russia.[2] The enforcement of artificial land scarcity was apparently essential to a skewed income distribution in pre-revolutionary Cuba:

> The great latifundists made no effort to cultivate all their land; on the contrary, they often bought up additional land and deliberately held it out of production. At the same time there were large numbers of landless peasants who would have liked nothing better than to work these idle lands, either as sharecroppers or wage laborers, and who continuously encroached upon them, or tried to encroach upon them, as squatters ... This seemed to many – and we must confess that we were among them – to be completely irrational ... The fact that some of the biggest of these 'feudal' lords had their offices in Wall Street should have been enough to suggest that there was something fishy about this theory; but apparently it wasn't. Now, in the light of actual historical experience, we can see what a silly theory it was. Without

[1] Eric Williams, *Capitalism and Slavery* (New York, 1966), pp. 3–30. J. H. Plumb ably demonstrates in a review article dealing with several books on race relations that the notion of the natural inferiority of the poor supported the English elite's exploitation of their fellow Englishmen. Hence a kind of racism can exist even within a racially homogeneous society. See *The New York Review of Books*, XII (13 March 1969), 3–5.

[2] Evsey D. Domar, 'The Causes of Slavery: A Hypothesis', (unpub. MS., 20 October 1966.) He cites among other works on this subject, Herman J. Neiboer, *Slavery as an Industrial System* ('sGravenhage, Martinus Mijhoff 1900), and Jerome Blum, 'The Rise of Serfdom in Eastern Europe', *American Historical Review*, LXII (1957), 807–83.

a landless proletariat in the countryside (and a high rate of unemployment in the cities), the latifundists would have had no one to cut their cane. *A poor half-starving peasantry and a national unemployment rate averaging a quarter of the labor force were of the very essence of capitalist rationality in pre-Revolutionary Cuba.*[1]

Realization of rents required that the cultivated land be kept out of the hands of workers lest the agrarian proletariat refuse to work on the sugar plantations.

Structural social problems in agriculture are avoided in medium-sized units. No radical division of function occurs, hence no class distinction or complex work system is required. There appear no incentives for oppression, power or social control since there are no economies of scale which would encourage the formation of large holdings. The path of further economic growth under such conditions lies rather in the shift away from small-scale agriculture into non-agricultural activities. And under these conditions the potential urban population and labor force emerge not from an oppressed rural proletariat but from a community of smallholders seeking an outlet for ambition. This difference in turn separates one pattern of urbanization and industrialization from another, particularly with regard to the social and political problems which rural-urban migration engenders. In this way, and others, the conditions of production in agriculture affect the process of economic change throughout the economy.

At this point I will state two hypotheses which derive from the model presented:

(1) The probability of economic development in a nation or region varies with the nation's or region's position on the matrix set out in Table 28. The matrix implies a set of isoprobability lines (see Figure 12) like a set of concentric circles converging on the center of the matrix, i.e. with unit size approximating the family farm producing some surplus and perhaps mid-way in the land availability continuum, thus encouraging some tendency to shift resources out of agriculture.

(2) The isoprobability distribution might resemble a bivariate normal distribution with an identifiable and small standard deviation. There is little likelihood of development under a regime of natural and technical conditions very different from those set out as optimum.

Figure 12 shows various possible types of enterprise and some possible isoprobability circles. These suggest one way in which the probabilities

[1] Leo Huberman and Paul M. Sweezy, 'Cuba's Economic Future', *Monthly Review*, xv (1964), 633–50. The quotation is from page 638.

might be distributed. As the probabilistic structure of the hypotheses indicates, there is no absolute assurance that a given set of conditions will or will not coincide with successful development. But once the general structure has been established, empirical investigation of many cases could lead to a more accurately drawn map.

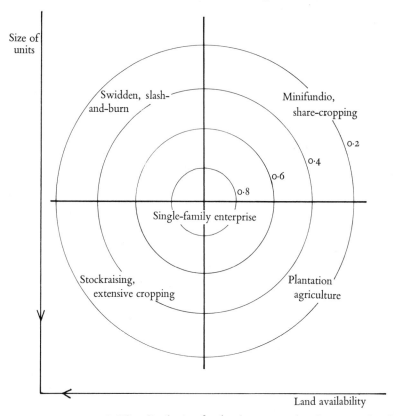

Figure 12 An isoprobability distribution for development under given natural and technical conditions.

Still another interpretation could be placed on the isoprobability lines. They could be regarded as indices of the rate of change of per capita product with the highest rates near the center. The hypotheses can then be checked by the correlation between matrix position (and hence iso-probability rating) and the level or rate of change of per capita product. One might begin with two maps of the world, one a shaded map of development or per capita income with darker colors for higher income,[1] the other a shaded map with coloring determined jointly by rural population density and the size of enterprises – darker colors for combinations with higher probabilities as suggested by these hypotheses. A coincidence of colors should result. One might perform a similar experiment in one country only, comparing regional, state or provincial data similar to that mentioned for the international experiment. Again a correlation should be apparent. One might finally analyze secular movement on the matrix from areas of low to high probability to see whether the timing of various countries' development is causally connected to position on the matrix. One might also study the history of those countries which have not developed to see whether characteristics of agricultural production may have been the principal deterrent to social and economic change. Once a country or region has moved from a condition of major dependence on agriculture and particularly on agricultural export products, this model would presumably no longer be operative. The rise of new sources of political and economic power, for example, could undercut the influence of a planter class and even withdraw legal sanctions from the monopoly privilege historically enjoyed by the planter class.

Despite the intriguing possibilities offered by these general empirical tests, I would like now to turn to the development experience with two crops, coffee and tobacco, in Colombia during the past century. I sketch out in some detail what appear to have been the main factors affecting the development potential of these two agricultural exports from Colombia; they depend in the final analysis on just those natural and technical conditions which are the independent variables which have occupied us so far in this chapter.

COLOMBIAN COUNTERPOINT

The history of tobacco cultivation in Colombia can be divided into three periods: the first, 1776–1845, was distinguished by operation of a government monopoly; the second, 1845–57, was the period of 'rationalization' of tobacco cultivation as the monopoly was first turned over to the firm of Montoya, Saenz y Cía.: then free production was permitted after 1850. There occurred during that period a dramatic expansion of production and exports, ended in 1857 by a leveling off of demand in Germany. The third period of Colombian tobacco exports, 1857–75, was marked

---

[1] See, for example, the maps included in Norton Ginzburg, *Atlas of Economic Development* (Chicago 1961).

Agriculture, exports, economic development

by only moderate further growth in exports and finally a decline after the latter date as a result of new competition from Dutch tobacco plantations in Java brought into production in the last quarter of the century. Government policy favored monopolization and large-scale operation in tobacco cultivation through 1850; after that date techniques of production were so fixed by previous historical development that large units continued to be the rule. Moreover, there was but little of the alluvial mud flows along the Río Recio on which the high-quality Colombian leaf was grown, and this was controlled by large estate owners – an English commercial house after 1857.

A majority of the tobacco they handled was grown along the old course of the Rio Lagunilla in the *vegas* of the Río Recio and in the bottom lands of the district of Guayabal. Most of this region had been enriched by the great mud flow of 1845 that had forced the Lagunilla into a new channel. This seems to have been the source of the tobacco that so captivated the German consumer.[1]

This situation was the genesis of a low-wage, high-rent income distribution which concentrated income and the gains from trade in the hands of the landowners. Scarcity of land and technical and historical conditions combined to produce plantation agriculture. Economic and social results were much as those expected from the preceding theoretical analysis.

Expansion of tobacco exports had the effect of enlarging the share of income of the large landowners. Rents rose due to expansion onto lower quality lands and more intensive cultivation of the alluvial soils. Moreover, export expansion permitted a higher level of imports so that artisan weavers were driven out of business by foreign competition. In some situations such redistributions of income have generated increased savings and investment, the key to sustained economic growth. In nineteenth-century Colombia, however, the income acquired by the landed class was largely devoted to luxury consumption and luxury importing; consequently, there was no immediate national gain from this redistribution of income.[2]

The conditions of production for Colombian tobacco were not unlike those which obtained in Virginia. Both were very different from the Cuban situation as outlined by Ortiz:

Virginia ... employed the system of large plantations ... In the Anglo-American colonies there were never small growers nor any concern with the distinctive qualities

---

[1] Harrison, 'The Colombian Tobacco Industry', p. 275.
[2] Living quarters and meeting rooms of the first large commercial house in the Ambalema tobacco zone were all lined with expensive Italian marble – these decorations were completed in the late 1840s when the marble had to be brought up the river in *champanes* or pole-boats.

of the leaf . . Tobacco there was never rolled or made into cigars, which were unknown, but only into plugs for chewing, into twist for pipe smoking, and later into snuff for inhaling. For this mass industrial production the fine skill of the cigar worker was not necessary.[1]

Tobacco cultivation in Colombia fits more closely the Virginian model than the Cuban. Cigars were sometimes made, but tobacco for export usually left the country in leaf form so there was little development of skills as in Cuba. There the growing of tobacco was 'treated as a small-scale garden product'. Workers in the cigar factories as well as these small-scale growers played an important role in the 'transculturation' which Ortiz views as a main source of the distinctive Cuban culture. Ambalema tobacco growing was carried out by share-cropping arrangements. Land was concentrated in the hands of a few Bogotá merchants and wealthy hacendados who also controlled marketing. Although the size of the production unit was probably similar in Cuba and Colombia, the size of the ownership unit was much larger in the latter and the organization of marketing was such as to isolate the producer from experience with the market and to concentrate profits in the hands of a few merchants. Small agricultural producers of Colombian tobacco had little chance or incentive to integrate vertically and hence diversify their economic activity. In contrast the Cuban *tabacalero* tended to move into processing activities associated with tobacco growing.

Substantial expansion of coffee exports from Colombia came nearly a score of years after the end of the tobacco export period. Production grew rapidly in the 1890s and again in the decade 1905–14, especially in Antioquia and areas of Antioqueño colonization. Further growth in production in the 1920s occurred largely in the rich Quindío region from where exports moved through the Pacific port of Buenaventura to foreign markets.

The growth of coffee cultivation was a natural response to the great profitability of the activity. A projection of future prices and output made in 1893 indicates that a rate of return on investment above 50 per cent was envisioned in spite of the long gestation period of the coffee bush.[2] Not that high a return could in fact have been realized since there was a dramatic fall in prices in the 1890s which was not fully reversed until 1910. How-

---

[1] Ortiz, *Cuban Counterpoint* p. 59.

[2] I calculated the internal rate of return on the investment discussed in the Bureau of the American Republics *Bulletin*, 1 (October 1893), 25–8. An expert gave there the necessary data for the calculation of the internal rate of return. The same procedure was followed as that used below in Chapter 10 in calculating the internal rate of return on railway investments in the 1920s.

ever, I have calculated that an investment in coffee cultivation in 1893 would have brought a real rate of return over the next 20 years of over 35 per cent to the investor. No other investment, save perhaps in the early railways, could have been so enticing. Little wonder that coffee expanded so rapidly.

Coffee cultivation in Colombia has historically been a smallholder enterprise. In the mid-1950s, less than 7 per cent of total coffee production came from farms larger than 50 hectares.[1] Intermediate or steep slopes on which some 80 per cent of all coffee-plantings are located offer the best ecological conditions for coffee but do not lend themselves to production in large units. Natural conditions favor a minuscule breaking up of production units into small plots. In areas of Antioqueño colonization (which accounted for well over half of all Colombian production by the end of the 1920s), the cycle of frontier activity included slash-and-burn maize planting, an intermediate period of interplanting which included corn, beans, manioc, plantains and coffee, then finally a more complete dependence on coffee alone.

> The tradition of an independent yeoman class, [writes Parsons] from which title to a few hectares of land has become the ambition of every campesino, has fitted the new crop extraordinarily well. Most of the small growers have continued to provide for their own subsistence on part of their fincas, sometimes disposing of small surpluses of plantains, maize, or garden fruits at the nearest market. The common adage that '*maiz comprado no engorda*' (purchased maize does not fatten) merely emphasizes the integrated role of the independent farm.[2]

In discussing Indonesian experience with coffee Clifford Geertz had made the point that

> Coffee did not demand the periodic efforts of great hordes of peasant-coolies organized ant-like into short, intensive 'campaigns', but the steady, painstaking application of at least semiskilled labor, and so it was cultivated by a labor force less massive and less fluctuating than the one employed in sugar.
> Such a system naturally leads to the formation of enclave estates, manned by permanent, fully-proletarianized workers.[3]

At the same time, coffee fitted well into the ecosystem of swidden, or roving, slash-and-burn agriculture also typical of the Antioqueño colonization. Geertz's observations about the derived cultural conditions of swidden *vs. sawah* or wet-rice plantation agricultural systems apply to the Antioqueños *vs.* the hacienda–plantation syndrome:

[1] United Nations, ECLA/FAO Joint Program, *Coffee in Latin America, I. Colombia and El Salvador* (New York 1958), p. 27, Table 18.

[2] Parsons, *Antioqueño Colonization*, p. 111.

[3] *Agricultural Involution* (Berkeley 1963), pp. 58 ff.

Expansion of coffee

As the bulk of the Javanese peasants moved toward agricultural revolution, shared poverty, social elasticity, and cultural vagueness, a small minority of the Outer Island peasants moved toward agricultural specialization, frank individualism, social conflict, and cultural rationalisation. The second course was the more perilous, and to some minds it may seem both less defensible morally and less attractive aesthetically. But at least it did not foredoom the future.[1]

Because of ecological independence the areas and peasants which became committed to coffee agriculture in Indonesia were more successfully integrated into patterns of international trade than were those ecological areas where a symbiotic relationship between rice and sugar had been formed. In Geertz's analysis the culturally derived conditions of a form of production depend on the ecological relationships which are established. Ecological independence, such as that established in coffee-growing areas, contributes to cultural forms conducive to social change:

The isolation of coffee cultivation on enclave European estates, like that of rubber later on, made the barrier to the drift of a commercial orientation to agriculture into the peasant sector much less formidable in the long run than did the mutualistic integration of sugar with wet-rice growing. Here ecological separation eventually reduced economic contrast, at least in the sense that peasant agriculture became a functioning element in the Indies' export economy rather than merely its backstop; peasant agriculture was developed, at least in part, into a business proposition rather than becoming frozen into a kind of outdoor relief.[2]

Antioquia with its hilly terrain proved to be particularly adaptable to this integration of peasant agriculture into the pattern of international trade. The social transition from a state of backwardness to one of integration into a larger economic system was smoothed. Many of the social characteristics of the Antioqueño are similar to those of the Outer Islanders of Indonesia; this parallelism in turn relates to the ecological relationships of subsistence and coffee agriculture. The apparent similarity between the two agricultural systems – that of Outer Islands peasants and Antioqueños – is illustrated in the accompanying quotations, first from Geertz, then from the ECLA/FAO coffee study of Colombia:

Indonesia

Coffee-growing fitted well with swidden, particularly on hillsides, where small gardens could be cared for without any real pressure on subsistence cultivation and, in fact, as the trees helped with the closed-cover problem, perhaps with some benefit to it. Coffee trees could be planted in swiddens and, taking three or four years before they became productive, could be maintained as gardens after the other swidden crops – grains, legumes, roots – had ceased to be economic and had been

[1] *Agricultural Involution*, p. 123.
[2] *Agricultural Involution*, p. 60.

232

'shifted' to another plot, thus fitting neatly into the phased inter-cropping pattern of swidden generally.[1]

Antioquia

The practice of interplanting other crops between the rows of coffee trees is quite common, especially on young coffee-plantings. Such crops often provide the shade needed by coffee-trees . . .
About one-third of all coffee-plantings in the country support other interplanted crops. The situation contrasts sharply with that prevailing in El Salvador where interplanting is virtually unknown . . .
On the smaller farms, coffee seems to serve rather as a source of cash income once the family's food requirements have been satisfied. Diversification is still very pronounced in relative terms on farms with between 1 and 10 hectares under coffee. Beyond this size, coffee farms become more specialized.[2]

The Antioqueño's experience with opening land and employing his own labor in coffee cultivation, as well as the contacts which many established with urban coffee buyers, was an important factor in establishing a set of social and psychological attitudes favorable to development. The fact that Geertz found that the Indonesian Outer Islanders were the most important group in the emerging development of that nation would suggest that some significance lies in the social patterns surrounding coffee cultivation in the two areas. These natural and technical conditions

enabled the Antioqueño to open the new frontier. . . . In this combination of elements – the existence side by side of good untouched free mountain land and a large number of ambitious mountain farmers with frontier blood in their veins – coffee operated like a catalytic agent. It provided an acceleration and enthusiasm which lifted the movement to a fever pitch making the participants feel that they were being beckoned on to a promised land to fulfill Colombia's historic destiny.[3]

The combination in Antioquia of freely available land and limited economies of scale led to a more equitable size distribution of income, which was favorable to development. Available data indicate that literacy rate and school attendance have been higher in Antioquia than in other

[1] Geertz, *Agricultural Involution*, pp. 59–60.
[2] United Nations ECLA/FAO joint study, *Coffee in Latin America*, pp. 31, 34.
[3] Robert Carlyle Beyer, 'The Colombian Coffee Industry: Origins and Major Trends', p. 183. The experience with coffee in three other regions of the Americas is discussed respectively in Sanford Mosk, 'The Coffee Economy of Guatemala', *Inter-American Economic Affairs*, IX (1955), 6–20; Stanley Stein, *Vassouras, A Brazilian Coffee County, 1850–1900* (Cambridge, Mass. 1957), and Eric Wolf, 'San José: Subcultures of a "Traditional" Coffee Municipality', *The People of Puerto Rico* (ed. Julian Steward et al.), pp. 171–264. I find nothing in their analyses of the conditions of production for coffee to contradict my analysis. A reading of their work makes clear, however, that coffee can be grown in a multitude of conditions with respect to scale of enterprise and labor intensity. For further information on the same subject see Vernon D. Wickizer, 'The Smallholder in Tropical Export-Crop Production', *Food Research Institute Studies*, I (1960), 49–99.

regions of Colombia. At the time of the 1918 census, Antioqueños were 30 per cent above the national average with respect to the literacy rate. (See Table 29). Data for earlier periods are not too reliable, but they tend to confirm that the Antioqueños were ahead of other regions in schooling. More than other Colombians they invested in education to raise productivity and perhaps to facilitate social mobility. Thus, as coffee cultivation expanded, the quality of labor inputs in coffee production was

Table 29 *Index of schooling given by region, 1847, 1874, and literacy, 1918, 1938* (national average = 100).

Region	Schooling		Literacy	
	1847	1874	1918	1938
Antioquia	143	189	131	130
Bolívar	132	81	89	85
Boyacá	62	71 ⎫	99	97
Cundinamarca	102	164 ⎭		
Cauca	126	83	108	106
Tolima	71	54	89	85
Santander	61	111	84	84

Source: computed from census data and data in *Anuario estadístico, 1875*. Number of children in school as a per cent of total population was the index used for 1847 because no age break exists for that early period. Number of children in school over number of school-age children used as the index for 1874. (Literacy rates based on censuses of 1918 and 1838.)

also improving. The combination of greater concern with industrialization and experience in coffee made the Antioqueño particularly able to deal with the problems of urbanization and industrialization and helps explain the early lead of Antioquia in industrial development. The spread of industrial development to other parts of Colombia has many causes, to be sure, but one of importance may be the inculcation of values similar to those fostered among the Antioqueños as coffee growing spread to other areas.

Pressure on land grew as the Antioqueño population expanded. As early as the 1920s migrants moving southward in Caldas, Tolima and Valle del Cauca, were reaching areas populated by other Colombians.[1]

[1] Parsons, *Antioqueño Colonization*, pp. 69–95.

Agriculture, exports, economic development

Consequently, industrial activities proved to be increasingly more attractive, and the nascent Medellín textile and food-processing industries drew their labor force from the ranks of rural–urban migrants. Antioqueño recruits for urbanization proved more adaptable and more skilled than their counterparts in Eastern Colombia because of the greater involvement of Antioqueño smallholders in a market economy and the process of rural–urban exchange.

The preceding brief description of tobacco and coffee production in Colombia sets the stage for a comparative analysis of the two agricultural export economies. The role of income distribution as a determinant of import demand requires special emphasis in the analysis. However once a pattern of development is under way, such factors as transport innovations and changing technology prove to be of consequence. Contrasts in the patterns of development induced by tobacco and coffee show up most clearly in a discussion of these factors as determinants of demand which flow from an initiating set of natural and technical supply conditions in the export sector. Such an approach emphasizes the inherent interdependence of the key sectors of a dual or enclave economy.

The demand for imports is a crucial determinant of the amount of domestic income expansion that will result from a given expansion of exports. Since the import-demand functions of various economic groups – workers, entrepreneurs and rentiers – are likely to differ considerably, the functional distribution of income influences import demand. When imports in turn are considered in functional classes (consumer goods, capital goods and raw materials) the import propensities of the various groups are probably even more different than with regard to aggregate imports. Workers devote a certain share of their income to the importation of cheap cotton textiles; entrepreneurs are most interested in machinery and equipment; rentiers live and spend abroad on luxury goods.

Because tobacco income was concentrated in the hands of the rentier class (particularly after 1857 when substantial further growth of the industry came to an end), a large share of the foreign exchange proceeds was spent on luxury imports. English merchants who gained control of the best Ambalema tobacco fields fostered a substantial capital outflow as well: 'The old landowners and foreign elements gained control of tobacco production after 1858. The result was, that except for supporting steam navigation on the Magdalena River, the funds made available by the export of tobacco were not used productively for Colombia's material benefit.'[1] The domestic income-generating effects of increasing

[1] Harrison, 'The Colombian Tobacco Industry', pp. xi–xii.

235

tobacco exports were thus smaller than they might have been had the foreign exchange income – or even income from domestic production – flowed into the hands of workers and potential entrepreneurs.

The distribution of income arising from expansion in coffee cultivation proved to be much more favorable with respect to the potential domestic income-generating effects. Since income was equitably distributed, import demand was higher for cheap cotton textiles than for luxuries which could not be produced locally. Importers and traders were aware that the market for such goods existed.[1] As importing firms were faced with growing demand for imported textiles, they saw the budding opportunities for import substitution by domestic production in modern and large-scale plants. When foreign exchange grew scarce in 1930, some importers switched over to domestic production of the goods they had been importing.[2] Industrial development was underway – even if on a limited scale and without an impressive capital-goods industry. While it had been possible by 1930 to cross the threshold permitting domestic production of cotton textiles and a variety of other consumers' manufactures, those thresholds may not have been reached had the pattern of demand called for more luxury goods. The pattern of demand would have been decidedly different if coffee had been grown on large plantations.

Development of the export commodity may pre-empt development in other activities; at the same time it may make import substitution more difficult by lowering transport costs which permit foreign producers to deliver their goods at a lower unit cost. Tobacco cultivation fostered only one kind of transport improvement – steam navigation on the Magdalena River – a change which did nothing to promote other sorts of exports or promote regional integration by trade.[3]

The building of roads or railroads to the main population centers in the highlands was unnecessary for the export of tobacco. Thus the urban centers remained more or less isolated from the world since the most arduous part of the journey from outside the country was still the overland trip from river port to the cities in the mountains. There was no encouragement to producers of exportable products in the highlands to export, for the advent of tobacco exports, far from opening up opportunities for other export products, served to concentrate dependence on that product

---

[1] Ospina Vásquez, *Industria y protección en Colombia* p. 263.

[2] Based perhaps on his Colombian experience, Albert O. Hirschman made this cyclical import substitution argument practically a rule of thumb for industrialization in his *Strategy of Economic Development* (New York 1958), esp. pp. 173 ff.

[3] See Gilmore and Harrison, 'Juan Bernardo Elbers and the Development of Steam Navigation on the Magdalena River', *passim*.

and others which could be grown or gathered in *tierra caliente*. A tendency to risk aversion by plantation owners was thus reinforced by objective conditions which made alternatives to investment in tobacco even less appealing. During this same third quarter of the nineteenth century ocean steamers with iron hulls and screw propellers were lowering freight rates and the delivered price of English textiles. This improvement left highland artisans in eastern Colombia at such a competitive disadvantage that they lost a large share of the market. Manufacturing investment could hardly have looked less appealing.

Transport costs were a significant share of the delivered cost of production for coffee from Colombia in the nineteenth century, but they fell from some 20 per cent of delivered price to less than 5 per cent after introduction of the railway. The railway permitted a freer range of cultivation, particularly in western Colombia after the Pacifico Railway and Panama Canal were opened in 1915. The tendency for transport costs to rise as the location of production moved away from the rivers was more than overcome in Antioqueño territory; in fact the railway effectively improved land availability in the first decade of this century and again in the 1920s. As a result, over-parcelization into inefficiently small production units was put off until the 1930s when a large part of excess rural population could be shifted into non-agricultural activities.

But the railway played an equally important role in promoting the Medellín textile industry. Although lower transport costs cut the price of imported manufactures, the price of raw materials and machinery fell even more; and since Medellín relied initially on the importation of almost all the components required for textile manufacture, transport improvements favored industrial growth. This effect was greatest, moreover, in coarse grades of cotton cloth of the kind in which Medellín came to specialize. Thus in this special case in which costs of manufacturing inputs fell more than manufactures, transport improvements induced by export expansion favored the growth of local industry.

Tariff legislation and import controls can shift the import-demand function downward by raising the costs of imported goods relative to domestic goods. There will be an increase in the domestic effect of any increase in income since a larger share will be spent on domestic products. Whether real income can be raised by such a policy depends on the relative efficiency of foreign and home industry in the protected activities.

Liberal governments in command during the expansion of tobacco exports avoided government interference with trade and allowed expanding imports to exert price pressure on artisan industrial activity.

Expansion of coffee

Since the domestic effects of income expansion were being extinguished in part by the rapid expansion of luxury imports, the income-generating effects of tobacco exports were less than they might have been had government protected selected industries. The ideology of classical liberalism (accepted as government policy after the Reforms of 1850) and the interests of planters and merchants melded to produce unyielding opposition to two groups – the traditional highland artisans engaged in a combination of cottage industry and subsistence agriculture, and the potential industrial entrepreneurs who tried without success to start small industrial enterprises. Neither group was able to get tariff legislation supporting their efforts.

The Reyes tariff established in 1905 served the new industrial interests of Medellín, but it was also favored by Antioqueño coffee growers since they often belonged to the same family. This coincidence of interest and the possibility of cooperation occasioned by it proved to be key factors in the process of industrial development in Antioquia. The internecine conflicts of the tobacco period gave way to accommodation as both industrialists and coffee growers were favorable to a more rapid expansion of manufacturing with protection.

In general, the growth of exports requires certain political adjustments as the export sector claims its due in the political arena. When the exporters and the import-competing groups are distinct individuals (and perhaps regional groups) who have in the past been antagonistic (as was the case with the artisans of Santander vs. the merchants and landowners of Bogotá and Cundinamarca), one can have little hope that agreement on tariff policy can be reached. For the artisan, there may be little solace in the contention that total national welfare is increased by a no-tariff policy that proves to be personally disastrous. The result may be regional conflict, rural unrest and civil war – as it was in Colombia in the years from 1853 to 1902. But when the expanding export sector and budding import-competing sector are in fact intertwined in family relationships, friendships and business alliances of long standing, one may expect accommodation rather than conflict, visible personal benefits to accompany (or replace) vague general ones. The tariff of 1905 was a success, for it answered the intertwined needs of the Antioqueños who were, at the same time, the most important exporting and import-competing groups.[1]

---

[1] Cf. Ospina Vásquez, *Industria y protección*, pp. 276–345, and Luis Eduardo Nieto Arteta, *El café en la sociedad colombiana* (Bogotá 1958), pp. 45 ff. In this essay Nieto Arteta moved away from his earlier favorable appraisal of the Reforms of 1850 and the role of tobacco in Colombian economic history as presented in *Economía y cultura*.

Agriculture, exports, economic development

Industrialization can achieve an irreversible and permanent shift in the import function that is of crucial importance for development. However, there appears to have been no successful industrial development during the period of tobacco's zenith as Colombia's principal export:

> The money brought into the country by the successful export of tobacco during 1845–75 did not support any industrial improvements save the introduction of steam navigation on the Magdalena. After 1857, the only commercial group that benefited from tobacco was situated in Barranquilla and they were oriented more outwards in the direction of Europe than inwards toward Cundinamarca, Tolima or Antioquia. The active commercial interests, with their abiding faith in *laissez-faire* and operating in an expanding capitalistic economy, dominated the tobacco industry from 1846 to 1857. After this date the landowners, with their high interest rate and static society controlled the cultivation and marketing of tobacco.[1]

Artisan industrial activity was of considerable importance and may have thwarted any efforts designed to initiate cost-reducing innovations. Safford makes clear in his review of Colombian and foreign enterprise in Colombia that members of the landed upper class did try their hands at manufacture; nonetheless, except for one or two isolated individuals this landed class was devoid of innovational talent. The plantation-hacienda complex did not produce innovating entrepreneurs. One might try to explain difficulties with artisan competition by reference to the universal problem of mechanizing wool cloth production. Certainly the cool climate of eastern Colombia requires woolens to a greater degree than Antioquia or Valle; still, innovational failure related to a variant of planter-class mentality seems a more likely explanation of the paucity of industrial growth.

Industrial development in the area of coffee cultivation did effect a downward shift of import demand which included recognizable structural changes at the end of the 1920s and again at the beginning of the 1940s. The downward shift in demand for consumer goods as shown in Figure 13 is even more impressive than that for total imports. Industrial growth in cotton textiles (but in other light manufactures as well) lessened the strain on the balance of payments and permitted capital goods imports and raw materials to continue to flow in for other economic activities.[2]

[1] Harrison, 'The Colombian Tobacco Industry', pp. 356–7.

[2] Early Antioqueño leadership is demonstrated in the informal census of manufacturing of 1915 reported in Informe del Ministro de Hacienda, *Memoria de Hacienda, 1916*, pp. xcvi–cxvii. These data were summarized and supplemented in United States Department of Commerce, Bureau of Foreign and Domestic Commerce, Special Agent Series no. 206, *Colombia: A Commercial and Industrial Handbook* (author P. L. Bell, Washington 1921), p. 180. Neither source provides complete coverage.

Expansion of coffee

Rapid response to growing domestic demand helped keep a larger share of the multiplied effects of coffee expansion within the country. Artisan industry, though out-competed by modern methods in cotton textiles, was able to shift into the fabrication of coffee bags from domestic fique fiber. Reduction of artisan employment was thus cushioned by the possibility of shifting into processing activities directly related to export production.

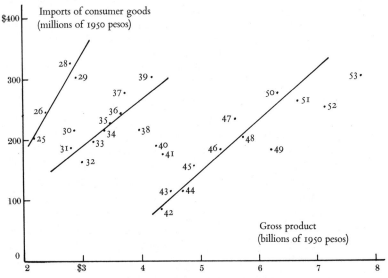

Figure 13 Relation between gross product and imports of consumer goods, 1925–53. Source: ECLA Study, Statistical Appendix, Tables 1, 14 and 30. Lines were drawn by eye and are not true regression lines.

There are more than enough differences between tobacco and coffee as they affected Colombian economic history to explain the different development outcomes. However, the differences sprang in large part from the natural and technical conditions of export production. The effects of income distribution, which have been analyzed in detail by other scholars, can be shown to be the result of the conditions which obtain with respect to land availability and scale potential.[1] Foreign demand played a role in tobacco's difficulties, but the failure to effect improvements in production was a result of the planter mentality. The relative

[1] See, for example, Alexandre Kafka, 'The Theoretical Interpretation of Latin American Economic Development', Economic Development for Latin America (ed. Ellis, New York 1962), pp. 1–25.

success of manufacturing in the coffee period flows from the Antioqueño entrepreneur's ability to introduce cost-reducing innovations and to domesticate those in use abroad. Success in the import-competing sector stemmed in turn from a better socio-political environment which grew up with the Antioqueño colonization and coffee cultivation. The different play of these forces in the tobacco and coffee periods of Colombian economic history tell much of the story.

SOME TENTATIVE CONCLUSIONS

A useful theory should suggest testable hypotheses about the relationship between variables. A theory of economic change should, moreover, relate the probability of economic development to conceptually measurable variables which constitute given data for economic analysis. The theory offered here meets these criteria; it also helps balance excessive concern with deficiencies and fluctuations of external demand for agricultural exports. Instead of seeking exogenous explanations for internal difficulties, we are led to look inside at the structure of the local economy and society.[1]

(1) Tobacco growing for export occurred under natural and technical conditions which caused a high-rent, low-wage income distribution, concentration of power in the hands of plantation owners, and a rigid two-class social stratification with little social mobility. The result was a high import coefficient, largely of luxury goods. Moreover, there was no substantial development of labor force skills or comparable educational investments; transport improvements did not reach to the highland cities; no technical linkages to the export sector permitted domestic exploitation, and domestic industrial development was discouraged by the possibility of importing foreign manufactures bought with increased export earnings. The tobacco export industry developed under conditions inimical to sustained economic expansion.

(2) The cultivation of coffee expanded in a framework of natural and technical conditions which created a class of agricultural smallholders in Antioquia and Caldas. The Antioqueños employed their surplus above needs of subsistence in investment in education and diversification of their economic interests to include processing of food products and substitution of domestic manufacturing for cotton textile imports. Lack of effective

---

[1] This is indeed the counsel offered by Kindleberger in *Foreign Trade and the National Economy* (New Haven 1962) when he emphasizes capacity to transform as the real measure of development potential.

demands for products which could be produced by local manufacture was no curb to industrial growth. Transport improvements occasioned by export growth lowered the costs of import manufactures, but the costs of raw materials for use in local industry fell even more. Coffee cultivation developed in natural and technical conditions at least moderately favorable to sustained economic growth. Parcelization and fragmentation of landholdings in Caldas and the Quindío limited the development response in agriculture. The lack of substantial technical linkages to coffee processing inhibited manufacturing growth without precluding the development of some light industry.

(3) In sum, tobacco cultivation provided the wrong conditions for development, coffee at least some of the right ones. A general model emphasizing the given natural and technical conditions as determinants of the development outcome provided a sound method for examining agricultural development and export expansion in this comparative study. There is good reason to hope it has more general applicability. As comparisons with other export economies indicated, there is nothing which inheres in particular crops which produces conditions necessarily favorable or unfavorable to development. The scale of farm enterprises in both tobacco and coffee has had great variability over time and space. Marketing and credit organization, in part independent of natural and technical conditions in the production process, can influence economies of scale. These additional factors help explain why a given crop does not have a predictable development potential.

(4) Emphasis on *given* natural and technical conditions should not lead one to infer that other factors must be ignored in analyzing this model. Other exogenous elements – marketing organization, credit availability, the existence of independent political power – can all be more accurately appraised for their impact on development potential. For example, slavery, land monopolization and debt peonage can be analyzed as means of creating false land scarcity which produces rents for the rentier class. Some system of slavery or forced labor is required if there are no natural land scarcities which can create rents. If the conditions of production are such that large production units are not possible (as in the American South after the Civil War), then an elite may employ some method of creating large ownership units while at the same time continuing with small production units. The system of share-cropping is the most obvious of such systems. If natural and technical conditions are not favorable to exploitation, then they have to be altered by some pre-existing elite. But the alteration is itself difficult; hence, I hypo-

thesize that natural and technical conditions in the middle of Figure 12 will usually not lead to exploitative labor and tenure systems.

If this analysis suggests ways in which some groups may bend given conditions to their own interests, it also offers guides to social policy. Once sources of power exist outside the landed elite in a plantation economy, they may introduce reforms to tax away rents and use revenues to provide domestic investment and educational improvement. Determined government policy can overcome the stagnation typical of the plantation system.

This comparative study of coffee and tobacco provides but a limited test of the model. Only two of many types of enterprise, only two of many sets of natural and technical conditions, received consideration. Many more cases of both successful and arrested development would need to be examined for a reliable test. It might be useful to examine several cases in which the independent variables are apparently the same but development outcomes are different. Alternatively, one might examine several cases of successful development to see whether they conform to hypotheses presented here. Other factors, such as terms of trade conditions, foreign demand, the initial political power of some groups would prove important: at issue is how much would be explained by natural and technical conditions and how much by factors extraneous to this model. If there is much which cannot be explained, the model ought to be discarded.

As analysis of historical processes of change grows more sophisticated, it should prove possible to examine the simultaneous change of technology, land availability and economic growth. The railway, barbed wire, the agricultural holding company and population growth rapidly changed the underlying variables all over the world in the nineteenth century. The chances for development must have varied substantially with those innovations. We turn now to an examination of the innovations in one area – transport – to measure in a more exact manner their impact on the economic development of Colombia.

THE DEVELOPMENT OF TRANSPORTATION

The population centers of Colombia found themselves in the middle of the nineteenth century far from the country's ports of entry and hence subject to the 'tyranny of distance'. The achievement of economic development after the War of a Thousand Days, and particularly the expansion of coffee exports depended crucially on significant technological improvements in the system of transportation which lowered the costs of moving goods and people to and from the highland population centers. These improvements – most obviously the growth of the railway network – gradually reduced the tyranny of distance by shrinking the effective distance to ports of entry.

The changes which occurred altered dramatically the internal movement of goods and people, the growth prospects of cities and regions and the use of various modes of transport. Internal improvements altered the balance between internal and external commerce in favor of the latter. In this chapter I will explore the changes wrought in the system of transportation between 1850 and 1930. Such an exploration must take into account the decline of transportation costs by various modes, the revolutionary implications of the opening of the Panama Canal and the great input of government funds which resulted in construction of numerous railway lines between 1870 and 1930. Perhaps most interesting from the point of view of comparative economic history is my attempt to analyze the benefits (and costs) associated with the construction and use of the Colombian railways. As the reader will note below, I am led to the conclusion that the coffee railways, begun in the four decades before World War I, played a significant role in the economic development of Colombia. In contrast, the investments of the 1920s in new lines not devoted to coffee transport had a lesser social return. Finally, considering the railways of Colombia as a whole, they were in relative terms as beneficial to that country as were the railways of the United States.[1]

---

[1] On the quantitative evaluation of American railways see Robert Fogel, *Railroads and American Economic Growth* (Baltimore 1964); and Albert Fishlow, *Railroads in the Antebellum Period* (Cambridge, Mass. 1965).

The development of transportation

At midcentury many of the principal overland routes had to be traversed by human carriers (*tercios*) because the poor quality of the ways prevented passage by mules or other beasts of burden. During rainy periods (which are to some extent unpredictable in mountainous areas of the country) many paths proved almost unpassable even by the human carriers. Still, mules were the more typical beasts of burden.

Over fairly flat areas – such as the sabana around Bogotá – wagon roads were available, though only after the mid-1850s. As late as the 1920s a reporter could write that 'the Departments of Antioquia and Cundinamarca are the only ones in Colombia where wagon roads of any length extending outside of the towns are found'.[1] The report of an English plantation owner in a letter dated 9 October 1862, though perhaps melodramatic, gives a flavor of the state of transport:

> Bolivar was a warrior, and conquered the Spaniards, but political economy being a sealed book to Bolivar, he failed to conquer even one road – Honda to the capital. Thus the country has continued poor from the very day of its independence. The United States is an empire caused by her cobwebbed roads. . . . Roads . . . mean wealth matured in the sunshine of simplicity of operation, making agriculture fat, and thus engendering manufactures, commerce, navy, churches, colleges, schools and – a nation is born.[2]

A civil engineer, Mr Evan Hopkins, reported that U.S. products were often cheaper in the inland river port of Honda than goods from the highlands 160 kilometers away, and gave the following reason: 'The so-called road from the capital to Honda is almost impassable during the rainy season, and at best it is but a very rough and excessively steep mule track.'[3] The British consul was no more complimentary almost half a century later in 1889:

> Perhaps the chief impediment to the extension of trade in Colombia during the past year has been the terrible condition of the chief roads of the country. The road between Honda and Bogotá, certainly the most important in Colombia, has been allowed, through neglect, to fall into such a condition as to be almost impassable.

---

[1] U.S. Department of Commerce, 'Colombia: Commerce and Industries, 1922 and 1923', *Trade Information Bulletin Number 223* (Washington 28 April 1924), p. 20.

[2] Letter from Robert Haldane to J. D. Powles, in J. D. Powles, Esq., *New Granada: Its Internal Resources* (London 1863), p. 149. Powles was chairman of the Committee of Spanish-American Bondholders.

[3] Powles, *New Granada: Its Internal Resources*, p. 10.

Expansion of coffee

... The time occupied in transporting the goods over that short distance has been greater than that taken from Europe to Honda.[1]

The first carriage road was built in 1851. 'Within the next fifteen years, the capital was surrounded by 150 kilometers of macadamized highway.'[2] Probably only the level roads leading out from Bogotá toward Honda and La Dorada were included in the paving program. The difficult passes and grades (which added most to costs, time and inconvenience of travel) remained unimproved until later.

Despite the obvious difficulties, there was a fairly brisk internal trade as indicated in the estimates of internal commerce prepared by the Chorographic Commission under the direction of Agustín Codazzi.[3] The Commission published estimates of internal and foreign commerce for 10 out of 31 provinces. Only slightly more than half of all trading relations between provinces occurred between contiguous provinces. Although the difficulties of transport inhibited long distance movement of goods, there was apparently a meaningful division of labour and regional specialization which had gotten its start in the colonial period. The maps prepared by Robert West show the movement of a number of important products into mining areas. They are reproduced here as Figure 14. Interprovincial trade in such products as artisan crafts, agricultural products, mining products and forest and fishery products apparently exceeded the trade of those same provinces with foreign countries. Total foreign trade per capita was only Ps$3·20, this figure combining both imports and exports. Low per capita income, the high cost of overland transport and the long distances of population centers from the sea were the principal inhibitors of trade expansion. It was particularly costly to move goods overland from the river ports to the highland cities. For example, the cost of moving a *carga* (*ca.* 250 pounds) upriver some 920 km. to Honda was Ps$7, whereas the next 160 km. overland to Bogotá cost Ps$4 to Ps$6 with even higher rates in the rainy season.[4] Given the high cost of overland movement and the relatively lower cost of river and sea transport one should not be surprised at finding North American flour sold in the river towns.

[1] Great Britain, Foreign Office, Diplomatic and Consular Reports, *Report on the Trade of Colombia for the year 1889*, Number 804 of the Annual Series, p. 3.

[2] Henao and Arrubla, *History of Colombia*, p. 461.

[3] *Jeografía física i política de las provincias de la Nueva Granada*, originally published, Bogotá 1857; published as volumes 21, 22 and 23 of the series, Archivo de la Economía Nacional, Banco de la República, Bogotá, 1957, 1958.

[4] See Table 6 above. Transport rates are taken from contemporary newspaper accounts.

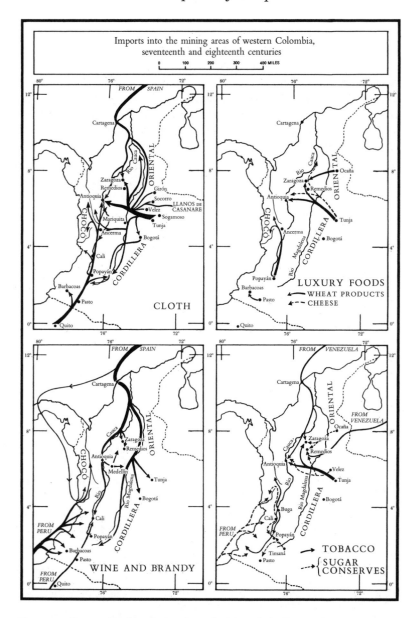

Figure 14 Interregional trade in the colonial period. *Source:* Robert C. West, *Colonial Placer Mining in Colombia* (Baton Rouge, Louisiana 1952), Map 12.

Expansion of coffee

The four most populous Colombian municipios in 1851 were all distant from the sea: Bogotá, 1,088 km.; Medellín, 950 km.; Cali, 142 km. (to Buenaventura); and Bucaramanga, 714 km.[1] In contrast, the four major U.S. cities in 1860 (New York, Philadelphia, Baltimore and Boston) were all port cities.[2] From this comparison alone one might surmise that cheap overland transport could have a great effect on the volume of trade and the potential for economic development in Colombia – greater still than the impact of cheap land transportation on United States economic development.

Table 30 *Major routes, distances and transport costs, interregional and international trade, 1850–80.*

Route	Distance (km.)	Total cost per ton
1. Bogotá–Barranquilla	1,088	$120
2. Medellín–Barranquilla	950	94
3. Bucaramanga–Barranquilla	714	90
4. Bogotá–Medellín	520	104[a]

Sources: Parsons, *Antioqueño Colonization*, pp. 156, 162; von Schenck, *Viajes por Antioquia*, p. 22; Valderrama Benítez, 'La industria cafetera santandereana', *Estudio*, II, pp. 1270–4.

[a] Estimated. No contemporary reports available.

In Table 30 I present estimates of the distances and costs of transport on some major routes for the year 1850. If one assumes as an example that goods which can bear transport rates as high as (but no higher than) 25 per cent of their value at the point of production or importation, then by knowing the prices of various products we can judge which could move in interregional or international trade. Only products worth perhaps Ps$400 per ton or more could have moved in international trade under this assumption. As of 1850 these would have included such items

---

[1] For city populations see Table 15 above; distances are from contemporary sources. Routes have changed to some extent over time; for example, the distance from Medellín to Cartagena by road is today only 692 km. See República de Colombia, Dirección General de Vias y Estructuras, *Mapa general de ferrocarriles* (Bogotá 1962).

[2] George Rogers Taylor, *The Transportation Revolution, 1815–1860* (New York 1968), p. 389. Data are from *Eighth Census of the United States: Mortality and Miscellaneous Statistics*, p. xviii.

as cotton textiles, tobacco, cocoa and stearine candles, among a list of articles for which I have prices available. Such items as sugar or *panela*, rice, meat and flour were probably too bulky to support a lengthy shipment from point of production. It was not by accident that the first major export product was grown in the Magdalena valley. The advent of steam navigation lowered river transport costs well before improvements in land transportation cheapened the movement of goods into the highlands. In an economic sense the river valley grew relatively closer to international commerce and farther from the highlands. The export products which followed tobacco – even including coffee in its early stages of development – came from areas on the slopes not too distant from cheap water transportation. The plantings in Antioquia listed by Cisneros in his survey of prospects for shipments via the proposed Ferrocarril de Antioquia were almost all located up the slopes of Magdalena tributaries (Yolombó, Yarumal) or near the navigable Cauca River (Titiribí, Concordia).[1] 'The promise of early completion of the new railroad seems to have attracted several early planters to the eastern slopes of the Antioqueño massif (e.g. Yolombó). Along the old Nare road, too, plantings began to appear in new clearings below San Carlos and it was here that Tulio Ospina, a young graduate of the University of California, first established a plantation.'[2] The event which was to change dependence on water transport alone was the advent of the railway.

THE DECLINE OF TRANSPORT COSTS

The application of steam power to transport goods within Colombia did not have the same impact on both river and rail transport. The evidence is scanty to be sure, but it would appear that transport rates did not fall very much either as a result of the simple appearance of steam navigation on the river, or its development through the competition of several companies after 1850. Steamboats of that era were not particularly efficient from an engineering point of view and in Colombia they only came to compete with a system of *champanes* or pole-boats which were not much less efficient (or, more exactly, more costly) than the early steamers. The situation may have been similar to that which prevailed on the Mississippi and its tributaries, as described by Taylor:

---

[1] Francisco J. Cisneros, *Report on the Construction of a Railway from Puerto Berrío to Barbosa, Antioquia* (New York 1878), p. 38.
[2] Parsons, *Antioqueño Colonization*, p. 137.

Expansion of coffee

It should not be supposed that the older river craft were immediately put out of business by the introduction of steam power. Quite the contrary, for the steamboat to a very considerable extent stimulated and facilitated flatboat operation. With steamboat transportation available, rivermen no longer had to walk back across country or laboriously to pole their keelboats upriver. ... By 1830 the steamboat was clearly the predominant means of transportation on western rivers, but the number of flatboats continued to increase, reaching a peak in 1846–1847.[1]

The steamboat provided the same function of easing upriver movements on the Magdalena. Juan Bernardo Elbers signed a contract in 1832 for 'two boats which would carry only passengers and tow *champanes* against a current of twelve miles an hour'.[2] The pole-boats continued in use on the Magdalena well after 1850. The reasons may in part have been technical (difficult currents and sandbars; scarcity of wood, and later, of coal; 'ignorance of the mechanical arts', and the lack of spare parts for engines),[3] but the differences in wage rates and levels of income between the United States and Colombia would certainly have favored the longer maintenance of the labor-intensive pole-boat in Colombia.[4]

Travelers' descriptions (that of Holton, for example) indicate that the steamers had to stop each day going upstream in order to take on wood for fuel. And travel at night was impossible above Banco.[5] Since even the smallest steamers drew more water than the pole-boats, they constantly faced the difficulties of going aground – a problem which grew in scope as the Magdalena filled up with the soil eroded by the gradual expansion of the agrarian population farming the slopes. In Isaac Holton's journey up the Magdalena in 1852, he was forced to switch from a steamer to a pole-boat just above Nare because the steamer had gone aground on a sand bar. Another feature of the voyage reminiscent of Taylor's comment above was that the same pole-boat had been pulled along behind the steamer from the river port at Mompóx. Holton had the bad luck of having to leave the relative comfort of the steamer for the unpleasant *champan*,

---

[1] George Rogers Taylor, *The Transportation Revolution*, pp. 64–5.

[2] Robert L. Gilmore and John P. Harrison, 'Juan Bernardo Elbers and the Introduction of Steam Navigation on the Magdalena River', *Hispanic American Historical Review*, xxviii (1948), 335–59. The quotation is from p. 352.

[3] For commentary along these lines see Salvador Camacho Roldán, *Notas de viaje* (Bogotá 1898), p. 167.

[4] On the difficulties faced in the initial establishment of steam navigation in Colombia see Gilmore and Harrison, 'Elbers and the Introduction of Steam Navigation'. A steamboat was in operation at least as early as 1824, but in many years thereafter the river was without service, and regular operation was not established until after 1850.

[5] For a sketch map of river navigation see Gilmore and Harrison, 'Elbers and the Introduction of Steam Navigation', p. 337.

The development of transportation

but we would not otherwise have had an account of river travel so complete and rich in comparison of the two modes of travel.[1] The evidence available on freight rates on the Magdalena – limited though it may be – paints a picture of falling rates. However, those for the years after 1845 and until 1880 were only about 23 per cent lower than the pre-1845 rates. There is no question that the decline was important, but it was dwarfed by the impact of the railways in later decades.

The improvement of mule trails and other public ways lagged behind the demand for such improvements. The difficulties with such construction in Colombia must be put in the perspective of its time. In the United States, 'turnpikes generally did not cheapen and stimulate land transportation sufficiently to provide satisfactory earnings from tolls. ... Turnpikes were being abandoned in Massachusetts as early as 1819, and by 1835 more than half of those built were either partially or completely abandoned.'[2] In other areas as well traffic was not sufficient to bear the high costs of construction and maintenance. Neither concrete, asphalt nor the internal-combustion engine were available to cheapen the cost of overland transportation until much later. France is said to have had 34,000 km. of 'national' roads in 1840; a year later Prussia had no more than 10,000. 'Not until the motor-transport age of the twentieth century did standards of grading and surface, on the best roads anywhere, get much beyond those of Telford, Macadam, and the engineers of the first Napoleon.'[3] Roads nowhere approached twentieth-century standards, but those of Colombia were decidedly poorer than those of the North Atlantic area. As late as 1907 a North American could write: 'Whatever route is taken it can be understood why freight from the point of shipment in the United States or Europe to Bogotá sometimes has cost $100 per ton. Locomotives sold at $10,000 in Philadelphia have cost the Facatativa Railway $30,000 when the freight up the river and across the Cordilleras was paid.'[4]

[1] Isaac F. Holton, *New Granada: Twenty Months in the Andes*, pp. 23–59. Holton's journey up the Magdalena occurred late in 1852; his account was published in 1857.
  For summaries of other travelers' accounts see Gilmore and Harrison, 'J. B. Elbers and the Introduction of Steam Navigation', p. 350, footnote 51, and *passim*.
[2] Taylor, *The Transportation Revolution*, pp. 27, 28.
[3] J. H. Clapham, *Economic Development of France and Germany, 1815–1914* (4th ed., Cambridge, England 1936), pp. 349, 350. See also the review of transport by L. Girard which appears as Chapter IV of vol. VI, *The Industrial Revolution and After* (ed. H. J. Habukkuk and M. Postan) of *The Cambridge Economic History of Europe* (Cambridge, England 1965), pp. 212–73.
[4] United States Congress, Senate Records, 'Report on Trade Conditions in Colombia', submitted by Charles M. Pepper; Senate Document 152, 60th Congress, 1st Session, vol. 11, 13 January 1908, p. 13.

Expansion of coffee

Colombian politicians attempted to leave the construction and operations of roadways to private entrepreneurs. They were in some cases to be given special subsidies, usually in the form of public land grants, but outright contracting for construction was virtually unknown in the nineteenth century.[1] Special land grants of over 10,000 hectares were used effectively in assuring construction of a bridge over the Cauca

Table 31 *An international comparison of the expansion of railways; lines in service as a percentage of lines ever built, 1850–1950* (per cent).

Country	1850	1880	1910	1930	1950
Great Britain	30·0	78·0	99	100	100
France	7·0	57·0	94	100	100
United States	2·5	26·0	89	100	100
U.S.S.R.	0·9	20·0	60	66	100
Argentina	0·1	5·8	65	88	100
Mexico	0·1	5·0	84	100	100
Canada	0·0	10·0	54	98	100
Brazil	0·0	9·2	58	88	100
Colombia	0·0	5·0	26	87	87
Japan	0·0	0·8	34	73	100

Sources: see the Note on Sources.

River and several trails from highland Antioquia to the south and east.[2] Significant public investments in road transportation were made in the decade 1905–14. Approximately Ps$300,000 annually were invested in new road construction in the years 1905 to 1910, somewhat more in subsequent years.[3] But the public incentives offered for road construction and tollway operation proved to be too limited to encourage much improvement in roadways. Given the near universal failure of tollroad companies in the United States and Europe, perhaps little could have been expected.

[1] Juan Bernardo Elbers was given monopoly rights for steam navigation on the Magdalena and other rivers as early as 1823. In exchange for this privilege he was to build and maintain a carriage road from the river port at Honda to Bogotá. The road was built but not maintained after Elbers forfeited his monopoly privileges. See Gilmore and Harrison, 'Elbers and the Introduction of Steam Navigation', pp. 340, 342, 351.

[2] República de Colombia, Ministerio de Industrias, *Memoria del Ministerio de Industrias* (Bogotá 1931), vols. 4, 6; Parsons, *Antioqueño Colonization*, p. 100.

[3] See República de Colombia, Ministerio de las Obras Públicas, *Memoria del Ministerio de las Obras Públicas, 1930* (Bogotá 1931), p. 95.

The development of transportation

Colombia was slow to build railways. A line was built across the Isthmus of Panama and completed in 1855, but it had no impact on the country as a whole. The next line was not put into operation until 1871. Table 31 presents for several countries one measure of responsiveness to the technological innovation presented by the invention of the railway. The data given at selected dates between 1850 and 1950 are the length of lines in operation in a given year as a percentage of the total length ever built within the country. Thus at any given point in time the country showing the highest percentage had responded most rapidly to the railway building potential of that country.

Colombia ranked well down on the list of ten countries in 1850 and 1880, but the same was true of other Latin American countries, most notably Argentina which was later to build such an extensive network of rail lines. The real measure of Colombia's slowness to adopt the railways is shown in the period 1880–1910. In that period Colombia built an additional 21 per cent of its total; during the same interval Mexico added 79 per cent of its railways, Argentina added 59 per cent, and Brazil added 49 per cent. The availability of foreign funds for direct investment during those years brought great opportunities to add to the infrastructure of the transport system all over the Americas (note the impressive gains of the United States and Canada), opportunities which were only partly taken advantage of by Colombia and the Colombians.

A measure of the relationship between coffee exports and the railway in Colombia is presented in Figure 15. The two variables – quantum of coffee exports and kilometers of railway in use – moved upward together in the period 1885 through 1934. The simple correlation between these two variables in the years for which data were available is a high and significant +0.98. Statistical relationships do not by themselves establish the direction of causality. A correlation of this magnitude indicates that some 95 per cent of the variation in coffee exports may be explained by variations in the number of kilometers of railway in use. This is not to say that the construction of the railways caused the expansion of coffee exports or vice versa; however, the statistical relation indicated does show strong mutual interdependence of coffee and the railways during the years indicated.

Given the mountainous configuration of the populated highlands of Colombia to which the railways would have to be built it is not difficult to understand the diffidence of government leaders and entrepreneurs alike in facing the decision to build railways. Technical constraints recommended that grades no greater than 1.5 per cent were maximum for efficient operation. The railway seemed almost impossible to many nineteenth-century Colombians as an answer to their transport problems.[1] But as in other countries the first lines built were not developed as part

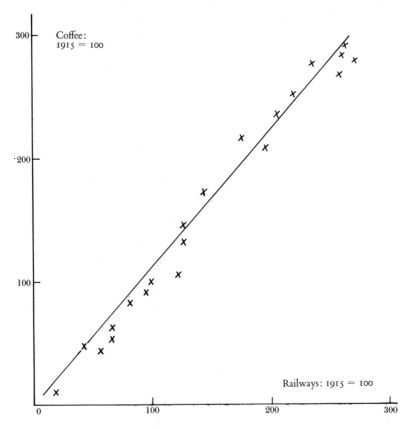

Figure 15 Relation between kilometers of railway in use and quantum of coffee exports, 1885–1934.

$$C = 0.13 + 1.11R, \quad n = 21, \quad r = +0.98.$$

of an integrated and complete system of internal transportation. The first line opened within the current borders of Colombia (i.e. excluding the Panama Railroad built after the California Gold Rush) was the Ferro-

---

[1] On problems of early railway construction and the experience of North American engineers see J. Fred Rippy, 'Dawn of the Railway Era in Colombia', *Hispanic American Historical Review*, XXIII (1943), 650–63.

The development of transportation

carril de Bolívar which ran 27 km. from Barranquilla, then a river port to Sabanilla, a port on the open ocean. As late as 1860 there was no wagon road, 'travel being on donkey back over precipitous hills and through dust and sand drifts, rendering the carriage of heavy packages dangerous and almost impossible'.[1] Ocean vessels occasionally called at Barranquilla when the sandbar gave way to ocean currents and permitted the entry of ships through the *Bocas de Ceniza*.[2] But generally Barranquilla was closed to ocean-going ships. The railways thus eliminated the bottleneck of the mule road between two long stretches of water transport. The impact of the railway may be illustrated in the shifting balance of port receipts for the three Caribbean ports of Sabanilla (Barranquilla), Cartagena and Santa Marta. In the last year prior to the opening of the Ferrocarril de Bolívar, Sabanilla accounted for just 10 per cent of the total customs revenues of the three ports; three years later its share rose to over 80 per cent. The new railway captured nearly all the traffic which moved inland from the ports.[3] In 1893 a British group opened a steel pier at Puerto Colombia greatly increasing the efficiency of transport and hence the use of the railway.

By 1904 some 565 km. of railway were in operation in Colombia. The number of kilometers in use doubled in the next decade. Between 1922 and 1934 the total length more than doubled again. No further important additions were made until the late 1950s.[4]

Table 32 presents the details of the growth of the railway network. It is of course a misnomer to speak of a 'network', since these were generally separate lines built for specific traffic purposes rather than an integrated system. But their lack of integration and apparently insignificant

[1] United States Consul J. W. Magill to Assistant Secretary of State John Appleton, 30 March 1860, Consular Despatches–Sabanilla, vol. 1; cited in Nichols, 'The Rise of Barranquilla', p. 161.

[2] In 1963 engineers had practically given up eliminating the sandbars when one day in August a great and unexpected shift occurred and left a deep channel. It was then hypothesized that the bar gave way because of its own excessive weight and that consequently it would build up again. This theory would explain both the failure of engineering works to remove the bar and its occasional disappearance, as in the 1870s, and 1890s and late 1930s as well as in 1963.

[3] Nichols, 'The Rise of Barranquilla', p. 169. I calculated percentages from the data which he presented in footnote 54, and which the author extracted from the *Diario oficial*.

[4] The standard source on Colombian railways is the three-volume work by Alfredo Ortega, *Ferrocarriles colombianos*, published as volumes 26 (two parts) and 47 of the Biblioteca de Historia Nacional (Bogotá 1920, 1932). Much of the data on freight rates, costs of construction and other railroad data has been taken from Ortega's work. For details on railway contracts and building see H. Theodore Hoffman, 'A History of Railway Concessions and Railway Development Policy in Colombia to 1943', (Ph.D. diss., American University 1947).

Expansion of coffee

size (by 1910 Argentina had 28,000 km. of railroads in use) did not prevent them from having a dramatic impact on the cost of internal transport. For example, mule transport rates for 1879 and 1880 were about 60 cents per ton-km., whereas the rates to be charged on the Ferrocarril de Antioquia in the construction proposal prepared by Francisco

Table 32 *Growth of the railway network, kilometers in use, selected years, 1885–1949.*

Railways	1885	1890	1904	1909	1914	1922	1934	1949
Group I or coffee railways	176	215	279	549	783	992	1642	1701
FC de Antioquia	38	48	66	102	205	242	439	338
FC de Cúcuta	54	55	71	77	71	72	83	60
FC de La Dorada	15	29	33	119	111	111	111	111
FC de Girardot	31	31	49	132	132	132	132	132
FC del Pacífico	38	52	43	94	234	341	678	824
FC del Tolima	—	—	17	25	30	94	199	236
Group II railways	—	40	87	114	122	176	1134	1081
FC de Ambalema-Ibagué	—	—	—	—	—	—	65	65
FC de La Sabana	—	40	40	40	40	55	238	200
Central del Norte 1ª	—	—	—	12	20	20	109	117
Central del Norte 2ª	—	—	47	62	62	62	256	224
FC del Nordeste	—	—	—	—	—	—	252	253
FC de Caldas	—	—	—	—	—	39	117	111
FC de Nariño	—	—	—	—	—	—	97	111
Other railways	27	27	119	238	261	313	486	201
FC de Bolívar	27	27	27	27	28	28	28	—
FC de Cartagena	—	—	105	117	105	105	105	105
FC de Santa Marta	—	—	67	94	128	180	189	96
Others	—	—	—	—	—	—	164	—
Total, all lines	203	282	565	901	1,166	1,481	3,262	2,983

Sources: Ortega, *Ferrocarriles colombianos*, I, pp. 27, 43; *International American Conference: Reports and Recommendations*, p. 123; Great Britain Diplomatic and Consular Reports, 'Report on the Railways of Colombia', *Anuario estadístico, 1924*, pp. 180–97, *1934*, pp. 369–70; IBRD, *Basis of a Development Program for Colombia*, p. 105.

Cisneros were 17 cents for imports, 11 cents for exports and the special rate of 8·5 cents for coffee, tools and utensils.[1] The simple average for all rail rates quoted between 1905 and 1929 appearing in Table 6 is 15 cents per ton-km. The average of mule rates over the years 1845–80 was 41·6 cents per ton-km. Thus overland transport costs may have been some 65

[1] Francisco J. Cisneros, *Ferrocarril de Antioquia* (New York 1880).

256

The development of transportation

per cent lower on railways than they had been on other overland carriers.[1] A reduction even of this magnitude may underestimate the impact of the railways since rail rates sometimes fell well below 15 centavos per ton-km. The simple average of seventeen separate freight rates on six different lines in 1910 was only 7.3 centavos per ton-km., and none of these rates were included in the compilation of Table 6.[2] The last available quotation for a mule rate is for the carriage of coffee from Bucaramanga to Chuspas in 1928; at that time the rate was 80 cents per ton-km.[3] The railway brought sizable reduction in the cost of transport; its role was more analogous to the canals than the railroads in the United States.[4]

THE OPENING OF THE PANAMA CANAL

A major influence on the pattern of internal transport in Colombia was the Panama Canal. Since most of Colombia's foreign trade took place with countries facing on the Atlantic, Pacific outlets proved to be too distant by sea to make them useful. The opening of the canal changed the situation dramatically. Once ocean transport to the Pacific port of Buenaventura was possible without the long trip around South America, the superior location of that port brought it into active use.

In the period up to 1914 virtually all goods moved from highland Colombia out to the Atlantic ports of Cartagena, Barranquilla and Santa Marta. Some efforts were made to build a gravel road from Cali to Buenaventura in the 1870s, and more than 11 leagues (51 km.) were completed. In 1873 the road reached as far as Córdoba, but it was never completed because of the turn of interest to a railway.[5] Nor was the building of the railway rapidly prosecuted before the opening of the canal. Only 65.5 km. were completed and open to traffic in December

---

[1] These calculations are based on the transport rates presented in Table 6 and the averages of them which appear in Table 19. The reader should again be reminded that these figures are generally based on travelers' accounts and other sources which may contain biases and inaccuracies.

[2] See Great Britain, Diplomatic and Consular Reports, *Report on the Railways of Colombia*, Miscellaneous Series Number 678 (July 1910), *passim*.

[3] See Ernesto Valderrama Benitez, 'La industria cafetera santandereana', *Estudio*, II (Bucaramanga 1933), pp. 270–4; and by the same author, *Santander y su desarrollo económico en el año de 1929* (Bucaramanga 1930), and *Tierras de Santander* (Bucaramanga 1940).

[4] On U.S. canals see Harvey Segal, 'Canals and Economic Development', *Canals and American Economic Development* (ed. Carter Goodrich, New York 1961), pp. 216–48; and Taylor, *The Transportation Revolution*, pp. 132–44.

[5] Rufino Gutiérrez, *Monografías*, 2 vols. (vols. 29 and 30, Biblioteca de Historia Nacional, Bogotá 1929), vol. II, p. 168.

Expansion of coffee

of 1908.[1] The line was completed into the Cauca Valley, in time for the opening of the canal in 1914. (See Table 32.) Within two years exports by volume more than doubled, the number of passengers quadrupled and local cargo moved was six times greater in 1917 than it had been in 1915. Only the volume of imports failed to respond rapidly, increasing 17 per cent from 1915 to 1917.[2]

Table 33 *Percentage distribution of the volume of trade of major ports, selected periods, 1918–47.*

Year	Barranquilla	Cartagena[a]	Santa Marta	Buenaventura
1918–19	30·8	22·6	38·4	8·2
1922–4	34·2	15·3	38·9	11·6
1927–30	31·9	19·2	27·6	21·3
1943–7	35·5	17·0	4·2	43·0

Sources: 1918–30: República de Colombia, Departamento de Contraloría, *Anuario de estadística general*, xxx, xxxi (Bogota 1931, 1932); 1943–47: IBRD, *Basis of a Development Program for Colombia*, p. 128.
[a] Exports of petroleum from Cartagena have been excluded from calculations.

The shifting importance of the ports is indicated in Table 33 which presents the share of total traffic by volume for selected years from 1918 to 1947. Traffic moved through the Panama Canal as early as 1914, but the official opening did not occur until after World War I. In the early years of the canal's operation the port of Buenaventura handled less than 10 per cent of total trade by volume. By the middle 1940s the share had risen to 43 per cent, and the Pacific port was the busiest in the country. Since ocean transport is so inexpensive relative to land transport it made immediate sense to divert trade from the Atlantic ports to Buenaventura once the canal was opened. Moreover, the growing western regions were relatively more proximate to Buenaventura than was Bogotá.

The change in port volume was particularly important for the coffee industry. In 1944 nearly 60 per cent of Colombian coffee moved on the Ferrocarril del Pacífico and out of the port of Buenaventura.[3] Thirty years earlier the proportion moving on that route was negligible.

The opening of the Panama Canal brought opportunities to numerous

[1] Great Britain, Diplomatic and Consular Reports, *Report on the Railways of Colombia* (Miscellaneous Series no. 678, July 1910), p. 39. Authored by Victor Huckin.
[2] Rufino Gutiérrez, *Monografías*, vol. ii, p. 175.
[3] Parsons, *Antioqueño Colonization*, p. 146.

The development of transportation

producers of bulk exports on the Pacific – sugar from Peru, ores from Chile, bananas from Ecuador and lumber from the Pacific Northwest in the United States. For west to east movements of lumber, for example, the opening of the canal reduced steamer time from 70 to 20 days and made possible a reduction in rates of nearly 50 cer cent.[1] The west's share of total U.S. output of lumber rose from under a fifth prior to the canal's opening to over a third in the inter-war period.[2] Waterborne rates from west to east were generally but a half or two-thirds those of the railways. I know of no detailed studies of the external benefits enjoyed by Pacific producers as a result of the opening of the canal, but as the discussion of the lumber industry will indicate, they very likely were substantial. Because coffee was a fairly bulky commodity relative to its value, the benefits of the canal enjoyed by Colombia were great – whatever the costs in hurt pride, national territory lost and the infringement of sovereignty, none of them without significance. The final construction of the coffee railways is the only improvement which may be counted as comparable.

EFFECTIVENESS OF THE RAILWAY

The key innovation in the transport system of Colombia was the railway. In order to evaluate its effectiveness one may proceed with a variety of comparisons, the most important of which is an analysis of the benefits and costs associated with the innovation itself. It is to that task that I now turn.

Objective criteria for judging transport investments are impossible unless one is willing to disregard interpersonal comparisons and assume that a unit of income is equal in value for all.[3] But even within the restrictions of efficiency considerations independent of equity (i.e. abstracting from questions of income distribution or the distribution of benefits) criteria for judgment are not unambiguous because they may be in conflict, and their quantitative magnitudes are difficult to evaluate qualitatively. Private rate of return on investment and broadly conceived benefit/cost ratios are the principal criteria for judging the efficacy of investments. The concept of social saving used by Fogel, Fishlow and more recently McClelland are of interest as well as private and social rates of

---

[1] See Bayard O. Wheeler, 'An Analysis of Douglas Fir Lumber Prices and Factors Contributing to their Structure and Behavior' (Ph.D. diss., University of California, Berkeley 1942), p. 151.

[2] United States Bureau of the Census, *Historical Statistics of the United States, Colonial Times to 1957*, p. 313. These data were brought to my attention by Arthur Rockwell.

[3] Otto Eckstein, *Water Resource Development* (Cambridge 1961), p. 54.

return.[1] In assessing the railway's impact on the United States economy, Fogel measured transport costs with and (hypothetically) without the railway and expressed this saving as a share of gross national product in 1890.[2] He puts the social saving on the interregional distribution of four agricultural products at 0·6 per cent, makes an addition for intraregional movements of the same products and concludes that 'careful study will yield an estimate for all commodities that is well below 5 per cent of gross national product'.[3] Fishlow's investigations yield a much higher estimate of the social saving in 1890, some 15 per cent of GNP, because of the addition of passenger as well as freight movement benefits, and a more conservative estimate of the technical possibilities of extending inland waterways.[4] If it can be shown that the social saving of Colombian railways was in the range established by Fishlow and Fogel for American railways, one might tentatively conclude that the railway was as important in Colombia's development as it was in the United States – despite the fact that little more than 3,000 km. of railways were ever in operation before 1960.

None of the four criteria proposed for the evaluation of transport investments yields an unambiguous verdict about the efficacy of such investments. The private rate of return may be a poor indicator of social value; the benefit/cost ratio, even if it is greater than one, might be smaller than that yielded by an alternative investment if capital is being rationed; the social savings rate, though a good indicator of the size of the benefits relative to national product, tells nothing about the costs of the investment. Another measure, one which would permit comparison of the investment in railways with all alternative investments, is the achieved internal rate of return of capital – if that rate of return is equal to or greater than all alternatives, then it may be judged a success. If it falls short of the rates of return of other projects, then it may be regarded as a less-than-optimal investment.[5] Four criteria then – private rate of return on investment;

---

[1] Fogel's work was cited above: see for another application of the social savings concept, Peter D. McClelland, 'The Cost to America of British Imperial Policy', *The American Economic Review*, LIX (May 1969), 370–81.

[2] For a critique of the method of the counterfactual conditional in econometric history see E. H. Hunt, 'The New Economic History', *History*, LIII (1968), 3–23. The Hunt article is followed by an extended comment on the same subject by G. R. Hawke.

[3] Fogel, *Railroads and American Economic Growth*, pp. 47, 223.

[4] Fishlow, *Railroads*, pp. 47–57.

[5] The well-known study by Conrad and Meyer of American slaveholding judged the internal rate of return on slaveholding to be slightly superior to long-term government bonds; hence, they argued, slavery was profitable. Subsequent adjustments of their data, notably those by Richard Sutch, have tended to strengthen their argument. See Alfred Conrad and John Meyer, *The Economics of Slavery* (Chicago 1964).

The development of transportation

social savings; the ratio of benefits to costs and the internal rate of return on capital – may be used together to provide an overall evaluation of the effectiveness of the Colombian railways. The Colombian railways can usefully be considered in two groups as presented in Table 32. In these two groups are included all lines in operation except the specialized railways connecting Cartagena to the Magdalena River, Barranquilla to its ocean port and Santa Marta to the banana zone. A few other specialized lines were used privately by oil companies and sugar plantations. The lines included in Groups I and II comprised between 85 and 90 per cent of lines in operation from the 1920s through the 1940s. After the consolidation of railway lines in the early 1960s they represented the total of all lines in the country. (See Table 34.)

Table 34 *Group I and Group II railways, kilometers in service, estimated costs of construction and value of assets, 1922, 1934, 1949* (assets in millions of current dollars).

Group I	1922	1934	1949
Kilometers in service	922	1542	1701
Costs of construction and improvements	34·7	76·0	82·8
Estimated value of rollingstock	8·7	19·0	20·7
Total value of investment	43·4	95·0	103·5

Group II			
Kilometers in service	176	1134	1081
Costs of construction and improvements	6·2	78·1	78·1
Estimated value of rollingstock	1·6	19·5	19·5
Total value of investment	7·8	97·6	97·6

Sources: kilometers in service from Table 32; for lines included in each group see text; the Note on Sources discusses the basis for cost and investment estimates.

The six lines in Group I were built to lower transport costs for coffee, for the expansion of production was constantly moving the growing area for coffee further away from cheap river and sea transport. Some 300 km. of track were laid between 1885 and the turn of the century, mainly as a supplement to or replacement of river transport. Another expansion of railways took place between 1905 and 1914 when the Antioquia and Pacífico Railways were largely completed. These lines anticipated the opening of the Panama Canal. The world's longest aerial cable (72 km.) was opened for coffee shipment from Manizales to the Magdalena River in 1919.

Without these transport improvements coffee exports could not have expanded. Alternatively, transport improvements would not have been made without the potential of an export crop. In the first score of years of its operation the Ferrocarril de Antioquia must have depended on coffee. In any given year no less than two-thirds and as much as 80 per cent of its outbound freight by volume was coffee.[1] 'Priority was necessarily given to facilities for the transport of coffee; ... of public investment made in the second half of the 'twenties to improve communications, some fifty per cent was allocated to the province of Antioquia.'[2]

The railways in Group II were expanded from 176 km. in 1922 to over 1,000 km. in 1934. The Nordeste and Central del Norte 2ª were constructed for intraregional movements in the area around Bogotá, the others to facilitate imports. Before considering these lines further, however, it would be well to attempt a preliminary estimate of the four investment criteria for the Group I railways for an early year. Some data are available for the year 1910 on the several lines then in operation; however, except in one or two cases (Ferrocarril de Bolívar and Ferrocarril de La Sabana) railways were not then profitable investments nor did they seem to have a great future. The great expansion of exports (and hence of the volume of goods traffic) was not to occur until the second and third decades of this century. At the time of Victor Huckin's study in 1910 the returns on the railways seemed meager indeed. A better year for the investigation of the efficacy of the Group I railways is 1924, the first year for which reasonably full estimates of traffic movement are available. Since it precedes the great expansion of the later 1920s, the estimates of benefits will tend to be on the low side when compared to the post-1925 period. One can then anticipate that the results of this analysis will provide a lower-bound estimate of the efficacy of the coffee railways.

The coffee railways in 1924

The narrowest of the criteria to compute in evaluating the railways is the private rate of return. Private profitability is calculated as the ratio of net revenues (after deduction of current costs of operation) to the value of investment: $(S-E)/I$. Sales and expenditures are available in reported statistics (*Anuario estadístico, 1924*): revenues for Group I railways in

---

[1] Alejandro López, *Estadística de Antioquia*, p. 27; data from that source were adjusted in some respects by Beyer, 'The Colombian Coffee Industry', p. 202.

[2] ECLA, *Study*, p. 262.

1924 were Ps$7·4 million, expenses of operation, Ps$3·5 million. The estimated value of investment appears in Table 36; it was Ps$43·4 million. Thus the private rate of return is estimated at 9·0 per cent. This figure is probably too low if one is trying to assess the return received by actual owners of the railways. In many cases substantial costs of construction were incurred by individuals who went broke and were forced to sell their interest in the railways at a substantial loss. Those individuals fortunate enough to buy into the railways after 1910 obtained shares and bonded debt at low prices. Huckin reported on the market price of five different debenture bond issues by Colombian railways; in 1910 only one of them was selling at par, the others between 52 and 95. No share prices – neither common nor preferred – were above 77 per cent of their face value at issue, and several were mentioned as unsaleable.[1] Thus individuals who bought into enterprises after 1910 but before their profit potential was realized must have obtained a higher rate of return than that indicated here.[2]

The next easiest of the criteria to calculate is the social saving. It requires an estimate of the total benefits enjoyed by shippers. To make such an estimate one requires information about the total number of ton-kilometers of freight actually moved by the railways and the rates at which they were moved; and the number of ton-kilometers which would have been moved by the next best available transport technology and the rates for such movements. The problem then becomes one of determining the difference in the transport bill under real and hypothetically determined conditions. The difference can then be regarded as the net benefits accruing to shippers as a result of the railway. Fogel put the problem in the following terms in discussing the U.S. railways:

> If the reduction in cost achieved by the railroads was small, and if canals and rivers [mules in the Colombian situation] could have supplied all or most of the service that railroads were providing without increasing unit charges, then the presence of the railroads did not substantially widen the market, and their absence would not have kept it substantially narrower. The conclusion that the railroad was a necessary condition for the widening of the internal market flows not from a body of observed data, but from the assumption that the cost per unit of transportation service was significantly less by rail than by water.[3]

[1] Great Britain, Diplomatic and Consular Reports, Report on the Railways of Colombia, *passim*.

[2] It should be pointed out, however, that the mere excess of current receipts over current expenditures did not guarantee that the excess would be distributed as profits. However, retained earnings would presumably have been used to raise the value of railway assets and were thus the basis for a capital gain for shareholders.

[3] Robert W. Fogel, 'A Quantitative Approach to the Study of Railroads in American Economic Growth. A Report of Some Preliminary Findings', *Journal of Economic History*, XXII (2) (June 1962), 163–97. The quotation is from page 166.

Expansion of coffee

As Fogel explains, one cannot work with observed data alone but must enter some comparisons with relevant, but nonexistent, alternatives. This is the counterfactual conditional which some critics of the new economic history abhor and others regard as its central historical insight.[1]

Table 35   *Group I railways, kilometers in service, tons hauled, estimated ton-kilometers hauled, 1924.*

Name of line	Kilometers in service	Tons hauled (thousands)	Ton-kilometers hauled (millions)
Antioquia			
Amagá Section	58	80	4·6
Nus Section	109	117	12·8
Porce Section	75	132	9·9
Cúcuta	72	44	2·5
FC de Girardot	132	143	18·9
FC del Tolima	94	22	2·1
Pacífico	341	112	25·5
La Dorada	111	151	16·8
Total	992	801	93·1

Sources: kilometers in service – Table 32; tons hauled – *Anuario estadístico, 1924*, p. 54; ton-kilometers hauled – kilometers in service times number of tons hauled, except that certain reductions were made on the Pacífico and Cúcuta lines to take account of short hauls.

The first step in assessing the benefits to shippers is to determine total freight movements by railway. In 1924 all Colombian railways hauled 1·7 million tons of freight. The coffee railways themselves hauled 801,000 tons.[2] Estimates of ton-kilometers carried by the coffee railways appear in Table 35. The six lines carried an estimated 93 million ton-km. of freight that year. Published data on ton-kilometers hauled by railways did not begin to appear until the 1930s; thus the figures in Table 35 must be viewed with some reservation.[3]

[1] For a critique of the approach see E. H. Hunt, 'The New Economic History'.

[2] One cannot conclude that the coffee railways hauled just half of all freight moved by railway; considerable double counting would be involved in such a statement since goods might move first on one of the north coast railways, then on the Ferrocarril de La Dorada and perhaps two other lines. I estimate that the coffee railways hauled about two-thirds of total ton-kilometers moved by all Colombian railways.

[3] On the reforms which led to establishment of the Consejo Nacional de los Ferrocarriles and the fuller publication of railway data see Donald J. Barnhart, 'Colombian Transport and the Reforms of 1931: An Evaluation', *Hispanic American Historical Review*, XXXVIII (1958), 1–24.

The development of transportation

The effective alternative to rail transportation was carriage by mule. One might argue that there were cheaper alternatives available, particularly the construction of roads suitable for wheeled vehicles which presumably could have moved goods at lower ton-kilometer costs than mules. However, as was indicated earlier, road construction was not a particularly successful enterprise in the nineteenth and early twentieth centuries and always failed as a profit-making venture. Maintenance costs due to abuse of the road surface by wagon wheels must have been a main deterrent to the spread of surfaced roadways to judge from contemporary accounts. Thus it would appear that in Colombia (as in the United States) neither tollroads nor public roads provided feasible alternatives to the railway. The mule was the next best alternative to rails.

Mule rates may be roughly estimated at about 50 centavos per ton-km. The average of all mule rates listed in Table 6 for the years 1845–1930 was 41·6 centavos per ton-km. The later rates tended to be above the average; the last one listed was 80 centavos. Other data tend to confirm 50 centavos as a likely lower bound by the 1920s.[1] The railway made possible rates no higher than 15 centavos per ton-km.; the difference of 35 centavos may be taken as a minimum estimate of the saving per ton-kilometer realized by shippers as a result of the railway. For those shippers who would have used mule transport at the higher rates, the saving is equal to the rate reduction multiplied by the number of ton-kilometers shipped. It is not possible to get a direct estimate of ton-kilometers which would have been shipped at the higher rates, but my estimates indicate that mules probably moved about 22 million ton-km. in international trade alone in 1895, so that figure may set a lower bound for the savings enjoyed by shippers at the higher rates. A graphic presentation of benefits to old shippers appears as the hatched rectangle in Figure 16.[2] The benefits enjoyed by new shippers (those which enter the market for transport services as the price of those services declines) are shown in the hatched triangle in Figure 16. The total benefit for old and new shippers is thus estimated as Ps$20.1 million. Gross product was estimated by the E C L A

---

[1] See Donald S. Barnhart, 'Colombian Transportation Problems and Policies, 1923–1948' (Ph.D. diss., University of Chicago 1954), p. 189.

[2] In his presentation of benefit/cost analysis Eckstein notes that 'in evaluating the benefits and costs of a project, two situations must be compared: the development of the economy with the project and the development that would occur without it'. We cannot know how many ton-kilometers of freight would have been shipped without the railway; the alternative of using shipments 'before' and 'after' construction is logically fallacious; however, the arc elasticity of demand for transport derived from these figures is −1·15, a figure apparently in the appropriate range – neither very elastic nor very inelastic. For the quotation see Eckstein, *Water Resource Development*, p. 51.

Study to have been about Ps\$650 million in 1925.[1] Since gross product was growing about 5 per cent per annum at the time, the 1924 gross product would have been about Ps\$620 million. The social saving was thus on the order of 3·2 per cent of gross product for the coffee railways alone.

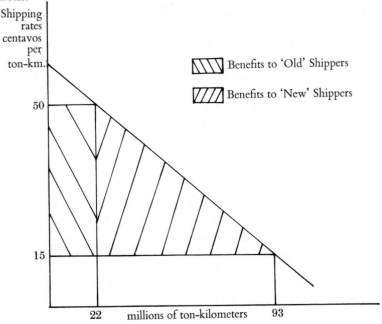

Shipping rates centavos per ton-km.

☒ Benefits to 'Old' Shippers

☒ Benefits to 'New' Shippers

Figure 16 Railway benefits to old and new shippers, 1924.

I have not made careful estimates of the benefits derived from the other railways; if those lines are included the rate of social saving as of 1924 may have been on the order of 4·8 per cent of gross product.[2] This

[1] ECLA *Study*, 'Statistical Appendix,' Tables 1 and 32. The ECLA estimate for gross product in 1925 (Ps\$2,189 million) is stated in 1950 pesos. I converted this estimate to current 1925 pesos for comparability with the other figures being used in this chapter, using the implicit deflator presented in the ECLA *Study*.

[2] One may estimate the average length of haul in 1924 at 75 km. (For 1935 the average length of haul was 90 km. rising to 110 km. in 1949. The average, available from Banco de la República, *Informe anual, 1960–62*, Part II, p. 264, was simply extrapolated backward.) The average length of haul multiplied by total tons hauled yielded an estimate of 137 million ton-km. for the year 1924.

By assuming the same conditions of demand for all railways as for the coffee railways alone one arrives at a simple outward expansion of the demand curve in Figure 16. The larger total benefits then come to Ps\$29·7 million or 4·8 per cent of gross product.

The development of transportation

figure, though comparable in magnitude to Fogel's estimate of the rate of social saving of American railroads, is conceptually different since it has been established as a lower rather than an upper bound estimate.

The concept of social saving examines only one side of the benefit/cost ratio; to compute that ratio we must also know costs incurred in the construction and operation of the Group I railways. Direct operating costs are derivable from railway reports; for Group I railways operating costs totaled Ps$3·5 million in 1924. Capital costs can only be derived indirectly. Estimated value of assets of Group I railways appears in Table 34 and totaled some Ps$43·4 million in 1924. Assuming a 10 per cent rate of interest or discount, capital costs may be estimated at Ps$4·3 million. Thus the benefit/cost ratio for Group I railways in 1924 works out as follows:

$$\frac{B}{C} = \frac{20·1}{3·5 + 0·1 \times 43·4} = \frac{20·1}{7·8} = 2·6$$

Benefits of the coffee railways exceeded costs (both fixed and variable) by a wide margin. Without knowing the exact price elasticity of demand for transport service, it is impossible to give an exact estimate of the ratio. However, the various biases discussed here are generally in the direction of underestimating benefits and overestimating costs, so that the benefit/cost ratio was probably higher than that indicated above. Moreover, passenger and animal traffic, which contributed about one-fourth of total rail revenue in 1924, have not been included in the calculation of benefits. There may have been unobserved nonuser benefits as well. Since traffic grew at a spectacular pace through the rest of the 1920s the ratio of benefits to costs must have improved through 1929. These additional factors favor the view that the ratio of benefits to costs on the coffee railways was quite favorable, and that the investment was well justified by the social returns. Eckstein suggested in his study of United States water resource development that a benefit/cost ratio of 1·4 : 1 was high enough to justify a proposed investment; the ratio is of course substantially higher in this case.[1] Though no final conclusions can be reached about the efficacy of transport investments up to 1924, it does seem that

[1] Eckstein, *Water Resource Development*, pp. 101–3. He also suggests use of an interest rate of 2·5 to 3 per cent in discounting future benefits, a rate well below the one used here in evaluating current capital costs.

The method is of course quite different since water resource projects entail the estimation of a stream of future costs and benefits all discounted at an appropriate rate to the starting point of the project. I have attempted that approach only for new railway investments for all lines after 1921.

on the three criteria used for analysis here the coffee railways did well: private rate of return, 9·0 per cent; social savings, 3·2 per cent and benefit/cost ratio, 2·6 : 1 Colombia's coffee railways seem to have done about as well as the United States railways and to have made an equally significant contribution to economic development.

Colombian railways under competition, 1936–49

Somewhat better data on rail traffic became available in the 1930s when most of the remaining foreign owners of Colombian railways were bought out by the Colombian government and operation of many of the lines passed to the *Consejo Administrativo de los Ferrocarriles*. For the years 1936–49 information is presented in publications of the *Consejo* as well as in the statistical yearbook in a form applicable to the present study. After 1949 a reorganization of the railways into sections obliterated some of the distinctions between those I have placed in Groups I and II. Hence the years 1936 through 1949, because of limitations of the data, are the only ones which provide the basis for further analysis and comparison of the two groups of railways.

Those years are far from ideal. During the 1930s the economy faced adverse terms of trade for coffee (low points were reached in 1937 and 1940), and the quantum of imports was actually lower in the late 1930s than it had been in the 1920s.[1] The volume of traffic on the railways in the 1920s, which reached a peak of 3·3 million tons hauled in 1928, was not surpassed until 1942.[2] The value added by truck transport actually surpassed that of the railways in 1940, according to ECLA estimates.[3] Hence, the impact of the Great Depression in the 1930s and the advent of serious competition from trucks and highway users puts something of a downward bias on any estimates of the efficacy of the railways during the years 1936–49. Such a bias may seem appropriate since it brings into bold relief the threat constituted to any mode of transport (particularly one so inflexible as the railway) by unexpected alternatives.

---

[1] ECLA *Study*, Appendix, p. 2. Exports by volume were up some 50 per cent, but the total volume of traffic was at best constant.

[2] Banco de la República, *Informe anual, 1960–1962*, p. 264.

[3] ECLA *Study*, Appendix, p. 158. The ECLA estimates are for gross product originating in the various sectors of transport. Since the railways carried bulkier commodities than trucks, more goods by volume may still have moved by railway. The ECLA estimates are based on assumptions about the number of vehicles in operation; the lack of sample surveys or other intensive studies of transport leads one to view the ECLA estimates with some skepticism.

The development of transportation

Table 36 *Estimates of efficacy of transport investments, Group I and Group II railways, average 1936–49.*

Averages of annual figures, 1936–49, except value of investment, 1949	Group I	Group II
1. Revenue or sales (millions)	$26·3	$8·8
2. Operating costs (millions)	$20·5	$8·9
3. Value of investment, 1949 (millions)	$103·5	$97·6
4. Benefits		
a. 'Old' users		
(1) Ton-kilometers (millions)	68	22
(2) Savings over mule rates	$0·35	$0·35
(3) Benefits to 'old' users (millions)	$23·8	$7·7
b. 'New' users		
(1) Ton-kilometers (millions)	231	80
(2) Savings over mule rates	$0·175	$0·175
(3) Benefits to 'new' users (millions)	$40·4	$14·0
c. Total benefits, 'old' and 'new' users (millions)	$64·2	$21·7
5. Gross product, 1943 (millions of current pesos)	$1819	$1819
6. Rate of return $(R-C)/I$	5·6%	—
7. Benefit/Cost ratio	2·1	1·2
8. Social saving	3·5%	1·2%

Sources: Consejo Administrativo de los Ferrocarriles Nacionales, *Revista del Consejo Administrativo*, *78*: 45 (Jan.–June 1950); *Anuario general de estadística, 1940, 1949;* ECLA Study, 'Statistical Appendix', Tables 1, 32.

Table 36 presents the relevant data for calculation of the evaluative criteria used here. The same assumptions about alternative rates apply in this analysis as were used for the coffee railways in 1924.[1] This assumption may seem inappropriate since freight movements by truck became common in the late 1930s. Truck rates were 10 to 22 centavos in 1949; rail rates were 6 to 8 centavos per ton-km.[2] However, the actual construction of the railways was ended by the early 1930s when the best alternative

---

[1] Roughly the same procedure as was used in examining the coffee railways in 1924 was used in determining the number of ton-kilometers shipped by 'old' and 'new' shippers. Similar price elasticities of demand derive from these estimates: −1·01 for the Group I railways and −1·06 for Group II. Again, these arc elasticities seem to be within the appropriate range.

[2] International Bank for Reconstruction and Development, *The Basis of a Development Program for Colombia* (Currie Mission Report, Baltimore 1950), pp. 115–25.

transport mode was still the mule. A fair evaluation would thus lead to comparison with the best feasible alternative of the 1920s rather than the innovation of the 1930s and 1940s.[1]

The private rate of return was negative for Group II railways but positive for Group I railways: the earliest railway investments were consistently the most profitable. The Group I railways were all initiated under a concession system which depended almost entirely on anticipation of high profit rates.[2] The secular growth of the Colombian economy and the expansion of exports almost guaranteed that the profit on such early ventures would be handsome. Group II railways were built up with easily available foreign funds during the highwater mark of U.S. foreign lending in the second half of the 1920s. The very fact that these lines were built relatively late in the game would suggest that private profits as high as those on earlier lines could not be expected. Even at that, had Colombian trade continued to expand in the 1930s and 1940s as it had in the few years prior to the building of the Group II lines, even they might have been profitable ventures.

The estimated rates of social saving are impressive. The apparent social saving of the Group I railways rose from 3·2 per cent of gross product in 1924 to 3·5 per cent of gross product for the average of years from 1936 to 1949. The railways in Group II failed to produce a rate of social saving approaching that of Group I railways. Though investment in these lines cannot be regarded as a social loss, as Barnhart and others have regarded it, the realized return was clearly not so great as Colombians had learned to expect from the railways built earlier.[3] The two groups of railways taken together produced a rate of social saving as high as Fogel's maximum estimate for U.S. railways in 1890. The figure is still well below Fishlow's estimate of 15 per cent for the social saving of American railroads.

---

[1] Fogel considers in his work such striking counterfactual situations as a sizable increase of navigable inland waterways and earlier appearance of the internal-combustion engine. The former plays a central role in his analysis of intraregional freight movements, the latter he holds out as a tantalizing possibility. His discussion illustrates some of the grave theoretical and empirical problems associated with making counterfactual conditional analyses.

[2] See Hoffman, 'A History of Railway Concessions in Colombia to 1943' (Ph.D. diss., American University 1945), p. 263. Hoffman intended in his thesis to contrast the success of the government program of railway construction after 1922 with the relatively ineffective system of concessions and land grants to private enterprise which had been the rule in preceding years. Although he was correct in observing that the government program built more railways more quickly than earlier procedures, he was unable to assess the decidedly different impact on the country's development of the two periods of construction.

[3] See Donald Barnhart, 'Colombian Transport and the Reforms of 1931: An Evaluation.' He repeats here the view of some contemporaries that three-quarters of the Ps$300 million invested in transport between 1923 and 1930 represented a total loss.

The development of transportation

The ratio of benefits to costs was high for the Group I railways but not so high as it had been in 1924. A number of additions to these lines were made in the 1920s, and it appears that they did not yield as great a return as the older investments. The benefit/cost ratio for the Group II railways was considerably lower than the Group I ratio, but it was still greater than one. Though the privately calculated profitability of these railways was negative, there was some social return.

The relative ineffectiveness of investments in the Group II railways explains the lower average ratio of benefits to costs when Groups I and II are combined. A higher rate of social saving might have been enjoyed had such investments been as successful as those in the coffee railways. This speculation is, however, illusory since it depends on the practical impossibility of a constant, rather than a declining marginal rate of return on capital. The further doses of investment in the Group II railways during the 1920s went to relatively inferior projects simply because the best projects (the coffee railways themselves) had already been undertaken.

Evaluation of the railway boom of the 1920s

There are not sufficient data on costs and benefits of the early investments in railways to justify further statistical analysis of their performance. The analysis of the coffee railways tends to show that they were wise investments with substantial returns, whether the investments were made before or after the boom of the 1920s. The preceding section has led to some doubt about the efficiency of railway investments of the 1920s when some Ps$143 million was devoted to enlarging and improving the system. In this section I will attempt to measure the present discounted value of the stream of costs and benefits ensuing from further railway expansion in the 1920s.

The procedure to be employed here differs in some respects from that used in previous sections. The analysis requires evaluation of the following formula:

$$\text{P.D.V.} = \sum_{i=1}^{t} \frac{B_i - C_i}{(1+r)^t}$$

where P.D.V. = present discounted value of the investment

B_i = benefits accruing from the investment in the ith year

C_i = costs of construction and operation in the ith year

r = the social rate of discount

t = assumed lifetime of the investment

Expansion of coffee

The internal rate of return is simply defined as that value of r in the preceding equation which will make the total expression on the right just equal to zero. In the following tables I will present the P.D.V. at various discount rates which in turn will provide a rough indication of the internal rate of return.

The following assumptions underlie the calculations:

(1) The extant railways in 1920 are assumed to have carried over the years 1921–57, 50 million ton-km. of goods per annum; that quantity has been deducted for all years from total ton-kilometers moved. The resultant movements are hence attributable to the railway investments made after 1921.

(2) The benefits (B_a) per ton-km. are estimated at 21·4 centavos. This figure is the weighted average of benefits of old and new shippers for both 1924 and for the average of years 1936–49. This estimate may appear too high, particularly for the years after 1945 when rail rates and truck rates were much closer together than 21·4 centavos. This assumption is compensated for by the implicit assumption that the railways end their useful life with no scrap value as of 1957.[1] An alternative estimate of benefits (B_b) equal to one-half those of B_a is also presented.

(3) Costs of construction were estimated on the basis of assumptions discussed in the Note on Sources and distributed over the years 1922–9. Operating costs were taken directly from published statistics for the years 1936–58 and interpolated on the basis of available data for earlier years. Two sets of operating cost estimates have been used, the first C_a based on current costs of the railways as published, the second C_b a deflated set of cost figures in 1925–9 prices. Current costs were deflated by the implicit gross domestic product price deflator used in the ECLA *Study* and the published reports of the Banco de la República.[2] This index is far from ideal for use in considering the railways, but it is the only one currently available. (An index of railway employee wage rates would be a superior index for use in deflating costs.) No deflation of benefits was needed since these were estimated in pesos of the 1920s in the first instance.

(4) Ton-kilometers hauled for years prior to 1934 were estimated by projecting backward the average length of haul and multiplying by total tons hauled.

---

[1] For a similar assumption used in analysis of the United States interstate highway system see Ann Fetter Friedlaender, *The Interstate Highway System, A Study in Public Investment* (Amsterdam 1965). I derived much of the guidelines for my investigation from the Friedlaender work.

[2] ECLA *Study*, Statistical Appendix', p. 38, Table 32; Banco de la República, *Informe anual*, 1 July 1960–31 December 1962, Part II (Bogotá 1963), pp. 192, 196.

The development of transportation

Table 37 *Costs and benefits of the Colombian railways, 1922–57* (millions of pesos).

Year	Benefits (a)	Benefits (b)	Costs of construction	Costs of operation (a)	Costs of operation (b)
	(1)	(2)	(3)	(4)	(5)
1922	3·9	1·9	9·4	7·1	7·1
1923	14·1	7·1	13·6	11·6	11·6
1924	18·6	9·3	20·0	13·2	13·2
1925	23·8	11·9	20·0	13·5	14·9
1926	33·6	16·8	20·0	18·8	18·4
1927	41·5	20·8	20·0	20·4	20·7
1928	46·9	23·5	20·0	24·2	22·1
1929	44·7	22·4	20·0	19·9	20·2
1930	31·7	15·9	—	10·0	12·8
1931	24·6	12·3	—	8·3	13·2
1932	28·9	14·5	—	6·9	13·0
1933	31·2	15·6	—	7·4	13·6
1934	35·7	17·9	—	11·0	14·5
1935	41·9	21·0	—	12·3	15·7
1936	48·2	24·1	—	13·2	15·9
1937	50·7	25·4	—	12·7	14·9
1938	55·9	28·0	—	14·0	14·6
1939	59·5	29·8	—	16·9	17·0
1940	62·1	31·0	—	19·4	19·2
1941	61·9	31·0	—	17·5	18·0
1942	73·8	36·9	—	18·6	17·5
1943	91·6	45·8	—	22·0	17·5
1944	93·1	46·6	—	26·6	18·4
1945	105·5	52·8	—	34·4	19·9
1946	116·4	58·2	—	43·5	23·2
1947	112·8	56·4	—	48·1	22·1
1948	120·5	60·2	—	53·9	21·7
1949	126·1	63·0	—	60·2	22·6
1950	117·7	58·8	—	66·3	21·9
1951	115·6	57·8	—	69·7	21·1
1952	115·1	57·5	—	72·1	21·3
1953	130·8	65·4	—	74·4	21·1
1954	131·4	65·7	—	77·1	19·6
1955	123·7	61·8	—	80·6	20·6
1956	125·4	62·7	—	85·5	20·2
1957	139·7	69·9	—	90·2	18·1

Sources: see the Note on Sources.

Expansion of coffee

It should already be apparent that I am seeking to provide only a very general estimate of the present discounted value of railway investments in the 1920s. In order to conduct a more careful study, one would have to disaggregate the railways and treat them individually with respect to their benefits and costs. Though such an analysis would have considerable utility in estimating the social return on individual railways, the available published data are altogether too sparse to justify that approach here.[1]

Table 38 *Present discounted value of Colombian railways, selected rates* (millions of pesos).

Benefits and costs used	Per cent					
	0	5	10	20	21	25
B_a, C_a	+1,254·8	+401·9	+137·7	+4·9	—	−12·3
B_a, C_b	+1,818·8	+521·5	+161·9	+3·1	−3·1	−14·3
B_b, C_a	−39·6	−59·5	−84·9	—	—	—
B_b, C_b	+519·0	+57·9	−52·1	—	—	—

Source: based on data in Table 37.

The estimated costs and benefits of the Colombian railways from 1922 through 1957 appear in Table 37. These data in turn serve as the basis for calculations of the present discounted value of the railways, under various assumptions about the social rate of discount, which appear in Table 38. The following conclusions may be drawn from that table.

(1) The internal rate of return on investments in the railways is very sensitive to the estimate of benefits. If the benefits were in fact equal to those hypothesized under B_a, then the internal rate of return was 20 to 21 per cent. In this case the internal rate of return proved not to be sensitive to the choice of current or constant prices. If the lower estimate of benefits is used, then the internal rate of return was between 5 and 10 per cent (if constant costs are used) or actually negative if one uses current pesos.

(2) Using social rates of discount in the neighborhood of 2 to 3 per cent as suggested by Eckstein, Friedlaender and others, one would conclude

---

[1] Direct access to railway archives could help in improving the reliability of estimates of costs and benefits. I would have been given access to the records of the Ferrocarril de Antioquia in 1964, but that line had destroyed all records prior to the mid-1950s when it was consolidated with the Ferrocarriles Nacionales in 1962. I am not sure what records might currently be available in unpublished form from other railways.

that the railway investments of the 1920s were beneficial to Colombia except in the case of the lower estimate of benefits and the use of current, undeflated operating costs. If costs are deflated to 1925–9 prices, then the present discounted value of the railways was positive even at a 5 per cent rate of discount. Since the peso declined in value so substantially after the mid-1940s, it would seem incorrect to give much attention either to the B_a, C_a or to the B_b, C_a estimates. The other two estimates using deflated, or constant peso, estimates should be deemed more meaningful in the analysis.

(3) The arguments presented up to this point suggest that the B_a, C_b estimate in Table 38 is the most accurate for use in evaluating the railway investments of the 1920s. At a low rate of social discount (and even 5 per cent is regarded by the theorists as a high rate) the railways proved to be immensely successful.

(4) Even if the real benefits were only half those posited by the B_a estimate the railways were still a good investment for the country.

(5) Since the overall return on railway investments of the 1920s was so high, and since the product of the Group II railways was so meager, we must conclude that the further doses of investment in the coffee railways were spectacularly successful. Those investments linked together the railways in the west (principally the Ferrocarril de Antioquia and the Ferrocarril del Pacífico) and made possible through service from the Magdalena River to the Pacific. The mechanism by which great benefits were realized was the shift of traffic to the port of Buenaventura, particularly the export of coffee, and the radical cheapening of transport costs. Data gathered by Robert Beyer suggests that the cost of overland transport as a percentage of delivered costs of coffee in New York fell from 15 to 24 per cent around 1870 to only 2 to 4 per cent by 1943.[1] After that date railway costs (expressed in constant pesos of 1925–9 purchasing power) per ton-kilometer continued to fall despite competition from trucking, difficulties in maintaining the volume of traffic and deterioration of rollingstock.[2] In short, the railway continued to perform its most important function: to cheapen the cost of moving bulky products. The investments of the 1920s did away with transshipments and the costly process of loading and unloading. For the coffee railways these proved to be very useful additions to the infrastructure already in place in 1920.

---

[1] Robert C. Beyer, 'Transportation and the Coffee Industry in Colombia', *Inter-American Economic Affairs*, II (1948), 18.

[2] Calculation of costs per ton-kilometer based on column 5 of Table 37 and ton-kilometers hauled. The source for the latter data appears in the Note on Sources.

Expansion of coffee

Summary of the railway experience

The initial improvements in the transport system wrought by the rail-roads had been in several cases almost obvious investment opportunities. Demand for improvement was so great that well-conceived projects were assured of success. By the 1920s, however, the most profitable lines had been built; careful planning would have been needed to get the best results of further transport investments. Unfortunately the Conserva-tive governments of the 1920s were unable to formulate such a policy. Pork-barrel legislation which required the national government to spread investment funds among the various departments made concentration on a few key projects impossible. The Colombian Congress parceled out the 25-million-dollar American indemnity among eleven different railroad projects, an aerial cable, a canal and an agricultural mortgage bank.[1] Some projects were brought to fruition, the best example being com-pletion of a two-mile tunnel connecting two sections of the Ferrocarril de Antioquia. More typical of the period, however, was the finding that a German firm, after the expenditure of Ps$4·5 million, had made no positive improvements in river navigation.[2] Perhaps foreign capital was too easily available: the national government felt it imperative in 1928 to forbid departmental and municipal government to sell any more bonds on the New York market (Law 6 of 1928).

It is not too surprising that costs of construction for the railways rose in the 1920s. (1) Prices of imported components, mainly rails and equip-ment, were apparently 20–25 per cent higher than in the pre-World War I period; (2) domestic prices had risen also; nonetheless a doubling of construction costs (from Ps$35,000 to Ps$75,000) per kilometer is re-markable. The quality of construction (ballasting, rail weights, grade and curvature specifications) was probably higher in the 1920s, thus adding to construction costs. Since construction costs fell during the 1930s to Ps$43,000 per kilometer, one is tempted to conclude that pork-barrel legislation and possible misfeasance in the railway construction program of the 1920s added significantly to the costs of that investment.[3] A 40 per

---

[1] United States Department of Commerce, Bureau of Foreign and Domestic Commerce, 'Colombia: Commerce and Industries, 1922 and 1923', Trade Information Bulletin no. 223 (Washington 28 April 1924).

[2] See Barnhart, 'Colombian Transport and the Reforms of 1931', p. 7.

[3] The index of U.S. export prices for manufactures declined from approximately 95 for the period 1925–9 to 65 for the years 1931–6. This change will explain perhaps 40 per cent in the fall in construction costs. Another 40 per cent could be accounted for by the fall in price of domestic inputs. The remaining 20 per cent decline in construction costs may be due to more careful project selection and quality control.

The development of transportation

cent reduction in initial construction costs of the railways in the 1920s would have raised the estimated benefit/cost ratio for Group II railways from 1·2 to about 1·5.

SUMMARY AND CONCLUSIONS

The backwardness of the transport system in 1850 was a real block to economic progress in Colombia. The gradual removal of that block by successive investments and innovations which reduced the cost of transport was a key element in the achievement of development in the years up to and even following 1930. If the cost of transport had been significantly higher the rate and level of economic development in the years after 1910 would probably have been significantly lower.

Improvements in water transport preceded improvements in overland transport by several decades, perhaps as much as half a century. As a result lowland areas near navigable rivers grew relatively closer to the outside world in the years between 1860 and 1910. Their effective distance from highland areas increased in relative terms. The result was an expansion in the trade of lowland areas with the outside world which began in the 1850s. Colombia's dependence on foreign trade thus got its start even before construction of the railways.

The effective distance between cities grew relatively great when compared to that between each city and the outside world. Consequently, internal trade faced increasing relative transport costs when compared to international trade. This tendency was exacerbated by the railways since all lines were built to facilitate external rather than internal trade. Bogotá and Medellín, the two largest cities, were not connected by direct rail service until 1960.

All during the second half of the nineteenth century transport innovations actually adopted by Colombia were biased in favor of the expansion of international trade and increased dependence on the vicissitudes of external markets. When the demand for Colombian tobacco suddenly fell off in 1875, the blow fell hard on an economy which earned a large share of its foreign exchange from that single product. Transport improvements made up to that time had done little to benefit alternative export products so that the transformation of the export economy proved most difficult: exports failed to perform well until the end of the first decade of the twentieth century. The inadequacy of the transport system bears a large part of the responsibility for the poor performance of exports.

Here it was only possible to make a quantitative assessment of improvements in rail transport. However, from 1905 onward the Colombian government was also making investments in a system of feeder roads and other highways tending to lower the nation's transport bill and to enlarge the size of market areas. These improvements may have had an even greater impact on Colombia's rate of economic development than did the railways.

Table 39 *Domestic freight movements by type of transportation, 1947, 1959–62* (millions of ton-kilometers and percentages).

Means of transport	1947		1959–62[a]	
	ton-km.	per cent	ton-km.	per cent
Railways	584·0	32·5	813	17·4
Highways	642·5	35·8	2,608	55·7
Inland waterways and coastal shipping	511·5	28·5	1,210	25·8
Airways	56·5	3·2	50	1·1
Totals	1794·5	100·0	4,681[b]	100·0

Sources: IBRD, *Basis of a Development Program for Colombia,* p. 103, for 1947 estimates. República de Colombia, Consejo Nacional de Política Económica y Planeación, Departamento Administrativo de Planeación y Servicios Técnicos, unpublished averages for four years, 1959–62.

[a] Four-year average.
[b] Excludes movements by crude oil and refinery pipelines.

The Liberal Party came to power in 1930 and promised to reform the transport system. Germán Uribe Hoyos, a prominent engineer, was appointed minister of public works; his task was to formulate the first national transport policy. The most striking aspect of the Liberal program passed by the Congress in 1931 was the shift in emphasis to highways. The new policy abandoned the former goal of a national trunk railway system; instead, it proposed a 6,400-km. network of highways. By 1942 only 391 km. were paved in any way and of these, 235 km. had only been treated with oil. The Liberals failed to complete even a third of their proposed program.[1] Nevertheless they began the reversal of an eighty-year-old trend favoring external over internal commerce. Since the indigenous development of manufacturing required the widening of domestic markets, that policy change was essential to the phase of development on which Colombia embarked in the 1930s.

[1] Barnhart, 'Colombian Transport and the Reforms of 1931', p. 12.

The development of transportation

The World Bank mission in the late 1940s provided the first comprehensive estimate of total freight traffic by type of transportation. In 1947, according to their estimates, more intercity traffic was moving on the highways than on the railways. The relative position of the railways was to decline even further in the 1950s. As the data in Table 39 indicate, the railway's share of total freight movements declined from 32·5 per cent in 1947 to 17·4 per cent in the years 1959–62. The railways were headed in the 1930s toward a secondary role in Colombia's transport system. But they had already done their job and repaid society well for the treasure and effort devoted to their construction.

There was a symbiotic relationship between coffee exports and transport improvements. One is tempted to conclude that had the railways been built earlier, in the 1880s rather than the 1920s, for example, coffee exports would have reached their 1920s level in that earlier decade. The country would have been four decades further along on its path of economic development that it in fact has been. An explanation of the failure to undertake railway construction earlier and with more vigor lies in the dominance of a *laissez-faire* ideology and the inability of the central government to perceive and appropriate the external benefits of railway construction. This statement is an 'as if' conditional which has no validity as a direct criticism of policies actually followed. It does, however, lead toward a search for the explanation of why the external benefits were not perceived and why development was delayed.

A THEORY OF THE TRANSITION

Sometime between the end of the nineteenth century and the beginning of World War I Colombia successfully reversed a long economic decline and began a spectacular period of economic development. Few countries achieved rates of growth of total and per capita output which exceeded that of Colombia's after 1910. Much of Chapter 8 was devoted to a detailed examination of the period of development, particularly the expansion of the economy of Antioquia. Chapter 7 before it, dealt with the previous era of decline. Here I will attempt to explain the transition.

The elements of the explanation are the following:

(1) An autonomous upward shift in the population growth potential occurred sometime after 1850. The shift apparently came earlier for Antioquia than for other areas of the country. This shift first had the effect of depressing income, then later of accelerating its growth.

(2) The upward shift of the population growth function expanded interdependence between individuals and regions and thus created new problems of adaptation and new opportunities for cost-reducing innovations, particularly in transport improvements and urbanization.

(3) Regions responded differently to these problems and opportunities so that interregional differences in income and product grew greater as some areas successfully developed while others stagnated.

(4) There was nothing automatic about the development process as differential regional development shows. Fortuitious circumstances will explain some of the difference; receptivity of a region's people is probably as important. Some regions made the most of their opportunities while others seem to have been overcome with the problems of population expansion and to have remained stagnant.

(5) An explanation must finally be pushed back to human motivation: Some regions developed because the people there wanted to.

In attempting a general explanation of the transition I will not try to describe events in detail but will instead deal with a 'stylized' reality not inconsistent with existing knowledge of what happened. Such a general interpretation is important because it will make the Colombian experience of the transition understandable as a particular case of the general problem

A theory of the transition

of transition to economic development faced by all countries and peoples at some time – either past or future – in their histories.

A MODEL OF AUTONOMOUS POPULATION EXPANSION

The reader already familiar with Figure 7 will recognize the general framework of explanation set out here in Figure 17. It includes the same assumptions about the production function and population growth

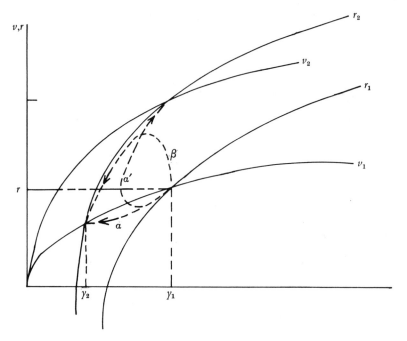

Figure 17 A model of autonomous population growth.

function typical of the literature mentioned earlier. One novelty is introduced, viz., the possibility of an autonomous shift of the population growth function upward from its initial position r_1 to r_2. A survey of the literature on economic growth indicates that no one has integrated this possibility into formal growth models.[1] Shifts of the production function

[1] For a general review see F. H. Hahn and R. C. O. Matthews, 'The Theory of Economic Growth: A Survey', *Economic Journal*, LXXIV (1964), 779–902. For an indication of some sensitivity to this question by a theorist see Nicholas Kaldor, *Essays on Economic Stability and Growth* (Cambridge, England 1960), p. 288.

have been a popular subject for analysis; shifts of the population growth function are perhaps due for at least equivalent attention.

An upward shift of the population growth function implies a fall in per capita income and possibly a reduction in the equilibrium rates of growth of income and population. This change is shown in Figure 17 as per capita income declines from y_1 to y_2. How then can an increase in the potential rate of population growth bring on a period of development? With the shift of the population growth function, the old equilibrium is upset and income depressed. This change may provide the stimulus for changes in the v function as people innovate in order to escape the exigencies of the decline in income. What is required is determination on the part of individuals to regain their former levels of income and to re-establish their expected levels of living. This is accomplished by moving the production function upward and outward from v_1 to v_2, a change which implies technical advance sufficient to offset the higher potential rate of population growth.

The greater potential for population growth poses a transcendant social and economic problem which may or may not be solved. If it is not solved per capita income will remain depressed permanently. If it is solved, however, the process of problem solving may become an ingrained social habit. The society may go on indefinitely shifting the production function upward and outward with new technical innovations. The larger scale of society and expectation of faster rates of growth for total demand became ancillary stimuli for even further innovation and problem solving. Regular economic growth may then be a permanent feature of the society.

The path on which the society tends to move from y_1 to y_2 may determine whether it will escape from the low-level equilibrium, regain the old level of income and then adapt itself to continuing technical change. Three possibilities are shown by the dashed curves labeled a, a', and β in Figure 17. The path of change labeled a shows an initial decline in the observed rate of population growth as per capita income declines. With the curve a' there is first the decline of the population growth-rate and decline in per capita income following the same path as a. But at some point the downward pressure on income is overcome by successful innovations and there is movement toward a new equilibrium with a higher rate of growth of income and population. From there the society may continue to innovate, or economies of scale can carry the society to higher levels of per capita income to the right of y_1. At some stage a standard-of-living effect may occur, lowering r_2 and permitting

A theory of the transition

further expansion of per capita income with lower rates of population growth.[1]

The key to the transition is the reversal implied in the movement off of the path α toward the low-level equilibrium at y_2. The reversal may itself be regarded as the result of actions taken to avoid the low-level trap. Thus innovation and change must appear to reduce the inevitable depressive influences of the upward shift of the population growth potential. The uniqueness of this analysis is in the hypothesis that there is a prior upward shift of the population potential which stimulates the innovations and economic change. One can examine this hypothesis in general terms by reference to the nineteenth-century experience of North-Atlantic countries.

The nineteenth-century experience

The path α' is the one which the developed countries of the North Atlantic have generally followed. There was an autonomous upward shift of the population growth function due to a variety of medical and institutional changes in Europe. In his review of the question Habukkuk lists the decline of epidemics, emancipation of the serfs in Germany, and certain aspects of the Napoleonic Civil Code as factors which brought on the shift after 1750.[2] The first effected dramatic mortality declines, especially among infants, the second and third mentioned reduced the effectiveness of the check of late marriages and thus may have raised birth and fertility rates. Improvements in medical knowledge in the century from 1750 to 1850 were not especially important since 'except for innoculation and vaccination, there were no additions to knowledge which had a significant effect on mortality during the century'. Factors endogenous to the models discussed here (increased productivity in agriculture, the growing relative influence of urbanization and industrialization) came too late to cause a movement of the v function *along* a fixed population growth function. Habakkuk concludes that

even where population growth was in some sense a response to autonomous economic changes, the most significant change was not any independent increase in per capita incomes, and that over most of Europe population growth was not in fact a response to economic changes even in a more general sense. There is a case, therefore, for regarding the population growth as in some measure fortuitous.[3]

[1] On the standard-of-living effect see E. E. Hagen, 'Population and Economic Growth', *American Economic Review*, XLIX (1959), 310–27.

[2] H. J. Habakkuk, 'Population Problems and European Economic Development in the Late Eighteenth and Nineteenth Centuries', *American Economic Review*, LIII (1963), 607–18.

[3] Habakkuk, 'Population Problems and European Economic Development', p. 612.

Expansion of coffee

He goes on then to provide an explanation for subsequent growth. 'The simple and initial effect of population increase was to reduce per capita income.' But then a number of other effects may derive from more rapid population growth: (1) a Ricardo-Lewis effect of cheap labor making possibly easy capital accumulation; (2) demand effects growing even with falling per capita income provided only that total income grows; (3) sectoral demand effects pushing up the need for housing, transport and other social overheads, at the same time shifting the marginal efficiency of investments; (4) entrepreneurial stimulation effects brought on by the changing factor-price ratios. These are a few possible beneficial effects of rapid population growth; others have been listed by Kuznets and Hirschman.[1] There is no logical necessity that lower per capita income will be the final result. Habakkuk asks the appropriate question:

Was the marked rise in per capita incomes in all advanced countries in the second half of the nineteenth century a rescue operation conducted by an independently generated leap in, e.g. technical progress? Or was it the response to population pressure of the kind which prompted Professor Hicks to speculate that 'perhaps the whole industrial revolution of the last two hundred years has been nothing but a vast spectacular boom, largely induced by the unparalleled rise in population.[2]

The prior acceleration of population could have been the primary inducement to the flurry of technological change and innovation which has been occurring since the eighteenth century. Although an autonomous upward shift in the population growth potential initially depresses income, it can be sufficient stimulus to bring on continuing change and improvements in the level of living.

The twentieth-century experience

The autonomous jump in the population potential apparently can follow a different path from that experienced in the North-Atlantic area. It is sketched as β in Figure 17. There is an initial surge of population, and the pressure on levels of living is much more severe. Consequently, the movement onto a path like α' may be much more difficult and less likely to occur.

One example of such failure is that described by Geertz as a condition of involution in which existing social forms are elaborated without being essentially changed. The density of population grows, per capita income stagnates or declines and interdependence is not exploited with social innovation:

[1] Simon Kuznets, *Economic Growth and Structure: Selected Essays* (New York 1965), pp. 123–41; Albert O. Hirscham, *Strategy of Economic Development*, pp. 176–82.
[2] Habakkuk, 'Population Problems and European Economic Development'.

A theory of the transition

Wet-rice cultivation, with its extraordinary ability to maintain levels of marginal labor productivity by always managing to work one more man in without a serious fall in per-capita income, soaked up almost the whole of the additional population that Western intrusion created, at least indirectly. ... What makes this development tragic rather than merely decadent is that around 1830 the Javanese (and, thus, the Indonesian) economy could have made the transition to modernism, never a painless experience, with more ease than it could today.[1]

Another example of ineffective response was the formation of the closed corporate peasant community.[2] This social form was devised to equalize life chances and life risks among peasants and for them to defend themselves from encroachments by the Spanish population. Every effort was made to slow down the rate of social change and preserve Indian culture from foreign domination. When the ravages of disease had passed and the Indian population began to grow again in the seventeenth century, the social forms did not change. The social structure of the peasant community was solidified into an unchanging relief which did not adapt to the reversal from declining to expanding population. As these examples illustrate, there is no guarantee that the expansion of population leads automatically to social and economic innovation.

The path of β moves a society much closer to the thin line of subsistence living. The observations of Coale and Hoover on the Indian economy are worth noting here:

(1) The decline of death rates from the high levels typical of peasant agrarian economies is occurring or is likely to occur more rapidly than it did in regions which industrialized earlier. Moreover, the decline is occurring in advance of (or in the absence of) profound changes in the economy and in per capita incomes. (2) The growth rates established, as mortality declines, are in excess of any observed in the records of areas industrializing earlier. (3) the prospect of rapid growth itself – particularly in areas where the current per capita incomes are very low – contributes to uncertainty about the likely course of fertility. The rapid growth rate may make it difficult to accomplish the economic and social changes that reduce fertility.[3]

It is the much greater rate at which the upward shift of the population growth function has occurred in the twentieth century which makes adaptation and successful innovation so difficult. Three principal differences exist between the experiences of the North Atlantic in the nineteenth century and the less developed world in the twentieth:

[1] Clifford Geertz, *Agricultural Involution, The Processes of Ecological Change in Indonesia* (Berkeley 1963), pp. 80, 82.

[2] Eric R. Wolf, 'Closed Corporate Peasant Communities in Meso-America and Central Java', *Southwestern Journal of Anthropology*, XIII (1957), 1–18; and *Sons of the Shaking Earth* (Chicago 1962), pp. 202–32.

[3] Ansley J. Coale and Edgar M. Hoover, *Population Growth and Economic Development in Low-Income Countries: A Case Study of India's Prospects* (Princeton 1958) .p. 17.

Expansion of coffee

(1) The rate of acceleration in population growth-rates – the rates are much higher today;

(2) the initial levels of per capita income – poor countries of today are much poorer at the moment of population acceleration than were the North-Atlantic areas a century ago;

(3) the causes of the acceleration – in the twentieth century the principal causes have been declines in infant and adult mortality, particularly the former; earlier, a rise in fertility played some role.

These differences may explain the responsiveness of the North Atlantic to the surge of population and the unresponsiveness of less developed areas in the twentieth century. In the terms of Figure 17 a population surge as great as β may not be reversible, whereas one following the aa' path can lead to continuing technological change and innovation.

The Colombian experience

Colombia fits in an intermediate position between the experience of spectacularly successful economic development achieved by the countries of the North Atlantic and the backwardness of most countries in Asia and Africa. Perhaps it is not by chance that the timing of population acceleration was also intermediate.

The Reforms of 1850 may have been sufficient to induce the sort of shift of the population growth function illustrated in Figure 17. The freeing of negro slaves and the increase of tobacco production in lowland areas could have changed radically the social and moral checks on the birth-rate among blacks and the lowland population. The freeing of the Indians from communal ties may have had similar effects. These changes could have occurred with no prior change in the level of per capita income among those groups. There is no data on fertility and population growth which will confirm or deny this possibility. These changes were of sufficient magnitude, however, to suggest that an upward shift of the population potential could have occurred, and that this shift might explain the fall in per capita income for some groups in the nineteenth century. The effort to return to the old level of income could then have stimulated the adoption of new techniques and production functions in agriculture (after 1890) and manufacturing (after 1900). Once the momentum of change was under way it continued and resulted in sustained growth.

Yet another feature of change during that period was the migratory movement of Antioqueños southward into open territory. That movement would not appropriately be described by any of the paths sketched in Figure 17. It involved, rather, a gradual growth in the scale of society

A theory of the transition

as population and resources (principally land) expanded together. At the point where the scale was large enough to finance transport innovations – the building of the railways – which required a large initial investment, the innovational possibilities were realized and growth through export expansion became a regular feature of the colonization movement.

Table 40   *Growth-rates, fertility-rates and standardized birth-rates, 1834–1964.*

Period	Intercensal population growth-rate, average annual cumulative percentage	Children 0–4 per 1,000 women 15–44, end years	Standardized birth-rate per 1,000 population
1834–43	1·4	—	—
1843–51	1·3	—	—
1851–70	1·6	—	—
1870–1905	1·2	—	—
1905–12	2·9	—	—
1912–18	2·4	649·3	40·9
1918–38	2·0	675·7	42·3
1938–51	2·5	744·9	43·4
1951–64	2·8	842·6	45·4

Sources: based principally on official census data and O. Andrew Collver, *Birth Rates in Latin America*, p. 90. See Note on Sources.

The first phase of the upward shift of the population growth potential was signaled by an actual decline in the rate of population growth in the intercensal period 1870–1905. In that long interval the rate of population growth was only 1·2 per cent per annum, lower than any of the three preceding intercensal periods (though only very slightly lower), and much lower than any of the growth-rates after the census of 1905.[1] As a glance at Figure 17 will confirm, an upward shift of the population growth function leads toward a new equilibrium at a *lower* rate of population than that pertaining to the old equilibrium. It is only after adjustments of the production function are effected that the observed rate of population growth can be sustained at higher levels. Since there were no censuses

[1] In a review of Latin American birth rates Collver suggests an 8 per cent underenumeration in the 1905 census (*Birth Rates in Latin America*, Berkeley 1965, p. 86). He presents no evidence to support his assertion other than the alleged implausibility of the estimate. But the violence of the war, 1899–1902, could have depressed the population. Thus I have accepted the official count in the estimates in Table 40.

287

taken between 1870 and 1905, it is impossible to give a more precise dating to the first phase of change in the population growth function.

A distinct rise in the rate of population growth is observed after 1905. This movement is along a path like a' from the initial lower rate of population expansion to a higher one made possible by the process of innovation which shifts the production function upward. The higher population growth-rate is paralleled by the rising fertility-rate. (Data on fertility are only available in the 1918 census and those which follow; vital statistics collected from parish registers are not reliable without very careful analysis and examination.) The fertility-rates were already high by North-Atlantic standards in 1918. The highest comparable fertility-rate ever experienced in the United States, for example, came in 1800 and was 546·4.[1] The fertility-rate in Colombia has continued to rise with some consistency in this century until it reached 842·6 at the time of the last census in 1964. Some of this increase may be attributable to more complete reporting in more recent censuses and to a fall in infant mortality.

The Antioqueño area led the upward movement in the population growth-rate and also experienced higher fertility-rates earlier than most other regions of Colombia. In 1918, for example, the fertility-rate for Antioquia was 711.0 children aged 0–4 per 1000 women aged 15–44, whereas the national average was 649·3. The gap was narrower by 1938 when Antioquia's fertility-rate was only 3·7 per cent greater than the national average. By the time of the 1964 census the Antioqueño area's fertility-rate was only 2·2 per cent above the average. All Colombian regions increased their fertility-rates in the years after 1918, but the increase was less in Antioquia suggesting that that area was further along the path of a demographic transition from very high fertility-rates.[2]

The foregoing demographic comparisons suggest that Colombia found itself both temporally and quantitatively intermediate between the nineteenth-century experience of the North-Atlantic area and the twentieth-century experience of Asia and Africa. Since equivalent population surges did not happen in most of Africa and Asia until after World War II, Colombia was ahead of those areas by perhaps four decades. This intermediate position suggests further that the Colombian experience of population growth as an inhibitor and then stimulant of the process of

---

[1] U.S. Bureau of the Census, *Historical Statistics of the United States, Colonial Times to 1957* (Washington 1960), p. 10.

[2] Data cited in this paragraph are all based on computations from census data. The Antioqueño area is taken to include the two departments of Antioquia and Caldas.

A theory of the transition

innovation may have been intermediate between the two paths sketched out as α' and β in Figure 17. But before pursuing that possibility it would be well to turn to another facet of the population expansion.

THE RISE OF INTERDEPENDENCE

With the expansion of population and aggregate output or an autonomous rise in the population growth potential, the share of interdependent in the total of all activities rises. Interdependent activities are those not mediated by the price system. They include all activities which require group rather than individual decisionmaking to achieve social optima. Economic interdependence always grows when specialization leads men to 'truck, barter and exchange'. Interdependence of a more 'social' nature is apt to grow as well.[1] In many cases, interdependence causes no problems that cannot be handled by a price mechanism allocating factor rewards and inducing output in an impersonal manner. But along with this development there grows another sort of interdependence which because of its technical nature or market imperfections cannot be handled adequately by the price mechanism.[2]

Some evidence of growing interdependence is the rising share of government in total expenditures as a country rises in the per capita income scale. A cross section of countries at different per capita income levels reveals a higher share of joint expenditures in the total at higher income levels.[3] The greater complexity of economic and social institutions in developed countries than in less developed countries is evidence of recognition and appropriation of the benefits – and avoidance of the costs – of interdependence. Greater complexity of social and economic organization is a hallmark of development: each example is a case of interdependence recognized.

All of the causes of 'market failure' – ownership externalities, technical externalities and public goods – are aspects of interdependence or jointness. Bator refers to such phenomena as 'interdependences that are external to the price system, hence unaccounted for by market valuation. Analytically, it [direct interaction] implies the nonindependence of various preference and production functions. Its effect is to cause divergence

[1] See, for example, Georg Simmel, 'The Sociology of Sociability', trans. by E. C. Hughes, *American Journal of Sociology*, LV (1949), 254–61.

[2] See Tibor Scitovsky, 'Two Concepts of External Economies', *Journal of Political Economy*, August 1954; reprinted in *The Economies of Underdevelopment* (eds., Agarwala and Singh, 1958), pp. 295–308.

[3] Simon Kuznets, *Modern Economic Growth: Rate, Structure and Spread*, pp. 234–43.

between private and social cost-benefit calculation.'[1] Group activity, politics and government originate in the realization that collective action yields greater satisfaction than individual action. The potential for greater satisfaction by group action exists whenever there is interdependence not mediated by the price mechanism.

The problem of the poor country is that interdependence often grows faster than the society's ability to cope with it. 'People are consistently reluctant to work with others toward group goals.'[2] In this atmosphere even the simplest of group decisions – primitive improvement of the water supply, for example – cannot be undertaken. Banfield attempts to explain the failure of political action in a peasant village in southern Italy. He rejects the facile hypothesis that poverty, ignorance, class conflict, land tenure, distrust of state, authority and fatalism are singly or together at the root of the problem of community development. He offers the following behaviour equation to explain political and social activity in the village: 'Maximize the material, short-run advantage of the nuclear family; assume that all others will do likewise.' With this pattern of behaviour successful appropriation of the benefits of interdependence would be difficult.[3]

Faced with expanding population and expanding problems the peasant community is not able at first to redirect behaviour from short-run personal ends to long-run community ends. On all the essential matters entailing cooperative action each man's hands are tied by mutual distrust. Communal organization fails to meet the challenge of expanded interdependence. The problem of transition from stagnation to rising per capita income is the sluggishness of the social organism in its adaptation to the changing environment.

The problem of response in the smallest units of peasant or traditional

[1] Francis M. Bator, 'The Anatomy of Market Failure', *Quarterly Journal of Economics*, LXIII (1958), 351–79. The quotation is from p. 358. There is a large literature on this subject; among the more interesting papers are those of Allyn A. Young, 'Increasing Returns and Economic Progress', *Economic Journal* (1928); Paul Rosenstein-Rodan, 'Problems of Industrialization of Eastern and South-Eastern Europe', *Economic Journal* (June–September 1943); rep. *The Economics of Underdevelopment* (eds., Agarwala and Singh), pp. 245–55; and Milton Friedman, *Capitalism and Freedom* (Chicago 1962), pp. 27–32. For a balanced and nontechnical account of interdependence and public goods see Samuelson, *Economics* (5th ed., New York 1961), pp. 187–93.

[2] George M. Foster, 'The Dyadic Contract: A Model for the Social Structure of a Mexican Peasant Village', *American Anthropologist*, LXIII (1961), 1173–92. The quotation is from page 1190. See by the same author, 'Peasant Society and the Image of Limited Good', *American Anthropologist*, and *Tzintzuntzan, Mexican Peasants in a Changing World* (Boston 1967).

[3] Edward C. Banfield, *The Moral Basis of a Backward Society* (Glencoe, Ill. 1956) p. 85 and Chapter v.

A theory of the transition

societies may be generalized to characterize the response of the society as a whole. On a countrywide level as well, there is no effective response to the costs and opportunities presented by the changed environment occasioned by the increase in the population potential. Interdependence grows and creates strains. New opportunities arise as well but they require cooperative action for effective response. For a time therefore, conditions may worsen, i.e. per capita income falls, social dislocations and conflict intensify, politics as a means of mediating group conflict fails.

The growth of population and interdependence brings with it disparate effects on the potential for economic development: the generation of interdependence creates positive opportunities for division of labor and greater productivity. As specialization and the division of labor make possible greater individual productivity one expects income per capita to rise. But at the same time there arise diseconomies which can only be dealt with by joint action. The list of these runs from rudimentary neighborhood effects – Pigou's smoke nuisance – to conflict of interest on the distribution of production and consumption both within and without the national group. Once again cooperative behaviour and mutual aid are necessary to overcome the diseconomies. The only alternative may be civil conflict.

The countries of Western Europe and areas settled by Europeans had by the nineteenth century a well-developed system of cooperation on issues of mutual or interdependent interest; but at the same time the ideology of individual liberty developed there, and some have assumed that the freeing of the individual underlay the success of European development. The analysis presented here would suggest that this view has been distorted. It was not so much individualism which promoted development as the combination of individualism (in those spheres where interdependence of a detrimental sort was minimal) and joint action (to curb the negative effects of interdependence and maximize the result of its positive effects), each operating in the appropriate sphere. Those countries which were successful in developing did combine individualism with joint action to benefit from rising interdependence. Colombia – and indeed most of Latin America – was so burdened with the ideology of individualism imported from Europe that it was difficult to perceive in the nineteenth century that some form of organization which could respond to growing interdependence was requisite to successful development. Hence the role of the central government and even of the several provinces was deficient in the provision of internal improvements, civil order and mechanisms for the mediation of private interests. A brief review of Colombian experience with the rise of interdependence will illustrate the process of transition to recognition of the need for joint action.

Initial experience with interdependence

A new interdependence came into existence in the second half of the nineteenth century with the expansion of international trade. It was bound to have differential effects on various groups in Colombia. The artisans faced with stiff competition from foreign textiles and manufactures suffered while traders and landowners in the export sector benefited. Since political power resided in the hands of the criollo landowning and trading class, they used it to enact a policy consonant with their interests even though it had deleterious effects on other groups. Interdependence expanded with the growth of trade, but political decisionmaking remained on a traditional rather than competitive basis. The decision to encourage trade expansion was made in spite of the fact that a better solution – in terms of total national welfare – might have been reached if all interested parties had been consulted.

The changing use of land involved other problems of interdependence for Colombia. The abandonment of the resguardo system probably led to more efficient use of Indian lands, but at the same time it had the effect of increasing the floating or marginal population. As land use changed from crops to livestock the demand for labor declined in the eastern highlands and magnified the problems of unemployment, vagrancy and crime. Church lands were also subject after 1861 to changing ownership and use in such manner as to reduce the demand for agricultural labor. The excess rural population was driven to marginal lands on the hillsides. They began the process of fragmentation of holdings and the spread of thousands of inefficiently small farming units. What began as a land policy designed to produce more efficient land utilization – and surely both the policy on Indian lands and Church lands were motivated by a desire to improve agricultural efficiency – ended in an inefficient misallocation of land and labor.

The elimination of the resguardos upset the social equilibrium of the Indian communities. The achievement of higher levels of living undoubtedly required that in the long run it be upset. But government policy failed miserably to limit transitional difficulties and did in fact exacerbate the problems of the Indian communities without at the same time seeking solutions for individual Indians in the larger mixed society. Merely eliminating one set of institutions was far from desirable – a new

A theory of the transition

set had to be created. In the institutional interregnum of the second half of the nineteenth century matters only got worse for the Indian whether on the reservation or off it.

During that phase of Colombian history the central government was not expanded to deal with the growing interdependence elicited by population growth. The Liberal governments promoted an extreme form of governmental decentralization which left the central government without sufficient revenues or power to undertake those activities within its sphere. No central authority commanded sufficient prestige to pull together and mediate disparate and conflicting interests. Civil conflict was an almost constant drain on energies which might have been better spent in problems of interdependence. It would be too much to argue that civil conflict was solely due to unrequited and growing interdependence since there were a number of issues of power politics and regional squabbles involved as well. Yet as a stylized interpretation of reality, the emphasis placed here on interdependence seems not to be misplaced. The failures and difficulties seem not to have been simply economic in nature but to have involved political decisionmaking which was not effectively directed toward achievement of the general interest. And because political power was so unequally distributed, violence proved to be the only option for the redress of grievances for many Colombians.

David Riesman sought in *The Lonely Crowd* to connect certain phases of economic development with the three 'parts' of a logistic curve of population growth. With high birth and death-rates, 'Change, while never completely absent in human affairs, is slowed down as the movement of molecules is slowed down at low temperature; and the social character comes as close as it ever does to looking like the matrix of the social forms themselves.'[1] In the phase of transition death rates are cut by improved sanitation and communications. But the transition itself

is likely to be violent, disrupting the stabilized paths of existence in societies in which tradition-direction has been the principal mode of insuring conformity. The imbalance of births and deaths puts pressure on the society's customary ways. A new slate of character structures is called for or finds its opportunity in coping with the rapid changes – and the need for still more changes – in the social organization.[2]

These are the characteristics of a new phase of human existence; they arose with the high population growth potential resulting from the spread between birth and death-rates. The violence and new forms of

[1] David Riesman and associates, *The Lonely Crowd* (Anchor ed., New York 1953), p. 27.
[2] Riesman, *The Lonely Crowd*, p. 29.

Expansion of coffee

behaviour result not only from larger aggregate population but from the increased interdependence which it has produced. The transition to the next stage in which fertility-rates are brought back into line with the lower death-rates can bring with it a measure of social order. But before that phase can begin (and as Colombia's inexorable fertility rise even up to the present indicates, that country has not made the last transition yet), mechanisms and institutions must come into existence which mediate conflict and take advantage of the opportunities arising from greater interdependence within society. If these problems are not solved violence and civil conflict will linger long after the first upward movement of the country's population potential. Here again Colombia is intermediate between developed and underdeveloped parts of the world since violence has not disappeared as a fact of life, nor has society failed to make substantial gains from the possibilities of interdependence.

Recognition of interdependence

Local government in the individual states had some success in meeting the challenge to society presented by growing interdependence; this was particularly true in Antioquia where the state government acted to promote research in coffee cultivation and subsidized initial experimental plantings.

An 1877 resolution went further, providing monetary awards of 50 pesos for each flock of two hundred or more sheep; 100 pesos for anyone producing fifty or more quintals of cotton; 500 pesos for the first producing at least one thousand liters annually of good wine; and, finally, 4 pesos for each one hundred coffee trees planted (maximum award, 100 pesos).[1]

The state also aided the process of development by providing roads and promoting railway construction. Early efforts were limited; one sees more success in the 1890s when a departmental board was established to take over railway promotion and succeeded in getting the first part of the line completed and some feeder roads constructed.[2]

Population was growing fastest in Antioquia: almost twice as fast as the national average in the nineteenth century; thus both the opportunities and difficulties generated by expanding interdependence were growing more rapidly there than in other regions. But the Antioqueños were always on the move southward in the colonization effort, and the frontier may have provided an outlet for many. Interdependence was

[1] Parsons, *Antioqueño Colonization*, pp. 111, 138. All but one of the subsidies paid in the first two years after their institution were for coffee growing.
[2] See Hoffman, 'A History of Railway Concessions', pp. 116–21.

A theory of the transition

recognized and dealt with earlier in Antioquia than in other regions, perhaps because of experience with joint ventures of mining, frontier life and pioneering or just that the stimulus of population growth was optimal in that region.

THE BEGINNINGS OF INNOVATION

Coffee as the catalyst

In an atmosphere of population growth, pioneering activity and growing recognition of interdependence in social and economic activities, coffee acted as a catalytic agent. In the context of downward pressure on income, it proved to be the means of regaining economic security and even of achieving new levels of economic development. But coffee cultivation was not by itself an initiating cause of development. It could have been exported at least half a century earlier – demand existed, prices were reasonably high and Brazilian growers had little trouble expanding output as early as the 1850s. But the development of coffee cultivation needed an inducement mechanism, a favorable setting, before it could get a strong start in Colombia. That mechanism was founded on the prior upward shift of the population potential. Coffee could not be the originating cause of economic change, but it did become a principal feature of the development process.

Coffee cultivation originated a shift of resources and required the integration of peasant smallholders into national and international markets. The result was an improvement of family-farm productivity as coffee claimed its ecological niche in the pattern of subsistence agriculture. The total effect expanded as more and more smallholders added coffee to their farming repertoire.

The cultivation of coffee in Colombia involved a number of innovations. On the farm itself the two most striking were the phased interplanting of coffee with subsistence crops which made it possible for the peasant to avoid the great risks of specialization which plagued coffee cultivation in Brazil, and the use of banana and plátano trees as shading for the bushes.[1] Harvest innovations included the picking of individual ripened beans as opposed to the crude stripping of the branch typical of Brazilian methods, and the development of small machines which stripped the outer hull from the beans before transporting them to urban markets.

[1] Peasant attitudes toward such risks are discussed in Eric R. Wolf, 'Types of Latin American Peasantry', *American Anthropologist*, LVII (1955), 452–71, esp. 464.

Expansion of coffee

This innovation was particularly important because local transport was so difficult and costly that it would hardly have paid to ship the bulky hulls from farm to local market towns. Marketing innovations at later stages in the process of production had also to be made: the cheapening of transport occasioned by the spread of the railway is the most obvious. In 1946 Colombia began to ship coffee to international markets via the Flota Mercante Grancolombiana owned by the Federación de Cafeteros and hence to save scarce foreign exchange. And from the early 1930s onward the Federación de Cafeteros provided a powerful bargaining agency which negotiated the price of Colombian coffee in international markets. These innovations are among thousands of new procedures which were adopted and diffused throughout the coffee zone as Colombia rose to its position of the world's leading producer of mild coffee.

Coffee cultivation performed an important political function as well.[1] By the mid-1920s coffee was the principal export earner for all the populated regions except the north coast and the south. The political differences between the eastern highland and Antioquia were lessened by mutual concern with the success of coffee exports. Moreover, the interests of cultivators, processors, merchants and industrialists became intertwined because there was no absolute specialization in these activities. The successful institution of higher tariffs in 1905 was the first sign that export interests were not adamantly opposed to the fledgling industrialists. The much more stringent protectionist tariff legislation introduced after the Crash of 1929 is even firmer evidence of the success of 'interest politics'.

The world-view of the eastern Colombian leadership in the nineteenth century was not conducive to compromise. Class stratification prevented decisions for development which could have been made had a greater sense of community between rich and poor, artisan and merchant, existed. The interdependence of economic life which arose with coffee emerged in a social atmosphere ripe for compromise essential to the tasks of development. Kinship ties continued to be of paramount importance, but at the same time there came to be less reliance on ascriptive status. In Antioquia at least, social mobility became easier in the twentieth century with greater educational and economic opportunities.[2] Greater mobility could be attributed in part to the new opportunities associated

---

[1] My argument here was suggested by the small pamphlet by L. E. Nieto Arteta, *El café en la sociedad colombiana* (published posthumously, Bogotá 1962).

[2] Some interesting folklore on social mobility appears in *Testamento del paisa* (ed., Agustín Jaramillo Londoño, ed., Bedout, Medellín 1962).

A theory of the transition

with coffee cultivation but equally as well to growing awareness of mutual interdependence and the benefits of cooperative decisionmaking.

Transport decisions

Perhaps the most obvious examples of interdependence appear in the category of internal improvements or social overhead capital. Such investments nearly always involve diffuse uncapturable benefits, long gestation periods for the investment project and an even lengthier pay-out period. Such projects also often involve a condition of falling marginal costs in which some form of subsidy or special taxing power must be invoked to achieve optimum results.

Colombia's experience with transport decisions fits this general picture. The instances of an effort to use private enterprise to make internal improvements were far from satisfactory. Roads were built too slowly or not at all. Construction of the railway dragged on from the 1870s until the 1920s with very little accomplished relative to the country's demand for transport. Only in Antioquia where the state government took over construction was the building program prosecuted with the requisite vigor.

The technology of the railway was already well-known by 1850; its applicability, even to South America's Andes, was established by Henry Meiggs in Chile and Peru in the 1860s.[1] Why was the application of the railway to the Colombian milieu so delayed? Why was railway construction so slow? Insufficiency of demand for improved transport facilities seems only a partially satisfying answer. The timing of the upward shift in the population growth potential would seem here as in the case of other innovations to have been important. The railway may be seen in light of this hypothesis as one result of the search for means of re-establishing expected levels of living. Since the railway produced very high social rates of return (as high as 20 per cent per annum for lines built in the 1920s, perhaps higher for earlier construction) by lowering transport costs for coffee and other goods, it was a natural complement to coffee cultivation. Had the complementarity of coffee and the railway been recognized earlier, the railways could have been built and coffee exported sooner and in greater volume but such speculation ignores the timing of the upward shift of the population potential. That shift had to occur before the florescence of innovation could begin. It is for that reason that the railways were not built earlier in Colombia – that and not insufficiency of demand or the limitations of existing technology.

[1] See Watt Stewart, *Henry Meiggs: Yankee Pizarro* (Durham, N.C. 1946); and J. V. Levin, *The Export Economies*.

Expansion of coffee

The flourish of the Wall Street bond market during the 1920s provided a financial mechanism by which the railways could be built and the beneficiaries effectively taxed by way of government assumption of the bonded debt. The central government was too weak to extract investable funds from the Colombian public who were the main beneficiaries of transport improvements. User fees alone were hardly sufficient to keep the existing railways running let alone to build more lines. Without strong institutions which could take into account the total social benefits (and costs) that would accrue from internal improvements the railways could not be built. The bond market made investments which were previously only feasible a reality. Real current resources were provided to the governments for railway construction against the prospect of future tax revenues. In the 1920s a government too weak to force investment on its own people found wealthy foreigners all too willing to build the railways. The bond market had long been a mechanism for mediating the interdependent objectives of savers and entrepreneurs in the North Atlantic area. The use of that institution for undertaking socially useful internal improvements in Colombia was perhaps the greatest contribution of foreign capital.

Shifting resources

The development of the coffee export sector was the means by which Colombians won back their traditional level of living and even improved on traditional expectations. Further development required the gradual shift of resources away from traditional activities and into modern ones. The most obvious of these shifts appears in the growth of manufacturing.

At the time of the census of 1870 only about 1 per cent of the Colombian labor force were located in activities that we may label as modern manufacturing. A much higher percentage were at work in less efficient artisan activities. The share in modern manufacturing expanded to 3·4 per cent in 1925 and continued to grow through the 1940s. (See Figure 18.) Since labor was more productive in modern manufacturing than in almost any other economic activity in Colombia, the transition to industrialization, however limited in scope, tended to raise average productivity and promote economic development. The ECLA *Study* estimated, for example, that in 1925 a worker in manufacturing was more than twice as productive as a worker in agriculture or artisan activities.[1] The institutionalization of economic development required not a single dramatic change but the inculcation of a regular process of change. The expansion of

[1] ECLA *Study*, 'Statistical Appendix', Tables 1, 5 and 8.

A theory of the transition

manufacturing – illustrated in the growth of labor force devoted to that activity and the much more rapid growth of output from it – proved to be one of the key indicators that such a change had become institutionalized.

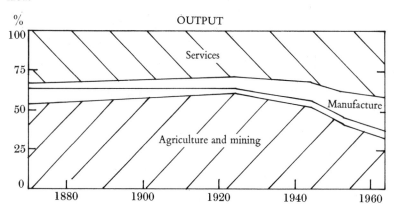

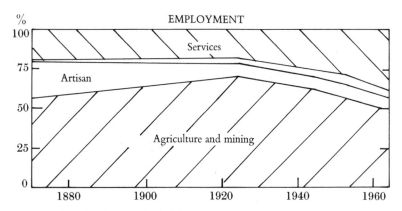

Figure 18 Distribution of output and employment by major sectors of the economy, 1870–1964. *Sources:* national censuses. See Note on Sources.

The share of output in manufacturing grew much more rapidly than employment because of rising productivity, in itself a sign of successful innovation. For example, between 1870 and 1925 the share of the labor force in modern manufacturing increased while that in artisan activities decreased; the result was a very considerable jump of average productivity

Expansion of coffee

in secondary or manufacturing activities.[1] It appears to have been particularly great in the years 1925–45. That period witnessed the rapid growth of the textile and food processing industries which experienced faster rates of growth in the 1930s than in any subsequent decades.[2]

Table 41 *Net interregional population movements, 1918–38* (thousands and per cent).

Region	Net change	Per cent of regional population in 1918
North coast	+ 48	+6·0
Gran Antioquia	− 5	−0·4
Pacific coast	+ 72	+8·5
Tolima–Huila	+ 9	+1·8
Boyacá–Cundinamarca	−113	−7·7
Santander	− 8	−1·2

Sources: population censuses. Expected population for each region was estimated on the basis of national average survival rates for each cohort. The difference between expected and actual population was then presented as net migration.

But innovations outside of the manufacturing and export sectors were also important. Among the rural population physical mobility was significant in the interwar period and was easing the friction caused by rapid economic change. Using the censuses of 1918 and 1938 one may estimate net interregional migration in the 1920s and 1930s.[3] A summary of those estimates appears in Table 41. The regions indicated tend to mask

[1] The construction of the 1870 output estimates assumes the same productivity in each sector for 1870 as existed in 1925. Thus the only explanation for increased average productivity in secondary activities as a whole had to be a change in the composition of employment from artisan to modern manufacturing.

[2] Labor productivity again increased in the years 1953–64, but the problem of automation and the inability of the manufacturing sector to absorb labor was even more serious than the problem of productivity. For a discussion of the productivity issue see H. J. Bruton, 'Productivity Growth in Latin America', *The American Economic Review*, LVII (1967), 1099–115.

[3] Unfortunately, the census taken in 1928 was never approved because of serious errors and the suggestion current at the time that some districts inflated their population statistics in order to increase their representation in congress.
    For a review and analysis of population censuses up to 1938 see Juan de D. Higuita, 'Estudio histórico analítico de la población colombiana en 170 años', *Anales de economía y estadística*, II (Bogotá April 1940), pp. 1–113.

A theory of the transition

important internal movements. For example, the Boyacá–Cundinamarca region contains a rural area of massive out-migration and the capital, Bogotá, a magnet for in-migrants. The Antioqueño area continued to have massive movements southward into the Quindío which were still within the Antioqueño region. These figures thus tend to be an understatement of the magnitude of internal migration. At the time of the 1951 census, the first to present any direct evidence on internal migration, 14 per cent of the Colombian population were living in a department different from the department of birth.[1] A comparison with comparable United States interstate migration statistics indicates that before 1950 at least, the rates of internal migration were perhaps higher in Colombia than they were in the United States.[2] Internal physical mobility was one means of lubricating the economic system and facilitating the process of economic change. Mobility made it relatively easy to shift human resources to new economic activities – certainly easier than would have been the case if no physical mobility had been occurring.

To a great extent physical mobility was coincident with the process of urbanization. Up to 1918 the population of the largest cities was increasing 2·7 per cent per annum; between 1918 and 1938 the rate of increase rose to 3·8 per cent.[3] The process of urbanization was speeding up to a rate more rapid than those being experienced in the more developed areas of southern South America.[4] But in contrast to the experience of the rest of Latin America, many secondary urban centers were growing as fast as Bogotá.[5] The more rapid development of western areas of the country which benefited most from the railways and the opening of the Panama Canal was the factor which made Colombian urbanization so different from the rest of Latin America.

The limited data available from the 1951 census on place of birth and residence suggest that internal population movements responded in

---

[1] The data are summarized in Banco de la República, Departamento de Investigaciones Económicas, *Atlas de economía colombiana, aspectos político, humano y administrativo* (Part II, Bogotá 1960), Tables 3 and 4, Map no. 17.

[2] See Everett S. Lee et al., *Population Redistribution and Economic Growth, United States 1870–1950* (3 vols., Philadelphia 1957), vol. I, p. 79. An unweighted average for all states and the District of Columbia for the intercensal periods 1920–30 and 1940, indicated that about 7 per cent of all Americans were living in states other than those in which they were born.

[3] Nineteen cities are included in this calculation. See Table 15.

[4] See Philip Hauser, ed., *Urbanization in Latin Amercia* (New York 1961), pp. 97–9. In both Argentina and Chile the capital cities were growing much faster than smaller cities – from the 1860s onward in Argentina, from 1907 onward in Chile.

[5] On city size distribution in Latin America see Harley L. Browning, 'Recent Trends in Latin American Urbanization', *Annals of the American Academy of Political and Social Science*, CCCXVI (1958), 111–20.

general to the pull of opportunities in those departments which were developing most rapidly. The data refer mostly to the years between 1935 and 1950, but the patterns were not essentially different for the earlier part of the interwar period. There is a significant positive correlation between the average level of departmental income and the percentage of that department's population who are in-migrants from other departments.[1] The department of Antioquia had a lower than expected degree of in-migration, given its high level of income per inhabitant. This is perhaps explained by the alleged cultural insularity of the Antioqueños and unwillingness to open opportunities to migrants from other areas of Colombia. But even given the cases of large deviations, the correlation between in-migration and economic opportunity was positive and significant in the decades before 1950. There is every reason to believe that the same pattern stretches back to the early years of the twentieth century.

The process of internal migration proved to be an important means of securing labor in the more rapidly developing areas of Colombia, and at the same time helped to draw off surplus population from backward areas. But the process was by no means successful if judged by the criteria of interregional equality.[2] Despite the high rates of internal physical mobility disparities between regions were exacerbated in the twentieth century. Economic conditions got better so fast in the developing areas, that the backward and overpopulated departments of Boyacá, Nariño, Cauca and Chocó were probably worse off as a result of the successful

[1] Income per inhabitant by department is from Misión Economía y Humanismo, *Estudio sobre las condiciones del desarrollo de Colombia*, Chart 237, Part II; birth and residence data from the 1951 census. Fifteen departments were ranked with respect to income per inhabitant and percentage of departmental population born in another department. The Spearman coefficient of rank correlation was calculated as $+0.64$, significant at the 0.01 level. There was no significant correlation between income per inhabitant and the percentage of a department's native-born population living in another department. The lack of correlation suggests that the factors promoting and inhibiting out-migration are much more general than relative economic opportunity alone would imply. For example, the department which deviates most from the generalized expectation for out-migration of the native-born is Nariño, a department still dominated by Indian culture. It sent fewer than expected native-born to other departments, a phenomenon probably explicable by the desire to maintain local cultural ties by many potential migrants.

[2] This problem has been examined theoretically and empirically in great detail. See in particular Jeffrey Williamson, 'Regional Inequality and the Process of National Development', Bernard Okun and Richard W. Richardson, 'Regional Income Inequality and Internal Population Migration', *Economic Development and Cultural Change*, IX (1961), 128–43. On Brazil and Mexico respectively see Werner Baer, 'Regional Inequality and Economic Growth in Brazil', *Economic Development and Cultural Change*, XII (1964), 268–85; James Wilkie, *The Mexican Revolution: Federal Expenditure and Social Change Since 1910* (Berkeley 1967), pp. 204–85.

A theory of the transition

development of Cundinamarca, Antioquia and Valle than they would have been if no development had taken place. This anomalous result stemmed chiefly from the out-migration of the ablest and best-educated residents of the backward departments, for they were the individuals most likely to succeed in the growing urban areas. The successful economic growth in some regions was multiplying the problems of others.

The interdependence of innovations

The expansion of coffee cultivation, the spread of internal improvements and the process of migration, urbanization and industrialization all interacted to yield a total result in terms of the rate of economic development which was larger than the sum of its parts. This feature of economic change stemmed from the interdependence of the innovations and increased mutual demand for the products of the several economic sectors of the country. An increase of coffee exports required an increased use of transport facilities. Greater use of transport stimulated further investment in internal improvements which in their turn lowered the cost of moving goods and hence permitted a greater volume of internal trade. Further economies of scale could be introduced with larger plant sizes in manufacturing and lower costs per unit of output. All these benefits can be summed up as the results of the increasing scale of the economy and society and appropriation of the benefits of interdependence.

With the gradual upward shift of per capita income and product there was an inexorable fall in the share of output contributed by primary agricultural activities and a rise in tertiary service activities. During the phase of expansion of the population potential, and because of economic changes discussed in Chapter 7, the share of labor force and output from primary activities actually rose, perhaps to levels even higher than those presented in Figure 18 for the year 1925. Perhaps through to the end of the nineteenth century the share of output attributable to secondary and tertiary activities was on the decline. But in this century opportunities in the cities expanded and the growth-rates picked up speed. Internal physical mobility grew as well so that the entire social system looked like a gas chamber which, heated from without, increases in molecular activity and attempts to expand beyond the confines of the chamber because of the increasing pressure of heightened activity within.

Throughout the 1920s Colombian development succeeded on the basis of innovation and interaction in the activities mentioned here. A transition had been made to self-reinforcing, mutually stimulating development.

One is driven finally to a motivational rather than a mechanical explanation of how the transition occurred.

[The economist always seeks to refer his analysis of a problem] back to some 'datum,' that is to say, to something which is *extra-economic*. This something may be apparently very remote from the problem which was first taken up, for the chains of economic causation are often very long. But he always wants to hand over the problem in the end to some sociologist or other – if there is a sociologist waiting for him. Very often there isn't.[1]

A complicated theory – Hagen's withdrawal of expected status, for example – has intuitive appeal, but a much simpler theory is possible: Colombians made the transition and began to develop because they wanted to. The population expansion was important and certainly innovations were essential. But the basic ingredient of the transition was the will to make it. Having recognized that element of motivation and will, the economist reaches the end of his own range of expertise.

[1] John R. Hicks, 'Economic Theory and the Social Sciences', *The Social Sciences, Their Relations in Theory and in Teaching* (London 1936), p. 135; quoted in Robert K. Merton, *Social Theory and Social Structure* (rev. ed., Glencoe, Ill. 1957), p. 89. The words bracketed are those of Merton.

A NOTE ON SOURCES

The reader of this book may find himself wishing for two kinds of further enlightenment. He may seek a guide for the further exploration of the extant literature on the economic history of Colombia, or he may wish for further details and clarification of the methods used in the construction of the many tables and figures used in my analysis. This note is designed to serve both ends in a brief space.

It is neither possible nor desirable here to provide a complete bibliographical survey of the subject. I am currently preparing an annotated bibliography of some 500 items on the economic history of Colombia between 1830 and 1930. That work is being sponsored by the Joint Committee on Latin American Studies of the Social Science Research Council and American Council of Learned Societies. It is part of a larger bibliographical effort including critical bibliographical essays on six Latin American countries under the joint direction of Roberto Cortes Conde and Stanley Stein. I restrict myself in this note to discussion of but a few major works and an explication of sources and methods of synthesis for statistical data employed in this book. For the sake of brevity all citations in this note are given in abbreviated form with bibliographical details provided in the list of sources on Colombia which follows.

AN INVITATION TO FURTHER READING

The best single work on Colombian economic history is the book of Luis Ospina Vásquez, *Industria y protección*. It covers the nineteenth century and the first three decades of the twentieth in more detail than any other work. Unfortunately, the book is not written to be read but serves better as a reference work. Other surveys are those of Nieto Arteta, *Economía y cultura*, first published in 1942, and Abel Cruz Santos, volume xv of the *Historia extensa de Colombia*, prepared under the auspices of the Academia Colombiana de Historia. The work of Indalecio Liévano Aguirre, particularly *Los grandes conflictos*, provides a stimulating entree into Colombian social history, even if one may quibble with his methods and approach to historical scholarship. A general review of recent historical research on the nineteenth century is provided in J. O. Melo, 'Los estudios históricos en Colombia.'

The nineteenth-century Radicals were prolific in their writings on economic questions. The works of Salvador Camacho Roldán, José Maria Samper and Miguel Samper are of particular interest because of their concern with social questions. The writings of the nineteenth century are very usefully reviewed in Jaime Jaramillo Uribe, *El pensamiento colombiano en el siglo XIX*. The role of the government is best studied through a careful reading of the *Memorias* of the several ministries which were on occasion written by the most competent men of affairs in the country. The *Memoria de hacienda, 1870*, written by Camacho Roldán, is particularly useful. See also Aníbal Galindo, *Historia económica i estadística de la hacienda nacional*.

Note on sources

Three nineteenth-century presidents dominated government policy and hence have occasioned careful studies of their incumbencies. The government of Santander is examined by David Bushnell in *The Santander Regime in Gran Colombia.* J. León Helguera concentrates on the critical period of change initiating the Reforms of 1850 in 'The First Mosquera Administration in New Granada, 1845–1849.' General Mosquera continued to be a dominant figure in Colombian politics into the 1860s, but that era has yet to receive the comprehensive treatment which Helguera accorded to the earlier period. Rafael Núñez, who was a major political figure among the Radicals in the 1850s, acceded to the presidency in 1880. In the course of several decades of political life he left the camp of the Radicals and found himself in the 1880s as the leader of a conservative reaction against Radical Liberalism. His life and political deeds are the subject of Indalecio Liévano's *Rafael Núñez*, perhaps the best biography of that enigmatic figure.

Private enterprise in the mid-nineteenth century has been studied by Frank R. Safford. Some of the results of his research appear in 'Foreign and National Enterprise' and 'Significación de los Antioqueños', both cited in the bibliography. His yet unpublished doctoral dissertation, 'Commerce and Enterprise in Central Colombia, 1821–1870', is replete with further useful details from Colombian business history. Enterprise and entrepreneurship were also the subject of interest to Everett Hagen, *On the Theory of Social Change.* His theory of economic development may prove to be of particular interest to those seeking psychological explanations for economic events.

Unfortunately, most of the treatment of nineteenth-century history has concentrated on political events and the activities of the political elites. Some exceptions do come to mind, however. Fals Borda has prepared a number of studies of rural life which have led him into archival research. Of particular interest is 'Indian Congregations in the New Kingdom of Granada', and *El hombre y la tierra en Boyacá.* His more recent foray into sociological history, *Subversion and Social Change in Colombia*, is less successful. One of the earliest publications of Juan Friede, *El indio en lucha por la tierra*, is a particularly enlightening study of the effects of nineteenth-century land policies in southern areas of the country. An interesting complement to these studies of land policy is the essay on land reform in Colombia in Albert O. Hirschman's *Journeys Toward Progress* which treats the successful implementation of the land reform law of 1961. R. Albert Berry has in preparation a massive study of Colombian agricultural problems in the twentieth century.

Banking and finance for the nineteenth and early twentieth centuries are reviewed in Torres García, *Historia de la moneda en Colombia.*

The highland artisans which have received so much attention in this book have not been dealt with in any detail elsewhere. The *Nueva geografía de Colombia* published by Vergara y Velasco in 1912 does provide some information on this group in the last decade of the nineteenth century, but it is by no means an adequate examination. The artisans are treated obliquely in the work of Ospina Vásquez, but his main concern is with the advent of modern industry and the factory system. A recent

Note on sources

study of the movement for union organization does discuss important developments among the artisans in the 1850s but then jumps discontinuously to the labor strife of the 1920s in the oil fields and banana zone. Still, Urrutia's *History of the Labor Movement in Colombia* (published in Spanish as *Historia del sindicalismo en Colombia*) is an outstanding beginning for the analysis of the social and economic history of social groups outside the narrow political elite.

There are many regional histories of Colombia but only one which commands universal respect as a work in social history. Parsons' *Antioqueño Colonization in Western Colombia* takes as its theme the movement of the Antioqueño frontier south then westward and the gradual rise of that regional group from a state of backwardness to leadership in industry, trade and finance. Perhaps it is because the Antioqueño story takes on near epic proportions that it has received the most successful historical treatment. Nonetheless, other regions – Santander, the Cauca, the north coast – await their historians who can escape the bounds of narrow political history.

The cutting edge of change in Colombian economic history from 1880 through the 1930s was provided by the interacting growth of coffee cultivation and internal transport improvements. Studies of coffee in Colombia seem almost unlimited in number; the Federación de Cafeteros issues a number of important serial publications. The ECLA/FAO Joint Study provides very useful information on the techniques of production that prevailed in the 1950s. Nieto Arteta's short essay, *El café en la sociedad colombiana* is a provocative analysis of the social role of coffee.

The work of Robert C. Beyer on coffee, because it appears in unpublished form in his doctoral dissertation, has unfortunately been overlooked. Beyer made important revisions and corrections in official data on coffee production and exports which should be brought to the attention of a wider audience. Only a small part of the results of his research appear in published form, principally in 'Transportation and the Coffee Industry in Colombia.'

Transportation and internal improvements have always been a source of problems in Colombia's economic history and have as a result produced a substantial literature. The work of Gilmore and Harrison, 'Juan Bernardo Elbers and the Introduction of Steam Navigation on the Magdalena', covers the period before steamboats got a good foothold. There have been no good studies of river navigation on the years between 1850 and the mid-1950s when diesel power overtook steam as a source of power on the river. The early railway period is treated in detail in Alfredo Ortega, *Ferrocarriles colombianos* and in a *Report on the Railways of Colombia* in Great Britain's series of Diplomatic and Consular Reports. Donald Barnhart, 'Colombian Transportation Problems and Policies', surveys the transport field for the years 1923 through 1948. The best source of data on transport for the late 1940s is the IBRD, *Basis of a Development Program for Colombia*.

The export sector – as in all Latin American countries – has received more detailed treatment than the domestic economy. On gold mining see Vicente Restrepo, *Estudio de las minas de oro*; on tobacco, John P. Harrison's dissertation, 'The Colombian Tobacco Industry'; on other nineteenth-century exports, see Nieto Arteta, *Economía*

Note on sources

y cultura, pp. 277–370. There are no satisfactory historical studies on the development of petroleum and bananas as export products. One might surmise that the domination of those industries by foreign firms almost from their inception will explain the absence of interest by Colombian scholars.

Some readers will be asking for a single work which might bring the story of this book up to the present. There is no adequate survey for the years of change since 1930. A number of books on politics have appeared, but they deal only marginally with economic matters. Perhaps the best of these is by Pat M. Holt, *Colombia, Today and Tomorrow* (New York 1964). A work on the economic history of the past forty years would require a very different structure from that employed in this book. Whereas in the century before 1930 the critical question was the integration of Colombians into local, national and international markets, in the more recent past the principal problems have been accelerating population growth, inelastic demand for Colombia's major exports, and development of a suitable mix of public and private enterprise for balanced economic growth.

SOURCES OF STATISTICAL DATA

To avoid cluttering the text and tables of this book with details of interest only to the specialist I have relegated to this section of the Note on Sources a discussion of the sources used and the processes of synthesis employed to bring them together. In the notes to the tables and figures themselves I have restricted references to those works which were the unique source of materials presented.

Transport rates for the nineteenth and twentieth centuries provide a valuable measure of the secular decline of economic distance and hence of the integration of markets. There is no single source for the rates shown in Table 6. They are drawn from a variety of travelers' accounts, the reports of contemporaries generally interested in transport problems and from the account books of merchants and trade organizations. Railway rates are drawn from proposed rates established in government construction contracts, from actual rates charged shippers, and from the data published during the 1930s and 40s by the Federación de Cafeteros on rates they paid to transport coffee.

All data are in current prices of the year in which rates were quoted. Where original sources provided information, routes have been given; otherwise, the rates are usually meant to refer to typical rates over principal routes in the country. Ordinarily, transport rates are given as the total fare for shipping a specified quantity over a given route. In all cases, I have changed those total fares to the common denominator of centavos per ton-kilometer.

Many of the rates for the years up to 1868 were first culled from contemporary documents by Professor Frank Safford, Northwestern University, and appear in Table I of his 'Commerce and Enterprise in Central Colombia, 1821–1870' (Ph.D. diss., Columbia University 1965). His ton-mile data were converted to ton-kilometers. I am indebted to him for permission to include his work with the others presented here.

Note on sources

Data on gold production which appears in Table 7 illustrate the depressed condition of the market for the three-score years following the unsettling events of the movement for independence. The series on the value of production in millions of current pesos are drawn from the work of Restrepo, *Estudio sobre las minas*. He had in turn revised the earlier estimates of Sötbeer and Humboldt in terms of information he culled from local sources. I simply divided his value-of-output series by the number of years in each of the periods he designated to arrive at an estimate of average annual output over the years 1537–1890. Figures on the quantity of output in thousands of fine ounces for the years 1537–1925 is drawn from the U.S. Department of Commerce, Office of the Metals Division, *Summary Data on Gold Production*, authored by Robert S. Ridway, and cited in Cruz Santos, *Economía y hacienda publica*, p. 141. Data for more recent years, 1923–66, is not production but rather export of gold in bars or dust form as reported in the statistical publication of the Banco de la República, *Informe anual del gerente a la junta directiva*, for the biennial period, 1 January 1965–31 December 1966, pp. 190–1. Since there was little difference between production and exports, the long-term series on the volume of output so constructed is a good index of activity in gold mining. It would of course be quite difficult to measure long-term changes either in the productivity of gold mining or in the buying power of gold produced in terms of Colombian imports.

No single source provides an estimate of the level of hostilities in Colombia over the past century and a half. Yet nearly everyone who has studied the country's history recognizes that civil strife, violence and alienation has formed an essential part of that history. I have tried with the able assistance of Mr Michael Conniff to draw together and sift such evidence there is to get a comprehensive but necessarily crude estimate of this important element. The principal sources are José Manuel Restrepo, *Historia de la revolución de la República de Colombia*, and *Diario político y militar*; Henao and Arrubla, *Historia de Colombia* and *History of Colombia* (trans. J. Fred Rippy); two anonymous works, *The Present State of Colombia* and *Recollections of a Service in Colombia*; Pérez Aguirre, *25 años de historia colombiana*; Payne, *Patterns of Conflict in Colombia* (for size of the military establishment); Briceño, *La revolución (1876–1877)*; Riascos Grueso, *Geografía guerrera colombiana*; Flórez Alvarez, *Campaña en Santander (1899–1900)*; Martínez Landinez, *Historia militar de Colombia*; Dix, *Colombia: The Political Dimensions of Change*; Guzmán Campos et al., *La violencia en Colombia*, and Quincy Wright, *A Study of War* (Chicago 1965). Even among these sources there are serious contradictions on the estimates of deaths and the real size of the official military establishment in the nineteenth century. The most serious discrepancies appear in the estimates for deaths in the War of a Thousand Days, 1899–1902 (the total for that conflict shown in the decade beginning January 1900). The estimate of 100,000 deaths is from p. 519 of the Rippy translation of Henao and Arrubla. Flórez Alvarez (p. 37) puts the total at 60,000 and Riascos Grueso (p. 335) at 150,000. Since there is some agreement that there were under 30,000 troops involved in the largest battle of that civil war, the deaths seem disproportionately large.

Note on sources

The late 1940s and 50s provide an equal puzzle since deaths by violence have been estimated as high as 300,000 (for the first time reportedly by Alfonso López Michelsen) though primary evidence in police and newspaper reports have never supported such an inflated total. An examination of the estimating procedure used in Guzmán Campos et al., *La violencia en Colombia*, I, 292, will show what an uncomfortably large role guessing and multipliers play in their total of 200,000. One is reminded of the body count for enemy casualties in the Vietnam war in which all the biases are upward.

Perhaps the most reliable series in Table 9 is column 5, Duration of conflict in months. The variations of that series probably provide a reasonable index of the intensity of conflict in an ordinal if not a cardinal sense.

Table 15 presents the population of Colombia's major cities, all of them with populations over 50,000 by the time of the 1964 census. Before 1938 there was no data distinguishing urban places within the municipio from the rural areas; for comparability these data thus include the total population of the municipio rather than just the cabecera. These data tend slightly to underestimate the rate of urbanization since the proportion of municipio population living in the cabecera (or built-up, urban area) has tended to increase over time. The difference is slight, however.

The data for 1851, 1870, 1905 and all years thereafter are based on population censuses. It should be noted that the 1928 census was never approved by the Colombia legislature because of irregularities. The estimates of city populations are probably more accurate than those for rural areas; nonetheless, one may still anticipate that there are inaccuracies. The Bogotá figures for years prior to 1851 derive from Republic of Colombia, Ministerio de Gobierno, *Estadística general de la República de Colombia*, p. 12. The 1884 figure, based on a local census; appears in the same place. The early figures for Medellín are from Restrepo Euse, *Historia de Antioquia*, pp. 136, 175, 236. López, *Estadística de Antioquia*, p. 76, presents higher but less credible figures, probably for a larger geographical area. The early figure for Cali appears without further reference in the 1912 census publication, p. 209. That for Bucaramanga is found on p. 263 of the same publication. The Cartagena figure appears in the French edition of Mollien's *Voyage dans la République de Colombia en 1822* (Paris 1825), I, 15–16.

The English version of Mollien's work, *Travels in the Republic of Colombia*, p. 373, provides the source for the earliest estimates of land values which appear in Table 16. Until more complete studies of local land prices are conducted, the scholar has available to him only the accounts of travelers and contemporaries on land values. One can anticipate that new data will become available from notarial archives; one problem discovered in the Santander region, however, is that the notarial records indicate the value of land sales along with contiguous properties but without a clear indication of the area, e.g. in hectares or fanegadas. Another approach may be the study of particular agricultural units such as the hacienda La Tena discussed in Smith, *Colombia. Social Structure and the Process of Development*. Other data in Table 16 are drawn from Powles, *New Granada: Its Internal Resources*; Parsons, *Antioqueño Colonization*, p. 83; Safford, 'Commerce and Enterprise', pp. 247–8; Henao and

Note on sources

Arrubla, History of Colombia, p. 640; Guerra Azuola, 'Apuntamientos de viaje', pp. 69–70; Restrepo, *Diario político y militar*, IV, 582–3; Holton, *New Granada: Twenty Months in the Andes*, p. 485; Restrepo Echavarría, *Una excursion al territorio de San Martin en Diciembre de 1869*, p. 139; Parra, *Memorias*, pp. 551–648; Camacho Roldan, *Escritos varios*, pp. 455–6.

Coffee production and its regional distribution has, as noted earlier, been the subject of numerous studies. The revisions of official data in Beyer, 'The Colombian Coffee Industry', Appendix Table XI, provide the basis for the 1874 and 1913 estimates in my Table 22. The data for 1932 and the average for 1953–6 appear in United Nations ECLA/FAO, *Coffee in Latin America*, p. 23; the earlier data were based on the first coffee census conducted by the Federación de Cafeteros. The 1943 figures are from Federación Nacional de Cafeteros, *Boletín de Estadística*, XI (April 1944). The Lorenz curve in Figure 9 is drawn from the same UN study mentioned above.

The data for an international comparison of railway expansion are drawn from the following sources: *Abstract of British Historical Statistics* (Cambridge 1967), pp. 225–6; Peyret, *Histoire des Chemins de Fer en France et dans le Monde* (Paris 1949), p. 185; *Historical Statistics of the United States* (Washington 1961), pp. 427, 429; Westwood, *A History of Russian Railways* (London 1964), p. 304; Hunter, *Soviet Transport Policy* (Cambridge 1957), p. 365; Ferrer, *The Argentine Economy* (Berkeley 1967), p. 228; Etcheguía, *Los ferrocarriles argentinos* (Buenos Aires 1938), pp. 47–8; Mexico, Director General de Estadística, *Anuario estadístico de los Estados Unidos Mexicanos 1941* (Mexico 1943), pp. 736–7; Villafuerte, *Ferrocarriles* (Mexico 1959), p. 34; *Historical Statistics of Canada* (Toronto 1965), pp. 528, 532; Instituto Nacional de Estatistica, *Anuario Estatistica do Brasil Ano II 1936* (Rio 1956), p. 3; Diretor Geral de Estatistica, *Resumo de varias Estatisticas Economico-Fianceiras* (Rio 1924), p. 80; Raul C. Migone, *Anuario Interamericano 1940* (New York 1940), p. 446; Bank of Japan, *100 years of Economic Statistics* (Tokyo 1966), pp. 115–16.

Investments in the railways as presented in Table 34 were estimated from a number of sources. The principal problem involves an appropriate estimate for the average cost of construction.

Estimates of cost of construction for 11 lines through 1910 are from Great Britain, Diplomatic and Consular Reports, *Report on the Railways of Colombia*, Miscellaneous Series Number 678, July 1910, by Mr Victor Huckin, Acting Consul-General at Bogotá. This 57-page report provides an informative and reasonably thorough discussion of Colombian railways up to that time. Included are both cost of construction and value of investment estimates. In all cases I took cost of construction rather than market value (uniformly lower in Huckin's report) as the measure of investment. The average cost of construction per kilometer for the 768 km. on which Huckin reports was $29,400. There was great variation around that mean, however, from $13,000 on the Ferrocarril de Cartagena to $53,000 per km. on the Ferrocarril del Pacífico. The weighted average for five of the coffee railways was $36,500 per km., attesting to the higher cost of construction in mountainous areas.

Note on sources

Later estimates are based on the studies of Ortega, Hoffman and Barnhart, cited elsewhere in the text. I have arrived at the following general averages for three periods based on the original research of these just mentioned: 1870–1920, $35,000 per km.; 1921–30, $75,000, and 1931–48, $43,000 per km. For a summary of construction costs data, 1922–48, see Barnhart, 'Colombian Transport and the Reforms of 1931: An Evaluation', p. 15. Applying these construction costs to the number of kilometers built on each line in the given period I derived the cost of capital in construction and improvements. The rolling stock is estimated here as simply one-fourth of the cost of construction.

The estimates of railway benefits and costs for the period 1922–57 which appear in Table 37 required even more complicated estimating procedures. The benefits estimate in column 1 was arrived at as follows: the estimated saving per ton-kilo-meter was put at 21·4 centavos, the weighted average of benefits accruing to old and new shippers as estimated in Table 36. That figure was then multiplied by the total ton-kilometers hauled by railways in each year. For years prior to 1936 (for which only tons hauled data is available) the average length of haul was extrapolated backward on total tons hauled. The underlying data appear in Banco de la República, *Informe anual* (Part II, July 1960–December 1962), p. 264. As indicated in the text the second estimate of benefits are just half of those in column 1 and are offered as an alternative which I believe to be unrealistically low.

Estimates of construction costs are discussed above. The costs were distributed over the years 1922–9 in rough accordance with the number of kilometers constructed in each year. Costs of operation and maintenance appear in various issues of the *Anuario general de estadística* for the years since 1936 and were extrapolated backward on the basis of partial data for those railways which constituted three-quarters of the costs of operations for the five years 1936–40. Since the Colombian peso declined in buying power over the interval considered it seemed appropriate to attempt to deflate current peso costs to the average of prices in the years 1925–9. I used the impli-cit gross domestic product deflator from the ECLA *Study*, 'Statistical Appendix', Table 38, and Banco de la República, *Informe anual* (Part II, July 1960–December 1961), pp. 192, 196. This deflation makes costs of operation roughly comparable to costs of construction and estimated benefits also expressed in pesos of the 1920s.

For the 1920s the average cost per ton-kilometer, 1930–56, was extrapolated backward on the total ton-kilometers hauled. These figures in constant pesos were then changed to current pesos by the gross domestic product deflator to complete the series in column 4.

Underenumeration in the 1951 census caused growth-rates calculated from official data to be too low in the intercensal period 1938–51, and too high, 1951–64. I used the ECLA estimate of 12·2 million for the 1951 population for the calculations in Table 41. See United Nations Economic Commission for Latin America, 'Some Aspects of Population Growth in Colombia', (unpub. MS., 10 November 1962), p. 6.

Calculations of fertility-rates are based on official data. No attempt was made to

Note on sources

correct for underenumeration of children under one year of age which the ECLA study previously mentioned notes as being particularly severe for the 1938 census. The rate being used here, i.e. number of children 0–4 helps escape the problem of underenumeration in the first year.

Crude birth rates are standardized for age and sex composition of the population.

Long-term trends in the sectoral distribution of output and employment is shown in Figure 18. It is based on data from *Anuario estadístico*, 1875; ECLA *Study*, pp. 16, 17, 'Statistical Appendix'; *Anuario general de estadística, 1962*, p. 768; *XIII Censo nacional de población*, Table 37; Banco de la República, Departamento de Investigaciones Económicas, *Series estadísticas y gráficas*, p. 98.

ECLA *Study* sectoral labor productivity estimates for 1925 were multiplied by the 1870 labor force to estimate the sectoral distribution of output. The assumption probably involves too high an estimate of labor productivity on average, but the distribution by sectors may be unbiased.

DANE conducted an industrial survey in 1962 and presented data on employment by size of firm, totaling about 240,000 employees in manufacturing firms with 10 or more employees. I estimated mid-1964 employment in firms with 10 or more employees at 280,000, thus leaving 375,961 employees in smaller firms (artisan activities) for that year. Total employment in 'industrias de transformación' was 655,961. Whatever figures one uses it appears that the share of the active population in secondary activities declined between 1950 and 1965.

LIST OF WORKS ON COLOMBIA CITED

Anon., *The Present State of Colombia*. By an officer late in the Colombian Service (London 1827).

Recollections of a Service in Colombia during the War of Extermination in the Republic of Venezuela and Colombia. By an officer of the Colombian Navy (London 1828).

Academia Colombiana de Historia, *Historia extensa de Colombia*, vol. 15; *Economía y hacienda*. By Abel Cruz Santos (Bogotá 1965).

Ancízar, Manuel, *Peregrinación de Alpha* (Bogotá 1956).

Banco Cafetero, *La industria cafetera y la agricultura de Colombia* (Bogotá 1962).

Banco de la República, *Informe anual del gerente a la junta directiva* (2 parts, Bogotá 1960–).

Departmento de Investigaciones Económicas, *Atlas de economía colombiana, aspectos político, humano y administrativo* (Bogotá 1960).

Barnhart, D. S., 'Colombian Transportation Problems and Policies, 1923–1948' (Ph.D. diss., University of Chicago 1958).

'Colombian Transport and the Reforms of 1931: An Evaluation', *Hispanic American Historical Review*, XXXVIII (1958), 1–24.

Berry, R. Albert, 'An Introduction to the Key Issues in Colombian Agriculture' (Mimeo, n.d.).

Beyer, Robert Carlyle, 'The Colombian Coffee Industry: Origins and Major Trends, 1774–1940' (Ph.D. diss., University of Minnesota 1947).

'Transportation and the Coffee Industry in Colombia', *Inter-American Economic Affairs*, II (1948), 17–30.

'Land Distribution and Tenure in Colombia', *Journal of Inter-American Studies*, III (1961), 281–90.

Blanco-Fombona, Rufino, *Bolívar y la guerra a muerte, época de Boves 1813–1814* (Caracas 1852).

Briceño, Manuel, *La revolución (1876–1877)* (2nd ed., Bogotá 1848).

Bureau of the American Republics, *Bulletin* (Washington, D.C. 1893–).

Bushnell, David, *The Santander Regime in Gran Colombia* (Newark, Delaware) 1954.

'Two stages in Colombian Tariff Policy: The Radical Era and the Return to Protection (1861–1885)', *Inter-American Economic Affairs*, IX (1956), 3–23.

Calderon, Clímaco, *Elementos de hacienda pública* (Bogotá 1911).

Camacho Roldán, Salvador, *Empresa del añil en grande escala. Escritos varios de Salvador Camacho Roldán* (Bogotá 1893).

Notas de viaje (Bogotá 1898).

Centro de Estudios sobre Desarrollo Económico, Universidad de los Andes, *Colombian Import Demand for Selected Agricultural Commodities 1964 and 1975* (Bogotá 1964).

Works cited

Cisneros, Francisco J., *Report on Construction of a Railway from Puerto Berrío to Barbosa* (New York, 1878).

Ferrocarril de Antioquia (New York 1880).

Collver, O. Andrew, *Birth Rates in Latin America. New Estimates of Historical Trends and Fluctuations* (Berkeley 1965).

Colmenares, Germán, *Encomienda y población en la Provincia de Pamplona* (Bogotá 1969).

Las haciendas de los jesuítas en el nuevo reino de Granada (Bogotá 1969).

Colombia, Republic of, *Reports of the Secretaries of State of the Republic of Colombia, First Constitutional Congress in the Year 1823* (London 1824).

Censo de población de la República de la Nueva Granada, levantado con arreglo a las disposiciones de la lei de 2 de junio de 1834 en los meses de enero, febrero i marzo del año de 1835 en las diferentes provincias que comprende su territorio. *Gaceta de la Nueva Granada* (1835), trim. 16, no. 211.

Resumen del censo jeneral de la población de la Nueva Granada, distribuido por provincias, cantones, i distritos parroquiales, con espresión del número de electores que a cada canton i provincia corresponde, con arreglo al articulo 17 de la constitución. *Gaceta de la Nueva Granada* (1844), trim. 50, no. 661, pp. 2–5.

Estadística jeneral de la Nueva Granada, que conforme al decreto ejecutivo de 18 de diciembre de 1846. Parte primera: *Población e instituciones* (Bogotá 1848).

Censo de población, 1905 (Bogotá 1905).

Ministerio de Gobierno, *Censo general de la República de Colombia, levantado el 5 de marzo de 1912* (Bogotá 1912).

Dirección General de Estadística, *Censo de población de la República de Colombia, 14 de octubre de 1918 y aprobado el 19 de septiembre de 1921 por la ley 8a del mismo año* (Bogotá 1924).

Dirección del Censo, Contraloría General, *Memorias y cuadros del censo de 1928* (Bogotá 1930).

Dirección Nacional de Estadística, Sección de Censos Nacionales, *Censo general de la población, 5 de julio de 1938* (1940–2).

Departamento Administrativo Nacional de Estadística, *Censo de población de 1951* (1954–9); *Censo de población 9 de mayo de 1951: Decreto-Ley Numero 1905 de 1954* (Bogotá 1954).

Departamento Administrativo Nacional de Estadística, *Anuario general de estadística* (Various years, title varies, some years missing, 1875–); *Anuario de comercio exterior* (Title varies, some years missing, Bogota 1905–); *Directorio de explotaciones agropecuarias (censo agropecuario), 1960, resumen nacional* (Bogotá 1962); *Censo agropecuario de 1960* (Bogotá 1964); *XIII Censo nacional de población* (Bogotá 1964).

Departamento de Contraloría, *Anales de economía y estadística* (Bogotá 1938–).

Dirección General de Vias y Estructuras, *Mapa general de ferrocarriles* (Bogotá 1962).

Dirección Nacional de Estadística, *Boletín mensual de estadística* (Bogotá 1951–).

Ministerio de Agricultura, *Economía agropecuaria de Colombia en 1950* (Bogotá 1952).

315

Works cited

Ministerio de Agricultura y Ganadería, *Economía agropecuaria de Colombia. División de Economía Rural* (Bogotá 1949–53).

Ministerio de Agricultura e Comercio, *Memoria del Ministro de Agricultura* (Title varies, Bogotá 1921–).

Ministerio de Fomento, *Memoria del Ministro de Fomento* (title varies, Bogotá 1880–).

Ministerio de Gobierno, *Estadística general de la República de Colombia*, Ed. Henrique Arboleda C. (Bogotá 1905).

Ministerio de Hacienda y Crédito Público, *Memoria del Ministro de Hacienda* (title varies, Bogotá 1823–).

Ministerio de Industrias y Trabajo, *Memoria* (Bogotá 1926–38).

Ministerio de Obras Públicas, *Memoria de Obras Públicas* (Bogotá 1905–).

Ministerio del Tesoro, *Memoria del Ministro del Tesoro* (title varies, Bogotá 1822–).

Presidencia de la República, Comité Nacional de Planeación, Dirección Ejecutiva, Misión 'Economía e Humanismo,' *Estudio sobre las condiciones del desarrollo de Colombia* (Bogotá 1958).

Lisímaco Palau, *Directorio general de Colombia, comercial, geográfico, administrativo y estadístico, Año 1* (Bogotá 1898).

Comisión Corográfica, *Jeografía física i política de las provincias de la Nueva Granada* (Bogotá 1856).

Jeografía física i política de las provincias de la Nueva Granada (Bogotá 1957, 1958). Originally published Bogotá 1857; Commission directed by Agustín Codazzi.

Comité Interamericano de Desenvolvimiento Agrícola, *Tenencia de la tierra y desarrollo socio-económico del sector agrícola* (vol. 1, Washington 1965).

Consejo Administrativo de los Ferrocarriles Nacionales, *Revista del Consejo Administrativo de los FFCC Nacionales* (Bogotá 1936–).

Cruz Santos, Abel, *Economía y Hacienda Pública*, vol. 15 of *Historia extensa de Colombia* (Academia Colombiana de Historia, Bogotá 1965).

Dix, Robert H., *Colombia: The Political Dimensions of Change* (New Haven 1967).

Echavarría, Enrique, *Historia de los textiles en Antioquia* (Medellín 1942).

Eder, Phanor J., *El fundador Santiago M. Eder* (Bogotá 1959).

Fals Borda, Orlando, 'Los orígenes del problema de la tierra en Chocontá, Colombia', *Boletín de historia y antigüedades*, LXI (1954), 36–50.

'Indian Congregations in the New Kingdom of Granada: Land Tenure Aspects, 1595–1850', *The Americas*, XIII (1957), 331–51.

El hombre y la tierra en Boyacá (Bogotá 1957).

Campesinos de los Andes: estudio sociológico de Saucío (Bogotá 1961).

La subversión en Colombia. Visión del cambio social en la historia (Bogotá 1967).

Subversion and Social Change in Colombia (New York 1969).

Federación Nacional de Cafeteros, *Boletín de estadística* (Bogotá 1932–).

Flórez Alvarez, Leonidas, *Campaña en Santander (1899–1900)* (imprenta del Estado Mayor General, Bogotá? 1938).

Fonnegra Sierra, Guillermo, *Los fundamentos de la ley sobre régimen de tierras* (Medellín 1930).

Works cited

Friede, Juan, *El indio en lucha por la tierra* (Bogotá 1944).

Los quimbayas bajo la dominación española (Bogotá 1963).

Gaitán Suarez, Alvaro, 'Acción indigenista en America ... métodos y resultados en Colombia', *XXXV Congreso Internacional de Americanistas* (n.d.).

Galindo, Aníbal, *Historia económica i estadística de la hacienda nacional, desde la colonia hasta nuestros dias* (Bogotá 1874).

Estudios económicos i fiscales (Bogotá 1880).

García, Antonio, *Legislación indigenista en Colombia* (Mexico 1952).

Gilmore, Robert L. and John P. Harrison, 'Juan Bernardo Elbers and the Introduction of Steam Navigation on the Magdalena River', *Hispanic American Historical Review*, XXVIII no. 3 (1948), 335–59.

Gomez Martinez, Fernando, and Arturo Puerta, *Biografía económica de las industrias de Antioquia* (Medellín 1945).

Great Britain, Foreign Office, Diplomatic and Consular Reports, *Report on Agriculture in Colombia*. Foreign Office Annual Series, no. 446 (London 1888). Submitted by W. J. Dickson.

Report on the Trade of Colombia for the Year 1889, no. 804 (London 1889).

Report on the Railways of Colombia. Submitted by Victor Huckin, Acting Consul General in Bogotá. No. 678 (London 1910).

Guerra Azuola, Ramon, 'Apuntamientos de viaje', *Boletín de historia y antigüedades*, IV (1906), no. 38.

Guhl, Ernesto, *Utilización de la tierra en Colombia*, Escuela Superior de Administración (Mimeo, Bogotá 1963).

Gutierrez Ponce, Ignacio, *Vida de Don Ignacio Gutierrez y episodios históricos de su tiempo, 1806–1877* (1900).

Gutiérrez, Rufino, *Monografías* (2 vols., Bogotá 1929).

Guzmán Campos, German, Orlando Fals Borda and Eduardo Umaña Luna, *La Violencia en Colombia* (2 vols., Bogotá 1962–4).

Hagen, Everett E., *On the Theory of Social Change* (Homewood, Illinois 1962).

El cambio social en Colombia (Bogotá 1963).

Harrison, John P., 'Introduction of Steam Navigation on the Magdalena River' (M.A. Thesis, University of California, Berkeley 1948).

'The Colombian Tobacco Industry from Government Monopoly to Free Trade, 1778–1876' (Ph.D. diss., University of California, Berkeley 1952).

'The Evolution of the Colombia Tobacco Trade, to 1875', *Hispanic American Historical Review*, XXXIII (1952), 163–74.

Helguera, J. León, *The First Mosquera Administration in New Granada, 1845–1849* (Ph.D. diss., University of North Carolina, Chapel Hill 1958).

Henao, Jesús María and Gerardo Arrubla, *History of Colombia*. Translated by J. Fred Rippy (Chapel Hill 1938).

Hermberg, Paul, 'El costo de la vida de la clase obrera en Bogotá', *Anales de economía y estadística*, I (Bogotá 1938).

Hernandez Rodrigues, Guillermo, *De los Chibchas a la colonia y a la república* (Universidad Nacional de Colombia. Sección de Extension Cultural, Bogota 1949).

Works cited

Higuita, Juan de D., 'Estudio histórico-analítico de la población colombiana en 170 años', *Anales de economía y estadística*, 3 (1940), supplement to no. 2, pp. 1–113.

Hirschman, Albert O., *The Strategy of Economic Development* (New Haven, 1957). *Journeys Toward Progress* (New York 1963).

Hoffman, H. Theodore, 'A History of Railway Concessions and Railway Development Policy in Colombia to 1943' (Ph.D. diss., American University 1947).

Holguín, Jorge, *Desde cerca (asuntos colombianos)* (Paris 1903).

Holton, Isaac, *New Granada: Twenty Months in the Andes* (New York 1857).

Instituto Colombiano de Reforma Agraria, *Segundo año de reforma agraria – 1963* (Bogotá 1964).

International American Conference, *Reports and Recommendations* (Washington, D.C. 1890).

International Bank for Reconstruction and Development, *The Basis of a Development Program for Colombia*. Report of a Mission, headed by Lauchlin Currie (Baltimore 1950).

Jaramillo Ocampo, Hernán, *Exegisis de nuestra economía agraria* (Manizales 1940).

Jaramillo Uribe, Jaime, *El pensamiento colombiano en el siglo XIX* (Bogotá 1964).

Leonard, David Phelps, *The Comunero Rebellion of New Granada in 1781, A Chapter in the Spanish Quest for Social Justice* (University of Michigan, Ann Arbor 1951).

Liévano Aguirre, Indalecio, *Rafael Núñez* (Bogotá 1946).

Los grandes conflictos sociales y económicos de nuestra historia (4 vols., Bogotá n.d.).

El proceso de Mosquera ante el senado (Bogotá 1966).

Londoño, Carlos Mario, *Economía agraria colombiana* (Madrid 1964).

López, Alejandro, *Estadística de Antioquia* (Medellín 1914).

López Toro, Alvaro, *Análisis demográfico de los censos colombianos: 1951 y 1964* (Bogotá 1968).

Migración y cambio social en Antioquia durante el siglo diez y nueve (Bogotá 1968).

Martínez Silva, Carlos, *Las emisiones clandestinas del Banco Nacional* (Bogotá 1937).

Martinez Landínez, Jorge, *Historia militar de Colombia*, vol. 1 (Bogotá 1956).

McGreevey, William Paul, 'The Economic Development of Colombia' (Ph.D. diss., Massachusetts Institute of Technology, 1965).

Medellín, Municipio de, *Anuario estadístico del Municipio de Medellín, relativo al año 1922* (Medellín 1923).

Melo, Jorge Orlando, 'Los estudios históricos en Colombia: Situación actual y tendencias predominantes', *U.N. Revista de la Dirección de Divulgación Cultural* (Universidad Nacional de Colombia), II (1969), 15–41.

Mollien, Gaspar, *Travels in the Republic of Colombia in the Years 1822 and 1823* (London 1824).

Mörner, Magnus, *Race Mixture in the History of Latin America* (Boston 1967).

Murphy, Robert Cushman, 'Racial Succession in the Colombian Chocó', *Geographical Review*, XXIX (1939), 461–71.

Works cited

Nichols, Theodore E., 'The Rise of Barranquilla', *Hispanic American Historical Review*, XXXIV: 2 (1954) 158–74.

Nieto Arteta, Luis Eduardo, *El café en la sociedad colombiana* (Bogotá 1958).

Economía y cultura en la historia de Colombia (Bogotá 1962).

Ortega, Alfredo, *Ferrocarriles colombianos*, Biblioteca de historia nacional (3 vols., Bogotá 1920, 1932). Vols. I and II appear as vol. XXVI of the series and vol. III appears as vol. LXVII.

Ospina Vásquez, Luis, *Industria y protección en Colombia, 1810–1930* (Medellín 1955).

'Perspectiva histórica de la economía colombiana', *Revista de ciencias económicas*, VI (1960), 5–32.

Plan Agrícola. Exposición sobre el Projecto de Resolución por la cual se dan bases para el Plan Agrícola, presentada al Consejo Nacional de Agricultura, Diciembre 1962 (Medellín 1963).

Ots y Capdequí, José María, *Nuevos aspectos del siglo XVIII española en América* (Bogotá 1946).

Palacio Delvalle, Guillermo, *Desarrollo agrícola de Colombia 1940–1952* (Bogotá 1953).

Parra, Aquileo, *Memorias de Aquileo Parra, Presidente de Colombia 1876 a 1878* (Bogotá 1912).

Parry, John H., *The Spanish Seaborne Empire* (New York 1966).

Parsons, James J., 'Antioqueño Colonization in Western Colombia', *Ibero-Americana*, XXXII (1949), Berkeley.

Payne, James L., *Patterns of Conflict in Colombia* (New Haven 1968).

Pereira, R. S., *Les Etats-Unis de Colombia, précis d'Histoire et la Géographie Physique, Politique et Comerciale* (Paris 1883).

Perez Aguirre, Antonio, *25 años de historia colombiana. 1853 a 1878. Del centralismo a la federación* (Bogotá 1929).

Pérez, Felipe, *Jeografía de las provincias del norte de la Nueva Granada* (Bogotá 1862). *Geografía general de los Estados Unidos de Colombia* (Bogotá 1883).

Pérez Ayala, José Manuel, *Antonio Caballero y Góngora, Virrey y Arzobispo de Santa Fe* (Bogotá 1951).

Perry, Oliverio (ed.), *Banco de Bogotá, trayectoria de una empresa de servicio, 1870–1960* (Bogotá 1960).

Posada, Eduardo and P. M. Ibáñez (eds.), *Relaciones de Mando. Memorias presentadas por los gobernantes del Nuevo Reino de Granada*, Biblioteca de Historia Nacional, vol. VIII (Bogotá 1910).

Posada Gutierrez, Joaquín, *Memorias histórico-políticas del General Joaquín Posada Gutierrez* (Bogotá 1929).

Powles, John, *New Granada: Its Internal Resources* (London 1863).

Restrepo Euse, Alvaro, *Historia de Antioquia* (Medellín 1903).

Restrepo Echavarría, Emiliano, *Una excursión al territorio de San Martín en Diciembre de 1869* (Bogotá 1955).

Restrepo, José Manuel, *Historia de la revolución de la República de Colombia* (2nd ed., Paris 1858).

Works cited

Restrepo, Jose Manuel, *Diario político y militar* (4 vols., Bogotá 1954).

Restrepo, Juan Pablo, *La iglesia y el estado en Colombia* (London 1885).

Restrepo, Vicente, *Estudio sobre las minas de oro y de plata de Colombia* (Bogotá 1952).

Riascos Grueso, Eduardo, *Geografía guerrera colombiana* (Cali 1950).

Rippy, J. Fred, *The Capitalists and Colombia* (New York 1931).

'Dawn of the Railway Era in Colombia', *Hispanic American Historical Review*, XXIII: 4 (1943), 650–63.

'Peak of British Investments in Latin American Mines', *Inter-American Economic Affairs*, II: 2 (1948), 41–8.

Globe and Hemisphere: Latin America's Place in the Postwar Foreign Relations of the United States (Chicago 1958).

Rivas, Medardo, *Los trabajadores de tierra caliente* (Bogotá 1946).

Robledo, Emilio, *Bosquejo biográfico del Señor Oidor Juan Antonio Mon y Velarde, Visitador de Antioquia 1785–1788* (2 vols., Bogotá 1954).

Rodríquez Plata, Horacio, *La inmigración alemana al estado soberano de Santander en el siglo XIX* (Bogotá 1968).

Rothman, Franklin, 'Abolition of the Tribute in New Granada' (unpub. MS., Berkeley 1966).

Safford, Frank R., 'Commerce and Enterprise in Central Colombia, 1821–1870' (Ph.D. diss., Columbia University 1965).

'Foreign and National Enterprise in Nineteenth Century Colombia', *Business History Review*, XXXIX: 4 (1965), 503–26.

'Significación de los antioqueños en el desarrollo económico colombiano', *Anuario colombiano de historia social y de la cultura*, V (1967), 49–69.

Salazar, Mardonio, *Proceso histórico de la propiedad en Colombia* (Bogotá 1948).

Samper, Miguel, *Escritos políticos-económicos* (3 vols., Bogotá 1925).

Schenck, Ferdinand von, *Viajes por Antioquia en el año de 1880* (Bogotá 1953).

Segovia, R. E., 'Crown Policy and the Precious Metals in New Granada, 1760–1810' (M.A. Thesis, University of California, Berkeley 1959).

Smith, T. Lynn, *Colombia: Social Structure and the Process of Development* (Gainesville, Florida, 1967).

Torres, Garcia, Guillermo, *Historia de la moneda en Colombia* (Bogotá 1945).

United Nations Economic Commission for Latin America, *Analyses and Projections of Economic Development*. Vol. III: *Economic Development of ̣Colombia* (Geneva 1957).

Some Aspects of Population Growth in Colombia (Santiago 1962).

Food and Agricultural Organization, *Coffee in Latin America. 1. Colombia and El Salvador* (New York 1958).

United States, Bureau of Foreign Commerce, *Monthly Consular Reports on Commerce, Manufacturing, etc.* Washington 1883–1900.

Congress, Senate Records, *Report on Trade Conditions in Colombia*. Submitted by C. M. Pepper, 1908. Senate Document 152, 60th Congress, 1st Session, vol. 11 (serial vol. 5244), 13 January.

Works cited

Department of Agriculture, Office of Foreign Agriculture Relations, *The Agriculture of Colombia*. By Kathryn H. Wylie. Foreign Agriculture Bulletin, no. 1 (Washington, D.C. 1942).

Department of Commerce, *Colombia: A Commercial and Industrial Handbook* (1921); *Colombia: Commerce and Industries, 1922 and 1923*, Trade Information Bulletin no. 223 (Washington, D.C. 1924).

Interdepartmental Committee on Nutrition for National Defense, *Nutritional Survey, May-August*, 1960 (Washington, D.C. 1961).

Urrutia, Miguel, *Estadísticas históricas de Colombia* (Bogotá n.d.). *History of the Labor Movement in Colombia* (New Haven 1969). *Historia del sindicalismo en Colombia* (Bogotá 1969).

Valderrama Benítez, Ernesto, *Santander y su desarrollo económico en el año de 1929* (Bucaramanga 1930).

'La industria cafetera santandereana,' *Estudio II* (Bucaramanga 1933), 1270-74.

Tierras de Santander (Bucaramanga 1940).

Van Young, Eric, 'The Común of Socorro' (unpub. MS., Berkeley 1968).

Vergara y Velasco, Javier, *Nueva geografía de Colombia* (Bogotá 1912).

Vicens Vives, Jaime (ed.), *Historia de España y América* (4 vols., Barcelona 1961).

West, Robert C., *Colonial Placer Mining in Colombia* (Baton Rouge, La. 1952).

Wurfel, Seymour W., *Foreign Enterprise in Colombia. Laws and Policies* (Chapel Hill, North Carolina 1965).

INDEX

Index

Index

Index

Hagen, Everett E., 149, 185–7, 189–90, 304, 306
Haldane, Robert, 160
Hamburg (Germany), 158
Handicrafts, 82, 147–8, 167. *See also* Artisans
Harrison, John P., 42n, 160–1
Helguera, J. León, 306
Hernandez Rodrigues, Guillermo, 73n
Hicks, John R., 284, 304n
Hirschman, Albert O., 199n, 236n, 284, 306
Hoffman, H. Theodore, 270n
Hoffman, Walther G., 213
Holguin, Jorge, 180–1
Holt, Pat M., 308
Holton, Isaac F., 128, 250, 251n
Honda, 43–4 (table), 161, 162, 245, 246, 252n
Hoover, Edgar M., 285
Hopkins, Evan, 245
Huckin, Victor, 262–3
Huila, 196 (table), 300 (table)
Human capital, 155
Human carriers (*tercios*), 245
Humboldt, Alexander von, 28, 31

Ibagué, 43 (table), 110 (table)
Imlah, Albert, 101n, 105n
Immigration, 203, 206
Import-competing sector: decline of, 1845–65, 170–1; in trade model, 149
Import merchants, success of, 163–4
Importables, sources of, 170–1, 170 (table)
Imports, 114, 163, 175; of capital goods, 213–14; decline in value of, 1866–85, 106; demand for, 111, 235, 240 (figure); impact on female artisans of, 165; of manufactures, 211–12; quantum of, 1930s, 268; structural composition of, 214
Imports per capita, 104–5, 104 (table)
Income adjustments, and trade deficits, 109
Income distribution: effect of, 154–7; relation to trade, 151; shift to merchants, 180; and structure of demand, 221
Income transfers, and analysis of welfare, 156–7
INCORA (Instituto Colombiana de Reforma Agraria), 64
Indemnity, U.S. payments of, 204–5
India: decline of handicrafts in, 148; population growth in, 285
Indians: Church dominance of policy toward, 126; effects of Reforms on, 123–4; poverty among, 124
Indigo, as export product, 98

Indonesia, 285; coffee cultivation in, 231–3. *See also* Java
Industrial development, 199, 213, 239, 298
Industrial Revolution, 284
Interdependence, 280, 289–95
Interest groups, 74–8, 90 (table)
Internal imperialism, 191
Internal rate of return, for railway investments, 272, 274 (table)
Internal trade, 138, 246, 247 (map), 277; and transport improvements, 162–3
International demonstration effect, 113
International trade, theory of, 97–8. *See also* Foreign trade
Interplanting, 295
Islitas, 44 (table)
Italy, 290

Jamaica, 6–7
Jambaló, 125, 126
Japan, 252 (table)
Jaramillo Uribe, Jaime, 20n, 89n
Java, 98, 112, 229, 285. *See also* Indonesia
Jenks, Leland H., 41n
Jesuits, expulsion in 1850, 75
Juez de Realengos, 56

Kemmerer mission, 205
Keynes, John Maynard (Lord), 222
Kopp Castello, Guillermo, 206
Kuznets, Simon, 10–11, 194n, 284

Labor force: mobility of, 174; policies affecting, 49–53, 176–7; protest by, 164–5, 208; sectoral distribution of, 165–6, 192, 198, 213–14, 298, 299 (figure), 303
La Dorada, 246
La Farge, Oliver, 198n
La Guama, 43 (table)
Lagunilla (river), 229
Laissez-faire, 2, 39, 138–41, 157–81, 279
La Mesa, 44 (table)
Lancaster, Kelvin, 151–2
Land policy, 49–50, 64–6, 71–2, 82–6, 131, 138
Land prices, 119–20, 120 (table)
Land tenure, 55, 119, 123–4, 140, 142, 177–8; categories of, 121–2, 122 (table); census of, 1960, 142; fragmentation of holdings, 124; and rental systems, 160; social functions of, 56; social implications of, 131–4
La Paila (hacienda), 160

326

Index

Index

Pacific Railway (Ferrocarril del Pacífico), 237
Paisas (Antioqueños), 186
Palmira, 110 (table)
Panama, 253; economic distance from Bogotá, 162; secession of, 204–5
Panama Canal, 237, 244, 257–60, 261, 301
Panama Railroad, 162, 254
Panic of 1873, 114
Pará (grass), 119n
Parcelization, 125
Paretian optimum, 151–2
Parra, Aquileo, 64n, 83, 87, 118, 168
Parry, John H., 38n
Parsons, James J., 62n, 191–2, 195, 200, 231, 307
Pasto, 110 (table)
Pastusos (citizens of Pasto), 190
Payaneses (citizens of Popayán), 186
Payne, James L., 164
Peñon de Conejo, 43–4 (table)
Peonage, among tobacco growers, 160
Pereira, 110 (table)
Pérez, Felipe, 72n, 159–60
Pérez Ayala, José Manuel, 22n
Peru, 31 (table), 32 (table), 198, 297
Pitayó, 125, 126
Plantation, requirements for, 221
Plata, José María, 71
Plátano, 295
Plumb, J. H., 225n
Popayán, 110 (table), 124, 186, 188
Population: in Antioquia, 193, 294–5; in artisan areas, 109; autonomous generation of, 281; colonial period, 3, 21–2, 51; and cropland, 143; density of, 50; and economic development, 193–4; growth of, 286–9, 287 (table); mobility of, 300–1, 300 (table); and per capita income, 284; regional distribution of, 136; shift in potential, 280; urban, 110 (table)
Powles, J. D., 245n
Presidents, tenure in office of, 92–3 (table)
Profit remittances, 208
Protection, of home industry, 152, 187
Prussia, roads in, 251
Public administration, as political issue, 72, 86–8
Public debt (bonds), used to purchase Church lands, 129
Public finance, Santander, 105
Public lands, conditions for purchase of, 131
Puerto Berrío, 44–5 (table)
Puerto Colombia, 44–5 (table), 255

Puerto Rico, 32 (table)
Quindío, 230, 301
Quinine bark, as export product, 98
Quito, artisan production in, 34

Radical Liberals, 66, 137, 139, 140, 168–9
Rail rates, 43–5 (table), 256–7
Railways: and coffee exports, 237, 253; construction of, 253–7, 276–7; effectiveness of, 260–2; profits, 263; promotion of, 294; reorganization of, 268–71
Recio (river), 157, 229
Reforms of 1850, 8, 69–70, 73–4, 95, 286
Rental income, concentration of, 133
Reos rematados, 175
Resguardo, 4, 51–4; abolition of, 52n, 83, 123–7, 138, 140; effects of abolition of, 292; treatment by republican governments, 03–6
Restrepo, Juan Pablo, 72n, 73
Restrepo, Vicente, 28n, 46n, 309
Restrepo Echavarría, Emiliano, 131
Revenues, central government, 40 (table); decline in, 1850–1, 86; as percentage of imports, 169–70
Reyes Tariff of 1905, 238
Reynolds, Clark, 7n
Ricardo-Lewis effect, 284
Rico, Luis Carlos, 107
Riesman, David, 293
Rio de la Plata (viceroyalty), 31 (table)
Rivas, Medardo, 158, 161n, 163, 190
River transport: decline in costs of, 162–3; rates, 43–5 (table), 163 (table)
Roads, 245, 251, 278
Robertson, William, 34n
Robinson, Joan, 50n
Robledo, Emilio, 29n, 61n
Rodríguez Piñeros, Eduardo, 129
Rodríguez Plata, Horacio, 12n
Rosenblat, Angel, 51n
Royal finances, comparisons for viceroyalties, 31 (table)
Russia, serfdom in, 225. *See also* U.S.S.R.

Sabana de Bogotá, 43 (table)
Sabanilla, 255
Safford, Frank Robinson, 73–4, 190–4, 239, 306, 308
Sainte Rose Cie., concession to, 71–2
Samper, José María, 140, 305
Samper, Miguel, 81, 126–7, 129, 305
San Antonio de Táchira, 43 (table)

Index

San Carlos (Antioquia), 249
San Gil, 43 (table)
San Martín, 120 (table)
Santa Marta, 43–4 (table), 109, 110 (table), 255, 257, 258 (table), 261
Santander (Department), 195–200, 234 (table), 300 (table); artisans of, 165–7, 238; Chorographic Commission in, 105; declining prosperity in, 105–6; formation of towns in, 22–3; and *laissez-faire*, 168–9; population growth in, 109; prosperity in, 61; tobacco cultivation in, 25, 138–9; vagrants in, 175
Santander, Francisco de Paula, 24, 64n, 72, 81, 92 (table), 130, 306
Santandereano, stereotype of, 190
São Paulo (Brazil), 206
Savings rate, related to income distribution, 154
Secondary (manufacturing) activities, 303
Second best, theory of, 140, 151–4
Segovia, Rodolfo E., 42n
Sharecroppers, conditions of, 159–60
Sheridan, Richard B., 97n
Silversmiths, 167
Sinú (river valley), 137
Slavery, causes of, 225
Social saving, 260, 263
Sociedad Democrática de los Artesanos, 79
Socorro, 105
Solow, Robert M., 218n
Soto, Francisco, 25n, 33
Status deprivation, 186, 189, 190
Steamboats, 41–2, 249–50
Stein, Stanley J., 233n
Stockmen, number in 1870, 177
Stockraising, 123–4, 127n, 132–7, 176–8; employment effects of, 179
Structural rigidities, nature of, 220
Suarez, Marco Fidel, 188
Sutch, Richard, 261n
Sweden, 193

Tariff: discrepancies between legal and actual, 170; government policy of, 169; and import demand, 237–8; and industrial development, 187; as political issue, 71, 78–82; rates, 33–4, 34 (table), 80 (table); and volume of trade, 36
TAT tests, 186
Taxation, early republican policies of, 39
Taylor, George Rogers, 42n, 249–50
Terms of trade, 115n, 180, 220, 268

Territorio Vásquez, 71n, 130
Tertiary (service) activities, 303
Textile industry, 199, 300; employment in, 214
Thomson-Urrutia Treaty, 204
Thousand Days War (1899–1902), 176
Tierradentro, 126
Titiribí, 249
Tobacco: cultivation of, 24–5, 118, 138–9, 157–60, 228–30; distribution of income in, 161; export of, 98, 111–13, 112 (figure), 151, 157, 163, 202, 217; and import demand, 113, 235; and industrial development, 239; monopoly of, 25, 33, 40, 117–18; productivity of, 103–4n, 157; scale economies in, 158
Tolima, 175, 195 196 (table), 234, 234 (table), 300 (table)
Torres García, Guillermo, 107n
Trade: distribution of gains and losses from, 149, 173; and income distribution, 151; multiplier effects of, 172–3; opening up of, 148–51; removal of restrictions on, 22; statistics on, 37–8, 98, 100, 106
Transfer mechanism, 4, 26–8, 30–2
Transportation, 41–2, 45, 86, 138, 178, 244–80, 297–8; costs of, 43–5 (table), 118, 161–2, 163 (table), 237, 248; and export expansion, 236–7, 279; and industrialization, 213–14
Truck transport, 45 (table), 268–9, 278 (table)
Tunja, 43 (table), 110 (table)
Turco (immigrant from Middle East), 206

U.S.S.R., 252 (table)
United Fruit Company, 207–8
United States of America, 7, 37 (table), 101, 193, 204–5, 224, 244, 250, 251, 252 (table), 253, 260, 263, 288, 301
Urbanization, 110 (table), 301
Uribe, Jaime Jaramillo, 305
Uribe Hoyos, Germán, 278
Urrutia Montoya, Miguel, 164, 307

Vagabonds, appearance in eighteenth century, 60
Vagrants, 174–5
Valle del Cauca, 168, 196 (table), 234, 303
Van Young, Eric, 26n
Vecinos (Spanish smallholders), 55
Vélez, 44 (table), 81, 118
Veliz, Claudio, 141
Venezuela, 32 (table)

Index